CARTESIAN QUESTIONS III

Cultural Memory | in the Present

Hent de Vries, Editor

CARTESIAN QUESTIONS III

Descartes Beneath the Mask of Cartesianism

Jean-Luc Marion

TRANSLATED BY
STEPHEN E. LEWIS AND
STEPHANIE RUMPZA

STANFORD UNIVERSITY PRESS
Stanford, California

Stanford University Press
Stanford, California

English translation © 2025 by the Board of Trustees of the Leland Stanford Junior University. All rights reserved.

Cartesian Questions III was originally published in French in 2021 under the title *Questions cartésiennes III. Descartes sous le masque du cartésianisme* © Presses Universitaires de France/Humensis, 2021.

 This book has been published with the support of the Centre national du livre.

Printed in the United States of America

Library of Congress Cataloging-in-Publication Data

Names: Marion, Jean-Luc, 1946- author. | Lewis, Stephen E. (Stephen Evarts), translator. | Rumpza, Stephanie, 1986- translator.
Title: Cartesian questions. III, Descartes beneath the mask of Cartesianism / Jean-Luc Marion ; translated by Stephen E. Lewis and Stephanie Rumpza.
Other titles: Descartes sous le masque du cartésianisme. English | Descartes beneath the mask of Cartesianism | Cultural memory in the present.
Description: Stanford, California : Stanford University Press, 2025. | Series: Cultural memory in the present | Originally published in French in 2021 under the title: Questions cartésiennes III, Descartes sous le masque du Cartésianisme. | Includes bibliographical references.
Identifiers: LCCN 2025003432 (print) | LCCN 2025003433 (ebook) | ISBN 9781503632851 (cloth) | ISBN 9781503643338 (paperback) | ISBN 9781503643345 (epub)
Subjects: LCSH: Descartes, René, 1596-1650. | Descartes, René, 1596-1650—Influence.
Classification: LCC B1875 .M335413 2025 (print) | LCC B1875 (ebook) | DDC 194—dc23/eng/20250310
LC record available at https://lccn.loc.gov/2025003432
LC ebook record available at https://lccn.loc.gov/2025003433

Cover design: Bob Aufuldish /aufuldish & warinner
Typeset by Newgen in Garamond Premier Pro 11/13.5

The authorized representative in the EU for product safety and compliance is: Mare Nostrum Group B.V. | Mauritskade 21D | 1091 GC Amsterdam | The Netherlands | Email address: gpsr@mare-nostrum.co.uk | KVK chamber of commerce number: 96249943

*To Jean-Robert Armogathe, Vincent Carraud,
and Dan Arbib – for the sequel.*

Contents

Foreword: Descartes Beneath the Mask — xi

Translators' Note — xv

I. DOUBT, THE SUPREME GAME — 1
　§1. Between Two Doubts — 1
　§2. The Cartesian Construction of Doubt — 4
　§3. A Review of Former Doubts — 8
　§4. The *Mathesis Universalis* and the Radical Pyrrhonian Argument — 13
　§5. From One Performative to the Other — 19
　§6. Doubt as First Principle — 26

II. *EGO SUM*, OUTSIDE THE SUBJECT — 30
　§1. The Privileged Formulation — 30
　§2. The Objection Starting from Substance — 32
　§3. The *Ego* as Substance under Reserve — 33
　§4. The Objection Starting from the Subject — 37
　§5. The Objection Starting from Representation — 40
　§6. The Non-reflexive *Cogito* — 43
　§7. The Objection Starting from the Cause — 50
　§8. The *Ego* Clear of All Cause — 53

III. KNOWING BY ESTEEM — 57
§1. The Aporias of Generosity — 57
§2. Esteem, a Mode of Thinking — 58
§3. "The True Office of Reason" — 62
§4. To Esteem, to Esteem Oneself (Montaigne) — 66
§5. Esteem in Love (Descartes) — 69
§6. Esteem and the *Moi* (Pascal) — 73
§7. A Practice of Doubt — 77

IV. THE INFINITE: THE UNFOLDING OF FINITUDE — 85
§1. Finitude as a Question — 85
§2. The Limits without Limits — 86
§3. Power and Incomprehensibility — 91
§4. The Indetermination of the Perfect — 95
§5. The Ontic Infinite — 97
§6. The Transcendental Infinite — 102
§7. Experience and the Infinite — 110
§8. The Will Reduced to Infinity — 116

V. FROM DESCARTES TO PHENOMENOLOGY, AND BACK — 121
§1. The Alleged Accord — 121
§2. Husserl's Disagreement — 122
§3. Heidegger's Disagreement — 124
§4. The Question of the Point of Departure — 126
§5. The Return to Phenomena *Quatenus Quidam Cogitandi Modi* — 128
§6. The Neutralization of the Origin and the Criterion of Evidence — 132
§7. The Doubling of the *Res* and the Correlation of Appearing — 135
§8. Thought as Decision — 140
§9. Thinking by Acts — 143

VI.	MONTAIGNE, OR DOUBT WITHOUT *EGO SUM, EGO EXISTO*	149
	§1. Without "Any Communication with Being"	149
	§2. The "Being Outside of Being," or the Dying "Moi"	152
	§3. The "Moi" without *Cogitatio* of Self	155
	§4. "Keeping to Oneself," or the Reduction	160
	§5. The "Entire Form"	165
	§6. "My Universal Being"	170
	§7. Being and "Life"	174
	§8. To God's Grace	177
VII.	HOBBES, OR THE IDEA AND BEING AS BODY	181
	§1. The Debate about the Idea	181
	§2. Unimaginable Ideas	184
	§3. Ideas of God and the Self	186
	§4. The Question of Substance	190
	§5. The Privilege of Simple Material Natures	192
	§6. Conceived Being, or the Body	195
	§7. The Irreducible Privilege of the *Cogitatio*	198
VIII.	SPINOZA, OR THE UNIFICATION OF THE PROOFS OF GOD'S EXISTENCE	202
	§1. Delay and Divergence	202
	§2. The Cartesian Origin of the Multiplication of Proofs	206
	§3. The Irreducible Plurality of Definitions	212
	§4. Perfection and Cause	218
	§5. Perfection and the Infinite	220
	§6. The Unification of Metaphysical Names	224
IX.	SPINOZA: ADEQUACY AND VISION	226
	§1. The Construction of Inadequacy	226
	§2. The Conditions of Adequacy: Spinoza's Agreement with Descartes	229

§3. Divine Knowledge and Adequacy: Spinoza's Disagreement
with Descartes   233
§4. The Conquest and the Aporia of Adequacy   235
§5. The First Challenge of the Recourse to Adequacy   238
§6. The Second Challenge of the Recourse to Adequacy   244
§7. Spinozist Thought and the Beatific Vision   249

CONCLUSION
THE DESCARTES TO COME   253

*Appendix: Montaigne, or the Proper Usage of the Skepticism
of Saint Augustine*   259

Notes   275

Index of Names   357

Foreword

Descartes Beneath the Mask

"*Larvatus prodeo*," Descartes announced, or rather, did not announce (since he never published this text): "Just as actors, taught not to let any embarrassment show on their faces, put on a mask, so I, about to mount the stage of this theater which is the world, where to this point I have hung back as a spectator—I appear masked."[1] Thus he masked even his mask, and remained masked. He remained so at least until 1637, postponing every prior publication; and he remained masked until 1641, when he finally declared himself as author under his own name. Why did he decide, voluntarily in contrast to us, to wear this mask and keep it on for so long?

There are many hypotheses, and they do not exclude one another. To begin with, Descartes was not one of those authors who wants above all else to make himself known, even if he has nothing to make known; with time passing quickly, he devoted it to research, or even discovery, and not first and foremost to publication. Whence the cult of his "solitude, away from which it is difficult ... to make any advances in the search for truth" (AT V.430.23–25; CSMK, 383). Next, he had understood very early (and explained in the *Discourse on the Method*) a fundamental rule of research, or rather of its reception: institutions easily accept what is true but already known; and the public enthusiastically receives what is new, even if it is false; but neither institutions nor the public spontaneously welcome what is both new and true. Knowing this, with experience that had often confirmed it, Descartes sought to set up various protections: Bérulle, the residence in the United Provinces, the Sorbonne, the Jesuits, Huygens and Chanut, the Queen of Sweden, and so forth, each time with disappointing success. Whence this conviction that "peace and quiet . . . are benefits that the most powerful kings on earth cannot give to those who are unable to acquire them for themselves" (AT V.467.20–23; CSMK, 384). But there is more: in scientific, philosophical, and theological debate, no one advances without a mask, because this very debate constantly imposes on its actors the mask of an ideology, a particular doctrine, or even a coterie: in the eyes of adversaries, one becomes immediately other than oneself, an Aristotelian or a *novator*, a fanatic or an atheist, a Jesuit or a Calvinist, without ever being able to appear for what one truly says. Descartes had this experience but understood immediately that it was inevitable; and so he changed vocabulary, language, and even theoretical lexicons depending on the interlocutors; he treated the same questions in registers that were almost incompatible (thus, for example, that of the union of the soul and the body, addressed in Latin and in scholastic terms in *Meditatio VI* and the polemics with Regius and Voetius, and in French, with new terms, with Elisabeth, Chanut, and Christina). This was perhaps a final effort to take off the mask. We may doubt its success, since this last effort in his theoretical journey was also the least well received, even up to today.[2]

While changing it fairly frequently during his lifetime, the mask that Descartes retained was above all imposed on him by posterity. The rapid construction of the myth of Descartes multiplied its contradictory and entirely inadequate figures, beginning in the second half of the century: animal-machines, occasionalism, innate ideas, and then in the following century, Jansenism, deism, atheism, even materialism, and so on. These avatars have continued to accumulate, including in our time.[3] This situation has probably affected all the influential philosophers, and it is by this affect, among other indices, that they are recognized. A philosopher quickly becomes influential precisely because one clamors for him, and because the sum of the misinterpretations of his text that accumulate imprison him, like a sarcophagi, but so too do the constraints exerted by the philosophy in which he grew up and *against which* he had to think. It is *beneath* this or these masks that we must meet up with Descartes, without, of course, adding a new one, as is so easy to do.

For if we can say that understanding an author means understanding him better than he understood himself, understanding him in this way does not mean reinterpreting him under a new reading but rather freeing him from the readings that from the beginning have masked him. One cannot avoid such a deconstruction, for Descartes appears a victim of not only the misunderstandings of him that had accumulated but also the misunderstandings that, from the beginning, *before he had even begun* to think, constrained him, or even prevented him from formulating what he had thought. This endless deconstruction, this archeological uncovering, seems to me today to be the sole reasonable justification for my ever renewed and corrected effort to read and reread the Cartesian corpus from one end to the other, since 1975. Not an isolated effort, but rather one swept along by the swelling current of a half century of considerable progress in international erudition, especially French, Italian, and Dutch. The learned, not always distinguishing the importance of what they have discovered; the polemicists, not seeing what their caricatures are symptomatic of; the speculators, sometimes imprecise in detail or insufficiently informed, unfair, or excessive, but whose sword cuts to the heart of the affair, much deeper than the surface-skaters imagine—all of these contribute today to a more correct, serene, and respectful knowledge of Descartes.

From what do we need to free Descartes? From the misinterpretations that Cartesianism has imposed on him. To think about an author is not to justify him at any price, to criticize him, or to enclose him in dilemmas he knew nothing of; it is to recover what he truly said. Or rather, what he truly meant to say, because he thought it; or even what he thought, without being able to say it clearly and as such; in short, it is to meet up with the unthought that he *saw*. In working on this, here I have followed two routes.

First of all, I have attempted to recover Descartes' exact terms and intentions (on doubt, the *ego*, esteem, the infinite), against the conventional simplifications in which the Cartesianism of the commentaries has decked him out. The goal is not only to correct what the texts say and don't say† but also to provide them with every chance and thus, from the outset, to avoid underestimating them: for in the end, and in principle, every great philosopher remains more intelligent than his best commentator, who can justify his work only by admitting this is so; and a philosopher that one would understand well enough to correct him, or even improve upon him, would not be truly great. This route, then, follows *Descartes in opposition to Cartesianism*.

Next, we will reconstitute how (non-)*Cartesianism defined itself in opposition to Descartes*—whether prior to him, by not taking the direction that he will take (Montaigne), or in front of him (Hobbes), by refusing the one he took, or after him (Spinoza), by closing up the openings that he had made.[5]

This double and indirect approach was only possible because it proved to be necessary. If here I have taken up, corrected, and modified former sketches, I owe it to the ever-clearer awareness of the enigmatic character of the Cartesian *beginning*, which, previously, had not yet fully appeared to me. Every true beginning—and Descartes accomplished one, our own—must remain effectively hidden and undecided, all the more so as it unfolds its possibilities. Maurice Merleau-Ponty had seen this: "Why is Descartes the most difficult of authors? Because he is the most radically ambiguous, the one who spoke the most indirectly [. . .]. He has the greatest amount of latent content."[6] Husserl had said it better than Nietzsche and Heidegger: "Indeed, great and dark depths open up behind the seeming triviality of the notorious pronouncement '*Ego cogito, Ego sum*'"[7] (whence Chapter Five, the pivot point of my inquiry). We have hardly begun to venture there.

More than ever, I must thank my predecessors in the interpretation of Descartes; all of them are useful, for nothing is lost if one knows how to make good use of their work. In particular, I recognize once again my debt to the Centre d'Études Cartésiennes (Sorbonne Université), founded fifty years ago and continued by Jean-Robert Armogathe and Vincent Carraud. And, through it, to the *res publica litteraria* that it exemplifies, following the examples of two departed but unforgettable mentors, Tullio Gregory and Marc Fumaroli, who have framed all my work as an historian of philosophy.

J.-L. M.
March–October 2020

Translators' Note

The endnotes provide references to standard editions of the works of Descartes, Montaigne, Hobbes, and Spinoza, as well as numerous other authors, and in all necessary cases we lay out for the reader the abbreviations subsequently used parenthetically or in the endnotes. Sometimes we have made modifications to cited published English translations in order to follow Jean-Luc Marion's French translations more precisely. All such modifications have been made tacitly, in order to avoid overburdening the text.

CARTESIAN QUESTIONS III

ONE

Doubt, the Supreme Game

§1. Between Two Doubts

Descartes' usage of doubt is still debated and, in fact, ambiguous. On the one hand, it has long been held as established, from d'Alembert to Kant, that Descartes offers the emblematic example of dogmatic thinking, claiming, against the well-tempered empiricism of Bacon, Gassendi, Mersenne, Hobbes, Locke, and Hume, the absolute certitude obtained by truths known a priori through innate ideas. And today the stream of obviously ever victorious refutations of Cartesian arguments overflowing Anglo-Saxon production rests on the peaceful conviction that the author of the *Meditationes* departed from healthy skeptical discipline. Whence, particularly in France, the repeated attempts, for the most part in vain, to strengthen the albeit rather limited objections of Gassendi.

But the powerful renewal of studies of modern skepticism since Richard H. Popkin, Charles B. Schmitt, and Tullio Gregory offers another more balanced, and thus more complex, approach. The rebirth of skepticism can be summarily attributed to the Latin translation of Sextus Empiricus' *Outlines of Pyrrhonism* by Henri Estienne in 1562 (more than to the *Adversus mathematicos* by Gentian Hervet, in 1569), and above all to Montaigne's *Essais* (first edition 1580, third edition 1588), furthered widely by Charron's *La Sagesse* (first edition 1601, second edition 1604). We may suggest, then, that up to Malebranche (who was the first to undertake a truly dogmatic critique of Montaigne, starting in 1674),[1] all the century's philosophical thought, in parallel with the implementation of a mathematized science of *physis*, is constituted in an essential part by a discussion of the extent and the limits of skepticism. Descartes, between Mersenne and Pascal, forms and develops himself within this debate: from the dreams of November 1619 to the *Letter to Voetius* of 1643, at least, the question of doubt and of the limits of skepticism resounds like the basso continuo of his entire itinerary of thought. One of the symptoms of the *failed* reception of this thought marked essentially by the skeptical problematic is that his hyperbolic and preparatory usage of doubt counts among the most original of his doctrines "that will be challenged by all the great post-Cartesians."[2]

This misunderstanding, or rather these two misunderstandings, nevertheless should not be understood improperly: they find their common origin in the subtle complexity of Descartes' usage of skepticism, such that he reshapes it in his practice of doubt. In short, we must come to admit that he practices doubt and pushes it to its limits, or even surpasses the limits that the ancient (and contemporary) skeptics assigned it, only in order to ruin and overturn it. The point is not simply to underscore that one cannot claim to doubt everything, but above all to bring doubt to its paroxysm by discovering, through it and despite it, an *inconcussum*.[3] Such an overturning, brought back to the level of doxography, explains a Cartesian tactic that in sum is rather clear-cut. In effect, the project of founding a *Mathesis universalis* that would unify all the sciences (existing, but also possible) according to the certitude of the clear and distinct must confront the arguments coming out of the New Academy, renewed from Sextus Empiricus by Montaigne, Charron, or La Mothe le Vayer: they relativized each scientific statement by putting it into logical contradiction with itself according to one of the ten (or five, or three) *modes* of doubt.[4] For, against Aristotle, not only "are all things relative (*pros ti ara ta panta*)," but this relativity itself remains "relative to us alone (*pros ti pros hemas*)."[5] With each statement bearing each time on a *positum*, one can always restart the operation of putting into contradiction, and thus call for the suspension of assent. For Descartes, it is therefore a matter, each time (errors of sensation, madness, dreams, and so on), of confronting a doubt that is logically argued, that claims that there is no statement to be found that does not invalidate its contrary. Consequently, in order to respond to these skeptical arguments addressed to precise dogmatic theses, he often takes up Cicero's discussions in the *Academica*, and Saint Augustine's in *Contra Academicos*, playing both against and with the New Academy.

There remains another, more radical tactic, which comes from extreme Pyrrhonism: the questioning of logic itself, and thus of every truth, through the principle of mounting to the extremes of doubt, which refuses to define itself in order to exert itself even more: "In this sense, the skeptic will be found not to be defining anything, not even the slogan 'I define nothing' (*auto to 'ouden horizō'*)."[6] Descartes evokes it and clearly makes a claim to it:

> Enitar tamen et tentabo rursus eandem viam quam hieri fueram ingressus, removendo scilicet illud omne quod vel minimum dubitationis admittit, nihilo secius quam si omnino falsum esse comperissem; pergamque porro donec aliquid certi, vel, si nihil aliud, saltem hoc ipsum pro certo, nihil esse certi, cognoscam—Nevertheless I will make an effort and once more attempt the same path which I started on yesterday. Anything which admits of the slightest doubt I will set aside just as if I had found it to be wholly false; and I will proceed in this way until I recognize something certain, or, if nothing else, until I at least recognize for certain that there is no certainty. (*Meditatio II*, AT VII, 24.3–9; CSM II, 16)

To simplify, we will say that Descartes uses provisional Pyrrhonism as a backfire that extinguishes the materials of the logician's skepticism of the Academy: doubt, if it becomes radical and principial, renders useless the particular and argued doubts. But how does Descartes connect them, and how does he surpass them? In what sense is radicalized and properly Pyrrhonian doubt in line with what Descartes sometimes calls *Meditationes contra Scepticos*,[7] and does it avoid imitating "the Skeptics, who doubt only for the sake of doubting" (*Discourse on the Method*, AT VI, 29.2; CSM I, 125)?

The difficulty in interpreting Cartesian skepticism lies in this play between usages of skeptical arguments, on the one hand the still-logical arguments of the Academy, and on the other that of the Pyrrhonian overthrow: "the ignorance of Socrates or the uncertainty of the Pyrrhonians."[8] It is in this sense that Cartesian certainty could be brought together with what elsewhere I have introduced as negative certainty.

§2. The Cartesian Construction of Doubt

First we must take note of an essential difference between Descartes and his predecessors. In the ancient and Renaissance skepticisms, the goal is to support and follow a doctrine, more argued in each case as one intends to fight against opposed doctrines that are denounced as "dogmatic" (Aristotelianism, Stoicism, Epicureanism); and thus skepticism itself tends, by confronting these opposed doctrines dogmatically, to become another "dogmatism." Sextus offers the best example of this, whether through his logical, systematic, and formally similar refutations, or when, in order to challenge the claim that the skeptic is dogmatizing, he again maintains the principle of suspension in consequence of the principle of sole likelihood: "But the most important point is that in putting forward these slogans [of suspension] he is saying what seems likely to him (*to heautō phainomenon*) and is reporting his own affect without holding opinions (*adozastōs*), affirming nothing about external substrata."[9] Descartes, in contrast, does not consider the doubt of the skeptics (nor his own) as a doctrine but rather as an act of thought. Thus, he often suggests that the skeptics cannot in fact truly doubt, because doubt is not enough to constitute a doctrine; they claim to be skeptics by reason but are such only by obstinance: "Certainly I have never denied that the sceptics themselves, as long as they clearly perceive some truth, spontaneously assent to it. It is only in name (*nisi nomine tenus*), and perhaps in intention and resolve, that they adhere to their heresy of doubting everything."[10] Indeed, for Descartes, doubt (and by extension skepticism) implies no theory at all, even a negative one, and even less any sort of *Weltanschauung*. However far the "limits of doubt, *dubitationis limites*" extend (AT VII, 548.24), this doubt must never surpass (*nimia dubitatio*, AT VII, 549.25) what can actually be thought. Doubt must do what it says, no less, but also no more. In order to reconstitute this act of thought and measure its true bearing ("neither too much or too little"[11]), it makes sense to distinguish four characteristics.

First, doubt remains *theoretical*, never practical, according to a strict "distinctio [...] inter actiones vitæ et inquisitionem veritatis—the distinction [...] between the actions of life and the investigation of the truth" (*Væ Responsiones*, AT VII, 350.22–23; CSM II, 243); for "in practical life it is sometimes necessary to act upon opinions which one knows to be quite uncertain just as if they were indubitable. But since I now wished to devote myself solely to the search for truth, I thought it necessary to do the very opposite" (*Discourse on the Method*, AT VI, 31.21–26; CSM I, 126–27): thus, "quandoquidem nunc non rebus agendis, sed cognoscendis tantum incumbo—because now I am not occupied with doing things, but only with knowing them" (*Meditatio II*, AT VII, 22.20–22; CSM II, 15), I will doubt only because I wish to know: "hæc interim dubitatio ad solam contemplationem veritatis est restringenda—meanwhile, this doubt [...] should be employed solely in connection with the contemplation of the truth" (*Principia philosophiæ I*, §3; CSM I, 193). This calls for several remarks. (a) Neither political prudence nor a conservative reflex on the part of Descartes are to blame here, as has long been claimed out of ignorance. (b) In fact, Descartes is taking up a rather habitual argument of the skeptics in defense against the reproach made against them that they forbid the conduct of daily life through the suspension of judgment. Did not Pyrrho risk his life by ignoring daily dangers, and was he not protected from them only by the vigilance of his friends? But, according to the opinion of Aenesidemus, "it was only his philosophy that was based upon suspension (*epochē*) of judgement, and that he did not lack foresight in his everyday acts (*prattein*)."[12] Sextus also agreed to the exigencies of practical life: "For we do follow a certain rationale that, in accord with appearances (*to phainomenon*), points us toward a life in conformity with the customs of our country and its laws and institutions, and with our own particular feelings."[13] We found the same distinction in Charron: "This by no means concerns the divine truths that eternal Wisdom has revealed to us and which we must receive with complete humility and submission, and quite simply believe and adore; nor likewise the external actions and customs of life, the observance of the laws, customs, and that which constitutes ordinary usage [...], for in all these things we must agree with and accommodate ourselves to what is common."[14] (c) Nevertheless, Descartes takes up this distinction only by modifying it profoundly. For the skeptics, the conduct of practical life can be carried out according to the same principle as the conduct of knowledge: by suspending assent, by holding to likenesses and to appearances; this same criteria suffices just as well for doubting in theory and surviving in practice. Sextus emphasizes it: "That we hold to the appearances (*tois phainomenois*) is obvious from what we say about the criterion of the Skeptic Way. The word 'criterion' is used in two ways: first, for the criterion that is assumed in connection with belief about existence or nonexistence, [...] the second for the criterion of action (*tou prattein*)."¹⁵ Against an undifferentiated doubt, Charron likewise invokes the likely in practice as well as in theory: "There is a difference between what I say and the opinion of the Pyrrhonians, even though it has the same feel and smell, since I allow myself to agree with and adhere to that which seems better and closer in likeness, always ready and waiting to receive the better if it presents itself."¹⁶ In contrast, Descartes accepts the likely (as the probable) in practice precisely because, in theory, he excludes it and accepts only the true (which is to say, the certain). The distinction of domains corresponds to the opposition of the criteria, while the skeptics maintain the same criterion for the two domains. Consequently, doubt changes meaning: for Descartes I doubt solely when the issue is knowing, and knowing truly. From a goal and "criteria" that are uniform and universal, as for the skeptics, it becomes the means to eliminate what is not certain in the theory.¹⁷ Whence this paradox that doubt will lead one to no longer doubting: "dubitationis utilitas [. . .] denique efficiat ut [. . .] non amplius dubitare possimus—the usefulness of the doubt [. . .] finally makes it so that [. . .] we can no longer doubt" (*Synopsis*, AT VII, 12.5–10; CSM II, 9).

Secondly, the issue is that of a *generalized* doubt: that which deceives me once must be considered as always deceptive, without taking account of the probability of an error intervening among other more numerous correct judgments. There is no right to error, for an error in one experience is enough to disqualify every new experience. This rule is valid in 1637: "Thus, because they [our senses] *sometimes* deceive us, I decided to suppose that nothing was such as they [men] lead us to imagine" (*Discourse on Method*, AT VI, 32.103; CSM I, 127). And in 1631: "everyone knows that they [our senses] are *sometimes* deceptive, and that we have good reason *always* to distrust those who have deceived us *even once*" (*The Search for Truth*, AT X, 510.13–15; CSM II, 407). And in 1641: "prudentiæ est nunquam illis plane confidere qui nos *vel semel* deceperunt—it is prudent never to trust completely those who have deceived us *even once*" (AT VII, 18.17–18; CSM II, 12). And, finally, in 1644: "it would be imprudent to place too much trust in those who have deceived us *even once*" (*Principles of Philosophy I*, §4; CSM I, 194).¹⁸ The error induced by a sensation changes its status: it is no longer an occasional failure but a permanent incapacity; probability no longer has legitimacy and no longer arises from the truth, since it allows for no certitude at all. With the elimination of probability, which for Aristotle remains a mode of true knowledge (in the

Regula II, AT X, 362.14–16), Descartes finally also challenges likeness, the skeptical criterion of the true.[19]

Thirdly, *hyperbole* comes into play: in order to definitively challenge a statement or an experience, not even a single occurrence of patent error is needed; a mere suspicion of error is enough. Thus, in 1637, "I thought it necessary to [. . .] reject as if absolutely false everything in which I could imagine *the least doubt*, in order to see if I was left believing anything that was entirely indubitable" (*Discourse on the Method*, AT VI, 31.26–30; CSM I, 126–27). And likewise again in 1641: "Jam ratio persuadet, non minus accurate ab iis quæ non plane certa sunt atque indubitata, quam ab aperte falsis assentionem esse cohibendam, satis erit ad omnes rejiciendas, si *aliquam rationem* dubitandi in unaquaque reperero—Reason now leads me to think that I should hold back my assent from opinions which are not completely certain and indubitable just as carefully as I do from those which are patently false. So, for the purpose of rejecting all my opinions, it will be enough if I find in each of them at least some reason for doubt" (*Meditatio I*, AT VII, 18.6–10; CSM II, 17); or: "removendo scilicet illud omne quod *vel minimum* dubitationis admittit, nihilo secius quam si omnino falsum esse comperissem—Anything which admits of the *slightest* doubt I will set aside just as if I had found it to be wholly false" (AT VII, 24.4–7; CSM II, 16).[20] This final step crosses a limit: doubt does not put into question the difference between true and false, but that between the uncertain (which could truly remain, depending on the moment or the occasion) and the certain (which can encompass knowledge but also non-knowledge that is certain). Doubt eliminates uncertainty, and thus also the possibility of an uncertain truth, so as to retain only certainties, perhaps negative ones. The paradox, "donec aliquid certi, vel, si nihil aliud, saltem hoc ipsum pro certo, nihil esse certi, cognoscam—until I recognize something certain, or, if nothing else, until I at least recognize for certain that there is no certainty" (*Meditatio II*, AT VII, 24.7–9; CSM II, 16), does not merely take up (as we said earlier), nor for the first time, the dogmatic aporia of Pyrrhonism, but exposes the interpretation of the truth as certitude, or rather the subversion of the question of the truth through the demand of certitude. Uncertainty does not overlap with the false, since it also includes, besides the false, truth that is probable or likely. Certitude does not overlap with the true but only the certainly true, as well as the false, or even the unknown recognized as such. Truth is normalized according to the thing that shows itself, but certitude is decided starting from the one who possesses it—that is to say, following the criterion of evidence, held by the gaze of the *intuitus*.

Doubt in Descartes' sense (theoretical, generalized, hyperbolic) thus becomes, contrary to the *epochē* of the skeptics, if not an affair of obstinance at least in the final instance one of will: for it is not only the evil genius that the *ego* triggers by pure will ("voluntate plane in contrarium versa—turn my will in completely the opposite direction," *Meditatio I*, AT VII, 22.13; CSM II, 15), but doubt itself, which disqualifies every existence that can be suspected of incertitude *propria libertate utens* (*Synopsis*, AT VII, 12.10).[21] Only such a will to obey solely the unconditional demand of certitude allows the tactic of suspicion in which hyperbolic doubt culminates. One can even discern here an anticipation of the revolutionary theory of the "law of the suspects," recalled by Hegel in the *Phenomenology of Spirit*: the "widow" was able to claim for its Ockham's razor not only the avowed guilty of counter-revolution but also the mere suspects, and admitted only one penalty, death, without benefit of a lawyer or a contradictory trial. So it goes for the suspicion of uncertainty, which is enough for a placement outside of knowledge. The law does not aim at justice, but the establishment of order—revolutionary or certifying.[22]

The question thus becomes: what is Cartesian doubt going to put into question, and just how far will the demand for certitude push its destitution of the world? The difference between Cartesian doubt and the skeptical *epochē* will appear then all the more clearly— as that between destruction with an eye to certitude and the suspension of assent with an eye to the *ataraxia* of the wise man.

§3. A Review of Former Doubts

In the next moment of *Meditatio I*, after the Cartesian construction of doubt, Descartes repeats the arguments of the skeptical *epochē* in order to test them, "chewing again on this common meat (*istam crambem* [. . .] *recoquere*)."[23] Let us highlight them in order to follow this return.

First, let us consider the argument of the deception of the senses: "interdum sensus circa minuta quædam et remotiora nos fallant—the senses occasionally deceive us with respect to objects which are very small or in the distance" (AT VII, 18.19–20; CSM II, 12), "as when [. . .] stars or other very distant bodies appear to us much smaller than they are" (*Discourse on the Method*, AT VI, 39.23–26; CSM I, 130–31). Descartes takes up the traditional examples of the perception of far-away things, for example, "towers which had looked round from a distance appeared square from close up; and enormous statues standing on their pediments did not seem large when observed from the ground."[24] But, far from contenting himself with this in order to draw from it, like the ordinary skeptics (even Sextus and Montaigne), the conclusion *ad nauseum* of the definitive fallibility of all sensible perceptions, he defends, if not their certitude, at least a certain certitude in those that remain not far away, but *here* ("hìc," AT VII, 18.22), close to the body that is mine ("corpus meum," 18.25). These close perceptions (the place where I am seated, the paper that my hands are touching, the fire that warms the body's members, etc.) I cannot doubt. For as soon as one approaches oneself, it is not so easy to be truly doubtful, unless with vague rhetoric or sophistical quibbling (or both, as in Sextus, La Mothe le Vayer, and sometimes Montaigne). Descartes here doubts skeptical doubt, which he resists. And he resists by coming back from the exterior (the *remotiora*) to that which already finds itself closer to the *ego* (his own body).

A second skeptical attack, also traditional, follows: the argument involving the "madmen," "clothed in gold and purple."[25] As strange as it seems to us, this argument had an undeniable force for the contemporary reader because it very likely makes an allusion to the hero of Cervantes' *The Glass Graduate* (*El Licenciado Vidriera*): this graduate in law, soldier, and pilgrim to Our Lady of Loretto, practiced in Flanders, where he became famous for his judgment and his juridical knowledge; and yet, he believed himself to have a body made of glass and imagined that he could only live packed in straw[26] (one will of course note that, madness aside, all of the graduate's traits apply to Descartes himself). We understand the reasoning: the most lucid mind can (allow itself to) be deceived even in the closest sensations, in this case in those of one's own body, the flesh that it itself is (and not an automaton exterior to it, as *Meditatio VI* will confirm, AT VII, 81.1–14 = *Meditatio I*, AT VII, 18.25). Nevertheless, it is not convincing since, in order for the reader to accept it, it would be necessary that he consider that he too is mad; the argument manifests a performative contradiction: irrationality (of the senses) would be proven rationally only by supposing the irrationality of the interlocutor that one claims to convince rationally. Literally: "But such people are deranged in the mind (*amentes*) and I would seem not less deranged of mind (*demens*) as them if I transferred to myself (*ad me transferrem*) an example taken from them" (*Meditatio I*, AT VII, 19.5–7; CSM II, 13). Thus, the issue is not excluding on principle the madness of reason ("confinement"), but rather recognizing that the argument of the madmen, who alone in fact doubt even what is sensible close-up, disqualifies itself: the reader, whom Descartes wishes to convince, thinks rightly that he does not think like a madman (whether he is right or not, which is beside the question); he thus rejects in advance that the madman's doubt can also apply to him. In this way Descartes renounces this argument of the skeptics, which clearly does not imply that he excludes madmen or madness, but simply that he accepts the opinion of his reader.[27] Paradoxically, skepticism fails again, *for Descartes*, to put into doubt what he nevertheless claims to be able to disqualify most easily: sensation.

Consequently, to *reinforce* doubt beyond what ancient skepticism could accomplish, or in short to make himself more skeptical than the skeptics, Descartes introduces a third argument. It has to do with the impossibility of determining a sign by which to distinguish the waking state from sleep: "Nunquam certis indiciis vigiliam a somno posse distingui—there are never any sure signs by means of which being awake can be distinguished from being asleep."[28] This commonplace is likely taken from Montaigne: "Those who have compared our life to a dream were perhaps more right than they thought. When we dream, our soul lives, acts, exercises all her faculties, neither more nor less than when she is awake [. . .]. Sleeping we are awake, and waking asleep."[29] But it is found frequently; for example, in the poetry of Jean-Baptiste Chassignet: "Is there nothing more vain than a lying dream? / A dream that is fleeting, vagabond, and shifting? / Life to a dream we are always comparing, / To a vagabond, shifting, and fleeting dream."[30] It is also current in the theater by, among others, Garnier and Rotrou, but especially Calderón: his hero, Sigismond, constantly passing from prison to the throne and back again, no longer knows if he is dreaming or awake: after having sought in vain to know "If this is a dream or the truth—*si es sueño o si es verdad*," he gives up: "for this strange world / Is such that but to live here is to dream. / And now experience shows me that each man / Dreams what he is until he is awakened. / The king dreams he's a king and in this fiction / Lives, rules, administers with royal pomp. / [...] this life / Is but a dream, and dreams are only dreams—*toda la vida es sueño, / Y los sueños sueños son.*"³¹ But also and perhaps above all this has to do with a profound experience of Descartes himself:

Here [in Amsterdam] I sleep for ten hours every night, and with never a care to wake me. Once sleep has let my mind wander at length among groves, gardens and enchanted palaces, where I sample all the pleasures that are dreamt of in fables, I gradually intermingle my daydreams with my night dreams; and when it dawns on me that I am awake, it is only to make my contentment more perfect and to enable my senses to share it—for I am not so austere as to deny them anything a philosopher could grant without doing violence to his conscience.³²

But this indifference can be overturned into a privilege of thought, where he is always awake enough to interpret his dreams without even exiting them; Baillet notes this explicitly: "What is singular to notice is that, while doubting whether what he had just seen were a dream or vision, he decided *while sleeping* that it was a dream, but he made the interpretation *before sleep had left him* [...]. On that score, *doubting whether he was dreaming or meditating*, he woke himself up without emotion and continued, with open eyes, the interpretation of his dream on the same idea."³³ It is even first and foremost a positive theoretical discovery that is at stake here, since it allows for the validation of the theoretical results obtained while dreaming: "it is easy to recognize that the things we imagine in dreams should in no way make us doubt the truth of the thoughts we have when awake. For if one happened even in sleep to have some very distinct idea (if, say, a geometer devised some new proof), one's being asleep would not prevent the idea from being true."³⁴ It is, then, a doctrine proper to Descartes—that *cogitatio* is not modified *as such* by waking or sleeping and its dreams—that restarts a skeptical argument that was a little too traditional to have theoretical validity. Thus reinforced, doubt, which disqualifies a number of everyday particulars (*plera, usitata ista, particularia*, AT VII, 18.20, 19.11&23), no longer depends only on a negative thesis of the skeptical sort (being awake is only a dream), but instead on a positive thesis (the indifference of *cogitatio* to the difference between being awake and asleep).

Nevertheless, precisely because the issue is not a mere skeptical polemic but rather a machine to detect certitude, Descartes responds to the doubt that he has just reinforced. A fourth argument ensues, which in fact mobilizes one of the results of the theory of knowledge elaborated in the *Regulæ ad directionem ingenii*: by admitting that particular sensations (*particularia*), like such and such movement of the head or of the hand, remain deceptive, it nevertheless remains that the sensible elements of which they are composed ("*generalia hæc*, general kinds of things," AT VII, 19.29; 20.8; CSM II, 13) remain indubitable. In this way Descartes operates a first reduction—of the complex sensible into simpler elements that are also sensible: the compositions can deceive, but the elements that they bring together remain true, because simpler. A comparison ("nec dispari ratione," 20.8) explains it: just as even the most audacious painters ("sane pictores," 19.31) always refer to nature, even if only through the use of "real colors" (*veri colore*, 20.7), so the elements perceived by the senses ("*generalia haec*, general kinds of things") always presuppose "simpler and more universal things, *magis simplicia et universalia vera*" (20.11; CSM II, 14). Let us take note here of a second reduction, that of the sensible elements (resulting from the first reduction, of the particular sensible to the general sensible) to universal concepts that they presuppose. Moreover, it is inspired by a prior "comparison," which the *Optics* had made, between, on the one hand, the process of sensible vision (where the idea arises without "resemblance" to its physical cause, the object) and, on the other hand, intaglio engravings (where the perspective makes it so that circles and squares are represented by drawing ovals and rhombuses).[35] Now these "simpler and more universal things" indeed constitute notions that are simpler than the "general things": the elements of the sensible presuppose notions or concepts that in no way resemble them. Their list, here tallied by the *Meditatio I*, reproduces some of the "simple natures" already thematized in the *Regulæ*; it includes first of all the material simple natures, "shape, extension and motion, etc.," then certain of the simple natures termed "common," "existence, unity, duration and the like" (AT X 419.19–20; CSM I, 45 = AT VII 20.15–19; CSM II, 14). Thus, if the dream argument puts into doubt for the first time everything sensible, it runs up against the indubitable conditions of possibility of sensation, conditions that themselves are conceptual, as Cartesian epistemology fixed them in 1627 and developed them in 1637—namely on the elementary conceptions and the categories of the understanding, the *naturæ simplicissimæ*, about which one cannot doubt, since they alone make possible all sensible experience.

One will therefore conclude that if there are sciences that use only the simple natures that are material and common, like arithmetic and geometry "and the other sciences of this kind, *aliasque ejusmodi*" (AT VII, 20.24; CSM II, 14), which is to say, like the one and only *Mathesis universalis* (*Regula IV*, AT X, 377.9–380.25), they will turn out to be absolutely certain, outside of the reach of skepticism. All the other quasi-sciences must on the contrary allow "composite things"; indeed, physics, astronomy, medicine, music, and so on all compose simple natures with materiality and its imprecision; all "are concerned with an object [. . .] that experience might render uncertain" (*Regula II*, AT X, 365.17–18; CSM I, 12), and thus they alone fall to the blow of skeptical arguments. *Here and at this point* in the reasoning, Descartes has therefore contained skepticism and, like most of his successors including as far as Kant, would have victoriously opposed to it the mathematical or similar sciences because they remain insensible.

Whence follows this new paradox: after having reinforced the traditional arguments of the skepticism of the Academicians in opposition to sensible certitude, Descartes refutes them by virtue of his own founding of sensible perception on the *naturæ simplicissimæ*.

§4. *The* Mathesis Universalis *and the Radical Pyrrhonian Argument*

And yet, the doubt that Descartes carries out does not stop here, not even with the real but provisional triumph of the Cartesian theory of knowledge over the incertitude of sensible perception. For a new paradox restarts the investigation in 1641, moving it beyond what Descartes had gained in 1627.

While the four preceding arguments concerned solely the sensations and sensible knowledge, the arguments that follow undertake to doubt properly intellectual knowledge, as well. And the reason is very clear: if, in the final instance, the sensations turn out to be indubitable *in a way*, it is only indirectly so; for they owe it to their foundation on pure concepts of the understanding, the *naturæ simplicissimæ* or "simple natures" that make possible their encoding in shapes by inscribing them through *ordo et mensura* in the *Mathesis universalis*. In other words, sensible knowledge, even if in itself doubtful, always presupposes a rational underpinning, which duplicates it in terms of quantifiable and formalizable extension.[36] This surely surprising yet inevitable consequence follows: in order to end up thoroughly doubting sensible knowledge, it would first of all be necessary to come to doubt the intellectual knowledge itself that makes it possible. Take an example of this intellectual knowledge: the absolute certainty of the sum 5 when "duo et tria simul addo" (AT VII, 21.9–10; CSM II, 14), which attests that the mathematical truths remain evident "whether I am awake or asleep," and thus also that doubt, if it holds to the dream argument, falls before *Cartesian* science, the *Mathesis universalis*. However, such certainty about mathematical statements, even in their simplest case, 2 + 3 = 5, can be contested. It is enough to note that this preeminent example, such as it is mentioned in *Meditatio I*, quotes the answer that the notorious unbeliever, Maurice de Nassau, made on his death bed to the question about what he truly believed: "I will tell you simply and in a few words that I believe that 2 and 2 are 4 and 4 and 4 are 8."[37] At issue is the typical case of one of these "atheists, *athei*" that Descartes had declared to have the goal of refuting.[38] We can infer from this connection that, for Descartes, if mathematics and the simple natures that are material and common remained indubitable, then it would become thinkable here to subtract them from divine power or to dispense with divine power—in short, to give oneself up to what at the time was understood under the name of atheism.

Against this other dogmatism (which categorically and banally affirms the dogma of the absolute certitude of mathematical statements and formal tautologies[39]) Descartes forges a fifth skeptical argument, the strongest and the most unexpected. It is the strongest because it radicalizes the Academicians' *epochē* into an absolutely unconditioned doubt without any exceptions, bearing on the evidence as such, Pyrrhonian by its very excess and degrading the highest certitude attained by its own epistemological innovation, the *Mathesis universalis*. And it is the most surprising because it relies on a hypothesis that is clearly *theological*, and thus absolutely meta-scientific (in this way confirming that theological questions sometimes interact with those of philosophy, AT I, 143.25–144.18). Indeed, here there enters in, like a meteorite suddenly fallen to earth,[40] without any preparation or justification, "quaedam [. . .] vetus opinio Deum esse qui potest omnia" (AT VII, 21.1–2), "the long-standing opinion that there is a God who can do all things" (AT IX-1, 16.14–14; CSM II, 14); it will reappear in the Third Meditation ("hæc præconcepta de summa Dei potentia opinio," AT VII, 36.8–9) and in the *Principals of Philosophy* ("audivimus esse Deum, qui potest omnia,"

I, §5). But in fact, we should not be astonished that Descartes' argument might rely here on this simple opinion. Indeed, this opinion cannot fail to concern every reader, since it appears as a possibility that is perfectly likely (like the dream argument) and not unlikely (like the madness argument); what is more, it can concern almost every reader, if he is a Christian, provided that he had recited or heard recited this formula: "God who can do all things, *Deus omnipotens*." This fact, moreover, forbids any talk of a supposed "deceiving God" (or worse, of a "great deceiver"), a title that, despite a long tradition of commentary, has no textual basis.

On the other hand, one can assign to this opinion at least three origins that are neither contradictory, nor exclusive. (a) This is the Christian God, creator and all-powerful, known by every reader from having recited the *Credo* (the *Apostles' Creed*): "I believe in God the Father almighty, Creator of heaven and earth."[41] Which the mention of "heaven" and "earth" (*nullum cœulum, nullam terram*, AT VII, 21.4) would confirm, preceding what nevertheless it is solely a question of revoking in doubt, the simple material natures, that is, the concepts of extension, shape, size, and location. *The Search for Truth* confirms this liturgical origin: "You have learned that you were *created* by a superior being who, being all-powerful, would have found it no more difficult to *create* us just as I am describing [namely, deceiving ourselves], than to *create* us as you think you are" (AT X, 512; CSM II, 408, emphasis added). (b) There could also be an allusion here to the nominalist doctrine of absolute or extraordinary (and not just ordinary) all-mightiness, such as it would define the divine essence. Descartes seems to allude to this doctrine in the *VIæ Responsiones*, n. 7 (AT VII, 435.108). (c) But it was probably Montaigne who furnished Descartes with the synthesis of these two possible sources, when he attacked, precisely in the name of God's all-mightiness, the atheists who claim for themselves the mathematical statements: "Of all the ancient human opinions concerning religion, that one, it seems to me, was most probable and most excusable which recognized God as an incomprehensible power, origin and preserver of all things, all goodness, all perfection." Consequently, there would be "overweening arrogance" in wanting to "pass the deity through our sieve," and to claim, of God, that "*he cannot make two times ten not be twenty*. That is [. . .] what a Christian should avoid having pass out of his mouth."[42] Here, the simple faith in the first article of the *Credo* offers the decisive *theological* argument in favor of a radical skepticism, which disqualifies even and above all what appears for a finite rational mind as the ultimate possibility of unshakeable certitude: mathematical (and logical) statements.

The argument sharpens in this way. I observe (I who know for example that material things have no resemblance whatsoever to their sensible "ideas," but are composed and codified in terms of extension, shape, and movement), while others (not educated, nor philosophers, *ageōmetroi*) remain convinced by the immediate evidence that these things resemble their "ideas" (a situation criticized at length in *Regula XII*, AT X, 412.14–415.20, and by *Optics*, I and IV). Nevertheless, there remains another hypothesis: imagine that when I place myself in front of what is for me insurmountable evidence of the simple natures that are material and common, in other words mathematics (or rather, the *Mathesis universalis*, according to the *naturæ simplicissimæ*), I thoroughly deceive myself, but this time from the point of view (at least thinkable) of another rationality and of an evidence that is superior to my own, that of a "God who can do all things," of whom by definition I have no comprehension whatsoever. Whence the hypothesis that has been explicitly evoked (albeit of course revoked immediately after) under the name of "absolute falsity" in the *Second Set of Replies* (AT VII, 145.1–9; CSM II, 103). This hypothesis weighs all the more heavily because the nominalist doctrine of extraordinary divine power had developed the paradoxical but rigorously logical thesis that, instead of a simple abstractive knowledge like in the normal realm of knowledge, God could give to a finite mind the intuitive vision of a thing that is even *absent*; in short, furnish the finite mind with the intuitive knowledge of an absent thing as if it were present.[43]

Certainly one can question the significance of this argument: does a God who deceives me offer a credible motive for doubting? Isn't this instead a contradictory hypothesis, since I can only accept it by *not* understanding it (for it challenges the ultimate conditions of my comprehension, or of the rationality I have at my disposal)? For Descartes, the argument nevertheless remains valid, for at least three reasons. (a) First, and formally, we recognize that the extravagance and the unlikelihood of hyperbolic doubt respond exactly to the non-standard character of an authentically Pyrrhonian skepticism; inversely, respecting the criteria of likeness, probability, and possibility would imply precisely an unconscious dogmatism of the greatest sort. A doubt of the highest certitude comprehensible to us thus must really and truly exceed our finite understanding. (b) Next, precisely in this instance, God does not positively deceive me; rather, he makes or at least allows me to deceive *myself*; the verb *fallor* (and its derivations) that the Latin uses to describe the final situation can of course be understood as a passive, but the French translation always takes it as a middle voice (in English, it would have to be translated, *I am mistaken*); the issue then is less that of an error prompted by a positive cause, exterior and circumstantial, than what Kant will call a "transcendental illusion," a natural risk of error, inevitable and permanent, because tied to the transcendental limits of the finite mind. I can deceive *myself*, be mistaken, without God deceiving me, by the simple fact that I am not God: this is what the theodicy of *Meditatio IV* will develop (AT VII, 55.14–56.8). (c) Finally, Descartes notes that it would be enough for me to be deceived in this way "occasionally, *interdum*" (21.15 = AT IX-1, 16.31; CSM II, 14) for this doubt to continue to impose itself; no one will call into question the fundamental divine goodness simply on the pretext that I fall into occasional errors; we must then conclude that God who can do all things remains good even if it happens that I am sometimes mistaken.

Nevertheless, Descartes sees quite well the difficulty in maintaining the title of an *optimus Deus* and a *fons veritatis* (AT VII, 22.23–24 = "a true God, who is the sovereign source of truth," AT IX-1, 17.35) with that of the "God who can do all" (in that he does not positively deceive). Consequently, he turns to a sixth and last argument: the hypothesis of a *genius aliquis malignius*, which one must translate literally as *a certain evil genius*. The indetermination *aliquis* plays an essential role, since it allows the masking of the internal contradiction of an almighty power that would be directly deceptive. For Descartes perfectly identifies the difficulty:

Here we must distinguish between the true God, clearly known, and false gods. Once the true God is clearly known, not only is it not permissible, but it is not possible for the human mind to attribute anything false to him [...]. But the case is not the same with false divinities, i.e. evil spirits, or idols, or other such gods invented by the error of the human mind—all these are called gods in Holy Scripture—or with the true God, if he is known only in a confused way. To attribute to these something false as a hypothesis can be either good or bad, depending on whether the purpose of framing such a hypothesis is good or bad.⁴⁴

i

That the issue here is simply a fiction without any theoretical validity, with a solely pedagogical or psychological function, useful for confirming at any time the will in its design, salutary but uncomfortable, to resist the temptation of accepting as absolute *in itself* the certitude *for me* of the mathematical truths—this was established definitively by Henri Gouhier.[45] The gap between the "God who can do all" and the *aliquis genius malignius* was also confirmed, by remarking that the latter only remains qualified by the title of *summe potens* (AT VII, 22.25, merely "powerful," AT IX-1, 17.38), without ever receiving the attribute all-powerful, *omnipotentia*, that is proper of the true God.[46]

There is more: if Descartes doubles the argument involving God's omnipotence with the pedagogical fiction of the *aliquis genius malignius*, it is probably in order to avoid explicitly formulating the fundamental doctrine that makes the argument irrefutable to his eyes: the doctrine of the creation of the eternal truths, as formulated in the three letters to Mersenne of April and May 1630. It has moreover already been demonstrated that the formula of 1641, "Deum, fontem veritatis" (AT VII, 22.23), refers directly to a similar one, dating from 1644: "omnipotens, omnis bonitatis veritatisque fons" (*Principia philosophiae I*, §22), which in turn makes a clear allusion to the creator of the eternal truths: "the existence of God is the first and the most eternal of all possible truths and the one from which alone all others proceed."[47] Of course, God is the source of truth and of truths, but as "*efficiens et totalis causa*—efficient and total cause" (AT I, 152.2; CSMK, 25); now, this relation not only implies no likeness whatsoever between the cause and the effect (in contrast to formal and final causalities) but expressly prohibits it. Consequently, the truth as effect does not coincide with the "source of truth," and thus what appears absolutely evident in the truth carried out can perfectly remain uncertain (or founded under a condition, at a distance from the origin) from the point of view of this "source." In short, in the situation instituted by the doctrine of the creation of the eternal truths, a truth that is certain *for me* can quite perfectly not be so *in itself*, for God. Whence the ultimate paradox: that the genuine Pyrrhonism comes from a theological consideration in metaphysics.

Thus, we must conclude (a) that Descartes establishes, at least in *Meditatio I*, a radical skeptical argument: with complete success, he practices skepticism as a method. (b) Nevertheless, this skepticism does not put into doubt sensible givens (as ancient skepticism does), nor religious doctrines (as Enlightenment skepticism does), but rather (like a renewed Pyrrhonism) the scientific statements obtained by the *Mathesis universalis*, as defined by the *Regulæ* and the *Essays* on method: Descartes thus accomplishes skepticism (by adding arguments against the scientific statements to the commonly received arguments against the testimony of the senses), not only because he doubts *all* the truths but also because in the end he doubts his *own* as well. (c) Finally, this extraordinary critical exercise, which goes beyond all the skeptical dogmas of his time, still constitutes only a first moment, preliminary to the speculative construction of the *Meditations* to follow.

In the end, nothing will remain of the "hyperbolicæ superiorum dierum dubitationes [...] risu dignæ—the exaggerated doubts of the last few days [...] [which] are worthy of laughter" (AT VII, 89.19–20; CSM II, 61). Descartes doubts everything, even his own doctrine of science and its own positive results, but, in the final instance, he doubts his doubt itself. In this way he shows, better than any other philosopher, that skepticism cannot culminate in a doctrine (in which, as we know, it would contradict itself), but can serve to test every doctrine—doubting becomes a privileged form of *cogitatio*. Doubt defines thought when thought thinks short of certainty, when it thinks by *esteem*.[48]

§5. From One Performative to the Other

What does it mean to doubt doubt, doubt doubting *itself*? It may signify a defeat of doubt, a victory of certitude found once again, or found at last; but it may also signify the auto-affirmation of doubt through its intensification. Yet in looking at these two conclusions more closely, we see that they turn against each other. In the first hypothesis, that of a defeat of doubt and a victory of certitude, there is only an empty result: by disqualifying the mathematical truths (and the *naturæ simplicissimæ*), the omnipotence of God affirms nothing but itself; but, as it exerts itself under the title of his infinity, it remains "incomprehensible";[49] its fact translates into no thesis accessible to us; skepticism is thus reinforced instead of being annulled. As to the second hypothesis, that of an auto-affirmation of doubt through its intensification, it is exposed to the contradiction of making of this doubt a statement ("non-assertion, *aphasia*," "not more, *ou mallon*," "perhaps, *tacha*," "it is possible, *endechetai*," "I withhold assent, *epechō*," "I determine nothing, *ouden horizō*," "to every argument an equal argument is opposed," etc.)⁵⁰ of a certitude that is outside of doubt, and thus a transformation of the supposedly radical skepticism into a dogmatism comparable to that of Aristotle, the Stoics, and the Epicureans. Sextus was well aware of this, since he tried to respond to this contradiction by a dodge that, in fact, only emphasized it more: "For concerning all the Skeptic slogans it is necessary for this to be understood first of all: we absolutely do not firmly maintain (without doubting, *ou diabebaioumetha*) anything about their being true, especially since we say that they can be confuted by themselves, being suppressed at the same time (*sumperigraphomenas*) as that in regard to which they are said—just as cathartic drugs not only flush out the bodily humors but expel themselves as well."⁵¹ But what does a suspension of the statement of suspension really mean? The metaphor of the ladder that one kicks away after having climbed it explains nothing. Here Sextus limits himself in fact to putting into form the summary warning that Diogenes Laertius attributed to Pyrrho: "Concerning the skeptical statements, one speaks not positively but negatively, *ou thetikōs, all' anairetikōs*."⁵² The question cannot be avoided: if one must not speak affirmatively of doubt (and thus likewise one must not speak of it negatively), how can one say it? And, quite simply, can one say it? And if one cannot say it, can it be accomplished in thought?

This question goes all the way back to Socrates himself, as La Mothe le Vayer recognized:

> What? Are you able to find this doubtful restraint so strange in them [the skeptics], when you see Socrates, the common father of all philosophers, the source from whom, as from the heights of the Apennines, says Cicero, flowed all the sects of philosophy, and who never proposes in Plato his most resolute conclusions except with a question mark, as if he is inquiring rather than teaching the truth of things that he treats? To the point that he does not dare to assure that he is a man rather than some strange animal: *ego enim, inquit, nescio an sim homo, an alia fera Typhone magis multiplex et varia*; and makes this frank confession, *hoc unum scio, quod nihil scio*, Anaxarchus having since then gone further than him, saying, *se, ne id quidem scire, quod nihil sciret*.⁵³

Must we then say that one does not know or that one does not even know that one does not know? But how do we affirm that neither can one affirm (and thus also deny) without self-contradiction? Of course, one can simply not see the difficulty. Certain thinkers, like Charron, continued to practice affirmation in order to claim to liberate themselves from it: "I will say here that I had inscribed over the door of my little house that I had built in Condom in the year 1600 these words: *Je ne sais pas*. But they [the dogmatists?] want us to submit sovereignly and finally to certain principles, which is an unjust tyranny. I agree that one should employ such principles with judgment, and that we should be attentive; but without being able to resist or rebel? I am firmly and strongly opposed."[34] Only one, Montaigne, had seen in advance the difficulty and where it comes from: "Most of the occasions for the troubles of the world are grammatical." In principle, in order to say that one must affirm nothing, it is necessary neither to affirm or deny; that is to say, it is necessary to say without predicating, and thus nothing less than to renounce the Aristotelian apparatus of the *legein*, categorial predication, which says (or not) something of something. To speak as an authentic skeptic, one must practice a non-predicative *legein*. Montaigne, who as Malebranche accused him, "affects the air of a Pyrrhonist,"[35] understands this and he rectifies the ambiguity: "I can see why the Pyrrhonian philosophers cannot express their general conception in any manner of speaking; for they would need a new language. Ours is wholly formed of affirmative propositions, which to them are utterly repugnant; so that when they say 'I doubt,' immediately you have them by the throat to make them admit that at least they know and are sure of this fact, that they doubt." To speak as a skeptic one must no longer predicate; it is therefore necessary to interrogate, without saying nothing of nothing, or rather to speak to say nothing of nothing: "This idea is more firmly grasped in the form of interrogation: 'What do I know?'—the words I bear as a motto, inscribed over a pair of scales."[36] What motto is more fitting to inscribe on the wall of a true Pyrrhonian, "I don't know" or "What do I know?" Pascal, clearly, was not fooled.[57] He did not underestimate the movement from one motto to the other:

He [Montaigne] puts everything into a universal doubt, and this doubt is so widespread that it becomes carried away by its very self; *that is to say, he doubts whether he doubts, and doubting even this last proposition*, his uncertainty goes round in an endless and restless circle. [. . .] For if he says that he doubts, he betrays himself with saying at least that he does so, which was strictly not his intention. He could only explain his position by a question, so, not wanting to say: "I don't know," he says: "What do I know?" which he makes his motto, putting it on the scales which, weighing all the contradictions, are in perfect equilibrium. That is to say, he is a straightforward Pyrrhonist.[58]

Skepticism only becomes a Pyrrhonism, a radical skepticism, by becoming non-predicative—that is, interrogative.

But what does this interrogation mean to say? By predicating nothing of nothing, what does it still allow to be seen, supposing that it allows anything at all to be seen? We know Montaigne's response, which he gives beginning from his address "To the Reader": "it is myself that I portray. [. . .] I am myself the matter of my book."[59] Doubting to the point of doubting doubt means putting predication on hold, so that the one who speaks speaks to say nothing of nothing, and thus speaks by bearing speech on nothing, by letting speech say nothing—and so making appear, in the abolition of what is said and is no longer said, the one who nevertheless said it. By unveiling no thing at all, by referring to no referent, by undoing itself of its signifiers and signifieds, speech only speaks itself, in actuality [*en acte*]. And this act manifests the one who thus speaks. The one who thus speaks is he who speaks, *ego*. Montaigne held back this conclusion, probably for motives that I analyze elsewhere,[60] but Descartes took it up entirely. During the fourth and final sequence of the argument in the form of dialogue[61] that leads to the discovery of the *ego sum*, he effectively abolishes every predicative statement, since none can subsist within hyperbolic doubt under the hold of the "*deceptor nescio quis, summe potens, summe callidus, qui de industria me semper fallit*—a deceiver of supreme power and cunning who is deliberately and constantly deceiving me" (AT VII, 25.6–7; CSM II, 17). But "*Ego sum, ego existo*" necessarily remains true, not insofar as I could verify the predication of it through argument (reasoning or experience), but insofar as *I pronounce* it *in actuality*: "*hoc pronuntiatum, Ego sum, ego existo, quoties a me profertur*, vel mente concipitur, necessario esse verum—this pronouncement, *I am, I exist*, is necessarily true every time *I utter it* or conceive it in my mind" (AT VII, 25.10–13; CSM II, 17). For it is not a question of what I think, know, or represent to myself (for none of that, nothing that would be a *res*, is sure), but *of the fact* that I "utter" it (AT IX-1, 205.17), "pronounce" it (de Luynes' translation, AT IX-1, 19.38). "Conceiving it in thought" is thus deduced from the act of uttering, of pronouncing, and not the reverse; such that, in the most complete formulation of what is referred to as "the *cogito*," that of *Meditatio II*, not only does the habitual formula and its discursive reasoning disappear (*cogito, ergo sum*), but there is not even a mention of *cogito / cogitare*. And yet there is nothing more coherent: what makes the argument is not that the existence of the *ego* is deduced from the *cogitatio*, but rather that the *cogitatio* effectively takes place and in this way the *ego* is experienced *in actuality*. Now, an act is not said, nor does it make itself said, by another act; it is said and made itself. Thought is not thought as a content of thought but is performed and, as an act performing itself, it attests to an existence, which calls itself—*where* it calls itself—*ego*. Thought takes a body saying nothing, nothing other than self, in short by saying *itself*, by *self saying*. What abolishes "all the most extravagant suppositions of the sceptics" (*Discourse on the Method*, AT VI, 32.20–21; CSM I, 127) is precisely what Montaigne had accomplished by moving to interrogation: the testing of thought as the placement in actuality of the *ego* answers to his test as experimental observation of the *moi* (the two terms, *ego* and *moi*, are not identified with one another, even if they enter in at the end of a similar process).⁶²

This exit from predication to the act of thought, where Montaigne (in the skeptical line, but radicalized) meets Descartes (in the exceptional formula from *Meditatio II*), is marked in the latter more clearly than in the former. The decisive character of the passage from one mode of thinking to the other, from thinking that predicates, deduces, and concludes with a representation, to thinking that performs itself, makes itself become *actu* by saying itself, to the point that in this act being and saying become one. The *cogitatio* is said in actuality by the *ego*: "necessarium mihi videtur ut mens *semper actu cogitet*, quia cogitatio constituit ejus essentiam—it seems necessary that the mind should *always be actually engaged in thinking*, because thought constitutes its essence," as Descartes expressly emphasizes.⁶³ This is seen first by Descartes' insistence, against some readers who only reason formally, on the non-syllogistic character of what is known as the *cogito* argument; it does not have to do with "the work of your reasoning or information passed on to you by teachers; it is something that your mind sees, feels and handles" (Letter to Silhon, March or April 1648, AT V, 138.4–6; CSMK, 331): seeing it, or in other words, experiencing it through an *intuitus* (AT VII, 140.23).

The reason why "I am" is not deduced from a proposition in the form of "the one who thinks is" lies precisely in the fact that the universal premise here remains a proposition, which falls under doubt, while "I am" does not constitute a proposition and thus resists against doubt. In effect, "I am" says nothing about anything, but signs off on, so to speak, the experimental protocol of the "*actu primo*, first actuality" (AT VII, 356.17; CSM II, 246), which is executed and performed in it: "I notice that while I was trying thus to think everything false, it was necessary that I, who was thinking this, was something" (*Discourse on the Method*, AT VI, 32.15–18; CSM I, 127). I am what I am for as long as I accomplish an act and I can accomplish no other than that of thinking; it is in the act of "this *moi* who is thinking" (Letter to Colvius, November 14, 1640, AT III, 247.10; CSMK, 159) that in response I notice "this *moi*—that is, the soul by which I am what I am" (*Discourse*, AT VI, 33.7–8; CSM I, 127). The *ego* discovers itself as *thinking* thought (*cogito, res cogitans*), not as *thought* thought (*cogitatum*), and not through a representation (even of the self), but through an act outside of the self, outside of its thought; this "thing that thinks" sees itself as thing while thinking, and thinking anything at all, since, whether it breathes, whether it walks, and even whether it thinks whatever you like (*omnis*, AT VII, 181.7: *omne* 160.7: *cætera*, 352.18, etc.), it is always first of all (and sometimes only) it that it experiences. This is why *Meditatio II* repeats *ego* (which, in ordinary grammar, would be useless, since the two singular nominatives, *sum* and *existo*, already imply it), and omits *cogito* (for the act of thinking is not said there in a proposition but puts itself into actuality by pronouncing itself: *profetur*, or, without saying it, *concipitur*); the translation should be: *it is* moi, who am, *it is* moi who exists. Thus, we understand better that thinking implies not only *seeing* but also, as was said, *feeling* and *handling* (AT V, 138.6). Thinking feels itself like a thing, a thing insofar as it thinks: "sed etiam sentire, idem est hîc quod cogitare [. . .] mentem quæ sola sentit sive cogitat—also feeling [is] here the same thing as thinking [. . .] the mind, which alone is concerned with feeling or thinking" (*Principles of Philosophy I*, §9; CSM I, 195).[64]

Descartes takes over from Montaigne in challenging any philosophy that is dialectical, logical, formal (by categories and syllogisms, or following the "tree of Porphyry") for the sake of a philosophy "sine Logica, sine regula, sine argumentandi formula—not by means of logic, or a rule or pattern of argument." Nothing certain, but above all nothing original can be known by categorial definitions and logical deductions: "Philosophos in hoc errare, quod ea quæ simplicissima erant ac per se nota, Logicis definitionibus explicare conarentur; ita enim obscuriora reddebant—I have often noticed that philosophers make the mistake of employing logical definitions in an attempt to explain what was already very simple and self-evident; the result is that they only make matters more obscure."[65] Nothing is known except by experience: "non autem ita attendo ad generalem illam notionem, *quicquid cogitat, est*—I do not pay attention in the same way to the general notion, 'whatever thinks exists'" (*Conversation with Burman*, AT V, 147; CSMK, 333), by knowledge obtained immediately: "nulla quidem ratiocinatio vel comparatio ab aliis rebus petita, sed certissima et evidentissima experientia quotidie nobis ostendit—not by any reasoning or comparison with other matters, but by the surest and plainest everyday experience" (Letter for [Arnauld], 29 July 1648, AT V, 222.16–18; CSMK, 358).

Either the principle of contradiction, or the existence of the soul. One might hazard the risk of saying that Montaigne put Descartes on the skeptical path, or more exactly the ultra-skeptical path, leading to the suspending of predication, and thus formal logic, and not toward some sort of intuitionism (because, for Descartes, the *intuitus* does not intuit but sees, looks, safeguards and retains [*sauvegarde et garde*]), but instead toward what Schelling, in order to surmount the dialectic and logical knowledge, or in short "negative philosophy," will call "positive philosophy." We might spot it in the distinction between two possible meanings of the "principle." Descartes proposes to understand it in two senses: either we understand it logically, as the principle of non-contradiction that "can serve in general, not properly speaking to make known the existence of anything, but simply to bring it about that, when we know it, we confirm its truth by such reasoning"; put plainly, the logical principle never reaches existence, but presupposes it and, at best, formalizes it in connection with other conclusions. Or instead we understand it from existence itself and starting from its fact: "the first principle is that *our soul exists*, since there is nothing whose existence is better known to us" (Letter to Clerselier, June 1646, AT VII, 444.13–25; CSMK, 290); in other words, we never meet up with existence deductively, but, barring missing it (and most philosophies miss it), we must accept it before any deduction, before any concept, starting from its fact; this *factum* remains to be received without foreseeing it, unthinkable in advance and always already there (unprethinkable, *unvordenklich*, says Schelling).⁶⁶ With the unprethinkable of *ego sum, ego existo*, Descartes led skepticism beyond itself, up to "positive philosophy."

§6. Doubt as First Principle

Descartes thus repeats Montaigne: with doubt, pushed to its radicality, one transgresses all predication, and beyond what is said, there remains the *moi* who, in actuality, does the saying. But this speech act is not led by Montaigne to the point of existence, existence that is felt and conscious. Montaigne thus does not pose what Descartes poses.⁶⁷ We could conclude from this that, in the final instance, Descartes passes beyond doubt and abandons skepticism, its arguments, and its postures, as a provisional moment and means. Doubtless one can admit that the "first principle" (what is customarily called the *cogito*) had for only a moment taken the figure of doubt, after having held the role of the *mens* instituting the *Mathesis universalis* (in the *Regulæ*), and, before that, of the *res cogitans* of metaphysical establishment, ending up finally at that of the "soul" that feels itself (*Passions of the Soul*). However, it could be that the skeptical moment of the *cogito* maintains a privileged role, albeit a concealed one. For in the end, if we accept (following the convincing argumentation of Vincent Carraud and Gilles Olivo) that *The Search for Truth* dates from 1631, we must also admit that this dialogue, certainly transitional, left unfinished and unpublished (like, moreover, the *Regulæ*), not only offers the first formulation of the *cogito* but also claims for it the status of first principle. Now it does not do so by relying on the act of *cogitatio* in general, but on the particular act of doubt: "Es igitur, et te esse scis, et hoc exinde, quia dubitas scis—You are, therefore, and you know that you are, and you know this just because you are doubting" (AT X, 515, and Carraud and Olivo, 330; CSM II, 410). The objector is not mistaken and right away sees a "principle" here: "Non video, nec etiam qua ratione dubitatio ejusmodi possit principium esse—I do not see how this sort of doubt can be a principle, nor by what reason" (AT X, 515, and Carraud and Olivo, 329; CSM II, 409). In sum, the first principle institutes itself with the performance "sum, quatenus dubito—I am, in so far as I am doubting."⁶⁸ Is it the matter of a still imprecise, mere anticipation of the "first principle" that the *Discourse on the Method* will attribute to "this truth: *I think, therefore I am*" (AT VI,

32.23 and 18–19)? Does this meeting derive from chance, or does it harbor an essential point?

In fact, here there appears a difficulty that is so essential that it will raise ever growing polemics until the end of Descartes' stay in the United Provinces (and even further, after his death). To the *I think, therefore I am* one can object not only that a particular (and existential) statement can be raised into a universal principle, but that this statement itself assumes yet another universal principle. Certainly, Descartes always firmly denies that *I think, therefore I am* is concluded by a syllogism, the universal premise of which would pose that "fieri non potest, ut id quod cogitet non existat" (*Principia philosophiæ I*, §10), but that on the contrary it is deduced from the fact that I think. Nevertheless, even without the syllogism, does not this fact itself—thought is in as much as it thinks—already presuppose the universal rule that "repugnant enim, ut putemus id quod cogitat, eo ipso tempore quo cogitat, non existere—for it is a contradiction to suppose that what thinks does not, at the very time when it is thinking, exist" (*Principles of Philosophy*, I, §7 = AT IX-2, 27; CSM I, 195)? Doesn't this *logical* contradiction (*repugnant*) already rest on the principle of contradiction, transposed from *to be / not to be* to *to think / not to be*? It even sometimes happens that Descartes quotes these two propositions in parallel in the same text: "communis notio, sive axioma. Cujus generis sunt: *Impossibile est idem simul esse et non esse* [. . .]; *Is qui cogitat, non potest non existere dum cogitat*" as an example of the same logical necessity.[69] A second difficulty is added to this first one: what does the proposition *I think* imply? How can we define "quid sit cogitatio" (*Principia philosophiæ I*, §10 = *The Search for Truth*, AT X, 522, and Carraud and Olivo, 336), and, indeed, must we? What does this thinking think (walking, breathing, etc.: Gassendi)? Is it equivalent to *ego*, and in that case why distinguish between them? Or is this thinking distinguished as one of its properties (and then is it *ego* who thinks?). Or does it think in *ego* (Nietzsche)? Independently of the link between *I think* and existence (Kant, Schelling), it is the logical link between the *cogitatio* and the *ego* that is no longer self-evident.

Now, to these objections, the representative of Descartes at this point in the dialogue (*The Search for Truth*), far from discussing the principle of non-contradiction or retreating behind its authority, claims to be able to dispense with it purely and simply: "if someone knows how to make proper use of his doubt (*sua dubitatione*), he can use it to deduce facts which are known with complete certainty—facts which are even more certain and more useful than those which we commonly build upon that great principle (*vulgo magno isti principio*), as the basis to which they are all reduced, the fixed point on which they all terminate, namely, *It is impossible that one and the same thing should exist and at the same time (simul) not exist.*[70] How do we explain this assurance? There is only one explanation, simple and radical: doubt replaces the *cogitatio*, because it escapes the difficulties that the *cogitatio* will eventually seem to present.[71] Existence comes directly from doubt: "Es igitur, et te esse scis, et *hoc exinde*, quia dubitas scis—You are, therefore, and you know that you are, and you know this [starting] from *just [the fact] that* you are doubting" (AT X, 515, and *La Recherche*, 330; CSM II, 410). For doubt offers the freest form of thinking, since it states no proposition, does not engage in the least predication, assumes no signification, aims at no referent. The other modes that Descartes will integrate into the *cogitatio* in 1637 and 1641 are distinguished, and hierarchized, through their growing significant content: the *intellectus* assumes the simple intellectual, immaterial natures; the *voluntas* reaches the infinite, but incomprehensible; the *imagination* treats mathematics, rational but immanent in me and abstract; and, finally, the *sensus* comes from material things exterior to myself; in contrast, doubt is enough to engender a thought, but without any content. This absence of content, and even of meaning, frees it from having to decide what it doubts (as a result it could doubt everything) and frees it as well from any reason to doubt (consequently it could doubt hyperbolically). Doubt doubts everything, and therefore nothing puts it in doubt: "Quandoquidem itaque dubitare te negare nequis, et e contrario certum est te dubitare, et quidem adeo certum, ut de eo dubitare non possis: verum etiam est te, qui dubitas, esse; hocque ita etiam verum est, ut non magis de eo dubitare possis—You cannot deny that you have such doubts; rather it is certain that you have them, so certain in fact that you cannot doubt your doubting. Therefore it is also true that you who are doubting exist; this is so true that you can no longer have any doubts about it."[72] He doubts everything, but never doubts himself: "Pro certo affirmare queo, nunquam me de eo, quid sit dubitatio, dubitasse—I can only say for sure that I have never doubted what doubt is."[73] This is how he is the first to accomplish what will qualify the *cogitatio* when it declares *ego sum, ego existo* necessarily true—he performs it as a pure act, pure because absolutely empty, and thus absolutely unconditioned. Without quality, doubt performs absolutely the act of cogitating. Thus, skepticism is accomplished in certitude.[74]

Even later, in 1647, Descartes will maintain this privilege: "Quippe scripsi, nos non posse *dubitare*, quin mens nostra existat, quia, ex hoc ipso quod *dubitemus*, sequitur, illam existere—I wrote that we cannot doubt that our mind exists, because from the very fact that we are doubting, it follows that our mind exists."[75] For Descartes, doubt remains the supreme game.

TWO

Ego Sum, Outside the Subject

§1. *The Privileged Formulation*

The history of philosophy makes philosophy possible by furnishing it with arguments, or perhaps we ought to say instead, imposing them on it. The most powerful of these arguments cross eras, requiring that a decision be taken in front of them. Thus, every new figure in philosophy, in order to be formulated, not only must justify itself, positively or more often polemically, in relation to these arguments; but above all these arguments constitute the never-exhausted reserves of philosophy's new beginnings. Among these arguments, which do not cease to survive each time they are called into question, like Cadmus' teeth from which new shoots are reborn, one of the most powerful has proven to be the *cogito ergo sum* that Descartes imposed on philosophy—to the point that the question of the *ego* lays waste to every prospective post-modernity. And yet, this persistence is not without its ambiguities.

Indeed, they are massive and disconcerting ambiguities. The most worrisome, but not the only one as we shall see, stems from an unlikely distortion that leads the immense majority of discussions to base themselves on a formulation, *[ego] cogito, [ergo] sum*, whose variations appear in all the texts of Descartes with the exception—admittedly worthy of attention—of the second of the *Meditationes de prima philosophia* itself.[1] It is as if this separation from the Cartesian argument itself had absolutely no importance, or at least that the majority of readers, even (and perhaps above all) the most erudite or subtle, had considered as marginal or at least non-determinate the very different formula of the major text: "hoc pronuntiatum, *ego sum, ego existo*, quoties a me profertur vel mente concipitur, necessario esse verum— this pronouncement, *I am, I exist*, is necessarily true every time I utter it or conceive it in my mind" (or "haec [cogitatio] sola a me divelli nequit. Ego sum, ego existo; certum est—thought exists; it alone cannot be separated from me. I am; I exist—this is certain").[2] In the innumerable studies on "the *cogito* in the *Meditationes*," this privileged formulation fades into a mere variant of the standard formula (*[ego] cogito, [ergo] sum*). But they are clearly to be distinguished from one another, on two points (not only one). First, a lesser difference: the disappearance of *ergo*, thereby opening the field of debate on the discursive, or even syllogistic, interpretation of the formula, which will be the focus of the majority of the discussion (from Mersenne and Gassendi to Hintikka). Next, and above all, what is almost always met with silence:[3] the formulation of *Meditatio II* (and it alone) omits precisely nothing less than the term *cogito*, supposedly so decisive. Whence the paradox that *here*, the argument of the *cogito* does not include the term *cogito*.

Obviously, this is not just a detail, since by omitting to include that I think in the statement of the argument, the *Meditatio II* tears it from the status of a presupposition or logical condition of a conclusion that is also logical; it excludes *cogito* from the propositional statement, not in order to omit it but, on the contrary, to reinforce it by transforming a statement into the very act of enunciation; the *cogito* no longer says itself because it is done and accomplished in saying (*pronuntiatum*) or in thinking (*mente concipiatur*). This certainly opens the way to an interpretation of the argument that is pragmatic, or even in a sense performative, but also assumes this formulation and this displacement, so often missed and left without being questioned.

We will not take up the inquiry, pursued elsewhere, of this separation and its forgetting, considering its results as established;[4] but, henceforth more suspicious of the received interpretations, we will attempt to examine, starting from these attainments, some of the most accepted objections to the Cartesian argument. For it might be that they all derive, to one degree or another, from the same inattention to the act-character of the *cogito*, which accomplishes the proposition because it *is not* part of it, and from the same insistence on the *cogitatio*, taken as another of the terms of the proposition.[5] For if one takes care to hear (and to utter) *cogito* as a verb, without

32   *Chapter Two*

substantivizing it immediately as a *cogitatio* (among others), certain questions vanish, lacking pertinence. To do this, we will follow the objections as they have been discussed not only by the historians of philosophy, but above all by the actors of this history, the philosophers themselves. But here again, we must remain prudent. For if, as Heidegger recognizes, "Descartes anticipated the metaphysical ground of the modern age—which is not to say that all subsequent philosophy is simply Cartesianism,"[6] nor should we conclude that modern philosophy, even its greatest representatives, always correctly understood its Cartesian origin and what it owes to it.

§2. *The Objection Starting from Substance*

Of all the objections made to Descartes, the one that dominates the rest is that he interpreted the *ego*, which both provokes the *cogito* and comes from it, as a substance. No doubt this predominance is because it was repeated by the greatest authorities. Let us examine the different formulations.

Kant first argues that while the *I* can very well prove to be the logical support of all thought, nevertheless it cannot provide the "persistence (*Beharrlichkeit*)" of a substance that effectively requires a "standing and abiding (*stebende und bleibende*) intuition," of which the *I* is lacking in time. At best, what we have here is "a substance only in the idea but not in reality."[7] In a sense, Hobbes was already arguing that a thinking thing, in order to constitute the substratum of its acts, should become a substance, and in this case a *corporal* substance, a material that alone remains beneath any changes, "semper eamdem res, hoc est eadem materia, tot mutationibus subjecta—the same thing, that is, the same matter that is the subject of so many changes" (AT VII, 173.20–21; CSM II, 122).[8] In short, only the external sense, the materiality of the bodies in sensible intuition, could assure a persistence or permanence of the *ego*; as pure *cogitatio*, it remains held in the temporal flow of internal sense and thus does not reach substantiality. The being that the *ego* attains by discovering itself as *cogitans* remains a being that is thought rather than real, because it attains no substance at all. But how could we fail to notice that here Kant turns Descartes' very position against him? And first of all because *Meditatio II* underlines that the *ego* is and exists only for a time, within the temporal limits of the accomplishment of its act of thinking: not only am I only each time (*quoties*) that I think, and am not if I do not think;[9] but I am only for as long as (*quamdiu, dum*) I think, so that if I stopped myself from thinking, *right away* I would simply not be at all: "Certum est. Quamdiu autem? Nempe *quamdiu* cogito; nam forte etiam fieri posset, si cessarem ab omni cogitatione, ut *illico totus* esse desinerem—That is certain. But for how long? For as long as I am thinking. For it could be that were I totally to cease from thinking, I should totally cease to exist."[10] I am, only if and for as long as I am thinking and *inasmuch as* I think, as Schelling rightly insists: "The *Sum* which is contained in the *Cogito* is, therefore, only: *Sum qua cogitans*, 'I am as thinking (*ich bin als denkend*), i.e. in that specific way of being which is called thinking."[11] Descartes agrees: I am step by step, and this is why he maintains that in order to be, I must not cease thinking. The critique, then, amounts to reproaching the powerlessness of *ego sum, ego existo* to attain a true substance, stable and permanent.

Husserl took up Kant's accusation, but by reversing it: the weakness of the supposed *cogito* lay in having claimed to attain the rank of substance. "Unfortunately, a turning point takes place in Descartes, not terribly apparent of course [?], but of great consequence, which makes of the *ego* a *substantia cogitans*, an independent human *animus*, the point of departure for reasonings following the principle of causality; in short, a turning point through which he became the father of the self-contradictory transcendental realism." Here it is no longer contested that the *ego could* be established truly as a substance (against Kant's reproach), but that it *must* become a being understood within the world and assimilable to it: "This Ego, with his Ego-life, who necessarily remains permanent for me, by virtue of such epoché, is not a piece of the world; and if he says, 'I exist, *ego cogito*,' that no longer signifies, 'I, this man, exist.'"[12] In other words, by assuming the title of substance, the *ego* would put itself at the level of other substances, in the world (extended substances), as well as outside the world (God). And does not the *ego* in fact assume this title when he claims "Ego autem *substantia*—I too am a substance"?[13] One fact, however, should prompt a little prudence: the *ego* takes and claims the title of *substantia* only in *Meditatio III*, never in *Meditatio II*.[14]

§3. *The* Ego *as Substance under Reserve*

And in fact, these two contrary objections, apparently so evident, prove instead to be rather questionable because they converge in a single presupposition: Descartes supposedly claimed the rank of *substantia* for the *ego* that utters *ego sum, ego existo*. First, we will note that Descartes only qualifies the *ego* with the title of *substantia* with reservations. For example, the first two *Meditationes*, those that formulate the argument in its most complete version, do not use the term *substantia*, no more than do the *Principia I*, §1–10.[15] Even the *Discourse on the Method*, when it qualifies the *ego* as substance ("I knew I was a substance whose whole essence or nature is simply to think," AT VI, 33.3–5; CSM I, 127), does so only secondarily, in order to define its essence; and the "first principle of the philosophy I was seeking"[16] thus imposes itself before and without the use of the concept of "substance." In other words, one can support the argument that the *ego* existing insofar as thinking can perfectly be deployed and exert its function as principle *without* (at least without *yet*) claiming its status as substance. Indeed, the usage of this concept will only become indispensable to Descartes later, at the end of the first sequence in *Meditatio III*, when he borrows "alia quædam adhuc via—still another way" (AT VII, 40.5; CSM II, 27) and abandons the first way, which only considered the ideas "quatenus [. . .] cogitandi quidam modi tantum sunt—insofar as [. . .] simply modes of thought" (AT VII, 40.7–8; CSM II, 27), in order to undertake the demonstration of the existence of God from a hierarchy of realities represented between accidents and substances, between finite substances and infinite substances, and then by distinguishing the extent of thought as the principal attributes of two types of substances. But *substantia never* enters in before the demonstration of the existence of God, not even for the demonstration of the existence of the *ego*. Consequently, in front of this textual evidence, every objection to the possible substantiality of the *ego* (in order to contest this rank or reproach this goal) has absolutely no bearing, in fact or in principle.

We could stop at this conclusion. However, so many eminent critics either take no heed of it, or directly contradict it, that one might think there are several reasons to resist doing so.[17] Nevertheless, many arguments come to reinforce and justify what we might call "the secondary status of the thesis of the substantiality of the *moi*."[18] (a) When the *ego* attests its existence to itself, it questions its essence; yet it certainly does not formulate a question by aiming at a substance, but questions itself on its own identity: *quisnam sim ego ille*?[19] Or again: *who is this me* that I am when thinking?[20] The issue is not the definition of an ontic status, or even less of a substantial one, but rather of confirming that I am precisely insofar as I am thinking, that *cogitatio* suffices, alone, to define me.²¹ (b) Thus obtained, the definition consists only in itself: the terms that attempt to explain it (*mens, animus, intellectus, ratio*) add nothing to it, since without the *cogitatio* they would be words that previously were without known signification (*voces prius significationis ignotæ*, AT VII, 15). When later, under the constraints either of the demands of the demonstration of the existence of God (beginning from the *alia adhuc quædam via*), or of the objectors and their lexicon, he uses the term *substantia*, he will rethink it starting from the *res cogitans* and as its synonym, one that is as indeterminate as possible: "usum fuisse verbis quammaxime potui abstractis—I used the most abstract terms possible," by contrast with those of subject, matter, or substance (*subjectum, materia, substantia*).²² In fact, Descartes here still has no need for *cogitatio* to take upon itself more than a *res cogitans*; for him it is enough to affirm its irreducible reality (thinking is enough to make of my *ego* a *res* in itself), without already launching into or encumbering himself with the difficulties of defining substance.²³

For in his eyes, the concept of *substantia* offers too many aporias to allow it to reinforce or better comprehend existence and even the essence of the *ego* insofar as it thinks. All the *pro et contra* discussions on the substantiality of the *ego* seem, from Descartes' point of view, inept and senseless, because the concept of *substantia* appears to him to be highly problematic and, in any case, much less clear and distinct than that of *res cogitans*, which is to say, of the *ego sum, ego existo*. Let us recall in summary fashion these well-known other difficulties. (a) Substance remains immediately unknowable, for if it exists, its existence remains inaccessible to us: "hoc solum [. . .] nos non afficit—this alone [. . .] does not have any effect on us" (*Principia philosophiæ I*, §52; CSM I, 210); it is therefore known only mediately, from its accidents or attributes (Thomas Aquinas, Duns Scotus, Suarez, etc.), and for Descartes, as it happens, from its principal attribute, the *cogitatio*. It is enough, then, to be assured of this directly in order perhaps to infer from it the corresponding substance: "Certum est cogitationem non posse esse sine re cogitante—it is certain that a thought cannot exist without a thing that is thinking" (AT VII, 175.25; CSM II, 124). And there is no reason or need, aside from the obstinacy of Hobbes (or the simplism of Spinoza), to attribute to *cogitatio*, the principal attribute, a *substantia* corresponding to another principal attribute, *extensio*. Thus, there is for us an epistemic insufficiency of the concept of substance. (b) And there is more, or rather, less: if one holds to its strict sense, substance is defined, by opposition to its accidents, as a thing "quæ nulla alia re indigeat ad existendum—which depends on no other thing for its existence"; in this case, a single substance merits this title *univoce*, God, and all the others receive it only on the condition of God's ordinary concurrence, by the delegation and the procuration of the divine aseity (*Principia philosophiæ I*, §51 and 52; CSM I, 210). Finally, it will be necessary, if need be, to have recourse to a contradiction in terms ("fateor mihi contradictorium videri"), that of the *substantiæ incompletæ* (AT VII, 223.10–20). Thus, there is added, to the epistemic insufficiency of the concept of substance for us, its ontic insufficiency in itself. In fact, *substantia* does not constitute a critical stake for the *ego* of the *cogito*, because it offers only aporias and no evidence. We can conclude that in order to conceive of the essence of the *ego existo*, the concept of *substantia* proves to be so uncertain that it becomes useless.

Yet if, in order to respond to the philosophical debates of the time, it was necessary for Descartes to attempt to conceive a *substantia*, but said *substantia* could not be known in and through itself, nor in the case of the demonstration of the existence of God, nor in that of the demonstration of the existence of material things (each presupposing the mediation of the attributes and of the principal of causality), there remained only one possibility for him: to take into account the sole existence that *can* be demonstrated immediately, because it shows itself, that of the *ego*. Indeed, the *ego*, insofar as it is thinking (itself) and has an "innata [...] mihi idea mei ipsius—idea of myself [...] innate in me" (AT VII, 51.13–14; CSM II, 35), can discover, implicated and conjoined within them, other ideas: "quædam [*sc.* ideæ] ab idea mei ipsius videor mutuari potuisse, nempe substantiam, durationem, numerum et si quæ alia sint ejusmodi—I could have borrowed some of these [ideas] from my idea of myself, namely substance, duration, number and anything else of this kind" (AT VII, 44.19–21; CSM II, 30; see also 43.20). In the idea of myself as *res cogitans*, I can reach what the *Regulæ* had already identified as the simple common natures, to which *Meditatio III* nevertheless here adds, for the first time, *substantia*.[24] From itself, the *ego* can, or better from *ego ille*, from "this *moi*" that I am while thinking, *I* can conceive of a *ratio substantiæ* in general, and in this way "transfer [it] to other things—ad quasdamque alias res transferre" (AT VII, 44.27 and 45.1–2; CSM II, 31). It is as if, at the end of the long detour through the demonstration of the existence and despite the insufficiency of the current concept of *substantia*, but in considering himself as the sole *res* (*cogitans*) with an existence he can attain immediately, Descartes was attributing *in fine* to himself, so to speak, *another* concept of substitution, the concept of *substantia*[25] ("ego autem substantia—I am a substance"). In so doing, he validates in advance, by turning back the reproach as his own innovation, Nietzsche's remark, which Heidegger will put at the center of his interpretation of the *ego sum*: "The concept of substance is a consequence of the concept of the subject: not the reverse!"[26] Whence this double conclusion: not only does the common concept of *substantia* prove so uncertain as to become useless for defining the *ego*, but, if it is truly necessary to safeguard a general concept of substance for the other *res*, this concept must be deduced from the *ego* itself and, probably, be transferred (by analogy or metaphor?) to these other *res* that, it must be noted, do not think.

Descartes certainly substantivized the *ego* in an *ego ille* ("this I"), but he did not substantialize it.[27] Rather, he inversely redefined all substance starting from the *ego*, as one of its "ideas"—Kant will make of this one of the categories administering phenomena, and decidedly more, the badge of a thing in itself. If therefore substance as οὐσία begins to disappear with the *ego*, the objection made to the *ego* starting from substance falls flat.

§4. *The Objection Starting from the Subject*

On the occasion of this rectification of the role and the limits of the concept of *substantia*, we can also rectify the usage, regarding the Cartesian *corpus*, of *subjectum*, and thus also of the abusive uses of the modern "subject," and a fortiori of its derivatives "subjective" or "objective," for example in order to oppose an "objective *cogito*," an "objective certainty," to others that are merely "subjective."

To begin with, a remark that disqualifies this sort of opposition is necessary: several times *subjectum* and *objectum* appear in parallel and as terms substitutable for one another. For instance, the *Regula I* inaugurates the thesis of the unity of the sciences "quantumvis differentibus subjectis applicata—however applied to different subjects," in direct opposition to the Aristotelian sciences, which are distinguished "pro diversitate objectorum—by the differences in their objects."[28] Similarly, *Regula IV*, in its version A, assigns to the new science that it opposes to the *vulgaris Mathematica* the abstraction of truths "ex quovis objecto—from any object"; while version B defines this *Mathesis universalis* as suited for seeking order and measure not only in numbers, figures, sounds, and the stars (in other words, in the two areas of pure mathematics and the two applied mathematics, music and astronomy) but also in "aliovis objecto—any other object."²⁹ Again, on the same question, the *Discourse* defines the new science, which surpasses the "particular sciences commonly called 'mathematics'" by noting "that despite the diversity of their objects," they "agree in considering nothing but the various relations or proportions that hold between these objects"; thus one can study them directly, "supposing them to hold only between such items as would help me to know them more easily."³⁰ And yet, does Descartes call the *ego* a *subjectum*? Of course, it is often a subject insofar as subjected (adjective), for example, "subject to an error"; but this is not the same as *the* "subject." And, of course, we find at least one occurrence of relation between *subjectum* and the understanding: "Neque immensum est opus, res omnes in hac repræsentatione contentas cogitatione velle complecti, ut, quomodo singulæ *mentis nostræ examine subjectæ* sint, agnoscamus—And this is not an immense task to want to encompass in thought all known things in our universe so as to recognize, in what way each of them is *subjected to the investigation carried out by our mind.*"³¹ We note that here the understanding *is not* called *subjectum*, and it is only the things that are subject to it (*subjectæ*: participle with an adjectival function), subjected to its thought.

But what about the *Meditationes*? They use the term *subjectum* only twice. (a) The clearest instance happens second: in order to illustrate the principle that the cause must possess at least as much reality as its effect, the example of the heating of a stone is raised: "nec potest calor in *subjectum* quod prius non calebat induci, nisi a re quæ sit ordinis saltem æque perfecti atque est calor—heat cannot be produced in an object which was not previously hot, except by something of at least the same order of perfection as heat" (AT VII, 41.8–10; CSM II, 28); in order to heat a stone, it is necessary to have a "thing" of the same order and perfection that heats the *subjectum*, the "subject"; clearly there is no question here of the modern "subject" that receives, underlies, and sees the thing that it thinks, but rather of the *substratum* of the thing itself (here, the stone, unformed matter). This usage recalls, in its literal translation by *subjectum*, the Aristotelian *hypokeimenon*.³² (b) The other occurrence, which precedes the first one, concerns a distinction among "meæ cogitationes"; certain of them are worthy of the name of idea because they constitute "*tanquam rerum imagines*—as it were sorts of images"; others add to these images "*alias quasdam* [...] *formas*—various additional forms," for when I will, or fear, or affirm and deny, I also form a volition, an affect, or a judgment. And yet, in the two cases, it remains that "*aliquam rem ut subjectum meæ cogitationis apprehendo*—I apprehend a certain thing as the *subject of my thought*" (AT VII, 37.1–12; CSM II, 25, 26). The parallel of the two texts allows us to understand that here the *subjectum* designates the thing of which the *ego* thinks the idea, and not the *ego* itself; once again it is the doctrine of *Regula VIII* that is at issue: all things are found to be subject to the *cogitatio* and, in this sense, furnish it with a *subjectum*. We can conclude from this that at no time are the *ego* or its *cogitatio* called *subjectum*.[33]

Where, then, might the Cartesian attribution come from of a determination of the *ego* as *subjectum*, if not as "subject," that approaches the manner in which Kant assumes that the transcendental subject offers a "*substratum*" that "grounds all thoughts"?[34] Curiously, perhaps from an objection by Hobbes. Following the guiding thread of the Aristotelian meaning of *subjectum*, Hobbes repeats that "*Philosophi distinguunt subjectum a suis facultatibus et actibus*—all philosophers make a distinction between a subject and its faculties and acts"; from this he infers that the same goes for the act of thinking, and thus that "*potest ergo esse ut res cogitans sit subjectum mentis, rationis, vel intellectus, ideoque corporeum aliquid*—it may be that the thing that thinks is the subject to which mind, reason or intellect belong; and this subject may thus be something corporeal." Of course, it is astonishing that Hobbes here assumes, without any hesitation or demonstration, that the *res cogitans* can be a *res* only by being something corporeal.[35] But it is above all noteworthy that Descartes, to respond to him, had to come closer to the scholastic lexicon Hobbes uses. This happens in three stages. First, Descartes denies that a *cogitatio* may not serve as *subjectum* to another, and thus suggests that the *subjectum* could consist in a *cogitatio*; next, he specifies that a *res cogitans* functioning as substance would be the issue; and finally, he allows that the *res cogitans* would play the role of a *subjectum*.[36] The comparison between two types of acts or attributes (extension and thought) follows, which returns to two substances as to their two *subjecta*. Descartes nevertheless does not go any further: if he does indeed qualify the body with the name of *subjectum* (AT VII, 14), he does not do the same for the *res cogitans*, called *substantia*, not *subjectum*.[37] But he goes up to that point:

40 *Chapter Two*

tangentially, for the first time, the *res cogitans* would become the *subjectum* of its *cogitationes*.

In the still-to-be-clarified history of the emergence of the "subject" before Kant, Descartes certainly plays a role, but not the one that is commonly believed. He did not invent the "subject," though he did invent (to Pascal's benefit) "this *moi*," *ego ille*.[38] He instituted the *ego* as the *thinking* principle, the thought that exists first in as much as it is thinking. And, in order to say it, he had need of neither *substantia* nor *subjectum*. Not that he was unaware or missed the "subject," but the *ego* was able to say itself without it, or indeed, *against* it. And if by chance the "subject" seems retrospectively to come from the *ego*, the *ego* does not depend on it.[39]

§5. *The Objection Starting from Representation*

Now we must examine a third objection, one that is major among Descartes' successors and very much authorized through usage among his recent commentators. It takes various forms, insisting sometimes on the primacy of representation, and other times on the role of reflection (or reflexivity) in the argument of the *ego sum, ego cogito*. It will be necessary to show that Descartes resisted it in advance.

We encounter the objection at the highest philosophical degree in Heidegger (whom historians of metaphysics ought to read more frequently). He notes, quite rightly, a patent fact: *cogito* must not be translated, or at least (if we give up on correcting the unanimous translations of the contemporaries of Descartes, and of our own) must not be understood simply as "I think" (nor *cogitare* merely as "to think"); we must understand it as "to perceive—*percipere*," "to self-represent—*sich-vorstellen*" in the sense of "to place oneself in front of oneself" and thus "to take possession of . . . ."[40] Brutal as it may appear, this understanding finds an echo in authentically Cartesian determinations of thinking; whether as the *intuitus* that sees because it gazes, and gazes [*regarde*] because it retains [*garde*];[41] or that the *cogitatio* "encompasses, *complecto*" or "apprehends, *apprehendo*" (AT X, 401.28; VII, 37.9) what it never knows "without a method" (AT X, 371.16); or that it reduces the perceptions of the sensible to the simple natures in order to codify them (*Regulæ VI* and *XII-2*), in direct consequence of the decision to think only through ordering and measure (*Regulæ IV* and *V*); or that it prepares "useful knowledge" for a "practical" philosophy of "lords and masters," using a reason taken as a "universal instrument."[42] But the clearest example of this *cogitatio* of mastery is found once again in the analysis of the piece of wax: the *ego* knows the wax only through an *inspectio mentis*, which reduces it to *quia* by reducing it to "nihil aliud quam extensum *quid*, flexibile, mutabile—merely something extended, flexible and changeable," and which thus alienates it from itself and brings it back to the *ego*: "non nisi mente percipitur—it is perceived by the mind alone" (AT VII, 31.2–3, 20; CSM II, 20, 21). This re-presentation is carried out as a mastery and puts what is represented at the disposition of the representing; the primacy of the representing over the re-presented in the *cogitatio* is signaled and finally ends up radicalizing thought by the bracketing of all re-presented content, or in other words by the priority accorded among the modes of *cogitatio*, to doubt and in a doubt: "That every *cogitare* is essentially a *dubitare* says nothing other than this: representing is securement."[43] In effect, if thinking presupposes placing oneself in front of the thinkable in order to render it certain under the *intuitus* that gazes at it / re-retains it [*qui le (re-)garde*], everything thinkable finds itself mortgaged straightaway by the pre-position of thinking: before rendering it certain by its taking into possession, and so as to do so, thought disqualifies any self-sufficiency of what is thought; the precedence [*préséance*] of *cogitatio* rightfully makes every *cogitatum* doubtful. We have seen that the *res cogitans* is aways first defined as *dubitans*: "Res cogitans? Quid est hoc? Nempe dubitans. . .—A thing that thinks? What is that? A thing that doubts. . ."; and reciprocally, to doubt means first of all to think: "quid enim dubitare aliud est, quam certo quodam modo cogitare—for what is doubting if not thinking in a certain kind of way?"[44]

But there is more. For if it is doubt that first puts re-presentation into operation, if it manifests the absolute empire of the *ego* by suspending all *cogitatum*, then *cogitatio* in its entirety re-presents first and essentially the *ego* to itself: "Representing and the one who is representing are *co*-represented in human representing." In short, "representing is a co-representing of oneself,"[45] according to an essential connection, where the represented is rooted in the representation, and thus in representing, and not the reverse, as the natural attitude imagines. But, from such an implication of re-presenting in the representation of the represented, a radical understanding of the so-called argument of the *cogito* necessarily follows: the *ego* finds itself presupposed (thus posed as existing) by the simple fact that it thinks in re-presenting *itself* in and before any represented that it represents to itself (and even if it re-presents to itself nothing at all because it doubts). This is so not only by a necessity of knowledge, but by a metaphysical necessity. Whence this conclusion: in fact and in principle, *cogito sum* is equivalent at bottom to *cogito me cogitare*: "*cogito* is *cogito me cogitare*."[46] The argument of the *ego sum, ego existo* does not encounter existence first though a psychological and "subjective" experience, but rather through the necessity of the *cogitatio* understood at its depths, as it originates in the radical metaphysical demand of re-presentation, rather than grounding it.[47]

We should note, however, that by leading the Cartesian argument back to its ultimate metaphysical ground in this way, Heidegger does not entirely break new ground; rather (and this is his strength), he is in line with a double heritage, which as always he radicalizes brilliantly. (a) He reads the *cogito* of Descartes first by reference to Kant, who defined transcendental apperception according to the demands of representation: "The *I think* must *be able* to accompany all my representations; for otherwise something would be represented in *me* that could not be thought at all, which is as much as to say that the representations would either be impossible or else at least would be nothing for me."[48] Heidegger's *Mit-[vorgestellt]* therefore reproduces the function of Kant's *begleiten*. (b) Above all, Heidegger seems to remember a radical objection of Nietzsche to the Cartesian *ego*:

"I re-present, therefore there is being," *cogito ergo est*.—That *I* am this being that represents, and that representing is *my activity*, is no longer certain, any more than that all that I represent might be.—The only being that we know is the being that re-presents. [. . .] It is *change* that is inherent in representing, *not* the movement: certainly, [it is] all disappearance and arising, but in representing itself, all persistence is lacking; on the contrary, representing introduces two persistences, it *believes* in the persistence of 1) the *I*, and 2) of a content. This belief in the persistence of substance, that is, in the remaining *identical* of the same with itself, is directly opposed to the process of representation itself. [. . .] being, the only one that is guaranteed us, is changing, *non-identical to itself* [. . .]. Such is the *fundamental certitude regarding being*. So representation *affirms* precisely the opposite of being![49]

Here Nietzsche puts exactly at the ground of the *ego cogito* what Heidegger and Kant also assign it as its base. But there is a single difference: Nietzsche opposes representation to being, while in contrast Kant (following Berkeley) and Heidegger (according to his interpretation of the nihilism of metaphysics[50]) identify it with being.

§6. *The Non-reflexive* Cogito

This convergence of three philosophers who are decisive for interpreting the *ego cogito* starting from the essence of *Vorstellung* as meaning (or the opposite) of being merits serious attention. It raises at least two questions: first, to see whether, in detail, the Cartesian texts confirm the very terms *représentation* and *repræsentatio*; and next, whether, conceptually speaking, the *ego* of the *cogito* is presupposed in every *cogitatum*, in only certain *cogitata*, or in self-*cogitatio* (**cogitatio sui*).

Although significant, the usage of the term representation itself is measured. The *Regulæ* sometimes assume that the idea represents the thing ("res ipsa, quam hæc idea repræsentat," AT X, 417.2; "per veram ideam repræsentare," 444.26); but it can also have to do with a representation of thought in the mode of sensation (*idea corporea*, 419.13) or of imagination[51] (423.13, 25). On the other hand, the *Discourse* assures us that the "understanding represents."[52] A perfect illustration is found in the analysis of the piece of wax, where the *mentis inspectio* reveals that the object to know presupposes the existence of its re-presenter; but, indeed, this analysis does *not* use the term *repræsentatio* and is limited to repeating, in a more imaginable mode, the argument of the *cogito*. We must therefore search elsewhere for the full use of what the *Præfatio ad lectorem* expressly announces: the status of the thing known as *res repræsentata* (AT VII, 8.23), as "illud quod per istam ideam repræsentatur—what is represented by the idea" (8.19; CSM II, 7).

The principle of the representation of understanding, and thus of the *repræsentatio* of *cogitatio* in the most powerful sense, is not fully formulated until the opening of the "other way—alia quædam adhuc via" (AT VII, 40.5), where "una [*sc.* idea] unam rem, alia aliam repræsentat—different ideas represent different things" (40.10–11; CSM II, 28). This way will allow the proof of the existence of God by the effects, as is confirmed by its occurrence, at the same strategic point, in the *Principia philosophiæ*: "Una [*sc.* idea] unam rem, alia aliam repræsentat" (I, §17). Indeed, prior to this relaunch of the order of reasons, the *ego* had proceeded only to the analysis of its ideas as such, "quatenus [. . .] cogitandi quidam modi sunt—insofar as [. . .] simply modes of thought" (AT VII, 40.3–4; CSM II, 27); as such they remain similar among themselves, without distinction or hierarchy, all equally stitched from *cogitatio*, so that they refer back to their origin, the *ego*, still the sole existing thing, more than to things with an existence that is still perfectly doubtful. The new way allows in contrast to differentiate and to hierarchize the ideas following their respective objective realities: to each idea its thing, to each thing its idea, the ideas being hierarchized in parallel to the things. This is the place of representation: the new relation (binary correspondence) that allows the hierarchization (of objective realities) designs the function of the *repræsentatio*, which comes in as a term now, and only now.[53] Which is to say, the *repræsentatio*, and thus also the interpretation of the *cogitatio* as *Vorstellung* (Kant) and *vor-stellen* (Heidegger) has meaning and legitimacy only when, after the opening of the "other way," it is a question of a relation between the *res cogitans* and the other *res*, which are not the *ego* and which are not in its mode of being. We thus understand the fundamental reason why the term *repræsentatio* never appears in *Meditatio II*, nor in the entire first section of *Meditatio III* (until 40.5): an enumerated doctrine of representation can enter only if the *ego* turns its *cogitatio* towards the *res* and their (possible) objective realities. It is not enough to consider the *cogitatio* in actuality; it must be turned away from itself in order to turn toward (possible) objects. Without this turn, or rather, this face to face with the *res extra me* that opens an exterior to the *ego*, the very principle of the *cogitatio* as *Vorstellung*—namely that no thing can truly be known if not through the representation that appropriates it to the *ego*, or rather that makes it become a knowledge that is certain to the extent that representation appropriates it—cannot unfold. The first way of the *cogitatio* consists in a quasi-reduction, operates through the pure performance of the *cogitatio* and manifests the *ego* alone; the second way opens a quasi-intentionality, wherein the *cogitatio* proceeds through *repræsentatio* and constitutes certain things as *substantiæ*.

This result allows us to draw two conclusions. (a) In order that the thing (*res*) become representable, it must be considered in its objective reality (*realitas objectiva*); thus, the appearance of *repræsentatio* must coincide with that of *substantia* (of the accident, of the difference between the infinite substance and finite substances); and such is indeed the case, as we saw earlier (§3). A decisive moment in the history of metaphysics results: the *res*, henceforth *substantia*, paradoxically becomes so as an *object*, or even an *objective* for *repræsentatio*; with Descartes, the distinction between the thing and the object is instituted, and the decline of *ousia* until its disappearance will be enacted by Kant. From this point of view, one can thoroughly admit that the *cogitatio* that the *ego cogito* henceforth exerts unfolds indeed according to the logic of *Vorstellung* (Kant) and of *vor-stellen* (Heidegger) and that Descartes belongs to the metaphysical history of nihilism. (b) On the other hand, we understand that, if *repræsentatio* enters in only with the *res* and their objective realities, and thus with *substantia*, it can do so only for as long as the *ego* remains a "mens [. . .] in se conversa—human mind [. . .] directed towards itself" (AT VII, 7.20; CSM II, 7), which "[se] ipsum exhibet—gives a representation [of itself]" (42.30; CSM II, 29). The *ego*, as such and "se solum alloquendo" (34.15), without *substantia* or hierarchized objective reality, represents to itself nothing and does not put into action its *cogitatio* as a *Vorstellung*, nor enter into the nihilistic history of the *vor-stellen*. That it can or must, later and at times, *also* conceive itself as a substance when it discovers that "non me solum esse in mundo—I am not alone in the world" (42.22; CSM II, 29), does not contradict the fact that it is not one *to begin with* and that its *cogitatio* does not *first* think (itself) through *repræsentatio*. Once again it must be admitted that at base Descartes often does not end up with univocal conclusions, but instead with an alternative. At issue is not a failure of the system, but the concepts' coherence with the dimensions of the question.

Several arguments can be added that confirm this conclusion. Of course, Heidegger is not wrong to forge the formula *cogito me cogitare* [*rem*] in order to expose the essence of the *cogitatio*; but he should have distinguished between the two modes of this *cogitatio* and restrained the interpretation of the *repræsentatio* as *vor-stellen* solely to the *cogitatio* of things that "exist outside of" the *ego* (*extra me existant*, AT VII, 40.8). Indeed, Descartes is not unaware of the formulation that Heidegger applies to him, and he even quotes it (almost) literally by anticipation; but he does so in order to refuse the application to the *ego cogito*. In response to the *Sixth Set of Objections* by the Jesuit Fr. Bourdin, Descartes mentions just such a reflexivity of representation, but in order to disqualify it: "Item cum ait non sufficere quod substantia aliqua sit cogitans, ut sit posita supra materiam, et plane spiritualis [. . .], sed insuper requiri ut actu reflexo *cogitet se cogitare*, sive habeat cogitationis suæ conscientiam, æque hallucinatur. . .—And again, when he says that to enable a substance to be superior to matter and wholly spiritual [...], it is not sufficient for it to think: it is further required that it should *think that it is thinking*, by means of a reflexive act, or that it should have awareness of its own thought, this is as deluded. . ."[54] as if he claimed that one only possesses a science or an art by knowing that one has it. Descartes allows no ambiguity whatsoever to float here: when the *ego* thinks in order to be and thinks that it is thinking, it does not represent to itself its thought because it does not reflect on itself either:

ad hoc [*sc.* being certain of existing] non requiratur scientia *reflexa*, vel per demonstrationem acquisita, et multo *minus scientia scientiæ reflexæ*, per quam sciat se scire, iterumque se scire se scire, atque ita in infinitum, qualis de nulla unquam re haberi potest. Sed omnino sufficit ut id sciat *cognitione illa interna, quæ reflexam semper antecedit*, et quæ omnibus hominibus de cogitatione et existentia ita innata est, ut [. . .] non possumus tamen revera non habere—this does not require *reflective* knowledge, or the kind of knowledge that is acquired by means of demonstration; still *less does it require knowledge of reflective knowledge*, i.e. knowing that we know, and knowing that we know that we know, and so on *ad infinitum*. This kind of knowledge cannot possibly be obtained about anything. It is quite sufficient that we should *know it by that internal awareness which always precedes reflective knowledge*. This inner awareness of one's thought and existence is so innate in all men that [...] we cannot in fact fail to have it.[55]

Once again, when *cogitatio* turns toward the *ego*, it does not think by *repræsentatio*.

It would be wrong to want to counter-balance this thesis by invoking consciousness.[56] A first argument claims that *conscientia* remains explicitly immediate: "Cogitationis nomine complector illud omne quod sic *in nobis* est, ut ejus *immediate conscii simus*. Ita omnes voluntatis, intellectus, imaginationis et sensuum *operationes* sunt cogitationes.—Under the term thought I encompass everything that is *within us* in such a way that we are *immediately conscious of it*. Thus all the *operations* of the will, the intellect, the imagination and the senses are thoughts." We note that operations, not representations, are at issue, and that the consciousness that we have of them in no way implies a representational separation, but remains immediate. Similarly: "Ideæ nomine intelligo cujuslibet cogitationis formam illam, per cujus *immediatam perceptionem ipsius ejusdem cogitationis conscius* sum.—By the name of thought I mean this form of any thought, by the *immediate perception* of which I am *conscious of the thought*."[37] It is a matter of perceptions, not of representations, and the consciousness that we have of them remains without mediation, because the idea remains the idea of the *same* perception, henceforth put into form. The other occurrences of *conscientia / conscius* never contradict this immediacy of *cogitatio* to itself but rather underline it; for even and above all when the issue is exterior things, it is only through an internal *cogitatio* that I think them: "my own thought or consciousness" allows the justification that "I can have no knowledge of what is outside me except by means of the ideas I have *within me*."[38] And, when someone objects to him that one could perhaps deduce that I am from any other act (walking, for example), Descartes retorts that it is not certain that I am walking, but that only the thought (that I am walking, or otherwise) can be so, because it does not remain at a distance and suffers no separation (*repræsentatio, reflexio*); and he explains it by appealing precisely to consciousness: "Nec licet inferre, exempli causa: *Ego ambulo, ergo sum*, nisi quatenus ambulandi *conscientia* cogitatio est, de qua sola hæc illatio est certa—I may not, for example, make the inference 'I am walking, therefore I exist', except in so far as the consciousness of walking is a thought. The inference is certain only if applied to this consciousness."[39] Thus, consciousness has nothing reflexive or representative about it. It does not add itself to the *cogitatio*, as something secondary and in reinforcement, but qualifies it as such: by definition immediate and without distance from itself, *cogitatio* thinks as *conscientia* and *conscientia* of itself.

Doubtless there remains an obstacle to this conclusion, in the *Conversation with Burman*: "Conscium esse est quidem cogitare et *reflectere* supra suam cogitationem—to be conscious is both to think and to *reflect* on one's thought":[60] do consciousness and reflection go together, at least here? Aside from the fact that this text does *not* come from the hand of Descartes (it was probably written by Clauberg from Burman's notes), and we do not yet possess a genuinely critical edition of it, we can make note of several possible reservations. (a) At issue in this formula is a concession (*quidem*, "certainly") made by Descartes to his interlocutor, who objected from the outset that "mens nostra non potest *simul* nisi unam rem concipere—our mind can think of only one thing *at a time*"; in the formula quoted here, Descartes thus takes up Burman's terms (whence the surprising use of *reflectare*). (b) But this is in order to immediately correct an error: "Quod mens non possit nisi unam rem simul concipere *verum non est—it is not true* that our mind can think of only one thing at a time"; and he repeats it: it is not true that "reflection" can only be carried out if the first thought on which we reflect has disappeared ("id non possit fieri manente priori cogitatione, *falsum est— it is false* that this reflection cannot occur while the previous thought is still there"). With even a little joke as a bit of table talk: "Ego concipio et cogito *simul* me loqui et me edere—Me, I am conceiving and thinking at *the same time* that I am talking and eating." The thesis is clear: "anima plura *simul* cogitare [. . .] queat"; it makes us think not so much of reflective representation as of the doctrine of the *motus cogitationis*, which, according to the *Regulæ*, "singula attente intuentis *simul* et ad alia transeuntis—carefully intuit one thing and pass on *at once* to the others";[61] even when we think of objects, we can, within certain limits, think of several at once. (c) Finally, and above all, far from reestablishing the *repræsentatio* and the *cognito reflecta* and thus contradicting himself, Descartes here holds that *cogitatio*, when it concerns the *ego*, is never reduced to other *cogitationes* concerning objects, because it does not add anything to them, but makes them possible as an *a priori* condition.[62]

In any case, there is a second argument to confirm the identity of consciousness with *cogitatio*: if consciousness must become clearer, this will come about neither by the *repræsentio*, nor by reflection, and thus by a representative distancing, but on the contrary by the reinforced immediacy of a "feeling." Which is also evident in a canonical definition of *cogitatio*: "Cogitationis nomine intelligo illa omnia, quæ *nobis consciis in nobis* fiunt, quatenus eorum in nobis *conscientia* est. Atque ita non modo intelligere, velle, imaginari, sed etiam *sentire*, idem est hîc quod cogitare—By the term 'thought', I understand everything *which we are conscious of* as happening *within us*, in so far as we have *consciousness* of it. Hence, thinking is to be identified here not merely with understanding, willing and imagining, but also with *sensing*."[63] This passage insists on the implication of the self-consciousness of the *ego* in the thought of any thing at all, to the point that not only are the first two sequences redundant in relation to one another ("nobis consciis [. . .] in nobis conscientia est"), but each of them operates a redundancy to the benefit of the *ego* ("nobis [. . .] in nobis," and then "in nobis conscientia"); to the further point that, in fact, no consciousness of some thing can be accomplished without the more originating and immediate consciousness of the self by the self. And Descartes adds a commentary, which Heidegger ignores, on what makes walking or vision certain or not: "Sed si intelligam de ipso sensu sive *conscientia* videndi aut ambulandi, quia tunc refertur ad mentem, quae sola *sentit sive cogitat* se videre aut ambulare, est plane certa.—But if I take 'seeing' or 'walking' to apply to the actual sense or *consciousness* of seeing or walking, then the conclusion is quite certain, since it relates to the mind, which alone has the *sensation or thought* that it is seeing or walking."[64]

And there is probably an excellent reason for understanding *cogitatio* as an immediate consciousness and a "feeling" without representation: re-presentation implies a separation and an ecstasy in which the thing re-presented is distinguished from the re-presenting thought, and therefore from the re-presenter itself, and traces a separation between self-consciousness and the consciousness of something other than the self. The separation between the re-presenter and the re-presented thus ties the *ego* to the *res* in such a way that it distances them from one another all the more. Logically, this separation would make even the experience of the self by the self impossible, for if doubt is born from the separation between the idea (even evident) and the thing, and if the *ego* maintained with itself a relation of representative to the re-presented idea, would it not fall under the blow of hyperbolic doubt, just like every other re-presentation? Now the *ego* precisely does not maintain with itself a representation, but rather a "feeling": "sentire, idem est hîc quod cogitare." Thus, what guarantees the immediate experience of self at the heart of the mediated experience of the thing (and also of the worldly actions of the *mens*) does not belong to representation, nor even to the intellectual modes that could in appearance be the closest, but only to feeling—the original feeling of self through self, the *ego*'s ordeal of self and of its existence.[65]

Like Kant and Nietzsche, and indeed even like Husserl,[66] Heidegger, by privileging the representative interpretation of *cogitatio*, here remains more of a metaphysician than his non-metaphysician's reading of nihilism allowed him to hope. Descartes certainly was not unaware of this interpretation derived from *cogitatio* but held it to the thinking of the things of the world: the whole doctrine of science and its putting into operation in the *Regulæ*, and then by the *Essais*, testifies to this containment well enough. When the method constitutes things into objects, it indeed represents them, if only because it codes them according to *figuræ*. But this stage still concerns only the usage of the simple material (and common) natures, and not yet that of the simple intellectual (and common) natures. When the *Meditationes* step onto this terrain, *cogitatio* goes beyond simple representing, becoming immediate to itself and "feeling" itself. Moreover, it is not by chance if Heidegger tends to reduce, without any other form of proceedings, all *cogitatio* to that of the *res extensa*: "The principle that lifeless nature is *res extensa* is simply the essential consequence of the first principle. *Sum res cogitans* is the ground, the underlying, the *subiectum* for the determination of the material world as *res extensa*";[67] but the conclusion falls precisely because the premise is erroneous. This reduction by Heidegger of *cogitatio* not only limits the reach of the thinking of the world, taking no heed of the knowledge of the non-worldly beings that it claims (the *ego*, the possible other *egos*, and God); it above all misses the final essence: a first and more originating *cogitatio*, one that is non-representative, non-intentional of objects, immediately affected by itself in the mode of a primordial feeling. A new frontier is marked here in the interpretation of the *ego sum, ego existo*.[68]

§7. The Objection Starting from the Cause

There remains a last objection, which Nietzsche perfectly formulated; it merits an examination that is all the more attentive because, while the erudite critics have virtually passed over it in silence, it has had great fortune in post-modern thought. It involves the objection made to the *cogito* from the understanding of the *ego* as a cause. The argument is simply formulated:

The conception of a consciousness ("mind") as cause, and then that of the I (the "subject") as cause are just latecomers that appeared once causality of the will was established as given, as a fact *of experience* [. . .]. Man projected his three "inner facts" out of himself and onto the world—the facts he believed in most fervently, the will, the mind, and the I. He took the concept of being from the concept of the I, he posited "things" as beings in his own image, on the basis of his concept of I as cause (*nach seinem Begriff des Ichs als Ursache*).[69]

The case of substance, derived from the *ego*, can thus be generalized: the same goes not only for the thing, but also for causality. The *I* produces causality out of itself, which it then attributes to "things," because it attributes causality to itself first of all.

Nietzsche is not inventing what he denounces; it was enough to read Kant to find confirmation of his suspicion. To begin with, the *ego*, or as it happens, the subject in the practical use of reason, explicitly claims the function of cause: "The faculty of desire is a being's *faculty to be by means of its representations the cause of the reality (Vermögen [. . .] durch seine Vorstellungen Ursache der Wirklichkeit) of the objects of these representations*."[70] And the same goes in pure reason, where the determination of causality depends directly on the subject; not only does causality, as the second analogy of experience, count among the principles of the pure understanding, and thus by full right stem from transcendental subjectivity; but it is defined explicitly as an operation of the *I*, which renders *itself* intelligible in this way according to *its* rule, a becoming that would remain, otherwise, a rhapsodic succession:

> When, therefore, we experience that something happens (*etwas geschieht*), we always presuppose (*voraussetzen*) that something else precedes (*vorausgeht*) it, which it follows in accordance with a rule. For without this I would not say of the object that it follows, since the mere sequence in my apprehension, if it is not, by means of a rule, determined in relation to something preceding, does not justify any sequence in the object. [. . . T]he case is the same here as with other pure *a priori* representations (e.g., space and time) that we can extract as clear concepts from experience (*aus der Erfahrung als klare Begriffe herausziehen*) only because we have put them into experience (*in die Erfahrung gelegt haben*), and experience is hence first (*allererst*) brought about through them.[71]

Causality, or more precisely the relation of cause and effect, gives access to the knowledge of objects only because it does not characterize things (in themselves) but comes directly from the imposition of the human mind. In other words, and as always, *there is nothing more subjective than the object*.

But the objection can go yet further: if the *ego* claims to assure itself of the knowledge of objects by imposing on them its rule of a relation of causality, it can do so only by claiming to experience in itself this causality; in itself, which is to say starting from itself, and thus in its own ideas, representations, or its own thoughts. The *ego* in person thinks (through) its thoughts, because it evokes them *to itself* and causes them *to itself*. But precisely that could constitute an illusion, if one asks: Who is this *ego* that thinks, and do the thoughts come *from* it, or do they come *to it*? Ought I to say: *I* think, since I cause the succession of my thoughts? Or rather, should I say: *it* thinks, if some thoughts come to *me* without my foreseeing them, or controlling them; indeed, Descartes himself recognizes that he does not have enough attention to hold back his thoughts.[72] Must we conclude that when I think I am thinking, I am causing nothing, but that *it* thinks in me without me, and thus happens without a cause? "In this way each first 'I think' contains a belief, namely, that 'thinking' is an activity, for which a subject must be thought, at least an 'it'."[73] That the *cogitationes* or *ideæ* in me do not depend on the *ego*, nor on the *mens*: is this not, moreover, what Spinoza argued against Descartes? "When we say that the human Mind perceives this or that, we are saying nothing but that God, not insofar as he is infinite (*non quatenus infinitus est*) but insofar as he has explained through the nature of the human Mind, *or* insofar as he constitutes the essence of the human Mind (*sed quatenus per naturam mentis humanæ explicatur, sive quatenus humanæ mentis essentiam constituit*), has this or that idea": when man thinks (*homo cogitat*), no *ego* brings about or causes any idea, but it is God alone, as constituting the mind of man, who thinks, constitutes, and causes ideas, as the efficient cause of existences but also of essences.[74] By other paths, Malebranche corrected even the thesis attributed to Descartes: "from the fact that the ideas of things are present to their mind as soon as they [men] wish it, they must conclude only this, that in the order of nature their will is generally necessary for them to have these ideas, but not that the will is the true and principal cause that presents ideas to their mind, and still less that the will produces them from nothing or in the way they explain it."[75] No *ego* causes anything, especially not its *cogitationes*, because, in its place, there thinks an other than its *I*, and whether it is God or *it* matters little.

Going forward, this conclusion would impose itself generally: "There is no longer anyone innocent enough to put forward, like Descartes, the subject 'I' as the condition (*Bedingung*) of '[I] think'; rather, the skeptical movement of modern philosophy makes us believe the opposite, assuming thought as the cause and condition of the 'subject' just as well as of the 'object,' of 'substance' as well as of 'matter': which is perhaps simply the opposite kind of error (*vielleicht nur die umgekehrte Art des Irrthums ist*)."[76] The critique of the existence of the *ego cogito* now appears limpid: Descartes would suppose thought as a fact, and thus attribute to it a cause; he reduced it, then, to an effect, to a thought thought, the mere effect of thinking thought, which refers back to the *ego* as its thinking cause. Descartes would assume without proof that thought constitutes a fact, that this fact needs a cause, and that the *ego* subsists unchanging in time, in order to carry out in time, in the role of substrate, such a causality. But the critique of causality in general destroys the Cartesian reasoning about the *ego*, because the *ego* itself presupposes causality, first toward its *cogitationes*, in order next to deploy it with regard to the things of the world.

§8. The Ego *Clear of All Cause*

Can this hermeneutic, the modern posterity of which (from Freud to Foucault) pursues an older fortune (Spinoza, Leibniz, Kant, Nietzsche, etc.), be justified by Descartes' text? Here again, the facts present more than one difficulty.

First, Descartes himself anticipated Nietzsche's critique. Nietzsche observed, "We have absolutely no experience of a *cause* (absolut keine Erfahrung über eine *Ursache*). [...] *The causality interpretation is a deception*. [...] *There are neither causes nor effects*. [...] In short: *an event neither is effected nor itself effects* (In summa: *ein Geschehen ist weder bewirkt, noch bewirkend*)."[77] But this difficulty being only somewhat evident, Descartes indeed saw it and foresaw it; he defined it nearly in the same terms, as a simple hypothetical explanation of effects, which alone in fact exist; the effects receive a (possible) intelligibility from the presumed cause or causes, whose existence, not directly observable, they validate in return:

I take my reasonings [in the *Essays*, e.g. the *Optics* and the *Meteorology*] to be so closely interconnected that just as the last are proved by the first, which are their causes, so the first are proved by the last, which are their effects. It must not be supposed that I am here committing the fallacy that the logicians call "arguing in a circle". For as experience makes most of these effects quite certain, the causes from which I deduce them serve not so much to prove them as to explain them; indeed, quite to the contrary, it is the causes which are proved by the effects. And I have called them "suppositions" simply to make it known that I think I can deduce them from the primary truths I have expounded above.[78]

The causes explain effects whose experienced existence remains nevertheless unexplained; but the fact of the effects precedes and attests to the nevertheless hypothetical existence of the causes; the epistemological primacy of the causes goes hand in hand with their ontic secondariness and the ontic primacy of the effects. Descartes knows perfectly well that causality remains for us a principle of the understanding, and thus a principle of intelligibility, not an ontic principle.

The two demonstrations of existence (of God and of material things, *Meditationes III* and *VI*) are thus carried out by the effects, which are attested, in order to lead back to the causes (God and material things), which for their part remain not immediately accessible (one by virtue of its incomprehensibility, the others as substances that "do not affect us" as such). Let us take note of two paradoxes in the search for a possible cause of the objective reality of all the possible ideas, when the issue is that of finding another existence than that of the *ego*. (a) First, the *ego* will not reach such an existence (effect) unless it is convinced of *not being able* to furnish the cause; God exists because the *ego* does not cause its idea of God. (b) Next: the criteria of existence is clearly fixed: "nec [. . .] me ipsum ejus ideæ causam esse posse—nor could I myself be the cause of its idea" (AT VII, 42.22; CSM II, 29); in other words, the only case in which the *ego* sees itself attributed with causality is the one (a) in which it does not accomplish it, (b) in which the existence of the effect appears precisely because it is clear of any cause [*hors de cause*], *extra causam*. For me and in *cogitatio*, the cause explains the thing but does not exist as a thing.

A textual fact proves that, for Descartes, the *ego* does not operate as a *cause*, and therefore causality is not conceived starting from the *ego*: the first two *Meditationes* never use the concept of *causa*, much less the request of a cause for the thoughts; better, this concept appears only in the second half of *Meditatio III* (AT VII, 40.21ff), the one, moreover, that imposes the "*alia quædam adhuc via.*" Now, this new orientation of the order of reasons, which alone introduces the concept of *substantia* (see §3), here makes recourse as evidence to the principle of causality: "Jam vero lumine naturali manifestum est tantumdem ad minimum esse debere in causa efficiente et totali, quantum in ejusdem causæ effectu—Now it is manifest by the natural light that there must be at least as much in the efficient and total cause as in the effect of that cause" (40.21–23; CSM II, 28); which is going to be applied not only to the formal reality of things and ideas, but also to the objective reality of the ideas, "etiam in ideis" (41.3), for there must be at least as much being in the cause as in the effect of this objective being. And if this demand winds up extending itself (in the *Iæ* and *IVæ Responsiones*) to the essence of God, itself interpreted as *causa sui*, never is it applied, even retrospectively, to the *cogitationes* that the *ego* thinks, nor a fortiori to the argument that establishes the existence of the *ego* in as much as thinking. We were even able to integrate this rupture between the field of *cogitatio* (from 17.1 to 40.4) and the *causa* (starting from 40.5) among the arguments that culminate in distinguishing two non-superposable or reducible Cartesian onto-theo-logies: the one of the *ens* as *cogitatum* (and in which the supreme being would have the figure of a quasi **cogitatio sui*); the other, where the *ens* is offered as *causatum* (and in which the supreme being is figured as *causa sui*). Nietzsche, neglecting this separation, tries to reduce the first onto-theo-logy to the second.[79] He thus in fact is in line with most of the successors of Descartes, up to but not including Kant, who tirelessly sought to identify being [*l'étant*] as *cogitatum* with being as *causatum*, in order to reduce the gap between the two supreme beings that they imply, so as finally to identify God *causa sui* with a **cogitatio sui* (Hegel, of course, and, negatively, Nietzsche) that was torn from the autonomy of the finite. In this way, Nietzsche's final objection deepens and ratifies, albeit in a negative mode, the completion of metaphysics. It thus lacks the essential point of Descartes: the finitude of the *ego*.

Seen again in the light of its readings by Nietzsche and Heidegger (but also by Kant), readings that support more than they oppose one another, the *ego* of the *cogito* of Descartes appears in a more radical singularity than the common interpretations of most historians of philosophy would leave us to assume. To one who reads the Cartesian texts with any precision, it does not seem possible to accept as something that goes without saying that the so-called argument of the *cogito* rests on (or leads back to) the *ego* as a substance or as a subject; nor does it seem possible to make the *ego* depend on a representation, or even less on a reflection; nor, finally, to interpret it as a cause, even of its own *cogitationes*. Knowing that habits confronted by demonstrations or even by facts do not disappear, I am not naïve enough to imagine myself able to prevent or even retard the habitual banalities on "the *cogito* in the *Meditations*," since even the greatest readers—I mean philosophers themselves—sacrificed doing so. But they sacrificed with their genius, and in order to carry out their own innovations; other readers do not possess such grand excuses. At least I hope to prove two things: first, that the erudite and precise history of philosophy cannot take place without sustained attention to the interpretations that metaphysicians give to their predecessors, for they are determined by their relation to them and have a privileged intelligence about them. And second, that the reading of the text of the *Meditationes*, especially the second one, asks to be freed, with difficulty, from old paradigms, and to have new ones discovered. Descartes remains determinant precisely because his arguments appear, to the extent that one reads them and considers them, infinitely more complex and *indeterminate* than the vulgate suspects: he continues to be a subject of thought because he remains outside the subject and clear of all cause.

THREE

Knowing by Esteem

§1. The Aporias of Generosity

Generosity may be "the last fruit of Cartesian metaphysics,"¹ yet it presents us with several difficulties. The first and the most evident is that this passion allows one to "pursue virtue in a perfect manner" (*The Passions of the Soul*, §153, AT XI, 446.10; CSM I, 384), thus proving, against a dichotomy that goes back to Plato, that the same "thoughts" can bring about "both actions of virtue and at the same time passions of the soul" (§161, 453.15–17; CSM I, 387–88). That here the same term crowns virtue and passion at the summit of their two hierarchies is already surprising. The second difficulty lies in how generosity fulfills in the final instance and at the same time passivity, since it derives from the first of the passions, admiration, and activity, since it consists in "the control we have over our volitions" (§152, 445.15–16; CSM I, 384); and it will probably be necessary to understand these two difficulties together, or indeed one through the other. But before that, we must recognize a third difficulty, which precedes the other two, since it comes from the initial definition of generosity: if in generosity "it is our own merit for which we have esteem or contempt" (§151, 445.2–3; CSM I, 383), self-esteem presupposes that we can "give *good reason for esteeming ourselves*" (§152, 445.15–16; CSM I, 384), or in other words, "esteem ourselves in accordance with our *true value*" (§161, 451.19–20; CSM I, 388)—esteem being all the more requisite and decisive in that "pride and generosity consist simply in the good opinion we have of ourselves—the only difference being that this opinion is unjustified in the one case and justified in the other" (§160, 451.16–19; CSM I, 386–87). What do "esteem" and "value" mean here, and what "reason" could they put into operation?[2]

What is the "thing that makes one esteem oneself" (§160, 451.23–24; CSM I, 387)? Descartes tries to give an answer to this question: "*True* generosity, which makes a man *esteem himself* to the highest point that he can *legitimately* do so, has only two components. The first consists in his knowing that nothing *truly* belongs to him but this freedom to dispose his volitions, and that he ought to be praised or blamed for no other reason than his using this freedom well or badly. The second consists in his *feeling within himself* a firm and constant resolution to use it *well*—that is, never to lack the will to undertake and carry out whatever he judges to be best" (§153, 445.26–446.9; CSM I, 384). But this response presents as many questions as the theses that it advances. First, what does it mean *to feel* the resolution, and how indeed can this feeling assure us that the will will not fail us and will remain "constant"?[3] Next, and above all, what criteria allow us to distinguish between the good and the bad usage of this supposed power? In order to satisfy these questions, it is not enough to observe that "one of the principal parts of wisdom is *to know in what manner and for what reason* anyone ought to have esteem or contempt for himself" (§152, 445.12–13; CSM I, 384); it is necessary to explain each one—the reason and the manner. The response proposed here simply reformulates a persistent aporia: how do we *know* the reasons for esteem (or scorn), if these not only have to do with a self-appreciation (with all the illusions of self-love that it implies, voluntarily or not, consciously or not), but above all if esteem as such does not seem to rest on any know-how, in the strict sense?

§2. Esteem, a Mode of Thinking

This aporia can be confronted seriously only by attempting to define, if possible, the epistemological status of esteem in itself. We will therefore risk, provisionally and by anticipation, a hypothesis: that esteem also constitutes an operation of knowledge, or more exactly a quasi-mode of the *cogitatio*, as distant from (and thus comparable to) the understanding as are, for example, sensation, imagination, will, and doubt.

In the nomenclature of the passions, where it rightfully appears, esteem is doubled (like joy and love) either as one of the "opinions that one holds, *without passion*, of the *value* of each thing," or "*regarded as a passion*" as "the soul's inclination to represent to itself *the value of the object of its esteem* [...] caused by a special movement of the spirits" (§149, 443.14–15 and 443.29–444.3; CSM I, 383). This double status of esteem (with or without passion) determines its two epistemological schemes. In the first case, we follow without any more hesitation, in order to esteem value, or what "reason deems we ought" (§150, 44.15; CSM I, 383); this esteem is enough to produce an already rational argument and allows, by following this "*magna luce in intellectu*," a "*magna* [...] *propensio in voluntate*" (conforming to the standard definition of truth fixed by *Meditatio IV*, AT VII, 59.1–3[4]): esteem, like the will, validates the evidence that the understanding uncovers in the thing to be willed or esteemed.[5] But in the second case, when esteem becomes a passion, which is to say, when it does what all passions do—"move and dispose the soul to want the things for which they prepare the body" (*Passions*, §40, 359.8–10)— it pushes us to decide "according to [*à raison...de*] our more or less affection" for the thing (§150, 444.21–22; CSM I, 383). Esteem, then, no longer obeys a light in the understanding in order to ratify it by the will but obeys the will itself, directly, guided by affection. For thinking "according to [*à raison de*]," by comparison and proportion, by degree and appreciation, signifies in fact having available no clear and distinct and thus no restricting reason, or dispensing with it. Such an imprecise esteem is found, moreover, in admiration, or rather in what allows for "supplementing its deficiency": for, when no passion or no evidence of understanding attracts our attention to a "thing," we can nevertheless have recourse to a "particular [state of] reflection and attention upon which our *will* can always impose our *understanding*, when we *judge* the thing present before us to *be worth* the trouble" (§76, 385.14–17; CSM I, 355). In esteem, then (as in admiration, from which it stems), the will may not follow the understanding by a consequent *propensio* but restrict it or eliminate its authority through a preceding "inclination" (441.19).

Understood in this way, the oft-quoted definition (*Passions*, §149) tells us much. First of all, that to esteem, in passion, means that the understanding finds itself directly controlled by the will, contrary to the normal situation and to the standard definition of truth, according to which the will indirectly ratifies clear and distinct knowledge, which is first obtained directly by the understanding (AT VII, 59.1–4). Next, in esteem as a passion, we are nevertheless dealing with some form of knowledge, since it allows once again for "representing" something (*Passions*, AT X, 444.1); but a knowledge that is very particular, that bears less on the "thing" as such than on its "value," according to which "it is worth the trouble," and thus in as much as it is useful, "ad usum vitae" (*Principia philosophiæ I*, §3, section title). For example, one can, in the situations in which the result does not depend on us, "*consider* [*estimer*] the outcome to be wholly fated and immutable"; or, in the case of a danger that is at least possible, follow "the route *considered* [qu'on *estime*] safer" (§146, 439.18–19 and 26–27; CSM I, 380, 381).

Esteem also allows for representing to oneself, even in the case where one cannot know *stricto sensu*, or in other words know through a representation *like*. . . and *as*. . ., or, put another way, to know through an interpretation of the "thing"; whence the introduction of the "value" to mark this non-objective and properly *hermeneutical* knowledge, where the "thing" does indeed present itself, but at an angle [comme de biais], as soon as we succeed in "looking [. . .], considering *as if*. . ." (§90, 395.18, 26; CSM I, 360), or in "looking at everything from this point of view [*de ce biais*]" (*Discourse on the Method*, AT VI, 26.17; CSM I, 124)—with a look from a certain angle [*d'un regard biaisé*], since it sees without the guaranties of objectivity (the *magna lux in intellectu*). At issue, then, when we represent a thing through consideration [*estimation*] of its value, is a simple thought of esteem, without certitude of the object, without order or measure. Esteem knows insofar as it thinks—by estimation [*à l'estime*]. It thinks just like one navigates by estimation, without the landmarks or the calculations that instruments of navigation would allow, without being able to have recourse precisely "to the level of reason."[6] Thus defined as a quasi-knowledge, a knowledge without the method, its order and its measure, one understands that esteem or estimation can also enter in at the limits of objectivity; not only at its low-end limits, the usage of life, the events that do not depend on us, but also at its high-end limit, incomprehensibility by excess and not by default, namely that of God: "On the contrary, we cannot comprehend the greatness of God, even though we know it. But the very fact that we judge it to be incomprehensible makes us *esteem* it further."[7] Let us then conclude this first sketch: esteem constitutes a form of knowledge directly and immediately produced by the will (my will, or that which passion imposes on me through my body), when the understanding cannot propose to (or impose on) it a clear and distinct idea of the thing as such, and thus as object, and when one can no longer (quasi-)know it except inasmuch as it "is worth the bother," and thus by interpreting it "by reason" of its "value."

Such an epistemological status of esteem (and of value) receives confirmations from two chronological extremes of the arc of Cartesian publications, with *The Discourse on the Method* responding to *The Passions of the Soul*. Esteem, which defines the form of thought without certitude (*by esteem*, precisely), and which does not know the thing as such, but in its value "in relation to ourselves,"[8] is first applied in 1637 to the sciences, "even those full of superstition and falsehood, in order to know *their true value* and guard against being deceived by them" (AT VI, 6.14–16; CSM I, 113); clearly the issue here is not knowing that of which alchemy, astrology, or magic claim objective knowledge—they know nothing about objective knowledge—but of "knowing *their worth* well enough not to be liable to be deceived" (9.11–12), of recognizing their ignorance by estimating them at their true value (none whatsoever): here the estimation of value opposes the (false) truth by exceeding it. A similar judgment of esteem is next applied to "the histories": for even when they "do not alter or exaggerate the *value* of things" that they report in order to make them "more worthy of being read," they nevertheless miss the truth by omitting their "less notable circumstances" (7.3; CSM I, 114): here the estimation of value is opposed to the (false) truth by default.[9] And finally, the writings of the pagans, similarly, "make appear [. . .] *estimable*" the virtues that in fact their wise men could never either fulfill or make accessible to others (8.3; CSM I, 114). These writings sin against the truth by a pure and simple ineffectiveness. Nevertheless, there are also positive uses of esteem to be found; for it allows us to evaluate the usefulness (today we would say the rate of return) of a program of research, since it can evaluate even the factual truth of a "discovery" by submitting it to a non-theoretical criterion: thus, faced with the project of acquiring a still unknown truth, one can and must ask oneself if the required and still-to-be-carried-out experiments can "be *worth* the time" (73.15; CSM I, 148).

But, in all these cases, the "value" univocally designates what one thinks without knowing it with exactitude.[10] This characteristic fits money preeminently, currency that has neither smell nor origin because first and foremost it has no fixed rate that would establish its value *ne varietur*; it thus designates any sum of money, without consideration of its origin and neutral toward any determination, since its "value is no less when it comes from the purse of a peasant than when it comes from a bank."[11] Likewise, when one "*esteems*" someone's "knowledge,"[12] it's not about things as such, nor even as they are known, but rather about the person who knows them, esteemed in terms of being educated; and the person does not merit this esteem for the very things he knows, but for his capability of having known them, and thus the utility that follows from that capability. Indeed, "a man who is of no use to anyone else is strictly *worthless*."[13] Thus we can confirm that value does not concern the truth of things, but their utility for us.

§3. "The True Office of Reason"

Nevertheless, would it not have been more enlightening and less ambiguous to cease according to esteem any status of knowledge at all (even hermeneutic, even with the reserve of an *in so far as*...), since it no longer thinks the thing as such, but only in relation to us and according to its sole "value" for us? That is, to speak like Montaigne, do we only make recourse to esteem when reason fails, "what I consider [*ce que j'estime*] permissible when reason no longer guides"?[14] Reason or esteem: must we choose?

In a declaration that is precise and very firm, Descartes opposes this exclusion of esteem from knowledge and rationality: "This is why the *true office of reason* is to examine *the just value* of all the goods whose acquisition seems to depend in some way on our conduct."[15] A declaration that is not only confirmed but reinforced by another that is nearly the same: "*The true use of reason*, then, in the conduct of life is to examine and consider without passion *the value of all the perfections*."[16] Thus, it is in general and in these two senses (with or without passion) that esteem puts into operation "reason" in its "true office" and "true usage." Esteem, and thus the value that it puts into operation, defines in this way the *general* mode of knowledge of these "things" that do not have the status of possible objects for a clear and distinct knowledge, but that nevertheless concern us above all as perhaps obscure objects of desire and of fear, according to our interest. Indeed, interest concerns matter that serves or is detrimental to my body, but also the needs of reason—including the most elevated, moral interest, which legitimately pushes us "to examine *the right value* of all the things we can *desire or fear*, the state of soul after death, how far we ought to love life, and how we ought to live in order to have no reason to fear losing our life."[17] To consider or estimate value, even when I cannot know the thing in itself clearly and distinctly, becomes possible because it appears necessary to me in order to assure myself of its utility for me. Utility requires that esteem think and know even that which escapes the certitude of the object.

How should we understand this certitude? It is certitude about an object taken not in itself but in as much as it is useful or harmful: "the objects which stimulate the senses do not excite different passions in us because of differences in the objects, but only because of the various ways in which they may *harm or benefit* us, or in general *have importance* for us. The function of all the passions consists solely in this, that they dispose our soul to want the things which nature deems *useful for us.*"[18] Evidently, we find here what *Meditatio VI* first introduced: on the one hand the situation of the union of the soul and the body in the *meum corpus*,[19] and on the other the fundamental distinction between the knowledge of the things of the world as objects of extension (known clearly and distinctly by *cogitatio* in the mode of understanding), and a knowledge that is also completely legitimate of these same things of the world as *commoda/incommoda*, useful or harmful things; in the case of the sensible world, these turn out to be known by *cogitatio* in the mode of sensation; and, once brought to the criteria of utility, these sensible thoughts prove to be not less but "*much more* lively and vivid and even, in their own way, *more* distinct—*multo magis vividæ et expressæ, et suo etiam modo magis distinctæ*" (AT VII, 75.15–16; CSM II, 52) than the clear and distinct ideas of objective knowledge itself. I have shown elsewhere the essential impact of this distinction between the *modi cogitandi*, particularly between the (pure) understanding and sensation ("*sentir*"), which attests in Descartes to an at least double approach to worldly beings, not only as subsistent (*vorhandene*) but *also* as usable and easy to handle (*zuhandene*).[20] Thus, the Cartesian thesis becomes clear: it is precisely because esteem must manage the non-objectifiable domain, that which certitude and evidence can no longer govern, that it is fitting that "reason" comes to fill its most complete and "true office": to discern among the things of use, what it is useful to desire or to flee from, to acquire or to avoid in the conduct of our actions and without the guarantee of a clear and distinct knowledge. The "true use of our reason" thus consists in exercising reason *beyond* the domain of objectification (that of the method, of the *Mathesis universalis*, of placing in order and taking measurements), as far as the domain of the unobjectifiable, so as to understand it, too, through *esteem*.

This task is not without difficulty, precisely because the realm of the practical also implies the action of the passions (or more precisely, the action of our body, which causes passions in our soul actively and as if through a will that is other than our own); in this way the passions not only do not allow us to know any object clearly and distinctly, but they blur things by deforming their value: "all our passions represent to us the goods to whose pursuit they impel us as being much greater than they really are."[21] Or: "Next I observe that there is nothing that can make the soul *content* except its *belief* that it possesses some *good*, and that often this *belief* is only a *very confused representation* in the soul. Moreover, the soul's union with the body causes it commonly to *represent* certain *goods to itself as being incomparably greater* than they are; but if it *knew distinctly their just value*, its *contentment* would always be in proportion to the greatness of the good from which it proceeded."[22]

The heart of the debate thus appears: how to esteem correctly and become "one who is a great admirer [*grand estimateur*] of persons of merit"?[23] It seems unlikely that Descartes here is not consciously remembering a formula that Montaigne attributes to himself (while Descartes pays tribute to Chanut): "I who am as sincere and loyal an estimator [*estimateur*] of it [Plato's virtue], and of virtues of similar stamp, as a man can be."[24] In order to secure this role, it would be necessary to succeed in controlling esteem and to rectify the distortion of it provoked by the action of the passions on our judgment. But, since in the field of unclear representation in which esteem operates, the issue is not so much objective truth as practical (and thus "subjective") utility, rectification does not mean simply the reestablishment of an exactitude that is in fact impossible, but the compensation of one excess by another, as when one bends a rod in the opposite direction in which it was first distorted. In a word, it is necessary sometimes to use cunning with esteem, and modify it (for it has a margin) for our benefit: "because nearly all the things of the world are such that one can *look at* them from a side that makes them appear good, and another that makes us notice their faults, I believe that, if one must use one's cleverness of approach, it is principally for the purpose of knowing how to *look at them from an angle* that *makes them appear* to us the most advantageous, provided that this happens without making a mistake."[25] Indeed, to look [*regarder*] (*intueri*) is not defined here by a view (and even less by a "simple view"), but as a *way of keeping* [*manière de garder*] (*tueri*) for the gaze [*regard*] that secures itself (*intuitus*) and of taking care [*prendre garde*] of what one sees, by keeping *it for oneself* (if it is *fit for use* [*commode* à l'usage]) or keeping *oneself from it* (if it is *unfit* [*incommode*] for use). Nevertheless, contrary to the theoretical attitude, it cannot be a question here of conforming the thing to the exigencies of certitude by reducing it to a combination of simple natures, and by eliminating from it, as much as possible, everything that experience would make uncertain;[26] *here* it is only a question of what experience makes uncertain, and of the "things which do not depend on us in any way" (§145, 437.19–20; CSM I, 379). A fortiori the same goes when, "*looking* with a philosophical eye upon the various activities and undertakings of mankind," that is to say, when "one becomes accustomed to *looking* from this angle on everything" in the field of morality and the practical,[27] one succeeds, for example, in balancing a sadness with a joy.

Descartes puts forth the example of such a balance of the passions that would allow for a correct estimation. He distinguishes at least three cases in which joy can and must prevail over sadness: (a) when the two passions "proceed from a true knowledge," one must prefer the first, which is always useful, over the second, always harmful; (b) when, as is most often the case in daily practice, the one and the other remain "badly founded," even in this case and considered in themselves, love and joy remain preferable to sadness and hatred, which are always without certain foundation; (c) finally, one can even go so far as to affirm that "a false joy is often more valuable than a sadness whose cause is true" because even a false joy makes me more happy than a true sadness, if I "*look* [*regarde*] at it from this angle" that is purely practical that allows the consideration of the useful and the harmful in the *usus vitae*.[28] In fact, this rectification of the "value" of the objects of desire by the compensation of "esteem" can be extended to the whole of practical life and in front of all the misfortunes of life: "the greatest souls [. . .] do everything in their power to make their fortune favorable in this life, yet they nevertheless *esteem* it so little with regard to eternity that they almost judge the events of life as we do those of comedies."[29] Thus one can and must obtain from oneself the ability "to hold in low esteem all the good things which may be taken away, and on the other hand to hold in high esteem the liberty and absolute control over ourselves."[30]

Montaigne attempted a comparable approach. In principle, he hopes, "the philosophers, who are remote from all public occupation, [. . .] have little *esteem*" for the powerful, who believe they possess the world. In principle, he who "considers as in a painting the great picture of our mother Nature in her full majesty; whoever reads such *universal and constant variety* in her face; whoever finds himself there, and not merely himself, but a whole kingdom, as a dot made with a very fine brush; that man alone *estimates* things according to their true proportions."[31] And yet this possibility finds itself contradicted by the "examples of arguments not only false, but inept" that these same "philosophers make to one another regarding the dissensions of their opinions"; henceforth, "let us judge from this what we are to think of man"![32] Who can estimate rightly? Montaigne's last question meets up with that of Descartes: only a god could do what the philosophers cannot, namely, estimate rightly: "It is to this alone [the divine majesty] that knowledge and wisdom belong; it alone that can of itself *esteem* something, and from which we steal what we account and prize ourselves for."[33]

§4. To Esteem, to Esteem Oneself (Montaigne)

Our reading of Cartesian esteem has gradually, with each step, joined with Montaigne's path. A clear sign confirms it. The famous opening of the *Discourse on the Method* is well known: "Good sense is the best distributed thing in the world: for everyone *thinks* himself so well endowed with it that even those who are the hardest to please in everything else do not usually desire more of it than they possess. In this it is unlikely that everyone is mistaken. It indicates rather that the power of judging well and of distinguishing the true from the false—which is what we properly call 'good sense' or 'reason'—is naturally equal in all men" (AT VI, 1.17–.8; CSM I, 111). It is less noted that this is a return to an argument first formulated by Montaigne:

All in all, to return to myself, the only thing that makes me *esteem myself* is the thing in which no man ever *estimated himself* deficient: my recommendation is vulgar, common, and popular, for who ever thought he lacked sense? That would be a proposition implying its own contradiction. [...] There never was a porter or a silly woman who did not think they had enough sense to take care of themselves. We readily acknowledge in others an advantage in courage, in bodily strength, in experience, in agility, in beauty; but an advantage in judgment we yield to no one.[34]

The two authors indeed agree about the equality of minds under the relation among "good sense," "sense," or "judgment"; to deny it would lead to contradiction: if I lack good sense, this judgment itself proves nothing, since I do not have the good sense to deny my good sense. But they diverge on two points, to the benefit, it seems, of Montaigne. First: he alone says explicitly that the equality in everyone of "sense" results from an *estimation*, and even from an estimation *of oneself by oneself*, while Descartes only evokes an indeterminate *thought*. And next, Montaigne, speaking in the first person, proves with his particular case the proposition's validity, instead of formulating it as universal without furnishing its performative argument. These two particularities allow him, in "returning to myself," to pose the question of esteem in terms of *self*-estimation [*estime de soi*]. These two moments still need clarification: how does the "I" esteem, and how do its estimations depend on self-estimation?

The esteem of things has rules. First, it requires a certain evidence that clarifies the value of the things: in "*estimating* expense and value according to show,"³⁵ the "world" is not wrong, since only exposure allows, or should allow, for an estimation. Value is also measured by the exceptional character of the thing: "in anything rarity serves as *estimation*"; sometimes, perhaps, also by its purely symbolic significance: "If with the prize that should be simply one of honor you mingle other advantages and riches, this admixture, instead of augmenting the *estimation*, lowers it and cuts it down"; or indeed, value is measured by the secret that surrounds it: "concealment, reservation, circumscription, are factors in *esteem*."³⁶ Nevertheless, esteem retains its opacity, the "iniquitous *estimation* of vices," for "vulgar and popular esteem is seldom happy in its choice" and is mistaken, or tricks others.³⁷ At root, all the difficulty of esteem derives from the intrinsic obscurity of substance, as defined by the medievals (and, soon, Descartes): as that which is not known directly, but only through the intermediary of its accidents (or attributes), and which therefore is always hidden in the final instance. This inaccessibility of substance stands out in an exemplary way in the knowledge, or rather the non-knowledge, of the individual, in particular of the individual human being. Montaigne perfectly describes the aporia:

But apropos of the *estimation* of men, it is a wonder that, ourselves excepted, nothing is *esteemed* except by its own qualities. We praise a horse because it is vigorous and skillful [...], not for his harness; a greyhound for his speed, not for his collar; a bird for his wing, not for his jesses and bells. Why do we not likewise *estimate* a man by what is his own? [...] Why in *estimating* a man do you *estimate* him all wrapped up in a package? He displays to us only parts that are not at all his own, and hides from us those by which alone one can truly judge of his *estimation*. [...] You must judge him by himself, not by his finery. And as one of the ancients says very comically: "Do you know why you think him [*l'estimez*] to be tall? You are counting in the height of his heels."[38]

Esteem thus cannot attain, either in the things of the world or in the other man, "a display," a theme wherein it could be exercised rightly.

Thus the decisive step taken by Montaigne: if we must exercise esteem, let it be on the sole theme to which I should, in principle, have a direct rather than an indirect access (like the substance of things or the identity of another); namely, on myself. Applied to myself, thinking by esteem could—ought to be able to—directly reach its theme and correctly formulate a judgment of its value. Esteem is understood in this way, in principle, beginning from self-estimation. Prudence remains nevertheless a requirement: "I hold that a man should be cautious in making an *estimate of himself*."[39] For two reasons: first because it is necessary to be assured that I have access to myself; and second, because "there are two parties in this vainglory [self-estimation], namely, to esteem ourselves too highly, and not to esteem others highly enough."[40] To esteem another highly enough carries no particular difficulty, for "what beauty I see in others I praise and esteem very gladly."[41] Not to make too high an estimate of oneself seems also to encounter no obstacle, since the lucid and honest character of Montaigne prevents it: "When I am in a bad way, [...] I persist in growing worse, and *esteem* myself no longer worth my care."[42] To the point that it increases the lack of esteem [*la mésestime*] beyond the reasonable: "But to come to my own particular case, it would be very difficult, it seems to me, for anyone else to *esteem himself* less, or indeed for anyone else to *esteem me* less, than I *esteem myself*."[43] As if self-consciousness were passing through the turning back of esteem onto the self: first the turning back of esteem for others onto this particular other ("anyone else to *esteem himself*..."), then the turning back of this esteem by another onto me ("anyone else to *esteem me*..."), and finally the turning back of my esteem onto myself ("than I *esteem myself*"). Here is the fundamental discovery: the question of esteem and of the "sincere and loyal estimator"[44] becomes the question of self-estimation, the self [*le moi*] defining itself precisely by this return upon the self of esteem. The "moi" probably does not feel or experience itself except in the reflexive gesture of self-estimation; in practice, the "moi" *results and comes from* self-estimation, and not the inverse.

But there is more: the discovery of self through the inevitable recourse to self-estimation also leads to a performative contradiction. Indeed, how could one avoid esteeming himself too highly, and thereby succeed in operating as a "sincere and loyal estimator"? For this is what wisdom and God demand of us: "Holy Writ declares those of us wretches who *esteem ourselves highly*."[45] And yet, to despise oneself in order to prove thereby that one is wise only results in acquiring an even higher esteem from others: "Because Socrates alone had seriously digested the precept of his god—to know himself—and because by that study he had come to despise himself, he alone was deemed worthy of the name Wise."[46] The more I neglect my glory and humble myself, the more I appear as humble, non-ego-centric, and thus as a model of holiness worthy of praise—this paradox was clearly identified by Saint Augustine, who came to the contradictory conclusion that "Minus mihi in hac re notus sum ipse quam tu—I am less known to myself than you are."[47] Montaigne himself was aware of this contradiction: "The parts that *I most esteem in myself* derive more honor from self-accusation than from self-commendation. That is why I fall back into the former and dwell on it more often. But when all is said and done, you never speak about yourself without loss."[48] Or rather, and in addition, one never speaks badly about oneself without *gain*, for, if he who esteems himself makes himself despised, he who despises himself makes himself esteemed.

Is there another way to resolve self-estimation [*l'estime de soi*], and thus the estimation of everything else [*l'estime de tout le reste*]? Montaigne, perhaps involuntarily, suggested that love of "self [*moi*]" by others substitutes for esteem, for love does not love only qualities, as esteem estimates them.[49]

§5. Esteem in Love (Descartes)

Esteem, self-estimation, and love—it fell to Descartes to answer, with an extraordinary proficiency, the breakthrough and the aporia of Montaigne.

The example of an estimation that always prefers joy (even when unfounded) to sadness (even when founded) nevertheless shows that the ethic of esteem proceeds more by a hermeneutical practice than by a theoretical calculation; as it can neither be quantified nor calculated precisely, so too its rightness cannot be demonstrated. This essential difficulty first appeared (as we saw in §1) with the aporia of generosity, which "causes a person's *self-esteem* to be as great as it may legitimately be" (§153, 445.25; CSM I, 384): where is the line between the legitimate estimation of oneself and self-esteem without any basis? Doesn't self-estimation always slide into excess, even (or above all) when it switches into ostentatious humility? It is not enough to appeal to the "freedom to dispose one's volitions" (446.3; ibid.); for this freedom only reinforces the difficulty of a legitimation of esteem: how would one be able to judge, by oneself, that one is "using it well or badly" (446.5) without at once complacently giving in to self-justification, always exactly proportional to culpability, whether avowed or not? How do we tear generosity and self-esteem away from solipsism, which, in ethics, is called egoism?

In order to overcome this persistent objection, Descartes carries out a remarkable movement, though little-noticed by critics: he proposes to regulate esteem (and thus generosity itself) according to a new criterion, the consideration of others by the *ego*, instead of being confined to the consideration of the *ego* by itself; in short, the measure of self-esteem is established by reference to the esteem for others, such that generosity is modelled on love. And not the reverse.[50] Indeed, if the generous person can "use well" (446.8) his free will, that is the result not only of his feeling capable of willing "to undertake and carry out whatever he judges to be best" (446.8–9; CSM I, 384), but above all because in general the generous "*esteem* nothing more highly than *doing good to others* and *scorning* their own self-interest" (§156, 447.25–448.2; CSM I, 385). Self-esteem can be limited thanks to its relation to others, but above all it succeeds in just self-estimation because it also and to begin with esteems the *ego* in the gaze of the other. Here it becomes crucial to understand that the doctrine of love (§79–83) *precedes* that of generosity (§150–159), renders it possible, and regulates it.

Indeed, love can certainly allow a definition that is formally univocal: "philosophers are not accustomed to give different names to things which share the same definition, and I know no other definition of love save that it is a passion which makes us join ourselves willingly to some object, no matter whether the object is equal to or greater or less than us."[51] But it is nevertheless really and truly hierarchized according to whether the dignity of what the lover loves surpasses, equals, or remains less than him. It is necessary (because, for Descartes at least, it is possible) to "more *reasonably* distinguish kinds of love according to the *esteem* which we have for what we love [others, the third], as compared with ourselves" (*Passions*, §83, 389.28–390.2; CSM I, 357). So let us make distinctions. Take the first case, in which "we have *less esteem* for the object of love *than for ourselves*" (a thousand doubloons, a flower, a bird, a horse, or even wine for a "drunkard" or a woman for a "brutish man," etc.); here, "unless our mind is very disordered" (390.8–9), it is only a simple affection in question, where one never has to sacrifice oneself for what one loves like that. Esteem, with or without passion, sacrifices the object of love to the one who loves. Next is the second case: "when we *esteem* it [a good] equally with ourselves, that is called 'friendship'" (390.4–5); Aristotelian friendship between equals finds its place here, perhaps even expanded, since the equals include, for "the man of honor," his mistress and his friends, just as for a "good father," his children. The corrected esteem of passion thus respects equality, which consists in considering those one loves "as other selves,"[32] and which becomes friendship between *ego*s "equal to oneself" because they share the same value, namely the faculty of using, and using *well*, their free will. With or without passion, esteem regulates in this way the reciprocity of *ego*s, in equal measure according to the *usus vitae*. Finally, there is the third case: "when we have more *esteem* for it [a good], our passion may be called 'devotion'" (§83, 390.5–7; CSM I, 357).[53] Here one esteems more, even "much more than for ourselves" (390.21), what has more *value* than the loving *ego*: a town, one's country, one's prince, God, in short every *ego* (collective or individual and sacred) that has a regulating or governing function with relation to my own: "if some man were *worth more, by himself*, than all his fellow citizens," esteem would be lost "if someone saw everything in relation to himself" and not to that man.[54] Thus, in the love of devotion between two friends, "charity requires that each of the two should *esteem* his friend *above* himself."[55] From which an Augustinian conclusion follows: "In the case of simple affection, one always prefers oneself to what one loves," as the earthly city bases itself on the "amor sui ad contemptum Dei"; while "in the case of devotion, on the other hand, one prefers the thing one loves so strongly that one is not afraid to die in order to preserve it," as the heavenly city rests on the "amor Dei usque ad contemptum sui."[56] With or without passion, esteem subjects the certitude of the *ego* to a properly ethical duty that is decided according to the criteria of the *usus vitae*, but itself understood in all its practical (and thus non-egoistic) fullness.

In this latter case, esteem can take other names. When "we *esteem* more greatly" certain others than ourselves, for example God because we cannot understand him,[57] we can hardly say that "we love them" (a certain equality of condition would be necessary); it is rather more fitting to say that "we respect, honor, esteem them," with "devotion."[58] This would allow us a better understanding of *Meditatio III*'s concluding sequence, which enjoins "immensi hujus luminis pulchritudinem, quantum caligantis ingenii mei acies ferre poterit, intueri, admirari, adorare—to gaze with wonder and adoration on the beauty of this immense light, so far as the eye of my darkened intellect can bear it" (AT VII, 52.13–16; CSM II, 36). The difficulties here, of course, are not lacking. (a) *Intueri* does not seem to fit with the epistemological sense that the new usage of the *Regulæ* conferred upon it, designating the operation of taking possession of the object; it would need to resemble its rare use designating "the intuitive knowledge of God"; but, except for a miracle, this knowledge remains for us unknown "in this life," since it assumes "an illumination of the mind, by which it sees in the light of God whatever it pleases him to show it by a direct impress of the divine clarity on our understanding";[59] therefore, it becomes problematic to claim to *intueri* divine splendor in pure philosophy. (b) *Adorari*, a *hapax* in the *Meditationes*, moreover has most often only a derogatory meaning: either that one knows vaguely "what is meant by *Deus* in Latin, and is adored by men," which can lead to atheism; or that one in this way directly practices idolatry.[60] This term, central and redundant in Bérulle, seems neither precise nor decisive in Descartes. (c) There remains *admirari*, also a *hapax* in 1640, which will take on its full theoretical status in 1649, but in the moral philosophy: this "first encounter with some object that surprises us," and which happens to us "before we know [it]," is thus regulated by what is not me, and measures esteem against what is different from the *ego*: "wonder is joined to either *esteem* or contempt, depending on whether we wonder at the value of an object or at its insignificance."[61]

Thus, the degrees of esteem, and in particular the degrees of self-esteem, are not fixed, in the final analysis, by the *ego* alone (as when it exerts the conditions of clear and distinct knowledge in theory), but rather by that to which or to whom the *ego* relates itself in practice. The criterion, which hierarchizes the estimation of values, appears even all the more radical as it is withheld from the rule of the *ego*: when and for what things and which other may the *ego* sacrifice what it loves, or be obligated to sacrifice itself? The Cartesian esteem of value is astonishingly yet powerfully characterized, contrary to evaluation, for example, according to Nietzsche, by its *befalling* the *ego* from elsewhere than itself (from the things of the world, from other human beings, or from God), much more than its arising from the *ego*.

§6. Esteem and the Moi (Pascal)

Descartes in this way regulates self-esteem by the esteem that the *ego* renders to another; it decenters itself, while still beginning from itself and the love that it can feel. Pascal will radicalize and reverse this gesture: self-esteem (indeed, esteem for the *moi*) is regulated by the esteem that the other bears for it; if the *moi* is decentered, it is henceforth so beginning from the other (and from the love that he brings about). Let us note that an insertion by Descartes (to my knowledge the only one of this kind) points in the direction of the Pascalian reversal, by intensifying and complicating his habitual usage of esteem: "seeing that we are *esteemed* highly by others is a reason for *esteeming ourselves*."[62] According to the consistent doctrine of generosity, this doubling means that self-esteem is regulated (or at least *must* be regulated) by the opinion of a third, who spares the *ego* the delusion of auto-idolatry: if someone else esteems me highly, then I am better justified in esteeming myself. But one can also understand this the other way around: there is no greater satisfaction for the *ego* than to see itself highly esteemed or to make itself esteemed by another. It is in this sense that Pascal will understand Descartes' thesis on esteem. Let us then examine briefly this Pascalian appropriation of the Cartesian thesis, so as to confirm that Descartes did indeed raise esteem to the rank of a concept—since Pascal himself overturned it on this very point.

While it is never thematized as such, the concept of esteem nevertheless offers Pascal at least two precise determinations. First, it operates in the opposite direction from the Cartesian concept, starting from the other's esteem for the *ego* rather than beginning from the *ego*: henceforth centripetal rather than centrifugal, the other's esteem determines the *ego*, which results from it as a *moi*, rather than the *ego* exercising esteem on the other. The plot is no longer woven by the estimating judgment of the *ego*, but instead starts from the "desire for the esteem of those around us";[63] it unfolds according to the tyrannical authority that the other's gaze exerts, through his esteem, on the self-esteem that the *ego* can (or cannot) agree with as a consequence. "Greatness of man. Our idea of man's soul is so lofty that we cannot bear to be despised and not enjoy the *esteem* of a given soul. All the happiness of men lies in this *esteem*" (*Pensées*, L. 411; trans. Krailsheimer, 120). The empire of esteem brings to daylight the greatness of mankind, and doubly so: first because no man can remain indifferent to the gaze of another, proving thus first of all that no *ego* can limit itself to simply being, and that it is necessary for it also to be esteemed (looked at, loved, etc.); and next because only another *ego* can, with the esteem that its gaze dispenses (or not), assure or invalidate this greatness. Not only does man merit the title of *estimating* animal (Nietzsche), but he reveals himself above all as the esteemed animal, *esteemable*, who essentially needs to be esteemed, the only being who cannot do without an estimation come from elsewhere (according to the erotic reduction). Esteem attests, by doubling itself, to the double postulation of man and thus decidedly removes him from reduction to the status of an object, of a machine in movement wearing a waxen mask as his sole visage. The *ego cogitans* of Descartes is corrected here by Pascal's "moi" that is thought of, *cogitatus* insofar as *esteemed*. In this way, "The vilest feature of man is the quest for glory, but it is just this that most clearly shows his excellence. For whatever possession he may own on earth, whatever health or essential amenity he may enjoy, he is dissatisfied unless he enjoys the high *esteem* of his fellows. He so highly *esteems* human reason that, however privileged he may be on earth, if he does not also enjoy a privileged position in human reason he is not happy. This is the finest position on earth" (*Pensées*, L. 470, trans. Krailsheimer, 151–52). Man is neither a wolf nor a god nor an *alter ego* to man, but a center and a pole of esteem, estimating and above all esteemable—more myself than myself and other than myself.

A second determination of esteem follows. The very greatness of his role and the greatness likewise that this role makes appear in man (at once both estimator and esteemed) causes the suspicion to arise that man is not able to exercise esteem within the rules—neither distributing it nor meriting it. Can man will to inhabit the "finest position on earth" and claim, nevertheless, to open it to others? The evidence of his impotence is expressed by the gap between the immensity of the desire for esteem and the reality of the failure to conquer it: "We are so presumptuous that we should like to be known all over the world, even by people who will only come when we are no more. Such is our vanity that the *esteem* of half a dozen of the people around us gives us pleasure and satisfaction" (*Pensées*, L. 120, trans. Krailsheimer, 31). Such a contradiction between the desire for esteem and the possibility of receiving it or of distributing it leads from inconsequence to injustice: we endlessly clamor for others' esteem, and deceive ourselves by demanding more than we deserve; and we denounce others' desire for esteem, who nevertheless do not exaggerate their merit any more than we already do; and so we are doubly unjust: in desiring without limit excessive esteem, and in denouncing in others what we accept in ourselves. "We do not want others to deceive us; we do not think it right for them to want us to *esteem* them more than they deserve; it is therefore not right either that we should deceive them and want them to *esteem* us more than we deserve" (L. 978; trans. Krailsheimer, 324). Pascal prolongs what Descartes had seen clearly: esteem puts into play between me and myself, between I [*moi*] who estimate and I myself [*moi-même*] who esteem myself (generosity), a third, the other. But where Descartes sees only a witness or a referee, Pascal spots a partner, or rather a rival. Generosity is thus exposed to the risk of mimetic rivalry.

The opposition recognized here between Pascal and Descartes must not hide their initial agreement: Pascal sees perfectly that esteem plays an essential conceptual role for Descartes. And indeed, esteem for him as well allows for reasoning rigorously precisely in the place where the rules of ordinary rationality (formal logic, predicative proposition, clear and distinct ideas, *Mathesis universalis*, and so on) are lacking. Thus, in politics, the preeminent domain of contingency, we understand that, against every supposed "political science," that oxymoron, it is necessary to accept that "anything founded on sound reason is very ill-founded, like *esteem* for wisdom" (L. 26, trans. Krailsheimer, 6). For even philosophy finds itself overdetermined by the criterion of utility (as Descartes himself agrees): "Even if it [everything that, like Descartes' natural philosophy, is useless and uncertain] were true we do not think [*estimons*] that the whole of philosophy would be *worth* an hour's effort" (L. 84, trans. Krailsheimer, 22). Thus, considering that man can find his rest only in an esteem, does it not always appear illegitimate to "have greater *esteem* for men's *esteem* than for pursuing the truth"? (L. 151, trans. Krailsheimer, 50). The idolatrous difficulty and illusion consist not so much in the infinite search for an esteem coming from another as in the ignorance of what this other can and must be. For it is enough that "man *esteem himself* at his own worth" (L. 119, trans. Krailsheimer, 30) to understand that, except for God's esteem, he cannot find rest. And just so, access to God depends on a judgment of esteem, or more exactly a judgment of value, that only a thinking that is within the realm of esteem can bear. The fundamental scheme of the three orders allows for passage from the order of bodies, irrational but known rationally, to the order of minds, which knows rationally and no more, up to the order of charity, which, like the heart, knows what exceeds discursive rationality. Now these transitions, which are not reversible (no order sees the order immediately superior to it, but a superior order sees the order or orders below it), clearly do not arise from the "minds" (the scholars or philosophers), since they and their *res cogitans* constitute only one of the three orders. Where then do they come from? From a non-objectifying mode of *cogitatio* (like doubt, as we saw)—as it happens, esteem making the judgment of value:

All bodies, the firmament, the stars, the earth and its kingdoms are not *worth* the least of minds, for it knows them all and itself too, while bodies know nothing.

All bodies together and all minds together and all their products are not *worth* the least impulse of charity. This is of an infinitely superior order. (L. 308; trans. Krailsheimer, 97)

Pascal thus finds, to pass from one order to the other, the same thinking by esteem that Descartes, at the end of his journey, had conceptualized. The absolutely original and indispensable role of a thinking by esteem in this way becomes even more patent. By contrast, we can only make note of the misunderstanding of thinking and knowing by esteem among most of Descartes' successors, however Cartesian in origin they claim to be: the claim of adequate knowledge, including of the essence of God (Spinoza), the univocal evidence of order in God (Malebranche), the (divine) calculation of the possibles and the (divine) knowledge of the complete notions (Leibniz), or even the non-critical invocation of the laws of nature and of clear ideas (Locke) only serve to obscure Descartes' discovery, confirmed by Pascal. And, with the censure of esteem, the speculative dignity of love also disappears—for a long time.

§7. A Practice of Doubt

Confirmed in this way by esteem, the dignity of accomplishing a true exercise of thought provokes a new question: is the rise of esteem limited to the last period of Cartesian thought, and is its role a marginal one in the prior periods? The question has to do with not only its chronology but also its concept: its role in moral philosophy, in the doctrine of the passions and of love, which followed already from its function as "true office of *reason*," implies as well not only that it does indeed exercise a *cogitatio*, but that it registers among the *modi cogitandi*. And yet, this list, as Descartes completed it (doubt, intellect, will, imagination, and also sensation), makes no explicit mention of esteem. By what right, then, ought one to correct it? Unless there were no need to correct it, or add some new rubric, because in fact esteem is *already* included, at least indirectly.

Let us see if this may be the case. As we said (in §3), esteem concerns "the conduct of life," where it establishes the "right value of all the things we can desire or fear,"[64] that is, things insofar as they are useful or harmful, *commoda* or *incommoda*; thus, esteem contributes to the *usus vitæ* through the evaluation of the practical and ethical value of things. Now, such an inclusion in the *usus vitæ*, in life and things *in as much as* they are useful, cannot not make us think of another decision, taken at the very beginning by Descartes: the decision to limit doubt to theory and not to use it "in matters of morality, [where] one must sometimes follow opinions that one knows to be quite uncertain, just as if they were indubitable" (*Discourse on the Method*, AT VI, 31.21–24; CSM I, 126). The difference between the doubtful and the certain, which is of course crucial in theory where the truth is at stake, would become dangerous and counter-productive in practical life, where it is fitting to follow "the most moderate and the least extreme opinions, which are commonly accepted in practice by the most sensible of those with whom I should have to live" (AT VI, 23.4–7; CSM I, 122).[65] This *practical* decision taken by the *Discourse on the Method* with regard to "all that is useful in life" (4.24; CSM II, 113) is only validated *a contrario* by the *Meditationes*, which are limited to indicating that doubt can only come into play on the condition of ridding oneself of the worries and cares of practical life (*mentem curis omnibus exsolve*, AT VII, 17.13–18.1). But the *Principia philosophiæ* comment explicitly on the meaning of this ridding oneself: "As far as ordinary life is concerned, the chance for action would frequently pass us by if we waited until we could free ourselves from our doubts, and so we are often compelled to accept what is merely probable."[66] Thus, through prudence, one must enter into doubt only when one exits from the use of life, from the practice of the useful and the harmful.

But the distinction is not as simple as it appears, for the passage to theoretical doubt itself is imposed (even if simply through the restriction of suspending all the cares of life) only because theoretical certitude offers, *as well*, a utility for practical life. Indeed, Descartes does not hesitate to speak of a *dubitationis utilitas* (AT VII, 12.5), of the utility of doubt that he explains in this way: "Quin et illa etiam, de quibus dubitamus, *utile* erit habere pro falsis, ut tanto clarius, quidnam certissimum et cognitu facillimum sit, inveniamus—It is *useful* to hold the doubtful as false in order to find all the more clearly what is the most certain and the easiest to know."[67] Doubt about knowledge [*le savoir*] thus *also* has a utility in the practice of life [*l'usage de la vie*], because theoretical truth *also* has a utility in the practical realm. In this way, there is a *utilitas* in demonstrating the existence of God and the immortality of the soul (AT VII, 6.16), even if only in order to counter those who otherwise would prefer the useful (*utile*) to the correct (*rectum*, AT VII, 2.6). There are also "useful and important" "truths" (VI, 41.18), like the discovery of "certain laws which God has so established in nature, and of which he has implanted such notions in our minds, that after adequate reflection we cannot doubt" (AT VI, 41.11–14; CSM I, 131). To the point that the new philosophy, theoretically truer than the old "speculative philosophy" (AT VI, 61.30; CSM I, 142), nevertheless ends up in a result that is "practical" (62.1), since it "leads to knowledge [...] very useful in life" (61.29–30; CSM I, 142) by making us "as it were, the lords and masters of nature" (62.7–8; CSM I, 142–43). In this way even theory, the domain restricted from doubt, also comes under the principle that "it is strictly *worthless* to be no *use* to anyone" (66.20–21; CSM I, 145). Let us conclude that, since strictly theoretical doubt still retains a meaning in practice, it joins with one of the characteristics of esteem: accomplishing "the true use of reason" by judging even when the evident reasons for a decision are lacking.

In what sense, and up to what point, can doubt share points in common with esteem? Before entering into the detail of the texts, let us pose a hypothesis: doubt (like esteem) cannot by definition proceed by strictly conceptual argumentation, because if it did it would presume what it wants to suspend, namely rationality itself. After all, this was the contradiction in the skeptical arguments developed, for example, by Sextus Empiricus: in order to challenge logical statements, he persists in accumulating arguments that are logical, and thus categorical and that claim to be demonstrative in their very negations. From this Descartes, following Montaigne's example, drew a lesson: doubt must not presuppose logic, nor therefore the truth of its arguments; it can only advance hypotheses, suppositions, hyperboles, and evaluations of the limit, which claim no truth whatsoever, even formal, but impose themselves with likeness on the imagination (like Cervantes' narratives, or the plays of Calderón or Shakespeare, Rotrou or Corneille). Doubt debates without resorting to any other argumentation than the naked *possibility* of doubting (or causing doubt), even if irrational and unlikely (see Chapter One, §5). To be sure, it thinks, but without an affirmed or affirmative concept. It thinks just like esteem evaluates—by esteem [*à l'estime*]. And this is why, again like esteem since it thinks without positive representation of the object, its "ratio dubitandi" (AT VII, 18.9) is not brought to bear by the understanding, but directly by the power of its will and the choice of its free will. Now, thinking and doubting by will mean "assentionem cohibere" (AT VII, 18.8), withholding one's assent for as long as one can, by three increasing steps of power characteristic of the Cartesian strategy (Chapter One, §2). First, it is necessary to resist immediate evidence in order to avoid seeing more than what is doubtful, in whatever manner one can do so; next, it is necessary to assimilate by theoretical violence the doubtful to the false (AT VII, 18.6–10); and finally, it is necessary to consider what deceives us once as always deceptive, and therefore false (VII, 18.17). These operations take place first directly on the sensible; but, as the sensible resists these doubts (the madness argument would assume that of the reader, and the dream argument concludes only in a probability and leaves, in any case, the sense data intact), it is necessary to shift the attack onto the mathematical statements, which continue to resist (the simple material natures remain), and rise to the hyperbolic hypothesis of an almighty God[68] (itself reinforced by the psychological fiction of the evil genius). At each stage, the (ir)rational extravagance of the skeptical argument makes up for itself with a more radical decision of the will; for as an argument, it is only a matter of a supposition (*suppono*)[69] or of an unfounded thought (*putare*, VII, 22.26 and following; *considerabo*, 22.29). But only this arbitrary decision allows for holding the doubt properly—without any truly convincing reason, by a pure evaluation of the limit: "I *resolved* to pretend" (VI, 32.12–13; CSM I, 127), "I *was willing* thus to think everything false" (VI, 32.16–17; ibid.), "manebo *obstinate* in hac meditatione defixus—I shall *stubbornly* and firmly persist in this meditation" (VII, 23.4; CSM II, 15), "*obfirmata* mente—mind *closed*" (VII, 23.8–9; ibid.). And I can do so because "in nobis *libertatem* esse experimur, ut semper ab iis credendis, quæ non plane certa sunt et explorata, *possimus* abstinere—we experience within us the kind of *freedom* which *enables us* always to refrain from believing things which are not completely certain and thoroughly examined";[70] to the point of being able to go so far as to decide to voluntarily deceive oneself: "non male agam, si, *voluntate* plane in contrarium versa, me ipsum fallam—it will be a good plan to turn my *will* in completely the opposite direction and deceive myself" (VII, 22.12–14; CSM II, 15). But then, if doubt depends on the will to the point of borrowing from it its last power to resist evidence, how and for what *reason* will this *will* ever decide to yield to evidence that is *certain*?

Here the connection with esteem becomes even more pertinent. For, in order to explain how, in front of the same statement that, for a time, my will had been stubbornly able to challenge, I suddenly accept it, it is not enough to describe the simple fact that I gave in to the evidence, due to its strength: since in the final instance neither arguments nor clear and distinct ideas are at issue, but rather suppositions and arbitrary hypotheses, would it not be all the more necessary to know what *reason* could force me to doubt no longer? Moreover, how did Descartes (or you, or I) succeed in finally accepting to say: "omnibus *satis* superque *pensitatis*—after having *thought through and having carefully examined everything*—, denique *statuendum sit* hoc pronuntiatum 'Ego sum, ego existo' [. . .] necessario esse *verum*—finally *one must conclude and hold as constant* that this proposition 'I am, I exist' is necessarily true"?[71] Probably because I no longer had the strength to continue doubting, nor to go on claiming that I was "forced" to doubt (*cogor*, VII, 21.27). Yes; but why am I *now* "forced to assent, *cogimur* [. . .] *assentiri*" (V, 148), why do I no longer have this strength to doubt and why did I decide in the end that I resisted *more than enough* in thought ("*satis superque* pensitatis")? Of course, it is because I *cannot* not consent to the rule according to which what

I think clearly and distinctly is true: "ea certe est natura mentis meæ ut nihilominus *non possem* iis [these things] *non assentiri*, [...] quamdiu ea clare percipio—the nature of the mind is such that I cannot but assent to these things, at least so long as I clearly perceive them" (VII, 65.7–9; CSM II, 45).[72] But once again, for what *reason* must I, here and for the first time, give in to this *reason*—when I could not do so earlier and without any other *reason* than the stubborn decision of my will? From where does the idea come that "I *could not* pretend that I did not exist," while I very well could "pretend that I had no body" (VI, 32.25–28; CSM I, 127)? Where does this "firm and immutable conviction, *sive firma et immutabilis persuasio*" suddenly come from, that resists the hypothesis of an "absolute falsity, *falsitas absoluta*" (VII, 145.11 and 4–5; CSM II, 103) and overturns "the most extravagant suppositions of the sceptics" (VI, 32.20–21; CSM I, 127)? Once again, why would I accept, *this time and for the first time*, to give in to the evidence? Why does *this* very argument, *this* performative contradiction, *this* interlocution now make my will to doubt give in at any cost, and even (and above all) without an argument that I recognize as true (otherwise, my doubt would be proved correct and, having become dogmatic, would cancel itself)?

Doubtless because a reason enters in that imposes itself on me (the rule of evidence, heart of the *ego sum, ego existo*), but this very evidence does not result from any reasoning of the understanding. It comes from the sole authority of the *ego*, through another mode of thought that nevertheless knows, esteem; in other words, through the mode of thinking that thinks with reasons by esteem. And more exactly, from my no longer having occasion to *think* [*estimer*] of God as deceptive: "Et certe [...] nullam occasionem habeam *existimandi* aliquem Deum esse deceptorem—And certainly [...] I have no cause to think that there is a deceiving God" (VII, 36.21–23; CSM II, 25).[73] Doubtless I perceive the performative contradiction that would arise if I—who (by supposition) am always deceived because a certain omnipotence (perhaps non-existent and surely anonymous) could deceive me (by recoding his codes)—were *not*, and if my existence (*that* I am) were only in order for someone to deceive me. But I perceive it and I accept it only because *here* esteem for the first time makes good use of my free will and is regulated by the infinity of God, by his evidence that I estimate to be superior to all other evidence—"eas [*sc.* demonstrationes] quibus hîc utor, certitudine & evidentia Geometricas æquare, vel etiam *superare, existimem*—the proofs I employ here are in my view as certain and evident as the proofs of geometry."[74] In order to accept an evidence that "satisfies me entirely" (To Mersenne, 25 November 1630, AT I, 182.1–4; CSMK, 29), it is necessary to estimate it just *enough*, so that, barring bad usage, my free will must accept it. There is at least one reader judicious enough to have seen and made clear the last instance of esteem: Fénelon. Here he evokes "something invincible by pure reason," "a light that is in me, that is not me, that corrects me, that rectifies me" and even "that forces me to judge in spite of myself."[75] As a result there is an "absolute powerlessness to doubt," wherein "it is impossible for me to abstain from judging that I am," for "I am no longer free" to think it.[76] Esteem in this sense imposes itself irresistibly, because it comes from elsewhere, in this way confirming admiration, where "the first encounter with some object surprises us" (*Passions of the Soul*, AT XI, 373.5–6; CSM I, 350). For between doubt and esteem there remains a difference: doubt comes from the *ego*, while esteem, even if it is the *ego* that formulates it, befalls the *ego*. Esteem thus does constitute a mode of thought, but without adding itself to the list of those that Descartes constantly inventories, nor does it modify that list: it enters in under the cover of doubt and, like doubt, often pairs up with the will, likewise under the cover of this will. The final moment of Cartesian philosophy finds and makes intelligible its first: for in the two cases, the institution of the method on the one hand, the esteem of the contingency of the passions on the other, it is necessary to think without the guarantee of clear and distinct ideas; and this is precisely what doubt and esteem allow us to do, always in the name of the *cogitatio*, but a *cogitatio* in an extreme situation, on the borderlands of rationality, where one can no longer be guided except, precisely, by thinking *by esteem*.[77]

This is so at the end of the journey, certainly. But it could also be that the doctrine of esteem retrospectively sheds light on an episode of thought from the era of the very beginnings. At the time of the three dreams of November 1619, Baillet reports that the "terror with which he [Descartes] was struck in the second dream marked, in his view, the *synderesis*, that is, the remorse of his conscience regarding the sins that he thought he had committed during the course of his life up to that point" (AT X, 186). This moral conscience returns, explained but criticized, in 1637, when the issue is that of "freeing myself from all the regrets and remorse which usually trouble the consciences of those weak and faltering spirits who allow themselves to set out on some supposedly good course of action which later, in their inconstancy, they judge to be bad" (*Discourse on the Method*, AT VI, 25.14–19; CSM I, 123). Thus, in 1619, Descartes was, by his own admission, a weak and faltering spirit, exposed to regrets and remorse, because still incapable of distinguishing good things from bad in the practical conduct of his life. The (bad) conscience thus depends first on a bad decision regarding the good and the bad: "For nothing causes regret and remorse except *irresolution*."[78] Irresolution, which makes us act without certitude and thus exposes us to taking for goods those things that are not. What mode of *cogitatio* is here in operation? One can identify it in two points.

First, an historical point. The *synderesis* that the dream of 1619 evokes refers to a *habitus* clearly defined by Thomas Aquinas: practical reason must be able to imitate speculative reason by having access to principles, not of course speculative (those of logic) but practical; it proceeds to apply them to particular moral acts, with a triple function: to attest (*testificari*) what was done, to search for (*investigare*) what must be done, and according to the case to excuse it or take it up again (*excusare, remordere*), to reprimand the bad and incline toward the good ("remurmurare malo, et inclinare ad bonum").[79] *Synderesis* thus exercises a conscience (*Gewissen*, not *Bewußtsein*) and assumes an apprehension of (moral) principles that is immediate and without their theoretical knowledge, so as to apply them to moral cases. Consequently, it enters under prudence: "Prudentia, applicans universalia principia ad particulares conclusiones operabilium [...] dicitur synderesis—prudence, applying universal principles to the particular conclusions of practical matters [...] is called synderesis."[80] Prudence deliberates by connecting particular cases according to the universal (moral) principles, but this intellectual virtue does not attain the rank of science, as Aristotle showed, because it lacks the νοῦς τῶν ἀρχῶν, the immediate grasp of principles. How, then, does it proceed to apprehend these principles, as well as the particular cases, for which there is no science? Thomas Aquinas answers the question clearly: "Ad apprehendendum autem intentiones quæ per sensum non accipiuntur, ordinatur vis *æstimativa* [...] in hominibus dicitur [*sc.* æstimatio] cogitativa—for the apprehension of intentions which are not received through the senses, the *estimative* power is appointed [...] in man [it] is called the cogitative."[81] Estimation, in the field of contingency, which is that of prudence, takes the place of science. The moral conscience thus exercises its function only through esteem, not through a conclusion of science. Now then—this is the second point—Descartes seems to follow this doctrine: "Remorse of conscience is a kind of sadness which results from our *doubting* that something we are doing, or have done, is good. *It necessarily presupposes doubt.* For if we were wholly certain that what we are doing is bad, we would refrain from doing it, since the will tends only towards objects that have some semblance of goodness. And if we were certain that what we have already done was bad, we would feel repentance for it, not simply remorse" (*Passions of the Soul*, §177, AT XI, 464.3–11; CSM I, 392). Remorse comes under doubt, inasmuch as it does not know whether one has done an evil or not; thus, the reproach that synderesis makes cannot be known by a concept or a clear and distinct idea; like doubt, it proceeds by esteem (finding along the way a term already used by Thomas).

Might we not conclude that esteem encompasses the first moment of the *cogitatio* as well as its final one? As if all the other modes of this unique but multiform *cogitatio* constituted only variants and specializations? The Cartesian *cogitatio* would come, then, from much further back than representation and the concept, and would thus go well beyond both.

FOUR

The Infinite: The Unfolding of Finitude

§1. Finitude as a Question

Doubt as the first "first principle" (Chapter One), the *ego sum* outside the subject and clear of all cause (Chapter Two), esteem as the fundamental mode of the *cogitatio* (Chapter Three): these theses of Cartesian innovation, certainly unexpected but, it seems to me, hardly contestable, all imply at the very least some thought of finitude. This is all the more the case if we take seriously the final words of the *Meditationes de prima philosophia*: "fatendum est humanam vitam circa res particulares sæpe erroribus esse obnoxiam, et naturæ nostræ infirmitas est agnoscenda—it must be admitted that the life of man is subject to frequent mistakes in particular things; and in the end we must acknowledge the infirmity and weakness of our nature."[1] Is this just conventional humility, or must we instead see here the inverted ordeal of the infinite?

I will try to demonstrate that, under a rhetorical appearance, Descartes in this way seals his long conquest of a thinking of finitude. Let us understand well: a thinking not of finitude *in* Cartesian philosophy, but of the finitude *of* philosophy itself, according to Descartes. Others after him will think the finitude of knowledge, of Dasein, or even of being itself, but it could well be that it is the finitude of the *ego*, and in it, of all *cogitatio*, that fixed, in the history of philosophy, the figure and the measure of finitude. For—at least this will be my hypothesis—more than in a theory of science and of objectness, more than in a transcendental doctrine of the *ego*, indeed, more than in a constitution of an onto-theo-logy, philosophy according to

Descartes consists already in a critique of reason by itself, and thus a recognition of reason's finitude. And this decision, which opposes him in advance to all his successors, up to (but not including) Kant, anticipates one of contemporary philosophy's essential attainments. This conquest, however, was not straightforward, nor was it easy. Let us try to reconstitute it by distinguishing, first, two clearly different experiences of finitude: one, following the epistemological theory of the object that the *Regulæ* of 1627 construct, and the *Discourse* of 1637 prolongs, ends up at the indefinite; the other, inaugurated by the Letters to Mersenne of 1630 and unfolded throughout the *Meditationes* of 1641, ends up, not without false starts, in a finite thought of the infinite, or indeed an *infinite finitude*.[2] This double journey will prove itself to be complex, often restarted by objections that oblige Descartes to correct, to adjust, and sometimes to surpass himself. For in order to have declared, against Morin, "I have never treated the infinite except to submit myself to it" (AT III, 293.24–25; CSMK, 172), he will in the course of things still have to learn, with difficulty, to submit to it himself.

Now, to seriously consider infinite finitude demands nothing less than to conceive what Levinas calls "the coming or the descent or the contraction of the infinite into a *finite* thought";[3] in other words, it asks us to conceive how finitude also implies *a certain* knowledge of the limit that makes us experience it. And the limit can be understood in two senses. Either in its denial, following Wittgenstein: "In order to be able to draw a limit to thought, we should have to find both sides of the limit thinkable (i.e. we should have to be able to think what cannot be thought)." Or through the recognition, according to Kant, that "the limit of the phenomenon belongs to the phenomenon (*die Grenze der Erscheinungen gehört mit [der] zu der Erscheinung*), but the thing, which makes the limit, is outside of it. It follows that we have a reason (*Ursache*) to conclude that a being (*Wesen*) is the originating cause (*Ursache*) of the world and of a world to come, without, however, having the means to determine them."[4] To pass from one sense to the other: this was the long course that Descartes followed, and its difficult debate.

§2. The Limits without Limits

We can follow that course starting with the *Regulæ*, and it seems not insignificant that they never use the term *finitus* in any of its declensions. There is nothing random about this omission, since in a sense the finitude of the human spirit seems to be repealed there from the very opening. Indeed, by introducing, against the Aristotelian distinction of the sciences according to their respective genres and thus their irreducible plurality, the major thesis of their unity beginning from a common source—"humana sapientia, quæ semper una et eadem manet, quantumvis differentibus subjectis applicata— human wisdom, which always remains one and the same, however different the subjects to which it is applied" (X, 360.8–9; CSM I, 9)—*Regula I* right away draws what one could call a consequence of infinitude: since human wisdom is no more differentiated according to its objects than sunlight is by what it shines on,[5] it is necessary to conclude that it lacks all limits: "non opus est ingenia *limitibus ullis* cohibere—there is no need to impose *any boundaries* on our minds"[6] (X, 360.12; CSM I, 9). Thus, one cannot assign any limit to human minds, once they can apply the same "wisdom" to any domain of the sciences, henceforth structurally and formally alike whatever their objects may be. In a word, since science always deploys the same operations, which are indifferent to their various objects, the objects do not change it, and thus do not limit it, either; in short, the unicity of "human wisdom" makes of it also a "universali[s] Sapientia" (X, 360.19–20). And the unicity of the method, which culminates in the *Mathesis universalis*, produces a similar limitlessness, because it puts into operation the originating limitlessness of the *bona mens* from which it follows.

However, implementing this limitlessness, this epistemological non-finitude, raises a real difficulty. Indeed, after the *Regulæ I–VII* gave the first presentation of the method and of the *Mathesis universalis* (the theory of order, the subversion of the Aristotelian categories, the institution of the *series* starting from epistemologically absolute terms in order to deduce from them the knowledge of relative terms, and so on), the *Regula VIII* intends to explain that we must nevertheless "sistere—stop" (392, 11 = 400, 7) and even points out where this must be done. But why would it be necessary, since we have established that "there is no need to impose any limits on our minds— *limitibus ullis cohibere*"? The answer consists only in a fact of experience: "Neque res ardua aut difficilis videri debet, ejus, quod in nobis ipsis *sentimus*, ingenii *limites* definire—It should not be regarded as an arduous or even difficult task to define the *limits* of the mind that we *feel* within ourselves" (X, 398.11–12; CSM I, 31). On first view, this observation does not appear to shed light on the difficulty, but instead introduces a contradiction: the *ingenia* would be free from all limits (to the point of embracing all the things comprised *in hac universitates*), yet we ought to feel—even easily—the limits of our own *ingenium*, as if the absence of limits of the known were nevertheless suited to the limitation of the knower. Before too quickly concluding that there is incoherence here, let us keep in mind that a great philosopher never contradicts him or herself, above all when he or she proposes to us a paradox. The issue is, rather, to conceive of this paradox, in order to understand the first Cartesian meaning of finitude—in the theory of objectness [*objectité*] and of knowledge.

Why do *ingenii limites* suddenly arise? Precisely because the *ingenium* remains unique and always the same in all the sciences; for, if he receives no external limitation from the fact of his objects, he undergoes as such at least a double internal limitation: he can know only what falls under the jurisdiction of the two "intellectus nostri actiones—actions of the intellect" (368.10), namely the gaze (or *intuitus*), which grasps the simplest terms, and deduction, which constructs from them the *series*. It is indeed quite easy to spot the questions that give way before these two requirements. (a) The title of *Regula VIII* right away announces that we must "sistere—stop" when "we come across something at which our intellect is unable to sufficiently look, satis intueri" (392.11; CSM I, 28). The example of the search for the equation of the anaclastic follows: if one holds to mathematics alone, in fact to mathematics applied to optics, one observes that it depends on the value of the angles of refraction and of reflection; but, as these angles themselves depend on the difference of density of two media, it is necessary to study them, and such study no longer belongs to mathematics (the sole domain of the pure gaze), but to physics; it is necessary to go so far as to determine the nature of light, and thus "quid sit generaliter potentia naturalis—what a natural power in general is" (395.2–3; CSM I, 29). Now, one can reasonably doubt that, in the field of physics, at least as defined by Aristotle by the change of an irreducible "matter," we could ever reach a genuine *intuitus mentis* (395.4) and not be reduced to a mere *experientia* (394.4). If such were the case (and we know that the polemic has not truly ended over what the *Optics* genuinely achieved), it would be necessary to give up on searching for the equation of the anaclastic.[7] And thus, whatever the details of this precise question, it is clear that the lack of the *intuitus* imposes, legitimately, a limitation on the *ingenium*. Does this have to do with a finitude? Or rather, *what* finitude is at issue?

Before examining this point, let us consider a second operation, (b) the deduction. By principle, nothing can be put into evidence if it is not an object, whether absolute and separate from every other for the *intuitus*, or deduced from such an absolute in a *series* by one or several relations; in short, if it is not, to one or several degrees, a relative term (*respectivum*); this placement in *series* does not depend on ontic determinations (the categories of being according to Aristotle), but following the *naturæ simplicissimæ*, very simple natures, principally the "material" (extension, figure, movement, etc.) and the "common" (existence, unity, duration, etc.), privileged as a priori concepts of the understanding (in a sense already close to the pure categories of the understanding that Kant will formulate). Now, these very simple natures remain by hypothesis finite in number and perfectly known; consequently, since we can know only through them, we can also know if a question is reduced to them in one way or another (that is, lets itself be formulated, transcribed, in terms of them); thus, if the question is not reduced to very simple natures, we know that we will never be able to know it: "nihil enim tam multiplex esse potest aut dispersum, quod per illam [...] enumerationem certis *limitibus* circumscribi atque in aliquot capita disponi non possit—nothing can be so many-sided or diffuse that it cannot be encompassed within definite *limits* or arranged under a few headings by means of the method of enumeration" (398.17–20; CSM I, 31). Every question about an object has limits, those of the very simple natures and their span: either it comes under their domain, and thus of a possible knowledge (of experience in the Kantian sense), or not.

But does this second limitation attest to a finitude? Paradoxically, no: on the contrary, it opens the possibility of measuring the undefined field of experience, already according to the principle that the conditions of possibility of the objects of experience coincide exactly with the condition of possibility of experience itself—that is to say, with the concepts and the *intuitus* of the human mind. Indeed, Descartes does not hesitate to defend a proposition that would appear absurdly ambitious if it didn't have to be understood in the transcendental sense: "Neque immensum est opus, res omnes in hac *universitate* contentas cogitatione velle complecti—Nor is it an immeasurable task to seek to encompass in thought everything in our *universe*" (398.14–16; CSM I, 31). Is there indeed nothing impossible about measuring the universe? Certainly, if this only has to do with our universality (*haec universitas*) of the things *to know*, that is to say of *objects* alone, defined a priori, to the exclusion on the one hand of what no *intuitus* succeeds in clearly and distinctly looking at, and on the other of what does not enter into a *series*, itself always limited to the *certis limitibus* of the very simple natures. We must then conclude that the paradox is valid: the human mind, while or rather *because* limited by its two primitive epistemological operations, encounters no limit to its knowledge—for what it does not ultimately know quite simply does not belong to the transcendental field of possible knowledge. The limits of "human wisdom" thus do not contradict the claim of the *Mathesis universalis* to be set up as "universal wisdom," but delimit only the *universitas* of what can be known.

The limits of the mind thus imply no epistemic finitude at all. Many arguments confirm this foundational paradox of the Cartesian doctrine of science. Not only do the *Regulæ* never employ, as we saw, the term *finitus* (nor its possible derivations), or express suspicion that *finis* might signify the frontier of a territory (and not only a goal); but they make use of *infinitus* (only six times) in order to characterize a knowable object or an operator of its knowledge. In this way the *Mathesis universalis*—well named, since it claims to an endless knowledge of the *universitas* encompassed by the *cogitatio*—proceeds by putting into order and taking measure of what, most often, offers at first glance no order or any measurability. How does it do so? First, for order, because one can establish it among all objects by complicating it *infinitis modis* on the model of the complex woof and warp of weavers (404.2). Next, in terms of measure, because, first, "subjectum omnimode extensum—every subject extended in every sense" is rightly susceptible of *endless* dimensions ("*infinitarum* dimensionum capax," 453.14–15; CSM I, 66) that are themselves "*infinitely* diverse, *infinitæ* diversæ" (448.11–12); and above all, because we measure in this way not only the three actually measurable dimensions of natural space but also the weight, speed, and an *infinity* of other parameters ("et alia ejusmodi *infinita*," 447.29), which however come under no actual extension; to the point that the *infinita multitudo* of possible figures "*sufficare*—suffices" to give an account of (in fact to code in pure imagination) the specific characters of nothing less than "all the sensible things, *omnium rerum sensibilium*" (413.18–19).[8] Thus, the limits of the "operations" of the human mind do not impose on it any finitude at all, but on the contrary subject it to an infinity of objects, or indeed the infinite as a character of the objectness that is ever open to new conquests.

The Infinite: The Unfolding of Finitude 91

From this another conclusion inevitably follows: if the theory of the limits of knowledge offers no genuine experience of finitude, even less so does it give the experience of the infinite. Or better: the infinite has no reason to intervene in the constitution of objectness, which develops indefinitely paradoxically because the mind knows its limits. Finitude itself therefore cannot appear there. Endowed with the method, the *ingenium* indeed faces only three possible situations: either he "entirely, *omnino*" knows the thing to be known; or he observes that this knowledge depends on a definitively inaccessible experience and he "is forced to come to a halt, *sistere cog[i]tur*"; or, finally, "he will be able to demonstrate that the thing he wants to know wholly exceeds the grasp of the human mind (*humani ingenii captum excedere*), in which case he will not regard himself as more ignorant on that account, for this discovery amounts to knowledge no less than any other—*quia non minor scientia est hoc ipsum quam quodvis aliud cognovisse*" (400.3–11; CSM I, 32–33). Can one speak here, already, of negative certainty? At the very least one can think, by anticipation, of a similar conclusion of Kant's:

> The consciousness of my ignorance (if this is not at the same time known to be necessary) should not end my inquiries, but is rather the proper cause to arouse them. All ignorance is either that of things or of the determination and boundaries (*Grenzen*) of my cognition. Now if the ignorance is contingent, then in the first case it must drive me to investigate the things (objects, *Gegenständen*) *dogmatically*, in the second case to investigate the boundaries (*Grenzen*) of my possible cognition *critically* (*kritisch*). But that my ignorance is absolutely necessary and hence absolves me from all further investigation can never be made out empirically, from *observation*, but only critically, by *getting to the bottom of* the primary sources of our cognition. [...] The former cognition of ignorance, which is possible only by means of the critique of reason itself, is thus *science—Jene durch Kritik der Vernunft selbst allein mögliche Erkenntnis seiner Unwissenheit ist also* Wissenschaft.[9]

§3. Power and Incomprehensibility

The doctrine of science treats of limits, but for that very reason is ignorant of finitude and thus of the infinite. With this result from the *Regulæ*, Descartes had almost himself verified what he will stigmatize, several years later, as the "main fault" of Jean-Baptiste Morin, that of always treating "the

Infinite as if his mind was above it"; it is only in 1630 that he will be able by contrast to pride himself on not having "ever treated of the Infinite except to submit [him]self to it, and not to determine what it is or is not."[10] For this critical advice excludes one from being able to think the infinite (and therefore finitude) from "above," by looking down on it; but since here looking down is equivalent to thinking an object (for the object is constituted, measured, and ordered by a master *ingenium*), this advice forbids one from thinking the infinite as an object—an object of the method, constituted according to order and measure, according to the *Mathesis universalis*. But can one know without knowing objects?

It is precisely this hypothesis that the three *Letters to Mersenne* from 15 April and 6 and 27 May 1630 formulate; it arises from them suddenly, like a meteorite in the Cartesian *corpus* that, despite some allusions in the works published after, will never receive explicit elucidations.[11] Moreover, the very question of the infinite appears there only discretely, almost marginally. The attack (for indeed we are talking about an attack against the dominant opinion, from Suarez or Bérulle to Kepler and Galileo, probably elicited by a question from Mersenne) contests that the mathematical (but also logical or even ethical) truths, "which *you* call eternal," can be imposed on the understanding, or indeed even on God's will. On the contrary, Descartes holds that they "have been laid down by God and depend on him entirely no less than the rest of his creatures" (AT I, 145.8–10; CSMK, 23). The fact, which Descartes accepts, that "I understand them [these truths] to be eternal and unchangeable," is not opposed to their creaturely status, since "I make the same judgement about God" (146.2–3; ibid.): besides that their *possible* eternity would not exempt them from being created (one thinks of the argument of Saint Thomas on the created eternity of the world), even with this eternity, they "proceed" in any case from "the existence of God [. . .] the first and most eternal of all the truths" (150.2–4; CSMK, 24). "Sole author on whom all things depend" (150.7–8; CSMK, 25) and "author of everything" (152.7; CSMK, 25), "it is certain that he [God] is the author" (152.2–3; ibid.) of these truths; their possible eternity proceeds from his own and they are only necessary for us, not for God, since it cannot be that "the truth of anything is prior to the knowledge which God has of it" (149.26–27; CSMK, 24). This doctrine has an epistemological function that is clear, but negative: we must renounce thinking of God according to the same conditions as those that allow for the clear and distinct knowing, by *intuitus* and deduction, of the objects of the method. Here the mathematical truths, but also and above all the simple natures, at least the material ones, lose their validity, since the two criteria of the *Mathesis universalis* prove to be, in the case of God, inapplicable, literally *without object*. For God does not come under the *mensura*: "We cannot comprehend the *greatness* of God, even though we know it" (145.21–22; CSMK, 23); and the imagination (the faculty of mathematics) does not have "as much *extension* as his power" (146.9–10; ibid.). God escapes as well from every *ordo*, from every ordering that would begin from another anterior truth: "they [men] could never say without blasphemy that the truth of anything *is prior* to the knowledge which God has of it" (149.25–27; CSMK, 24), since at issue is "the *first* truth" (150.2; ibid.). Whence the epistemological irrationality of atheists, who confuse the truths produced by order and measure with the truth of God: "because they perfectly comprehend mathematical truths and do not perfectly comprehend the truth of God's existence, it is no wonder they do not think the former depend on the latter. But they should rather take the opposite view, that since God is a cause whose power surpasses the *bounds* of human knowledge, and since the necessity of these truths does not exceed our knowledge, these truths are therefore something lesser" (150.14–21; CSMK, 25). To think of God outside of *Mathesis universalis* thus amounts, paradoxically but rigorously, to *not* "comprehending" him (146.6, 8; 150.14; 152.10, 12); for "to comprehend something is to embrace it with thought" (152.17–18; CSMK, 25), while the point is only that of "touching it with thought" (152.19; ibid.).[12] Otherwise, one would speak of God only like "the common and almost universal way of imagining him as a *finite* thing" (146.18–19; CSMK, 23). Here, and here only, the infinite finally emerges, but *backwards*.

Why so late? Because the excess of God in relation to common (and even, initially, *Cartesian*) rationality manifests itself through the im-*mens*ity and the extra-*ordinar*iness [le dé-*mesure* et le dés-*ordre*] that an "incomprehensible power" imposes (146.4–5; 150.22). Power, because it contrasts with science (*Mathesis universalis*) insofar as it attests to a state of fact (a creation). Incomprehensible, because this state of fact, independent of all human knowledge, does not result from human knowledge but rather fixes its conditions of possibility. It is then only by consequence of its denomination as infinite power that the infinite finally enters in, in the second position among the "highest thoughts" (150.12) about God: "God is infinite and all powerful" (152.11; CSMK, 25). It is under the relation of omnipotence that God appears infinite; or rather, the infinity of his power explains his incomprehensibility and renders it thinkable. It is necessary to think "God as a being who is infinite and incomprehensible" (150.7; CSMK, 24–25), if one does not want to think of him as an "idol, *aliquod idolum*" (VII, 139.6) and blaspheme him as other than himself. His incomprehensibility excepted, his power would be lowered to the rank of a derived truth, because as intelligible as those produced by the *Mathesis universalis*. Thus, incomprehensibility becomes a *positive* mark of knowledge only if it bears, in the *final* instance, on the infinite; for, as Descartes will only say later (in 1646), "since this word *comprehend* implies some limitation, a finite mind cannot comprehend God, who is *infinite*. But that does not prevent him having a perception of God, just as one can touch a mountain without being able to put one's arms round it."[13] To remain thinkable outside of all comprehension, power thus implies the infinite—and this proposition is analytic.

With the extraordinary (literally: outside of any *ordo*) doctrine of the creation of the eternal truths, the essential probably does not lie first of all in the recognition of the divine transcendence and its creative power, and therefore not in an ontic thesis but in an epistemological overturning: knowing does not always amount to constituting an object of *Mathesis universalis*, or to counting on the limits of "human wisdom" in order to increase it to the point of knowing "all the things contained by thought in the entire *universitas*" (X, 398.15; CSM I, 31); knowing requires, at least once, the suspending of comprehension. The infinite appears, and thus also the finitude of my mind, only if the epistemological obstacle of a *cogitatio* bounded by mere objectness falls away. The infinite does not arise through the increase of comprehension, but by its *reduction*, its bounding, or rather its suspension: to know the infinite means to not comprehend it, or rather, to no longer think in the mode of comprehension. If later Descartes will underscore the ontic positivity of the infinite, he here first reaches it only by an epistemological denial (if not an epistemological negation). And this is why the only mention of the *infinite* as a substantive is not found in the very discussion of the creation of the eternal truths but, by contrast, in the discussion of mathematical infinity (AT I, 146.20): Mersenne asks if an infinite line can be measured; Descartes concedes that it can; but, goes the objection, the infinite number in fathoms would not itself be infinite; which Descartes challenges. For "what basis have we for judging whether one infinity can be greater than another or not? It would no longer be infinity if we could grasp it" (147.2–5; CSMK, 23). Here Descartes does not yet distinguish the (mathematical) indefinite from the (properly philosophical and positive) infinite, because he holds to its meaning through epistemological contrast, which rests on its privilege of incomprehensibility.[14]

The first intervention of the infinite, in 1630, presents several characteristics that still limit its function. (a) The infinite is not mentioned directly as a substantive (except in one case, ontically very different, of infinite number, outside the exposition of the doctrine itself). (b) It enters in only through association with and by derivation from power (without *mensura*) and incomprehensibility (outside *ordo*). (c) It is requisite only in order to explain that one can think divine power even while it remains incomprehensible, and thus with a strictly epistemological function. Not yet an autonomous concept, but merely derived, with an epistemological role and without ontic status, the infinite pokes out, but does not yet break through. Nevertheless, and above all, its doctrine directly contradicts the theory of knowledge of the *Regulæ*, without our being able to envisage any conciliation between them.

§4. *The Indetermination of the Perfect*

This indetermination and this relative marginality of the notion of the infinite is clearly manifested in the *Discourse on the Method*. Used parsimoniously, the term often retains the everyday sense of the indefinite, in speaking of "an infinity of devices" (AT VI, 62.9; CSM I, 143), "an infinity of diseases" (62.27; ibid.), "an infinity" of forms or species (64.18; ibid., 144), or "an infinity of observations" (75.3; ibid., 149). Only two occurrences mark a progress. First, the fourth part of the *Discourse*, in the outline of the a posteriori proof, refers to "a perfect and infinite being" (39.4–5; CSM I, 130). Next, the fifth part invokes, so as to ground the "laws of nature" (as in AT I, 150.2–4), the "infinite perfections" of God (VI, 43.7–8; CSM I, 132). What should we retain from these rare indications? More than there seems.[15] (a) This time the word *infinite*, while it still remains an adjective, as in 1630, constitutes an ontic qualification—that, precisely, of an "infinite being," no longer only an epistemological qualification. (b) This ontic qualification becomes possible because one passes distinctly from the theory of knowledge (of the *Regulæ*) to the rational theology of "metaphysics" that in 1630 Descartes still wanted to avoid (AT I, 144.3–18; 145.5–6). (c) This shifting of the *infinite* becomes possible because it is tied with a positive and categorical statement on God, conceived as a "*perfect* and infinite being," about whom one can state "infinite *perfections*." As we shall see in 1641, the *infinite* enters positively into play only in its link (or even its identification) with divine perfection, which will not occur without raising other difficulties (see §4–5). But this new (ontic) connection of the *infinite* with the divine perfections implies the disappearance of its previous assimilation to (epistemological) incomprehensibility alone, since the point going forward is to prove positively the existence of God on the basis of the perfection of his essence; and, indeed, no mention remains in 1637 of the "being who is infinite and incomprehensible" (AT I, 150.7), or of the "incomprehensible power" of 1630 (146.4–5; 150.22).

From this, a new question arises: if the divine infinity no longer uncovers itself through (epistemological) contrast with the *Mathesis universalis*, how will a finite mind be able to have access to it? Overturning these terms leads to the possible difficulty of an encounter between human perfection, which is incomplete by definition, and the divine infinite, literally always unlimited. The question, moreover, is explicitly posed: where does the "idea of a being more perfect than my own" come from? (VI, 34.13, omitting the infinite; CSM II, 128). How is it that "it had been put into me by a nature truly more perfect than I was and even possessing in itself all the perfection of which I could have any idea" (34.19–23; CSM II, 128)? If this idea, "which was God" (34.24; CSM II, 128), counts among perfections that I do not have, how could I have it? Between comprehension and incomprehension, a relation that is, so to speak, dialectical between contraries would still remain, but between perfections, positive but *infinitely* unequal, what transition could remain? Without any doubt, a sequence lets us glimpse a more complex plot: according to the hypothesis that I am "alone and independent of every other," I could possibly imagine "myself being infinite, eternal, immutable, omniscient, omnipotent; in short, having all the perfections which I could observe to be in God" (34.30–35.6; CSM II, 128). But besides the fact this hypothesis does not stand up to critique (I am precisely not "independent," but in "dependence," 35.26), the concern here is only one of simple ontic comparison of perfections, without any direct link being established between finitude and the infinite. The principal question remains not only without an answer, but hardly even posed: how, if I am imperfect, could there be "put into me" (34.20) the idea of a perfect and even infinite nature? The argument still assumes a climb from the finite (confused with the imperfect) to the infinite (assimilated to the perfect); but from the finite to the infinite, the consequence is never a good one, since by definition there is no common *mensura* between them; how then would an epistemological transition be thinkable with the "incomprehensible," and how could the idea of an "infinite being" reside ontically in a finite mind? And furthermore, does it go without saying that the infinite—without bounds, without a comprehensible concept, without a definable essence—can directly *define* an individuated essence, even that of God?

In short, the succinct metaphysics that the *Discourse on the Method* outlines leaves intact the principal difficulties of a thinking of the infinite that conforms exactly to finitude; worse, it practically inventories them. Let us formulate them. (a) How can the infinite inhabit—affect, reach, shed light on, however one would like to put it—the finite? (b) Can the infinite name the divine essence, or even simply open the indistinct horizon of the incomprehensible?

§5. *The Ontic Infinite*

It is these difficulties that the *Meditationes de prima philosophia* finally confront. Or rather, that they finish by confronting, since it is necessary to await the great caesura, which divides *Meditatio III* (starting from AT VII, 40.5), and where, for the first time, *cause* and *substance* arise, in order to see the terms *infinite* and *finite* appear (still as simple adjectives).[16] The point is to construct a hierarchy here among ideas (those of the *res cogitans*) according to how they are distinguished by their respective objective realities, instead of being confined to their equality as modes of thought (following their equal formal reality as *cogitationes*); as a result, we obtain the ideas that represent accidents (40.14), then those that show *finitæ substantiæ* (40.20), and finally that idea by which I understand "summum aliquem Deum, æternum, *infinitum*, omniscium, omnipotentem, rerumque omnium, quæ præter ipsum sunt, creatorem—a supreme God, eternal, *infinite*, omniscient, omnipotent and the creator of all things that exist apart from him" (40.16–18). This still composite definition will be found later in similar terms: "Dei nomine intelligo substantiam quamdam *infinitam*, independentem, summe intelligentem, summe potentem, et a qua tum ego ipse, tum aliud omne, si quid aliud exstat, quodcumque exstat, est creatum—By the word 'God' I understand a substance that is *infinite*, independent, supremely intelligent, supremely powerful, and which created both myself and everything else (if anything else there be) that exists" (45.12–14; CSM II, 31),[17] and the formula *substantia infinita* is confirmed elsewhere (45.21, 22, 23, 27). In this way the first version of the a posteriori proof of the existence of God becomes possible: each objective reality must have a cause ("etiam de ideis," 41.3), since it is not simply nothing ("non tamen profecto plane nihil est," 41.28–29). Now, this cause must have as much formal "being, *esse*" as its effect, the objective reality, has objectively; thus, the infinite objective reality of the idea of God can have only the infinite formal reality of God as its cause, not that of the finite *res cogitans*.

This formulation nevertheless calls for at least two remarks. First, we note that the *infinite* never appears here as such, nor has it become an *idea infiniti*, but instead it qualifies either a substance or an *ens*; next, we note that it immediately receives another qualification, namely perfection: "hæc idea entis perfecti et infiniti"; finally, this formula in the end supports all the weight of the proof, since it alone is found enthroned as the idea that is "maxime clara et distincta" and "maxime vera" (46.8, 12, 28). Furthermore, no sooner is this privileged idea mentioned, which covers, so to speak, the infinite with perfection, but *infinite*, even as an adjective, disappears to the benefit of perfection: "idea entis perfectioris" (46.2; 47.28), *ens perfectius* (47.29), "nihil perfectius" (48.5), "idea entis perfectissimi, hoc est Dei" (51.3–4).[18] What motive explains this substitution? There is at least a clue: the last mention of the infinite occurs precisely in order to mark its insufficiency, if not its *epistemological* weakness:

Nec obstat quod *non comprehendam infinitum*, vel quod alia innumera in Deo sint, quæ nec *comprehendere*, nec forte etiam attingere cogitatione, ullo modo possum; est enim de ratione infiniti, ut a me, qui sum finitus, *non comprehendatur*—It does not matter that *I do not comprehend the infinite*, or that there are countless additional attributes of God which I cannot in any way *comprehend*, and perhaps cannot even reach in my thought; for it is in the nature of the infinite *not to be comprehended* by a finite being like myself. (46.18–23 = IX-1, 37; CSM II, 32)

We find here, almost to the letter, the warnings of 1630 about the inevitable incomprehensibility of the infinite (AT I, 147.4–5; 152.9–19; see *supra*, §3). One could conclude from this that, having constructed the first version of the proof on the hierarchy of finite and infinite beings, the conclusion, certainly ontically positive, does not appear any less epistemologically fragile, since we have no comprehension of the infinite; and so it is necessary to transpose the infinite into perfection, for perfection can and even must be known positively. This substitution of the *ens perfectum* for the *ens infinitum*, or their assimilation in an *ens perfectum et infinitum*, would in this way validate the turn already outlined by the *Discourse on the Method*, by assuming the breakthrough of the Letters of 1630 towards a "being that is infinite and incomprehensible," while at the same time avoiding its epistemological difficulty.

Consequently, one could put forward another explanation to clarify this turn: Descartes would not have appealed to the *ens infinitum* and would not have interpreted it right away as an infinity of positive perfections unless he wanted to thus ensure an idea that is "maxime vera, et maxime clara et distincta—the truest and most clear and distinct" (46.28; CSM II, 32); in short, he would have taken up *another* tradition than the one that had led him, in the Letters of 1630, to think of "God as an infinite and incomprehensible being" (AT I, 150.6–7; CSMK, 24–25), that of the univocal concept of being, which immediately divides the object of *metaphysica* into *ens infinitum* and *ens finitum*. The entire merit of this hypothesis is due to Dan Arbib, who maintains that the "Cartesian infinite belongs to the metaphysical history of the infinite since Duns Scotus."[19] A rapid establishment of perspective is enough to give credit to this reading here. Thomas Aquinas, inheriting from the majority of his Greek and Latin predecessors on this topic, did not first define God by infinity, which he does not count among the divine names. He of course accepts that one can say that God is infinite, but only by consequence of his privilege of being the act of being: "Illud autem quod est maxime formale omnium, est ipsum esse [. . .]; cum igitur esse divinum non sit esse receptum in aliquo, sed ipse sit suum esse subsistens [. . .], manifestum est, quod ipse Deus sit infinitus et perfectus—Now being is the most formal of all things [. . .]; since therefore the divine being is not a being received in anything, but He is His own subsistent being [. . .], it is clear that God Himself is infinite and perfect."[20] Thus, infinity does not define God in the first instance but derives from the ontic exception of the *ipsum esse*. Duns Scotus, in contrast, was the first to inaugurate the inverse way: to search for "some concept in which God is conceived in himself and quidditatively, *per se et quidditative concipiatur*." Now, since "the finite (*viator*) understanding can be certain, concerning God, that he is a being (*quod sit ens*), while at the same time it remains in doubt about whether he is a finite or an infinite being, a created or an uncreated being," it is necessary that its inquiry rely "on an identical, univocal concept (*conceptum eundem, univocum*), taken from creatures"; and this will be that of being as being, common to the sensible but also to that which exceeds the physical, the properly metaphysical domain: "Ens ut ens est communius sensibili, per se intelligitur a nobis, alias metaphysica non esset magis scientia transcendens quam physica—Being as being is more common than the sensible and is *per se* understood by us, otherwise metaphysics would not be a more transcendental science than physics is."[21] If the concept of infinite being allows for a better conception of God ("conceptus perfectior simul et simplicior nobis possibilis est conceptus entis infiniti"), this is because it fits into the univocal concept of being, common to *all* beings and not to God alone: "Deus non est cognoscibilis a nobis naturaliter, nisi ens sit univocum creato et increato—God cannot be known to us [by concept] in the state of nature, if being is not taken in the same sense for the created and the uncreated."[22] The *ens* (which with Clauberg will become the first object of *ontologia*) furnishes the understanding with its object, the first insofar as conceivable even before it knows by itself and, as such, each other being, and allows it to include in a univocal ontic *pre*-vision (from the point of view of the understanding) all beings, and even God—but for him, the issue will be the concept of being as infinite. The infinite thus becomes a mere *variable* of the univocal concept of being, which is the first object of knowledge. When Suarez takes up the division of the (objective) concept of being into infinite and finite being, he too will do it, despite his protestations of Thomist orthodoxy and his semblance of a critique of Scotism, from the postulate of univocity: "ens potius revocari ad univoca quam ad æquivoca, [. . .] quia et potest esse medium demonstrationis, et simpliciter ac sine addito dicitur de ente creato et increato—being can be reduced to univocal rather than equivocal [terms], [. . .] because it can both be a medium of demonstration and also simply and without addition it is said of finite and infinite being."[23]

Does Descartes take up this inheritance? He does indeed accept the division between the finite and the infinite as a first and radical distinction between God and creatures. But he does not do so on the basis of the least univocal concept, if only because of his constant refusal of univocity of any sort between God and any creature: "nomen *substantiæ* non convenit Deo et illis [*sc.* finite substances] *univoce*—the term 'substance' does not apply *univocally* [. . .] to God and to other things"; "nihil [. . .] univoce illi [*sc.* divine attributes] et nobis convenire—none belong to God and to ourselves in the same sense" and "nulla essentia potest univoce Deo et creaturæ convenire—no essence can belong univocally to both God and his creatures"; and "nullum agendi modum Deo et creaturis univoce convenire—no mode of action belongs univocally to God and his creatures."[24] Furthermore, not only does he never refer the infinite to a *conceptus entis*, but he sometimes also happens to invoke it by substantivizing it directly, without referring it to the least *ens*: "perceptionem infiniti [. . .], hoc est Dei—my perception of the infinite, that is God" (AT VII, 45.28–29; CSM II, 31), and "me percipere infinitum—my perception of the infinite" (45.23; ibid.); or "non comprehendam infinitum—I do not comprehend the infinite" (46.19; ibid., 32).[25] In short, even in the first formulation of the a posteriori proof, the perfect does not completely take control of the infinite, which frees itself sometimes not only from the perfect, but from the *ens* as well—the *conceptus entis* is never cited. What conclusion should we draw from this? Perhaps only one, but it is decisive: when in the line of Duns Scotus and Suarez the infinite is found to be assigned to God, it allows one to think God from the univocal concept of being, with the goal of fixing his quiddative concept, that is, defining his essence, or at the very least, comprehending him. But the Cartesian infinite is characterized precisely—exactly of concern is the *ratio infiniti*—by the *positive* impossibility of comprehending God: "est enim de ratione infiniti, ut a me, qui sum finitus, non comprehendatur—the nature of the infinite is such that it is not comprehended by a being such as I, who am finite" (46.21–23; CSM II, 32). Whatever the difficulties of this statement may be, Descartes faces and accepts them, since it is on this condition that he can hold, in the *idea infiniti*, an idea that is "maxime vera, et maxime clara et distincta" (46.28), which ensures the proof. The infinite of Descartes presupposes and *reposes* on its incomprehensibility, in exact opposition to the *ens infinitum* of Duns Scotus and Suarez, who keep comprehensibility at their disposal. While his modern readers (or contemporaries, as we shall see) struggle to conceive it, we can allow it without being surprised. The fact remains that Descartes claimed to conceive and demonstrate this paradox. Such must be our task.

§6. *The Transcendental Infinite*

If the paradox of the infinite cannot be conceived correctly either from the perfection of God or inclusion in the *conceptus univocus entis*, what *alia adhuc via* should we follow, *quod sectabor iter*?

We already know that it is not necessary to follow the way taken by Morin, who "always treats the infinite as if he had completely mastered it and could comprehend its properties" (AT III, 293.21–23; CSMK, 171–72). Not only does Morin "comprehend" the infinite and its properties, as if by overview and as *if he was there*, but above all he speaks of it from another point of departure than this infinite: the first definitions begin from *esse* (def. 1), from the *ens* (def. 2) of the *ens finitum* (def. 3), and not from the *ens infinitum* (def. 4); one must wait until axiom X for the infinite to be mentioned as that greater than which nothing can be conceived, well after the *nihil*, the *aliquid*, the *ens finitus*, and the *virtutis finitæ effectus*, and so on, has been conceived. The first theorem subjects the infinite, without examination or discussion, to the concepts that determine it: "Ens infinitum est in se, id omne quod est, vel esse potest."[26] In short, the infinite in fact is not at issue, but rather the infinite *ens*, and thus a concept of *infinitum* that is thinkable from the *conceptus entis*. Morin, no more than Spinoza, begins with neither the infinite nor even with God; he begins with concepts of the understanding that he inherits from the Scotist tradition, conveyed by Suarez. None of them think the infinite, because they comprehend it all at once as an object for metaphysics, without any critical precaution. In their almost brutal radicality, the Letters of 1630 at least had the merit of overturning the terms: the "incomprehensible and infinite being" (AT I, 150) imposed from the outset that one receive it starting from its "incomprehensible power" (150.22); thus, the infinite was thought *starting from* incomprehensibility, without which we would be dealing with something other than the infinite.

Looking closely, we see that Descartes had followed this negative way even before evoking the infinite in the second part of *Meditatio III*, by verifying finitude from *Meditationes I* and *II*, where it was uncovered in the two operations of doubt and of the existence of the *ego*. (a) In *Meditatio I*, doubt rests on the hypothesis that I can deceive *myself* (and not, as it is so often simplified, be deceived by a supposed "great deceiver," never mentioned by this name); this self-deception (*fallor*) is not equivalent to any sort of knowledge, but recognizes an imperfection. Descartes argues here with great precision: responding to an objection from Burman who held that doubt precedes all experience of the infinite, he effectively distinguishes the implicit from the explicit: if "explicitly we are able to recognize our own imperfection before we recognize the perfection of God, because we are able to direct our attention to ourselves before we direct our attention to God and infer our own finiteness before we arrive at his infiniteness" (such is indeed the case in *Meditatio I*), nevertheless "the knowledge of God and his perfection must implicitly always come before the knowledge of ourselves and our imperfections. For in reality the infinite perfection of God is prior to our imperfection, since our imperfection is a defect and negation of the perfection of God."[27] At base, *in re ipsa*, the exercise of doubt implicitly presupposes the infinite, for without it my finitude would not know itself; I would not even doubt, I would be ignorant *without doubt* (in the two senses of the formula), without even having consciousness of doubting. Following this authorized commentary, it would be necessary to conclude that from doubt to the infinite, the continuity suffers no solution. However, this first climb towards the infinite did not satisfy, because, even under Descartes' authority, it is limited to affirming what it would be necessary to show: that the issue is indeed a finitude, and that it already implies the infinite, that which doubt alone is not enough to demonstrate. (b) It is therefore necessary to prove the continuity between doubt and the infinite in another way. Now, the final hyperbole of doubt rests on the opinion rooted in my mind, "Deum esse qui potest omnia—that there is a God who can do all things" (AT VII, 21.2; CSM II, 14); from which two consequences immediately follow. First, omnipotence, even as a hypothesis, refers necessarily to the infinite: without even returning to the *Letters to Mersenne* of 1630, we know that the *Discourse* invoked "the perfect being [. . .,] *infinite*, eternal, immutable, omniscient, omnipotent . . ." (VI, 35.2–5), as the *Meditatio III* will confirm by defining God as "*infinitum*, omniscium, omnipotentem. . ." (VII, 40.16–17). Next, and above all, omnipotence implies incomprehensibility, which is attested by my powerlessness to *not* doubt mathematical truths; for the divine omnipotence, by disqualifying in 1641 through hyperbolic doubt the objective knowledges, reproduces the bracketing of the doctrine of science by the "incomprehensible power" of God the creator of the eternal truths (thus confirming the argument of 1630 against the atheist mathematicians; AT I, 150.12–22). *Meditatio I* thus takes up the guiding thread of omnipotence and, this time, almost explicitly the infinite.

Can one argue that *Meditatio II*, on the contrary, had to mask finitude, since it resists doubt (which would open finitude), by assuring itself of the existence of the *ego*, as a number of objectors claimed (from Gassendi to Voet)? Or better, how would this *res cogitans*, henceforth assured of existing, be able to recognize finitude better than the *Regulæ*, which already established that "nihil prius cognosci posse quam intellectum—nothing can be known prior to the intellect" (AT X, 395.23–24; CSM I, 30)? In short, how could a "pronuntiatum [...] necessario [...] verum" (VII, 25.12–13), or indeed a "first principle" (VI, 32.23 and X, 527), in their unshakeable certainty ("certum [...] et inconcussum," VII, 24.12–13), vouch for the least finitude? Here again, it is possible to interpret in two senses. (a) First, it does not go without saying that the certainty of the existence of the *ego* forbids access to its finitude, since Descartes sometimes obtains it, as we have seen, beginning not from the *cogitatio* in general, neutral and supposedly active, but from thought in the state of doubt, and therefore in imperfection and passivity: "verum etiam est te, qui dubitas, esse [. . .]. [S]i non essem, non possem dubitare—it is also true that you who are doubting exist [. . .]. [I]f I did not exist, I would not be able to doubt."[28] If then it is indeed in the mode of its doubt that the *cogitatio* performs its existence, it well and truly also testifies to finitude in that same way. (b) But one can demonstrate the finitude of the *res cogitans* more directly: since the *ego* performs its unconditioned existence only temporally—notably "quoties—each time" (VII, 25.12; 36.12), and "quamdiu—for as long as" it thinks (25.9; 27.10; 36.16), it does not testify to itself once and for all by observation, nor by *intuitus*; instead, it must perform it by a temporalized act (the *Principia I*, §7, adds, "eo tempore quo cogitat"), and thus repeat it unceasingly in contingency; indeed, "si cessarem ab omni cogitatione, [. . .] *illico* totus *esse desinerem*—I would cease *at the same time to be or to exist*" (VII, 27.11–12, and IX-1, 21, as Luynes translates it). My existence of course remains absolutely certain, but in the very time of and at the same time as its cogitated performance; that is, for a time: its contingency remains patent. It is not an anticipation of the most banal thesis of the discontinuity of time (49.12–20; 53.15) that is at issue here, but an announcement of the Kantian determination of finitude—by the temporality of thought (as much as by its sensibility).

Thus, the first two *Meditations* free up finitude more than indirectly, first by repeating the incomprehensibility of what exceeds the science of objectness, and then by temporalizing the act of the *cogitatio*. Nevertheless, it remains that these overtures never mention the finite (*finitus*) or the infinite (*infinitus*) as such. That falls to *Meditatio III*.

As I have already emphasized, it is the second part of that meditation (starting from AT VII, 40.12) that finally explicitly inaugurates the infinite ("summum aliquem Deum [. . .] infinitum," 40.16–17), and then the finite ("finitæ substantiæ," 40.20). Consequently, the *res incompleta et ab alio dependens* (51.24–25; see 53.10), the *substania incompleta* (222.15), is demarcated (strictly speaking, is de*fined*) with relation to God and in contrast with him, considered as *substantia infinita* (45.11, etc.), according to a pairing that opposes the "idea substantiæ infinitæ" to the "idea [substantiæ] finitæ" (166.1–2), the "substantia infinita et independens" to the "res finita et dependens" (185.26–27). But setting this relation also allows, for the first time, its center of gravity to pass from the finite (the thought of the *ego*, implicitly finite insofar as it doubts) to the infinite (first insofar as the sole absolutely independent substance): "Nam contra manifeste intelligo plus realitatis esse in substantia infinita quam in finita, ac proinde priorem quodammodo in me esse perceptionem infiniti quam finiti, hoc est Dei quam mei ipsius—On the contrary, I clearly understand that there is more reality in an infinite substance than in a finite one, and hence that my perception of the infinite, that is God, is in some way prior to my perception of the finite, that is myself" (45.26–29; CSM II, 31). This reversal of priority in fact irrevocably deposes [*destitue*] the *ego* of an anteriority that only resulted from its function as first knower, but which disappears as soon as one considers the first term as such, the infinite. It is not by chance that the *ego* and God are, so to speak, laid bare, abandoning at the same moment the provisional characters of two "substances," no longer to be confronted except under the titles (substantivized but not substantialized) of *finitum* and of *infinitum*: "priorem in me esse perceptionem *infiniti* quam *finite*, hoc est Dei quam mei ipsius."[29] The paradox of the knowledge of the infinite without its comprehension, or indeed *thanks to* incomprehension, can also be unfolded all the more clearly in the nudity of the term: "Est enim de ratione *infiniti*, ut a me, qui sum finitus, non comprehendatur—it is in the reason of the infinite not to be comprehended by a finite being like myself" (46.21–23; CSM II, 32).[30] It will be while repeating this paradox to Gassendi (see *infra*, §7) that Descartes will make the *idea infiniti* arise without reserve and in all its clarity: "Idea enim infiniti, ut sit vera, nullo modo debet comprehendi, quoniam ipsa incomprehensibilitas in ratione formali infiniti continetur—the incomprehensibility itself is contained in the formal reason of the infinite" (368, 2–4; CSM II, 253). Henceforth, the infinite does not delimit the finite by marking its borders, nor by stigmatizing it with incomprehensibility (like a Kantian "humiliation" of reason); instead, it is manifested *as such insofar as it is incomprehensible*. And this manifestation of the infinite *as such*, with its *fitting* epistemological effect, also constitutes a manifestation to itself of the finite *as such*: the *fold of the infinite also unfolds the fold of finitude*. The same fold unfolds the infinite and the finite.

Even so it still remains necessary to specify how the fold of finitude is unfolded in order that the *ego* is not only found there, but finds there in some way (*quodammodo*) the infinite itself, yet without ever comprehending it. It is not enough to conclude that, even without comprehending divine perfection, "our mind indeed can *quocunque modo* attingere cogitatione possum, have *some* idea of it" (VII, 52.5 = IX-1, 41.27–28). For this mode itself is in no way stable, since right before, regarding the idea that is *maxime vera et maxime clara et distincta*, the mere possibility of "touching [it] by thought" did not seem guaranteed: "alia innumera in Deo sint, quæ nec comprehendere, nec forte *etiam attingere cogitatione, ullo modo* possum—countless additional attributes of God which I cannot in any way comprehend, and *perhaps cannot even reach* in my thought" (VII, 46.19–21 = AT IX-1, 37; CSM II, 32). The warning, which we will find again later,[31] comes from far back, from 1630: "it is possible to know that God is infinite and all powerful although our soul, being finite, cannot *comprehend or conceive* him." So what does it mean here that "it is sufficient to touch it without one's thought" (AT I, 152.10–13 and 19; CSMK, 25)? Can we explain how this *modus* could join two incommensurables? To declare the ideas of the finite and of the infinite as simply innate (AT VII, 51.13–14) is not enough to render them commensurable, nor to join them to one another. Even mobilizing the biblical theme of man created *ad imaginem et similitudinem* of God is not enough, either, to clarify it, since the reserve of a *quodammodo* (51.20, *in some fashion*, IX-1, 41) maintains the gulf that separates them.

Nevertheless, we must follow this road. By proposing that the image and likeness of God that I bear is equivalent to his idea as the infinite ("*similitudinem*, in qua Dei *idea* continetur—that *likeness*, which includes the *idea* of God," 51.21; CSM II, 35), Descartes claims not only that, among other ideas, I also have such an idea in the "treasure house of my mind" (67.23; ibid., 46) (even though he had claimed it earlier: *rursus*, VII, 40.16; *sola restat idea Dei*, 45.9); he claims as well that this idea, that of an infinite, that of God, is *also* at once and identically my own. And he can argue for this claim and this paradox. First, because all my finitude tends toward it, irresistibly (48, 7–24; 51, 23–29): what gives me access to the idea of the infinite consists in precisely that which seems to the objectors to close it off, in the fact that being only finite, I cannot avoid endlessly desiring the infinite; for not being able to do without aiming at the infinite, because one is not infinite, itself *also* makes one rise to the infinite. The proof is that, if I had not already some notion of the infinite in my finitude, nothing would be lacking to this finitude, of which, moreover, I would not even be conscious. Next: because the idea of the infinite (God) and the idea of myself (*ego*) do not make two different ideas but rather *one*; a claim that is proved by the fact that I conceive the finite and the infinite by the exercise of a single, same faculty (left, moreover, without another name): "Dei idea [. . .], a me percipi *per eandem facultatem*, per quam ego ipse a me percipior—I perceive [. . .] the idea of God, *by the same faculty* which enables me to perceive myself" (51.21–22 = IX-1, 41; CSM II, 35). The fold of finitude is unfolded by the operation of a sole faculty, which must then perceive in it "*simul etiam*, at the very same time" (51.27=IX-1, 41), the two faces, finite and infinite.

What do these first two arguments assume? That when I look "me ipsum," *I see double*—through this sole *cogitatio*, I do not see one (a being?), I see two; on the one hand, I, *ego*, an imperfect thing, and thus one "aspiring indefinitely, *indefinite aspirans*" (51.26) to what is always more than oneself, but *also* all these perfections accomplished *re ipsa* and so no longer *indefinite*, thus the infinite and *ita Deum* (51.24, 26, 28, and 29). The infinite is perceived *at the same time and through the same gaze* as the finite. And this claim has only one acceptable meaning: the finite *within* its limits frees itself *from* its very limits (assuming that one can trace them clearly and distinctly); thus, the infinite, so to speak, surrounds the limits and in this way makes them visible by opening the horizon where they are inscribed. Particular to Descartes is, first, his serious thinking of the *limits* of finitude, instead of accepting, like Hobbes or Gassendi, the brute fact and then supposing it intelligible, when it is not so in itself. Descartes takes on the necessity of thinking both sides of the finite; he postulates that one can ascend to finitude backwards in order thus to gain access to the infinite, or rather to enter there *as* the infinite. The infinite (God) does not add to the finite (the *ego*), he does not even double it, but comes upon it, like the condition of its being brought to light. The *ego* can assure its finitude only by recognizing its limits; but it can experience them only by experiencing their resistance, and thus by pushing them back unceasingly and by attempting (always *indefinite*, of course) to cross over them—"ad majora et majora [. . .] indefinite aspirantem—aspiring indefinitely to greater and greater things" (51.26; CSM II, 35). This movement, in the end immobile, advances without end in the excess of the infinite over the finite.

This single idea with a double entry, the unfolding of the infinite *as* finitude and vice versa, finds another explicit confirmation in the first entry in *Meditatio III* of the biblical theme (Gen. 1:26), according to which "quite probably, *valde credibile*" God created the *ego*, that is, "me [. . .] ad imaginem et similitudinem ejus—me in his image and likeness" (VIII, 51.19–20; CSM II, 35). But *ad imaginem et similitudinem* indeed does not mean—a capital point—that God had produced, next to me or even in me, as an addition distinct from me, another image than me myself, taken globally; he did not produce another image than the *ego*; he did not add his signature somewhere, at the bottom or to the right of myself, like a new representable idea, like a thing apart from me: "Nec etiam opus est ut nota illa sit *aliqua res* ab opere ipso *diversa*—not that this signature need be *anything distinct* from the work itself" (51.17–18; ibid.). Like the great artists (the greatest never sign their canvas, for one recognizes "a Cézanne" at the first glance), God has no need to sign his creations, especially the most successful, for it jumps right out that this is "a God," manifesting in itself and globally the style, the touch, and, if we may dare to say so, the fine hand of God. God by his inimitable gesture illuminates his creature with an infinite brightness, co-extensive and indissociable from his finished work, taken in its totality. The signature does not need to be written separately, because the *ego* retains in itself a resemblance to God, since it recognizes itself on the basis of the divine infinite; the *ego* breathes the infinite by the grace of the artist, God. Just as one no more *comprehends* the idea of the infinite even when one nevertheless sees it as the truest, clearest, and most evident idea, so one does not seize upon the *ego* a mark, a signature, a label from the infinite, that would come to add to its finitude or subvert it. The *ego* does not comprehend the infinite as an object any more than it comprehends God, but it finds itself *in* the infinite, all the more evidently surrounded by it as by contrast it detaches itself from the finite. The infinite appears as the transcendental horizon of the finite.[32]

This endless advance, into what is beyond the already-known limits, toward a cogitable ever greater than the already cogitated, offers two characteristics. First, it takes its place a priori within the horizon of the infinite, without which the *ego* would not conceive even itself. Next, by definition it never possesses the infinite, nor comprehends it, since the infinite in actuality excludes all progress; and yet the advance experiences that no cogitated exhausts the cogitable, and thus it accepts a limitless excess that is always already given, and in short demands the infinite. The undeniable *vis argumenti* (VII, 51.30) is due to the fact that the finite, in order to be conceived simply as finite, certainly has no need to claim to be infinite (which is what the misinterpretation of the objectors assumes), but implies no less certainly the unfolding of the two sides of the fold of finitude, and thus the infinite as its condition of possibility. The finite calls for ever more than itself in order to think itself as such. Every finite cries for the infinite: "clamant, quod facta sint [. . .], clamant etiam, quod se ipsa non fecerint—they cry out that they were made [. . .], they also cry out that they did not make themselves" (Saint Augustine).[33] The *ego*, which also cries that it is not *a se* (VII, 48.7), cries out, if only in order to conceive its finitude, for nothing less than the infinite.

However, this result raises a difficulty to the very extent that it is convincing; for the infinite, such as the finite implies it as its condition of possibility, henceforth takes on a *transcendental* function.[34] Now the term "transcendental" never qualifies the knowledge of an object or a phenomenon given in experience, but always and only that which makes the experience possible: "I call all cognition transcendental that is occupied not so much with objects but rather with our mode of cognition of objects *insofar as this is to be possible* a priori."[35] If, then, Descartes claims to reach the idea of the infinite as a transcendental condition of the experience of the *ego sum*—such is indeed the case, since it has to do only with the two sides of a sole and unique faculty, and not of two distinct sorts of knowledge—then the infinite cannot designate a being distinct from the *ego*, nor name God, since it renders possible an experience, but includes within it nothing real. Can the transcendental function of the infinite nevertheless forbid an experienced phenomenon of the infinite? It remains for us to attempt to show how a phenomenon, or as it happens an act of the *ego*, can indeed put on stage and into play what is here the transcendental function of the infinite.

§7. Experience and the Infinite

A symptom of this difficulty reappears in the continual resistance of the objectors to the *idea infiniti*. Starting from *Meditatio III*, Descartes had formulated his principal argument in favor of the knowledge of such an idea: "Nec obstat quod *non comprehendam infinitum*, vel quod alia innumera in Deo sint, quæ nec comprehendere, nec *forte* etiam attingere cogitatione, ullo modo possum; est enim de ratione infiniti, ut a me, qui sum finitus, *non comprehendatur*—It does not matter that *I do not comprehend the infinite*, or that there are countless additional attributes of God which I cannot in any way comprehend, and *perhaps* cannot even reach in my thought; for it is in the nature of the infinite *not to be comprehended* by a finite being like myself" (VII, 46.18–23 = IX-1, 37; CSM II, 32). An innovation was not at stake, but rather the adoption of other similar formulations.[36]

The first objector, Caterus, confines himself to what seems to him clearly evident: if one wants *mordicus* a reason to refuse this idea, one will say that "imperfectio est intellectus nostri, qui infinitus non est—imperfect is our intellect, which is not infinite" (VII, 93.16–17; CSM II, 67); consequently, the habitual defensive argument sinks into triviality: "Someone [. . .] will ask '*Are* you clearly and distinctly aware of an infinite being? What, in that case, is the meaning of that well-worn maxim which is common knowledge (*tritum illud et vulgo notum*): *infinitum, qua infinitum, est ignotum*—*the infinite qua infinite is unknown*?'" (IX-1, 77.18–21 = VII, 96.12–13). It seems that Descartes takes close note of this blunt refusal when he reformulates his former defense ("hic dicam infinitum, qua infinitum est, nullo quidem modo comprehendi, sed nihilominus tamen intelligi, quatenus scilicet clare et distincte intelligere aliquem rem talem esse, ut nulli plane in ea limites posse reperiri, est clare intelligere illam esse infinitam," AT VII, 112.21–25),[37] merely by changing "things": already in the new reply the issue was no longer the idea of the infinite, but rather of its specification as *immensa et incomprehensibilis potentia*—immense and incomprehensible power (110.26; CSM II, 79). This displacement will lead to a new proof, according to causality, or indeed, with a few adjustments, according to the *causa sui* (111.1 and following), but which in fact falls back on the position of 1630. The sole genuine innovation consists in the warning that the non-comprehension and the inadequate knowledge of God does not prevent us from "reaching, *attingere*" it (113.15–19) without encompassing it, because "Deum ab humana mente capi non posse—God cannot be taken in by the human mind" (113.28; CSM II, 81); and, on the contrary, his perfections are such that we can "non tam *capere* quam ab ipsis *capi*—not so much take hold of them as be taken hold of by them" (114.7; CSM II, 82). Now this formula comes from William of Saint-Thierry: "Quod enim naturali intellectu intelligit anima, capit; illo autem intellectu [*sc.* the Holy Spirit, according to Romans 5:5] non tam capit, quam capitur—For what it [the mind] understands by natural understanding it grasps; but through this understanding it does not so much grasp as it itself is grasped."[38] The passage to a register that is neither epistemological (*comprehendere / intelligere*), nor ontic (no *ens*), nor even transcendental (the condition of possibility is reversed), marks well at once both the blocking of Caterus and Descartes' turn toward a new interpretation of the infinite. The *IIæ Responsiones*, which continue on the path of infinite power (142.2) and perfection (135.27), ratify the truce in the debate on the *idea infiniti*. In the *IIIæ Responsiones*, Hobbes, always peremptory, strikes without any argument: "ad nomen *infiniti* non oriri ideam infinitatis divinæ, sed meorum ipsius finium, sive limitum—what arises in connection with the term 'infinite' is not the idea of the infinity of God but the idea of my own boundaries or limits" (186.20–22; CSM II, 131); he therefore receives only an incidental response: "Cum dicitur Deus inconceptibilis, intelligitur de conceptu adæquate illum comprehendente—When they say that God 'cannot be conceived of', this refers to conceiving in such a way as to have a fully adequate comprehension of him" (189.17–18; CSM II, 133), which is a simple repetition of a response to the *IIæ Objectiones*: "Ac proinde satis est quod ea pauca, quæ de Deo percipimus, clare et distincte intelligamus, etsi nullo modo adæquate—Hence in the case of the few attributes of God which we do perceive, it is enough that we understand them clearly and distinctly, even though our understanding is in no way adequate" (152.20–22; CSM II, 108). Nothing decisive, then, comes into play here, any more than in the *IVæ Responsiones*, where Arnauld is not surprised by the idea of an *ens infinitum* but, more pertinent, debates the difficulties of the hypothesis of a *causa sui*.

The debate would have remained at the *status quo* if, for once, Gassendi had not put into question (and he was probably the first) the possibility of an infinite intellection of the infinite. In 1641, he had advanced a principal objection, fairly effective because rather succinct: "cum humanus intellectus non sit concipiendæ infinitatis capax, ideo neque habet neque respicit ideam infinitæ rei repræsentatricem. Quare et qui infinitum quid dicit, attribuit rei, quam non capit, nomen quod non intelligit—since the human intellect is not capable of conceiving of infinity, it therefore neither has nor can contemplate any idea representing an infinite thing. This is why if someone calls something 'infinite' he attributes to a thing which he does not grasp a label which he does not understand" (VII, 286.22–26; CSM II, 200). After having quoted this argument, Descartes had responded that

non distinguis intellectionem *modulo* ingenii nostri conformem, qualem de infinito nos habere unusquisque apud se satis experitur, a conceptu rerum adæquato, qualem nemo habet, non modo de infinito, sed nec forte etiam de ulla alia re quantumvis parva—Here you fail to distinguish between, on the one hand, an understanding which is suited to our *little mode* (and each of us knows by his own experience quite well that he has this sort of understanding of the infinite) and, on the other hand, a fully adequate conception of things (and no one has this sort of conception either of the infinite or of anything else, however small it may be). (365.1–5; CSM II, 252)

This distinction between adequate knowledge and sufficient knowledge had moreover been the object of a rather detailed development in the responses to Arnauld (220.1–221.24). In 1644, three years later, in order to support his first objection ("Dei, cum infinitus sit, non haberi vera idea—since God is infinite, we cannot have a true idea of him"), Gassendi bluntly attacks the response of Descartes in 1641 through this finite *modulum* of the infinite in us: "Quare tantum abest ut ego non distinguam intellectionis *modulum*, quin potius nihil agnosco præter *modulum*; [. . .] conceptum de Deo, seu Ente infinito, non modo non modulum, sed ne minimuli quidem *moduli* umbellissimam umbellulam esse—This is why I am so far from missing the distinction of the *little mode* of intellection: I recognize nothing other than this *little mode*; [. . .] a concept of God, or of the infinite Being, is not only not a *little mode*, but is not even the smallest shade of the shadow of a *little mode*."³⁹ In fact, there is indeed a deep conviction that supports this opposition, but it remains implicit and shows itself only rarely. It is the supposed evidence that: "Dicis [. . .] te intelligere *infinitam* [*sc.* substantiam, see VII, 45.11]; at hoc ipsum est, quod tibi pernegatum est; quandoquidem *solius infiniti intellectus* est rem intelligere infinitam; quod ille solus tantum sit intellectivus, quantum re intelligibilis est—You say [. . .] to understand an infinite substance; but it is precisely this that you are refused; since it falls *solely to an infinite understanding* to understand an infinite thing; because it is as intelligent as the thing is intelligible."⁴⁰ In contrast, the *Iæ Responsiones* had already underscored precisely that the *modulum* implied only a *finita cognitio* (VII, 114.15–16), a *mens finita* (119.3). To Gassendi's eyes, his position nevertheless seems well-enough fortified that he can finally, and not without exasperation, pose the decisive question: "Ista idea, quam habemus entis infiniti, *comprehenditur-ne a nobis*, an non comprehenditur?—This idea that we have of the infinite being: *do we comprehend* it or do we not comprehend it?" Gassendi wants an idea of the infinite that is clear and distinct, *just as for all other things*; paradoxically a radical "Cartesian," he admits no exception to the clear and distinct knowledge of objects. Like a card player who *wants to see*, he would like *to see* in the *idea infiniti* yet another of "those things [that] can serve as the objects of true thoughts" (AT II, 597.14; CSMK, 139). To him, the stakes seem simple:

Nam id quidem, quod tibi repræsentatur per humanam ideam, ipse comprehendis, alioquin enim neque de eo loquereris, neque id aut assereres, aut assummeres aliis demonstrandum: atqui dixisti id, quod comprehenditur, non esse infinitum; [. . .] quare neque vera est illa idea, vel ex eo, quod dixeris ideam infiniti, ut sit vera, nullo modo debere comprehendi—For what is represented to you by a human idea you comprehend yourself, for if not you would not speak of it, nor would you assume the duty of demonstrating it to others: but you said that what one comprehends is not the infinite; which means this is not a true idea, either; from that, you said that the idea of the infinite, to be true, must in no way be comprehended.⁴¹

The opposition between Descartes and Gassendi thus becomes patent: on the one hand, it involves deciding whether the *idea infiniti* gives an object (according to the epistemology of the *Mathesis universalis*) or a being to be seen, through comprehension; while on the other hand, at issue is the transcendental unfolding of the infinite over the finite, without objectivization, but by definition of the infinite possibility of the finite. Descartes' habitual response, which arises again in the *Væ Responsiones*, takes on its full meaning: "idea enim infiniti, ut sit vera, nullo modo debet comprehendi, quoniam ipsa incomprehensibilitas in ratione formali infiniti continetur—the idea of the infinite, if it is to be a true idea, cannot be comprehended at all, since the incomprehensibility is contained in the formal definition of the infinite."[42] Here, the concern is no longer that of an *infinite being* that would oppose itself directly and without common measure to another being that is finite, nor an object that would find itself contradictorily constituted as infinite by a finite *ego*, but instead that which can be known *by* its very incomprehensibility.

The final blow in this sparring match was initiated by Descartes, in his Letter to Clerselier of 12 January 1646. There he recalls his consistent doctrine: "Since the word 'comprehend' implies some limitation, a finite mind cannot comprehend God, who is infinite. But that does not prevent him having a perception of God, just as one can touch a mountain without being able to put one's arms round it."[43] But this old distinction here receives a new justification: "to perceive" and "to touch" are not reduced to a metaphor allowing for a loophole; these terms have a precise and strong meaning: what I cannot explain I can experience. A few months before the explanation made to Clerselier (June 1646), Descartes gave another to Elizabeth, who questioned him on the relation between human free will and divine causality (3 November 1645). He admits that "if we think only of ourselves," we cannot help "regarding" our free will "as independent." However, if we consider "the infinite power of God, we cannot help believing that all things depend on him," otherwise it would be necessary to accept that "his power is *both finite and infinite*: finite, since there is something which does not depend on it; infinite, since he was able to create that independent thing." Before pursuing Descartes' argument, we will note (a) how strange the hypothesis appears of such a power that is both infinite and finite; and (b) that, if one indeed sees that a thing not depending on divine power would make that power finite, it seems counter-intuitive to say that this same power remains infinite when it creates this "independent thing"; one would think the reverse to be true. But Descartes suggests quite clearly that there is more (infinite) power in *creating* an independent finite thing than (finite) powerlessness in the observing of an independent thing. (c) Even more surprising: what real difference is there between "a thing that does not depend [on the infinite power]" and "creating this independent thing"? Does it not seem that here it is *the same* fact—creating—that produces *the two* effects? These surprises remain without apparent response. This is perhaps why Descartes honestly avows that "the knowledge of the existence of God should not take away our certainty of our free will," which of course does not resolve the theoretical difficulty.

The true difficulty then arises: the "infinite power" not only *seems* "both finite and infinite," it *is* so, since the actual situation where the power of God and the free will of man are found is described here—the former infinite, but creating a finite thing that makes it finite, the latter, finite, yet independent of the infinite. In this sense, Descartes' response simply brings into juxtaposition the two terms of the contradiction. How is he able to do it? There are two reasons. First, because the issue here is probably not a contradiction, but already a figure of the unfolding of the infinite in the finite. Next, because Descartes maintains the two elements of this unfolding by invoking a new term, experience: our "free will which we *experience* and feel in ourselves," to the point that "the independence which we experience and feel in ourselves [. . .] is not incompatible with a dependence of quite another kind, whereby all things are subject to God."[44] That which cannot be comprehended—the unfolding of the infinite in the finite—can nevertheless be well and truly *experienced*: here, under the aspect of the infinite power of God unfolding itself in the free will of man; elsewhere, under the aspect of the finite thought of the infinite, that "habere unusquisque apud se *satis experitur*—each of us *experiences well enough* in himself" (VII, 365.3; CSM II, 252). We find confirmation that this experience offers the true answer to the objection of Gassendi in the fact that Descartes makes recourse to it in order to justify the certainty of freedom: "Ego certe mea libertate gaudebo, cum et illam apud me *experiar*—but I am certainly very pleased with my freedom since I experience it within myself" (VII, 377.23–24; CSM II, 259).[45] Experience imposes, then, the unfolding of the infinite in the finite, under its various forms, and first of all those of the idea of the infinite and of the freedom of the will. Descartes, in the end, reveals himself as more empiricist than Gassendi.

§8. The Will Reduced to Infinity

Now we can finally return to the second entry of the biblical theme of the image and likeness, this time in *Meditatio IV*. We find it right away, explicitly placed in association with experience: "Sola est voluntas, sive arbitrii libertas, quam tantam *in me experior*, ut nullius majoris ideam apprehendam; adeo ut illa præcipue sit, ratione cujus imaginem quandam et similitudinem Dei me referre intelligo—It is only the will, or freedom of choice, which I experience within me to be so great that the idea of any greater faculty is beyond my grasp; so much so that it is above all in virtue of the will that I understand myself to bear in some way the image and likeness of God" (VII, 57.11–15; CSM II, 40). In its first entry, this theme remained indeterminate, assigned to a still anonymous *eadam facultas* (51.22), while it is identified henceforth as *facultas eligendi* (56.13); or even more exactly as a *voluntas sive arbitrii libertatem*, that "I know by experience [. . .] is not restricted in any way—sane nullis [. . .] limitibus circumscribi *experior*" (56.28–30; CSM II, 39). In short, from this point forward the *ego* experiences, at least in itself, an unlimited faculty. Unlimited in what sense? Before attempting a response, let us measure the step taken. In the *Meditatio III*, the *eadem facultas* through which I perceived both the infinite God and the finite me (45.29) nevertheless only opened the fold of the infinite in the finite in a transcendental mode (*supra*, §6), without giving access either to a knowledge or to an experience of some operation or phenomenon of any sort: the unfolding of the infinite manifested nothing, if not the condition of finitude. Here, in contrast, this unfolding is manifest in a faculty, a faculty that I experience and that makes me thus know something—as it happens, the heart of the "natura cogitans [. . .] quæ *ego ipse* sum—thinking nature [. . .] which *I myself* am" (59.8–9; CSM II, 41). Anticipating the objections of Hobbes and of Gassendi, which were focused solely on *Meditatio I*, interpreting it moreover wrongly according to an ontic rather than a transcendental approach to the infinite, *Meditatio IV* was already responding by rising, in addition, to the real experience and knowledge of the unfolding of the infinite in the exercise of the faculty of the nevertheless still finite *ego*.

However, the paradox remains: how can the infinite unfold itself in the exercise of a faculty of a *mens finita*? In other words, in what sense and to what extent can one qualify the finite *ego*'s will as infinite? For a long time it has been held as certain that Descartes considered the human will to be infinite;[46] today, however, it is emphasized that *Meditatio IV* does not literally confer the qualifier of infinite on the will[47] but is limited to acknowledging that "tantam in me experior, ut nullius majoris ideam apprehendam—I experience it within me to be so great that I do not apprehend the idea of any other that is greater" (57.12–13; CSM II, 40). It would become tempting, then, to consider it as certainly "ampla et perfecta" (56.27), "amplissima atque in suo genere perfecta" (58.16–17), greater than any other faculty, but nevertheless not positively infinite. Of course, one will always find loopholes to avoid accepting other such declarations that are clearly affirmative of this infinity. But some arguments in the contrary sense remain. (a) Take the clearest declaration: "The desire that each of us had to have all the perfections that he can conceive, and consequently all those that we believe to be in God, is due to his having given us a will that has no bounds. And it is principally because of that *infinite will that is in us*, that one can say that he created us in his image."[48] How could one disqualify this text? All these terms offer a patent Cartesian authenticity: the desire of the perfections that are in God is found in the *Discourse on the Method* (VI, 34.24 and following) as well as in *Meditatio III* (VII, 48.7–24; 51.23–29); the general resemblance to God is found located "principally" in the will, which we note is without "bounds" in us, just as, in 1641, "I experience it circumscribed by no limits, *nullis* [. . .] *limitibus circumscribi experior.*" As to the objection that this is a response to a question of Mersenne (in a letter that is today lost) and would therefore have no "theoretical justification," it would call into question nothing less than the entire doctrine of the creation of the eternal truths, which also appears in 1630 as the response to a question of Mersenne that we have lost.[49] The text thus appears to me to be impeccable. (b) Take another, from a later time: "Voluntas vero *infinita quodammodo* dici potest, quia nihil umquam advertimus, quod alicujus alterius voluntatis, *vel immensæ illius quæ in Deo est*, objectum esse possit, ad quod etiam nostra non se extendat—The will, on the other hand, can in a certain sense be called infinite, since we observe without exception that its scope extends to anything that can possibly be an object of any other will—*even the immeasurable will of God*" (*Principia philosophiæ I*,

§35; CSM I, 204). Can its weight be diminished by supposing the addition of "in a certain sense, *quodammodo*" as an attenuation of infinity? To begin with, it is neither the style nor the intention of the *Principia* to attenuate anything, indeed to the contrary; how would one treat as attenuation other uses that are similarly affirmative, such as: "*valde credibile* est me *quodammodo* ad imaginem et similitudinem ejus [*sc. Dei*] factum esse—a very strong basis for believing that I am somehow made in his image and likeness" (AT VII, 51.19; CSM II, 35); or "quatenus etiam *quodammodo* de nihilo, sive de non ente, participo—in so far as I participate in nothingness or non-being" (54.20–22; CSM II, 38); and "*major* in me *quodammodo* perfectio est, quod illos [*sc.* actus voluntatis] possim elicere, quam si non possem—there is in a sense more perfection in me than would be the case if I lacked this ability" (60.29–31; CSM II, 42)?[50] It is not a question here of restrictions, but rather of extreme, almost imprudent affirmations. And this is, moreover, the most striking trait of this text: the affirmation that even God's will cannot will something too great or infinite that our will, although finite, cannot also will. If *quodammodo* attenuates something here, it will be this audacity itself. To which two other audacities, in French, respond: (a) "the exercise of our free will [. . .] renders us *in a certain way* like God by making us masters of ourselves": progress toward likeness to God is no longer at issue here, but already to rightfully possess it (the danger would be to lose "through timidity" "the rights" already acquired); (b) "free will is in itself the noblest thing that can be in us, since it makes us *in a way* equal to God and seems *to exempt us from being his subjects*." Clearly, no longer being subject to God is in no way an attenuation, but a full radicalization of the power of the free will.[51] Let us conclude, then, that *Principia I*, §35, says not less but, rather, more than is ventured in *Meditatio IV*.

It is necessary, then, to come back to *Meditatio IV*, for it doubtless allows us to resolve the difficulty of the alleged hesitations of Descartes between the affirmation of the infinity of the will (1638), its absence (in 1641), and its supposed attenuation (in 1644). These three qualifications, indeed, do not contradict but complete one another, for they mark the degrees of accomplishment of a single operation: the reduction of the will to its status "in se formaliter et præcise spectate—looked at in the formal and precise sense" (57.20; CSM II, 40). The first moment of this reduction well and truly consists in *not* yet considering the will as infinite, but only in noting that no other faculty's idea is "greater" than the idea of the will. Still to be clarified is what must be understood "with precision, *præcise*" by this faculty. The concern is the act of the will in so far as it puts into operation freedom, as a property of the *res cogitans*, by making it real. It is therefore necessary to measure the actuality of the will, to *reduce* it to this actuality. To get there, one will first consider the *ratio cognitionis et potentiæ* and will conclude that the human will remains without comparison inferior to the divine will, as much due to what it knows of the goals of its action (it is unaware of the contingencies, which God knows, etc.) as with regard to the power to really attain them (it is only capable of the possible, while God is capable of what is impossible for us). And we cannot object that in God, will and understanding are not distinguished *ne quidem ratione* (AT I, 153.3), for the fact that they are not even distinguished from reason does not mean that they are not in God as much as in us and that the comparison could be made with our *ratio cognitionis et potentiæ* (subject to the incommensurability of the finite to the infinite). One can pursue and consider the *ratio objecti* (57.19); once again the conclusion will be that the divine will extends to more objectives than ours. What remains, then, of my will, once knowledge, power, and the objects that it can mobilize have been bracketed? Is it canceled, or even only attenuated "in some way"? Not at all, for in this last status, the will (the faculty of putting freedom into operation) is summed up and retracts, so to speak, into the free will [*le libre arbitre*], in the pure potential to pursue or flee, to deny or to affirm what the understanding proposes (57.21–26). Now, this potential, freed from its adjacent conditions (knowledge, power, objects), exerts itself as such without our "feeling—*sentiamus*" determined by any exterior force: I can decide heads or tails, even if I can do nothing about it, know nothing about it, have no objective, provided that I decide; and, free from every condition by this very reduction of the conditions, I *feel* myself, I *experience* myself as *absolutely* free in my decision. I will what I want to will, infinitely. Now, since "we have ideas not only of all that is in our intellect, but also of all that is in the will,"[32] we must conclude that we have, through exercise of the will reduced to the pure free will, the idea of this infinity.

Of course, we do not have an idea of the infinite as of an object in the field of theory; even its transcendental status of unfolding in the finite does not confer on the infinite a visibility for the understanding. But the understanding does not exhaust all the modalities of the *cogitatio*, which can also be experienced as a will: "plura tamen eadem de re nos posse velle quam cognoscere, satis *experientia* declarat—yet *experience* shows clearly that about any given thing our will may extend further than our knowledge" (III, 432.7–8; CSMK, 195). We experience willing *infinitely*.

FIVE

From Descartes to Phenomenology, and Back

§1. *The Alleged Accord*

At least since Hegel, who hailed him as a "hero," it seems to go without saying that Descartes was the true initiator of modern philosophy.[1] It would still be necessary to measure what essentially *reversible* relation this modernity in philosophy maintains with Descartes, or rather, with what the doxography has substituted for him, not without variations or contradictions between eras, under the title of "Cartesianism." Indeed, if "modern philosophy" has constantly laid claim to Descartes, it was almost always with the most complete duplicity, hailing the audacity of the innovator all the more as it challenged his most explicit theses.[2] It may be that phenomenology, precisely because it would be, according to Husserl, "the secret longing of modern philosophy,"[3] made no exception to this strange attitude; for its persistence constitutes in itself a philosophical question, doubtless crucial despite being up to this day unquestioned as such (which says not a little about our lack of self-awareness).

Of course, Husserl overwhelmingly laid claim to a decidedly Cartesian genealogy for the phenomenology that he founded: "The seeds of transcendental philosophy we find historically in Descartes."[4] Already present in the *Logical Investigations*,[5] this claim becomes the very opening of the *Cartesian Meditations*: "René Descartes gave transcendental phenomenology new impulses through his *Meditations*; their study acted quite directly on the transformation of an already developing phenomenology into a new kind of transcendental philosophy. Accordingly one might almost call transcendental phenomenology a neo-Cartesianism, even though it is obliged—and precisely so by its radical development of Cartesian motifs—to reject *almost* all the well-known doctrinal content of the Cartesian philosophy."[6] In truth a strange claim, which, in the same movement, both invokes the authority of Descartes and challenges it. For if the Cartesian *project* justified in advance the transcendental *project* of phenomenology (moreover, before it was itself perfectly decided), phenomenology nevertheless could boast of a community of intention only on the condition precisely of not confusing Descartes' project and its doctrine: the project confirms that phenomenology begins well before itself, that is to say at the Cartesian moment, but, regarding the doctrine, Descartes proves to be above all the "father of transcendental realism, an absurd position (*des wiedersinnigen transzendentalen Realismus*)."[7] Not only does phenomenology remain "almost (*fast*)" a neo-Cartesianism, but it would be necessary to say that it is due to the express condition of *not* holding onto the Cartesian doctrine that it can claim its filiation with the Cartesian project.

§2. Husserl's Disagreement

In fact, Husserl hardly waits to start criticizing Descartes' "failure to make the transcendental turn" and to detail at least four lapses. First, Descartes remains hiddenly but radically determined by scholastic theses. Next, he applies, in a dogmatic and non-critical manner, the methodological ideal of mathematics, to the point of extending to the whole of philosophy a deduction *more geometrico* from the *ego cogito* taken as "an apodictic 'axiom.'" Next, he has surreptitiously modified the *ego cogitans* into a *substantia cogitans*, constituted by the *mens sive animus* alone, and has connected it to the principle of causality. Which in the end conducts him not to transcendental philosophy but instead to the absurdity of "transcendental realism."[8] Instead, then, it is necessary to speak here, but in the strictest of terms, of the *anti*-Cartesian meditations of Husserl.

It remains that this diagnostic today appears to us to be much too approximative and summary to be convincing: in fact, none of the critiques formulated by Husserl rely on a textual argument precise enough to secure them. First, the medieval heritage of Descartes, which is certainly incontestable, remains perfectly ambiguous, attesting just as much, or indeed even more, to a contrast rather than a continuity: most of the time the same inherited questions are found to receive a totally new response, and the innovation is truly measured only by distinguishing with more precision the questions taken up and the difference of the responses: the more the medieval horizon emerges, the more the Cartesian novelty appears, not the reverse.[9] Next, one could easily return against Husserl himself the argument of the mathematical ideal imposed on the whole of philosophy, for it must be noted that Descartes precisely does not proceed *more geometrico* (the appendix to the *Second Set of Replies* remains a single exercise, granted to indulge Mersenne's zeal, and one that only Spinoza's naïveté will take as a paradigm); rather, Descartes opposes quite firmly mathematics to the *Mathesis universalis*.[10] Above all, the *ego cogito*, though sometimes called a "first principle," never receives the status of a logical axiom and only maintains its primacy provisionally. As to the supposed substantialization of the *res cogitans*, it in fact does not enter into the initial argument that establishes the existence of the *ego*, since *Meditatio II* is unaware of even the term *substantia*, which appears for the first time only in *Meditatio III*, and first in order to prove the existence not of the *ego* but of God; and the same goes for the principle of causality.[11] Finally, the qualification of "transcendental realism" (in fact an anachronism due to the simple fact of its heavily Kantian origins) does not serve to explain much here—not even *whether* the Cartesian *ego* remains a mere region of the world limited to subjective interiority; nor *how*: for the persistence of a "Cartesian way" in the *Ideen I* and the suspicion that the *ego* remains there a simple ontic *residuum* weighs at least as much on the "consciousness-region" of Husserl himself as on the *res cogitans* of Descartes. Thus, the relation of Husserl to Descartes (and therefore also that of Descartes to phenomenology) remains deeply ambiguous: the claim of Cartesian patronage contradicts the explicit critique of the Cartesian theses; but this critique remains, for a large part, without a real object, applied in order to refute positions that are foreign to the letter of the Cartesian texts. It is as if, at least in a first moment, Husserl missed the target and, at the same time, did not truly determine either his relation to Descartes or the relation of Descartes to phenomenology as such.

Evidently, Husserl was too faithful in following the results of the interpretation of Descartes by the Marburg School, more precisely of the *Regulæ* read as an attempt, only partially realized, at *Erkenntnistheorie*. After the approaches of J. E. Erdmann (1834) and K. Fischer (1865), he takes up the conclusions of Natorp's *Descartes' Erkenntnistheorie* (1882), and then those, even more decisive, of Cassirer ("Le développement de la pensée de Descartes depuis les *Regulæ* jusqu'aux *Meditationes*," *Revue de métaphysique et de morale*, and *Descartes' Kritik der mathematischen und naturwissenschaftlichen Erkenntnis*, 1899), and of Cohen (*Kants Theorie der Erfahrung*, second edition 1885). As sinuous and complex as it may appear, the Marburg School approach to Descartes is summed up in this single question: to what extent does the thinker of the *Meditationes*, unfortunately metaphysical and challenged in principle by Kant, nevertheless in the *Regulæ* anticipate critical thought through his breakthrough toward a pure theory of knowledge, free of any ontico-ontological assumption?[12] On this narrow basis, the debates turn around either the assimilation of this project to the ideal of mathematics, or the decline in the study of *substantia*, yet always remain within the restricted horizon of an epistemic modernity, and a principled ignorance of the *Seinsfrage*. Heidegger, for that matter, will rightly criticize these Marburgian points of fixation in Husserl—though that will not prevent him, too, from continuing to attribute them to Descartes, ever led back to an *Erkenntnistheorie*. For the Marburgers, well aimed but off target; for Husserl, too well aimed, and too successful.

§3. Heidegger's Disagreement

Heidegger in his own way confirms and prolongs this basic ambiguity. To begin with, one might hold that, like Husserl, he addresses criticisms to Descartes that, taken at the literal level of the texts, reflect only very approximately Descartes' authentic positions.

Looking solely at arguments developed in *Sein und Zeit*, we find that not a single one truly hits the mark. For instance, the thesis that every being is in the mode of *substantia* perhaps holds for Spinoza (the one and only *substantia*), or indeed for Leibniz (every unity assumes a *substantia*), but surely not for Descartes, who refers finite beings to substantiality only with parsimony (in the strict sense, only God merits the title of substance), and thus under the reserve of an essential non-univocity.[13] Or take the thesis that every substance, including the thinking substance, must be comprehended according to the paradigm of the *res extensa*, itself assimilated to the *Vorhandenheit*:

this directly contradicts the fact that *mens* is known before, without, and more easily than *extensio* (*Meditatio II*), which, on the contrary, is known belatedly and with difficulty (*Meditatio VI*). Moreover, Heidegger seems, at least once, to concede this, by admitting that Descartes leaves open a certain access to the ready-to-handedness (*Zuhandenheit*) of material beings.[14] Finally, Heidegger chooses to critique what Descartes states as *ego sum, ego existo* under the very different formulation *cogito me cogitare [rem]*; now, beyond the fact that this seems forged under the influence of "the thought that accompanies every other thought" according to Kant, it is explicitly challenged by Descartes when he reads such a formulation written by one of his objectors, Father Bourdin.[15] It could be, moreover, that these critiques apparently addressed to Descartes really, in the final instance, aim at Husserl himself, and him alone.[16] Thus, in following the surface of their first confrontation, one ought to conclude that, according to Heidegger even more than for Husserl, Descartes not only does not belong to the phenomenological enterprise, but, in the figure of the *ego cogito*, opposes to it a major obstacle, upon which the destruction of the history of metaphysics must be thoroughly carried out.

And yet this first approach, if one stopped there and went no further, remains deceptive.[17] Indeed, even and precisely as obstacle to the enterprise of re-opening the question of being, Descartes appears as an essential interlocutor for Heidegger, and more and more so as the destruction of his "omission" (*Versäumnis*) advances. For the elaboration of the concept of "metaphysics" in Heidegger's thought, as well as the emergence of *metaphysica* in the history of philosophy, depends essentially on Descartes. Indeed, after having maintained as programmatic a positive usage of "metaphysics" (at least until the *Introduction to Metaphysics*) and of (supposedly fundamental) "ontology," Heidegger ends up radically overturning it by redefining the "onto-theology" of Kant as the very constitution of *metaphysica* (as witnessed by the three stages in the writing of *What is Metaphysics?* from 1929 to 1949).[18] Now, this reversal depends on taking seriously and reevaluating the Cartesian concept of *causa sui*, accomplished in an exemplary way in 1957 by *Identity and Difference*.[19] For, how would Descartes have been able to introduce a concept whose logical contradiction had been challenged by all the medievals (and even neo-Platonism)—a contradiction that Descartes himself perfectly recognized—if not for a speculative motive that to his eyes was even more restrictive: to close *metaphysica* on itself in a system, assured by founding the principle of causality on causality raised to the status of supreme being? The fact that, with the rather naïve exception of Spinoza, all his successors had avoided this term does not mark the disappearance of the concept, but on the contrary prolongs its latent reign, which ends up as the final figure of onto-theo-logy consigned by Nietzsche in the relation of the will to power to the Eternal Return. By contrast, one must consider that the forced-march advance of Heidegger toward the *Ereignis* reflects, in proportion, the destruction of the *causa sui*, this seal imposed by Descartes on the constitution of *metaphysica*. And it is only in this context that the critical scope of the interpretation, attributed to Descartes in 1927, of being [*l'étant*] as *cogitatum*, and thus as *objectum*, is understood: it alone allows the onto-theo-logy exhibited by sufficient reason to dominate being [*l'étant*] in totality. In this way, the relation of Heidegger to Descartes appears in all its ambivalence, but also in all its importance: as much as Plato, Aristotle, or Kant, Descartes offers Heidegger a support and a point of resistance, which calls for and allows the destruction of the history of ontology.

While Husserl exhibited a filiation with Descartes, which he in fact destroyed in the detail of his analyses, Heidegger exhibits an antagonism toward Descartes, unceasingly presupposing the French philosopher's theses in order to destroy the entire history of ontology and of *metaphysica*. These two readings nevertheless hold a point in common: neither Husserl nor Heidegger reads Descartes *in* himself, and as a result their appreciations of his thought can teach us *almost* nothing about his relation to phenomenology, or to its project.

§4. The Question of the Point of Departure

How can we move beyond this aporia? The imprecision and the ambiguity of the responses brought by Husserl and Heidegger to the question of the status of Descartes in phenomenology doubtless come from the fact that they do not take up the Cartesian text at its central point, where the true beginning of its enterprise is determined.

Husserl assumes that Descartes begins with doubt, in which he recognizes only a failed effort at the reduction, which in the end is inaccessible: doubt remains provisional, while the reduction establishes itself definitively.

Moreover, the certitude attained *a contrario* by doubt defines only a region in contrast to the uncertain, while the consciousness-region doubles every world-region by the reduced given. Consequently, according to Husserl, Descartes can only privilege the *ego* as a *substantia cogitans*, and thus sink into transcendental realism. As to Heidegger, he assumes that, more essentially than with doubt, Descartes begins with the being that operates doubt: the *ego sum*; and above all, that Descartes omits determining its mode of being, because he remains obsessed by the conquest of its epistemic privilege, certitude, without measuring its ontological range. Now, this norm of certitude in turn imposes the acceptance of no other mode of being for all beings (*entia creata*) than subsistent substantiality (*substantia* as *Vorhandenheit*); and such a permanent subsistence is finally and pre-eminently displayed in material *extensio*.[20] As different as they remain in their conclusions, the readings of Descartes by Husserl and Heidegger thus share a common point of departure: it is necessary to read Descartes starting from the *ego* cogitating objects in view of epistemological certitude, and thus through the ordeal of doubt, the first figure of the *cogitatio*. And straightaway, inevitably, this point of departure misses the reduction, intentionality, the question of phenomenality itself, and the meaning of the being of beings.

This start goes so much without saying that one is *almost* unsurprised. It massively dominates French as well as international Cartesian studies, at least since the empiricist critiques and the neo-Kantian readings. For the essential debates developed in this field of investigation, during the last century in France under the influence of Léon Brunschvicg and Martial Gueroult,[21] and elsewhere under the influence of analytic philosophy.[22] To the point that even readings explicitly oriented by the authority of Heidegger toward an ontological (or at least metaphysical) approach to Descartes still privilege the epistemic (or indeed epistemological) point of departure.[23]

As for the principal dialogues of the two venerable initiators of phenomenology, they appeal more directly and positively to certain specific arguments of Descartes, but each time they impose on him, with a remarkable interpretive violence that, moreover, is fully acknowledged, points of departure or centers of gravity that suit them, but that have no explicit legitimacy in Descartes. For instance, Sartre transfers divine freedom to the human being without hesitating to make him carry the weight of the *causa sui*, which Descartes reserved exclusively for God (and, even in this case, not without precautions). And Levinas, through one of his fairly frequent imitations of Sartre, displaces the *idea infiniti* of the essence of God onto the face of the other, in order to correct the degradation of the "men crossing the square" (AT VII, 32.7; CSM II, 21) to the rank of simple objects determined by the *inspectio mentis*.[24] Henry redirects the formula *videre videor* (from a notation of AT VII, 33.12, picked up in passing and without consequence by Gueroult) in order to support the complete doctrine of a non-ecstatic phenomenality, which he opposes to that of Husserl and Heidegger, and even to all metaphysics.[25] And finally, the hermeneutics of Ricœur endlessly bandages the "wounded" *cogito* in order to restore to it a quasi-self-consciousness that Descartes nevertheless never claims for the *ego*.[26] While these forceful takeovers remain fertile—and they are unquestionably so—they clearly do not do justice to the Cartesian texts (nor do they claim to). But neither can they shed light on the relation, if there is one, between the phenomenological enterprise and that of Descartes.

Would it not then be necessary, in order to measure his possible affinity with phenomenology, to consider Descartes in a resolutely different way? Would it not be necessary to recognize in him another point of departure than that of doubt as a *failed* reduction?[27]

§5. *The Return to Phenomena* Quatenus Quidam Cogitandi Modi

Indeed, it could be that Descartes does not limit himself to beginning with doubt (see *supra*, Chapter One, §6, and Chapter Three, §7), and in this way fail the reduction from the very beginning. It could be that his breakthrough does not consist in doubt itself (as it does for most of his contemporaries), but instead in what makes it possible, or rather in what it makes possible—access to the phenomenality of the world. In this case, it may be that what doubt makes possible surpasses that which makes it possible itself, namely doctrinal or systematic skepticism, the mere suspension of belief, opinion, or assent, all of which are diminutive or restrictive operations. More essentially, the issue would be that of leading all perception, every idea, and every representation, whatever they may *be* and wherever they come from (through, in, or *without* the senses), back to another status—to the status of pure presentations, that represent in the final instance nothing other than themselves and must be distinguished only following their degree of clarity and of distinction, in light of their evidence alone. And this is exactly what the *regula generalis* claims to accomplish when *Meditatio III* surpasses doubt (which is still dominant in *Meditatio II*, where it remains within the horizon of the *ego sum, ego existo*) by defining the criteria of this first certitude:

Nunquid ergo etiam scio quid requiratur ut de aliqua re sim certus? Nempe in hac prima cognitione [*sc.* ego sum] nihil aliud est, quam clara quædam et distincta perceptio ejus quod affirmo [. . .]; ac proinde jam videor pro regula generali posse statuere, illud omne esse verum, quod valde clare et distincte percipio—But do I not therefore also know what is required for my being certain of anything? Surely in this first instance of knowledge [namely, I am], there is nothing but a clear and distinct perception of what I am. [. . .] And thus I now seem able to posit as a general rule that everything I very clearly and distinctly perceive is true. (AT VII, 35.7–15; CSM II, 24)

This leading back from doubt (henceforth provisional) to evidence thus implements a (quasi-)*reduction* (henceforth permanent) to everything that comes, whatever it may *be*, to the *mens* with the rank and status of *cogitatum*. From which there follows this definitive and exemplary conclusion: "quamvis illa quæ sentio vel imaginor extra me fortasse nihil sint, illos tamen cogitandi modos, quos sensus et imaginationes appello, quatenus *cogitandi quidam modi* tantum sunt, in me esse sum certus—even though these things that I sense or imagine may perhaps be nothing at all outside me, nonetheless I am certain that these *modes of thinking* which I refer to as cases of sensing and imagining, in so far as they are simply modes of thinking, do exist within me."[28] Putting into doubt has no value in itself, but as a means to and an index of putting into evidence—not only of that which appears in full evidence, but also, by contrast, of that which remains obscure and/or unclear. For in every case, that which appears to the *cogitatio* as one of its modes *appears* to it; real or not, ontically qualified or not, certain or not, it appears with certainty; even if what appears has nothing of a thing about it, its appearance still appears and, as such, offers a certainty—of appearing: *videre videor*. Before doubt and in order for it to become possible, appearing itself is necessary.

Let us consider now the reduction as Husserl ends up formulating it, after many approximations: it does not have to do with a simple suspension of adhesion to the suggestion of the natural attitude, allowing resistance to the illusions of knowledge in order to concentrate on the spaces of certitude alone; rather, it has to do with neutralizing an interrogation, considered as a priori by the ontology of *metaphysica*, but in fact derived and secondary—that which asks if what appears to me is true or not, or better: whether it is or not—to the benefit of a response that is more originary and always already assured—that which gives me what appears *as such* a phenomenon of its own right. In principle, the reduction consists in suspending, if not definitively eliminating, the supposedly first question but in principle the merely second one, in order to be open to the final assurance of the appearing of the phenomenon as such. The epistemic question of the object's certitude fades before the restitution of the phenomenal appearing as such. The reduction consists in substituting one question for the other, in transforming the ontic object into a phenomenon appearing in and by itself. Husserl says it over and over, very clearly: "We now understand that, by our universal epoché with respect to the being or non-being of the world, we have not simply lost the world for phenomenology; we retain it, after all, *qua cogitatum*."[29] Or again: "This universal depriving of acceptance [. . .], or, as it is also called, this '*phenomenological epoché*' and 'parenthesizing' of the Objective world—therefore does not leave us confronting nothing. On the contrary we gain possession of something by it; and what we (or, to speak more precisely, what I, the one who is meditating) acquire by it is my pure living, with all the pure subjective processes making this up, and everything meant in them, *purely* as meant in them: the universe of '*phenomena*' in the (particular and also the wider) phenomenological sense."[30] The reduction does not *subtract* anything, not even with a subtraction more radical (universal, permanent, etc.) than doubt; it does not fold back, simply more than doubt and by an exclusive will for certitude, on objects that are even rarer but more assured, or indeed on a *residuum* that would be summed up in empty consciousness. On the contrary, it *adds* to consciousness the immensity of what appears to it, on the sole condition of accepting the appearing within the limits in which it appears. The world is transformed: from an unstable chaos (sometimes certain, sometimes uncertain, or both successively), it is transmuted into a universal appearing, albeit of a reliability that varies and is still to be experienced. This transformation of appearance into appearing, and thus of things into phenomena, provokes, in return or rather in response, the transformation of the representative *ego* into a phenomenal subject: "through the epochē [. . .]

I stand *above* the world, which has now become for me, in a quite peculiar sense, a *phenomenon*."[31] Or further: "But immediately it [the phenomenological-transcendental philosophy] achieves the possibility of creating a ground for itself through its own powers, namely, in mastering, through original self-reflection, the naïve world as transformed into a phenomenon or rather a *universum* of phenomena."[32] Indeed—and we must insist here against the facile interpretations that suggest the supposed principle, "So much appearing, so much being"—far from phenomenology converting appearing into being (thus leading phenomenality back to an unquestioned ontic presupposition), the inverse is true: phenomenology leads the actual and habitual ontic qualifications (those that privilege common *metaphysica*: being or not being, what truly is or is only in appearance, etc.) back to their phenomenal determination (what degree of evidence to grant to what shows itself?). Phenomenology does not offer the final version of phenomenalism, nor attempt to save the appearances by rehabilitating the ontic dignity of the appearing, if only because *a minima* it metamorphoses the appearing into phenomena. Not by transforming it from one form to another, but simply by abstaining from conforming it to anything other than itself—not even to an object, or indeed even to a real being. It reduces the phenomenon to itself by leading it back to its appearing, and nothing else.

Now this is precisely what Descartes more than sketches, and of course in his own way. But Descartes does not accomplish this leading back with doubt (doubt that he picks up from the philosophical situation of his time, in order, moreover, to return it "quamprimum occurret occasio—as soon as the opportunity arises"[33]); thus, he does not expose himself, either, to its consequences imposed by the common interpretation (solipsism, substantialism, dualism, etc.); but he already practices a kind of reduction of things as they are (in the scientific attitude, that is, in the natural attitude) to pure and simple *cogitationes*. In this way, an exemplary formula, already quoted—"even though these things that I sense or imagine may perhaps be nothing at all outside me, nonetheless I am certain that these *modes of thinking* which I refer to as cases of sensing and imagining, in so far as they are simply modes of thinking, do exist within me"[34]—literally anticipates that of Husserl, quoted earlier: "We now understand that, by our universal epochē with respect to the being or non-being of the world, we have not simply lost the world for phenomenology; we retain it, after all, *qua cogitatum*."[35] Descartes already operates a kind of reduction, not because he doubts, but because he leads things (sensations, imagination) across doubt and beyond appearing, back to their status if not already as phenomena, then at least as modes of the *cogitatio*, valid as such.

§6. *The Neutralization of the Origin and the Criterion of Evidence*

Even if, as we saw (Chapter One, §6, and Chapter Three, §7), doubt appears as the first and perhaps the most radical mode of the *cogitatio*, to the point of providing the first occurrence of the "first principle," this status depends on a more original rule of the *cogitatio* itself: in order to distinguish the *cogitationes* and establish their degree of validity, it is not their origin that must be considered, but solely their degree of evidence.

This thesis seems all the more fundamental because it arises chronologically as the first that can be assigned to Descartes; even though it was not directly written (much less published), we know it through the faithful and precise transmission of his biographer, Adrien Baillet. Reporting in detail three dreams Descartes had during the night of the feast of St. Martin, 10–11 November 1619, while he was wintering in Neuburg an der Donau, Baillet was astonished by their contents (directly related to theses on the unity of the sciences, which will be worked out only during the following ten years), but above all by their immediate interpretation as inspired "dreams":

What he found especially remarkable is that, doubting whether what he had happened to see was dream or vision, he not only *decided while sleeping* that it was a dream, but he also pursued the interpretation *before breaking his slumber*. He *judged* that the *Dictionary* could not be called anything else than all the Sciences gathered together [. . .]. M. Descartes continued to interpret his dream in slumber, *surmising* [*estimant*] that the piece of verse on the uncertainty of what kind of life one ought to choose, & which begins with *Quod vitæ sectabor iter*, marked the good counsel of a wise person, or even moral theology. On that, *doubtful whether he was dreaming or musing*, he awoke without emotion; & *continued, with open eyes, the interpretation* of his dream on the same train of thought. [. . .] Seeing that the application of all these things turned out so well to his taste, he was bold enough *to persuade himself*, that it was the Spirit of Truth which had wanted to open to him "the treasures of all the sciences" by this dream.[36]

In other words, the distinction between waking and sleeping, which is to say the consideration of the origin, has no pertinence at all for thought, because the validity of a *cogitatio* depends only on its clarity and distinction. The absolute immanence of the *cogitatio* to itself disqualifies the prior question on the transcendence (the origin and the ontic status) of its contents, making their certitude depend only on their evidence for thought. Such an absolutely decisive discovery implies that the immanence of the *cogitatio* to itself is accomplished exclusively in clear and distinct ideas and according to the extent of this clarity and distinction; that is, what takes place is a reduction of the thinkable to the sole evidence of the clear and the distinct.

It is in the final sequence of the fourth part of the *Discourse on the Method* that the immanence of the *cogitatio* to itself receives its explicit development, in a manner that for once is sharper than in the parallel sequence from *Meditationes II–III*. Take the difficulty of distinguishing waking from sleeping: "Lastly, considering that the very thoughts we have while awake may also occur while we sleep without any of them being at that time true, I resolved to pretend that all the things that had ever entered my mind were no more true than the illusions of my dreams."[37] In this first stage, the impossibility of finding a criterion for distinguishing waking from sleeping (as in AT VII, 19.17–22) leads through precaution to holding waking thoughts as just as false as those in dreams. But this universalization of falsehood stumbles over the truth of this "I, that thought it," of this "something" that is, of the *I think therefore I am*. In a second stage, one thus observes that this truth—there exists an *I think*—remains just as valid for false thoughts as for true ones; and therefore also that, as such and however they may be, awake or asleep, all thoughts appear only through and for this that (or *he who*) thinks them. Now, as the evidence of this "first principle" holds only for the clarity and distinctness of my perception (that of my existence as thinking), and not at all for its origin (sensation or concept, waking or sleeping, revery or dream), one must infer in it the "general rule that the things we conceive very clearly and very distinctly are all true," only in so far as they are thoughts as such; the difficulty no longer lies in their provenance (as in ancient skepticism), but "in recognizing which are the things that we distinctly conceive."[38] Thoughts must be referred to and decided in relation to the instance that thinks them, and not by their origin or their supposed content: the criterion of clarity and distinction thus annuls the difference (psychological or empirical) between waking and sleeping. The truth of thoughts is decided by their reduction to clarity and distinction, which is to say, by their being led back to the pure appearing in them. The best confirmation of this change of criterion is found in the mathematical demonstrations (a privileged example, to be sure, but simply one among others, since it occurs in 1637 after the existence of the *ego* and of God):

> For if one happened *even in sleep* to have some very distinct idea (if, say, a geometer devised some new proof), one's being asleep would not prevent the idea from being true. And as to the most common error of our dreams, which consists in their representing various objects to us in the same way as our external senses do, it does not matter that this gives us occasion to doubt the truth of such ideas, for *often they can also mislead us without our being asleep* [. . .]. For after all, *whether we are awake or asleep*, we ought never to let ourselves be convinced except by the evidence of our reason.[39]

This sequence refers back to the discovery of 1619 and raises it to a concept.

The conclusion of this reduction and the presupposition of the "general rule" of truth (that is, the equivalence between truth and the clarity and distinctness of ideas) is summed up in the Cartesian affirmation of the *reality* of thoughts: "It follows that our ideas or notions, being *real things* and coming from God, cannot be anything but true, in every respect in which they are clear and distinct."[40] This is confirmed by the *Meditationes*: "Imo etiam hoc nihil mutat; nam certe, quamvis somniarem, *si quid intellectui meo sit evidens*, illud omnino est verum—Yet even this does not change anything. For even though I might be dreaming, *if there is anything which is evident to my intellect*, then it is wholly true."[41] The entire and sole difficulty lies in the reduction of the ideas that appear in the *cogitatio* to that which, in them, truly appears clearly and distinctly.

I will therefore hazard a conclusion that is as audacious as it is inevitable: the *regula generalis* offers the Cartesian equivalent to, if not the reduction, at least the "principle of all principles": "illud omne esse verum, quod valde clare et distincte percipio"[42] could indeed be translated as: "whatever appears, provided that it is reduced to that which appears very clearly and distinctly in the immanence of the phenomenological *cogitatio*, must be received as what it gives of itself, that is, as true," and in this way connect with the terms of Husserl: "*each originary giving intuition* is *a legitimate source of knowledge*, [. . .]

whatever presents itself to us *in intuition* in an *originary way* (so to speak, in its fleshly actuality) *is to be taken simply as what it gives itself as*, but *only within the limitations in which it gives itself there*."[43] We can assert that (a) the legitimation by intuition of whatever appears corresponds to the equivalence between the true thought and the clear and distinct perception; and (b) the delimitation of whatever actually gives itself within the limits of intuition corresponds to the precise degree of clarity and distinctness of each of the thoughts. According to Husserl's terms recognizing that "the essence of the difference [. . .] between inner and outer perception [. . .] is the operative factor in the Cartesian treatment of doubt," one can also say of Descartes:

I can doubt the truth of an inadequate, merely projective perception: the intended, or, if one likes, intentional, object is not immanent in the act of appearing. The intention is there, but the object itself, that is destined finally to fulfil it, is not one with it. How could its existence be evident to me? But I cannot doubt an adequate, purely immanent perception, since there are no residual intentions in it that must yet achieve fulfilment. The whole intention, or the intention in all its aspects, is fulfilled. Or, [...] the object is not in our percept merely *believed to exist*, but is *also itself truly given*, and as what it is believed to be. It is of the essence of adequate perception that the intuited object itself really and truly dwells in it, which is merely another way of saying that *only the perception of one's own actual experiences is indubitable and evident*.[44]

Thus, the episode of the three dreams does not constitute a mere psychological anecdote but proves the decisive experience of the immanence of the *cogitatio* to itself, such that it allows and requires Descartes to jump ahead to the phenomenological reduction: for the *ego*, *cogitationes* are "real things," exactly like "our own actual experiences" for the perception accomplishing the reduction.

§7. *The Doubling of the* Res *and the Correlation of Appearing*

Yet another convergence between Husserl and Descartes could come to light, directly tied to the first, but more ambivalent.

Husserl always emphasizes that "the word 'phenomenon' (*Phänomen*) has a double meaning, in virtue of the essential correlation between *appearing and that which appears*."[45] Access to that which appears opens only in the appearing, and thus in the appearing to consciousness, which becomes the sole path toward the thing itself. In other words, "The transcendent object would not be the object of *this* presentation, if it was not *its* intentional object. This is plainly a merely analytic proposition. The object of the presentation, of the 'intention', *is* and *means* what is presented, the intentional object."[46] In other words, the point is to identify strictly the (intentional) immanent object (real in the sense of *reell*) with the transcendent object (real in the sense of *real*), so as to know the latter only through the former.[47] But this identity does not cancel out; on the contrary, it is only explained by the difference between two modes of reality that double and redouble this single object—to begin with, intentional and *reell*, and then transcendent and *real*.

Is it not the same for Descartes? For this doubling of the reality of the *res* is found in *Regula XII*, which already definitively seals the gap between the reduction already noticed in the dreams of 1619 and the *Discourse* of 1637, by doubling or indeed even eliminating *realitas* itself: it shows that things must not be thought according to their (transcendent) existence in reality (*revera*) in the world, as practiced by the natural attitude, which is to say following their essence as things in themselves (*in se*), but that they must be led back to the point of view that refers them (according to *ordo et mensura*) exclusively to knowledge (the *Mathesis universalis*), which considers them in their pure and simple appearing (immanent to the *mens*):

Dicimus igitur primo, aliter spectandas esse res singulas *in ordine ad cognitionem nostram*, quam si de iisdem loquamur *prout revera existunt*. [...] Quamobrem hic de rebus non agentes, *nisi quantum ab intellectu percipiuntur*, illas tantum simplices vocamus, quarum cognitio tam perspicua est et distincta, ut in plures *magis distincte cognitas mente* dividi non possint—First, when we consider things in the order that corresponds to our knowledge of them, our view of them must be different from what it would be if we were speaking of them in accordance with how they exist in reality. [...] That is why, since we are concerned here with things only in so far as they are perceived by the intellect, we term "simple" only those things which we know so clearly and distinctly that they cannot be divided by the mind into others which are more distinctly known.[48]

In this sense, things can appear in this way in their true simplicity, defined going forward from the sole point of view of clarity and distinctness (as independent objects, Husserl would say). The reduction of "things" as such (as they exist) to the point of view of knowledge is not limited to recomposing them from fundamental concepts (the simple natures) through a merely constructivist approach; it modifies their status, since henceforth, as known according to these simple natures, the "same things," reduced to objects, appear *as known*, to the intellect; this is why, as known, that is to say, *as appearing to it*, they can no longer contain the least error: "Dicimus tertio, naturas illas simplices esse omnes per se notas, et *nunquam ullam falsitatem continere*. Quod facile ostendetur, si distinguamus illam facultatem intellectus, per quam res intuetur et cognoscit, ab ea qua judicat affirmando vel negando—Thirdly, these simple natures are all self-evident and *never contain any falsity*. This can easily be shown if we distinguish between the faculty by which our intellect intuits and knows things and the faculty by which it makes affirmative or negative judgements."[49] The "same things," reduced to their appearing (their knowledge by the *mens*), are only in as much as known (*reell*), and no longer in as much as existing (*real*).

These decisions, while made in favor of a strict theory of knowledge and thus of the object, are not restricted to that theory. Indeed, they will not be put into question by the *philosophia prima*, which on the contrary finds them and validates them as soon as the conditions of their application are restored beyond hyperbolic doubt (from *Meditatio III*); when the *ego* of the *cogito* inventories its thought-acts, it concludes that, "cum volo, cum timeo, cum affirmo, cum nego, semper quidem *aliquam rem* ut subjectum meæ cogitationis apprehendo—when I will, or am afraid, or affirm, or deny, there is always *a particular thing* which I take as the object of my thoughts."[50] I cannot claim to apprehend directly the things themselves, but solely what is found included, as in its subject of immanence, in my thought, itself comprehended as the instance and the substrate (*subjectum*) of all appearing. In this sole immanence, everything becomes *at least* a phenomenon under the title of *modus cogitandi*: "Nempe, quatenus ideæ istæ cogitandi quidam modi tantum sunt, non agnosco ullam inter ipsas inæqualitatem—In so far as the ideas are simply modes of thought, there is no recognizable inequality among them."[51] This equality among the *modi cogitandi* as such justifies the previous observation that between dreaming and waking "nothing changes (*nihil mutat*)." Indeed, every *modus cogitandi*, even one that is empty or materially false, remains a mode of phenomenality and thus *as such* remains something, above all if it is not the thing to which the natural attitude refers: "Atqui quantumvis imperfectus sit iste essendi modus, quo *res* est objective in intellectu per ideam, *non tamen profecto plane nihil est*, nec proinde a nihilo esse potest—yet the mode of being by which *a thing* exists objectively in the intellect by way of an idea, imperfect though it may be, *is certainly not nothing*, and so it cannot come from nothing";[52] the *realitas* that is *thought and which thus appears* is not nothing, though it is not the *realitas* of the thing of the world. The best commentary on this Cartesian doubling is, unsurprisingly, given by Husserl: "But, no matter what the status of this phenomenon's claim to actuality and no matter whether, at some future time, I decide critically that the world exists or that it is an illusion, still this phenomenon itself, as mine, is not nothing (*als ein Phänomen ist es doch nicht nichts*) but is precisely what makes such critical decisions at all possible and accordingly makes possible whatever has for me sense and validity as 'true' being (*als* wahres *Sein*)—definitively decided or definitively decideable being." In fact, counter to his initial critiques, Husserl here admits that Descartes did indeed practice the reduction: "Descartes, as we know, indicated all that by the name *cogito*. The world is for me absolutely nothing else but the world existing for and accepted by me in such a conscious *cogito* (*als die in solchem* cogito *bewußt seiende und mir geltende*)."[53] Thus, here one can reasonably admit a Cartesian origin for phenomenology (at least, Husserlian phenomenology), provided at least that it recognizes, against certain declarations of Husserl himself, that Descartes anticipates the practice of the reduction, as a reduction of things to the *cogitatio*, without confusing it with doubt.[54] Here the radical immanence that, following Henry's remark, the *videre videor* implements takes on all its weight, grounding the certitude of the *ego sum* in an authentic practice of the reduction.[55]

Nevertheless, this encounter of Descartes with Husserl makes the difference all the clearer. If for both of them the transcendent reality (*real*) of the thing appears only through its reduced reality (*reell*), for Descartes it has to do with a division, which forces one to climb from essence to existence (of the *mens*, of God, and of material things); while for Husserl, not only does "the word 'phenomenon' (*Phänomen*) [have] a double meaning, *in virtue of the essential correlation* between appearing and that which appears,"[56] but it concerns the "correlation between the world (the world of which we always speak) and its subjective manners of givenness"; and even of an a priori correlation, which constitutes the initial "wonder of wonders" of phenomenology: "The first breakthrough of this universal a priori of correlation (*dieses universalen Korrelationsapriori*) between experienced object and manners of givenness (which occurred during work on my *Logical Investigations* around 1898) affected me so deeply that my whole subsequent life-work has been dominated by the task of systematically elaborating on this a priori of correlation."[57] Husserl conceives the distinction between appearing and that which appears on the basis of the correlation that connects, a priori and on principle, the transcendence of the phenomenon to its immanence in consciousness, and in this way manifests the reality of the *real* through the reality of the *reell*. Why, in contrast, is such a correlation lacking in Descartes? Because intentionality is missing in Descartes, which would forbid him his rupture with the thing itself, a rupture that results from his destruction of *ousia*, and thus also from his giving up of the play between *dynamis* and *energeia*, and from a negative doubt taken up from the renewed skepticism (Sextus more than Montaigne), or in short, from the grey ontology. What other *quasi*-correlation would nevertheless allow him to tie appearing to that which appears, under the name of the demonstrations of existence (of the *ego*, of God, and of material things), when no intentionality opens any direct (albeit teleological) access for him to the intentional object, through the adequate fulfillment of the noema? The most explicit response stems from the "general rule" of truth, which a priori ties the clarity and the distinctness of the *cogitatio* to the truth of the *cogitatum*. Or more precisely, since this liaison itself "is assured only for the reasons that God is or exists, that he is a perfect being, and that everything in us comes from him," it derives its a priori character only from "the existence of God [which] is the first and the most eternal of all possible truths and the one from which alone all others proceed."[58] In a word, what Husserl wants to obtain directly through intentionality, Descartes bases indirectly on the creation of the eternal truths. What the one aims for through intentional immanence, the other assures through the transcendence not of the thing itself, but of the causal principle (and soon, of the principle of reason). Here, on the basis of a singular correlation (between *cogitatio* and *cogitatum*, or between *appearing* and *that which appears*), *metaphysica* and phenomenology diverge.

§8. Thought as Decision

This first result—Descartes practiced, in his own way and by anticipation, a genuine reduction—suggests a second argument in favor of a fundamental affinity between his thought and the phenomenological approach. Indeed, the reduction would not benefit from any phenomenological privilege if it offered only one thesis among others; with the reduction, at issue is not a thesis, but rather a decision; otherwise, it is hard to understand why Husserl never stops emphasizing its difficulty and demanding to remake it so as to perfect it.

And if the reduction must be decided, this is because one can enter seriously into philosophy only by taking the initiative of practicing it by *making the decision to do so*: "Philosophy—wisdom (*sagesse*)—is the philosophizer's quite personal affair. It must arise as *his* wisdom, as his self-acquired knowledge tending toward universality, a knowledge for which he can answer from the beginning, and at each step, by virtue of his own absolute insights. If I have taken the resolution (*Entschluß*) to live with this as my aim—the resolution (*Entschluß*) that alone can start me on the course of a philosophical development—I have thereby chosen to begin in absolute poverty, with an absolute lack of knowledge."[59] And this resolution is accomplished initially by deciding for a reduction: "And so we make a new beginning, each for himself and in himself, with the resolution (*Entschluß*) of philosophers who begin radically: that at first we shall *put out of play (zunächst außer Spiel zu setzen)* all the convictions we have been accepting up to now, including all the sciences. Let the idea guiding our meditations be at first the Cartesian idea of a science that shall be established as radically genuine, ultimately an all-embracing science."[60] In what sense is this not so much a theoretical thesis but a decision, a resolution? In the sense that a thesis always remains a thesis for and through the *I* that poses it and puts it at his disposal; while a resolution in turn decides this *I* himself, who only takes it by letting himself be taken, who poses it only by also letting it dispose of him.

But it is to be noted that *this centering I is not an empty pole of identity*, any more than any *object* is such. Rather, according to a law of "transcendental generation", with every *act* emanating from him and having a *new* objective sense, he acquires *a new abiding property* (*eine neue bleibende Eigenheit*). For example: If, in an act of judgment, I make the resolution (*entscheide ich*) for the first time in favor of a being and a being-thus, the fleeting act passes; but from now on *I am abidingly the I who is thus and so decided (des so und so entscheidene Ich)*, "I am of this conviction". That, however, does not signify merely that I remember the act or can remember it later. This I can do, even if meanwhile I have "given up" my conviction. After cancellation it is no longer my conviction; but it has remained abidingly my conviction up to then. As long as it is accepted by me, I can "return" to it repeatedly, and repeatedly find it as mine, habitually my own (*mir habituelle eigene*) opinion or, correlatively, find myself as the *I* who *is* convinced (*beharrend*) [...]. Likewise in the case of resolutions of every other kind, value-decisions, volitional decisions. I decide (*Ich entschließe mich*); the act-process vanishes but the resolution persists; whether I become passive and sink into heavy sleep or live in other acts, the resolution continues to be accepted and, correlatively, I am so decided from then on, as long as I do not give the resolution up. [...] *I myself*, who am persisting in my abiding volition, *become changed* if I "cancel" my resolutions or repudiate my deeds.[61]

In a word, one enters into philosophy by a decision and one becomes a philosophizing *I* only by making decisions that, in return, alter, modify, and qualify this *I* as philosophizing. Without assimilating too quickly what diverges, one cannot avoid thinking here of the essential determination of Dasein. Heidegger indeed will remain a strict and even hyperbolically faithful inheritor of Husserl's initial "decision" when he will make it evident that Dasein is ultimately accomplished in the "anticipatory resolution (*vorlaufende Entschloßenheit*)." It appears as the privileged mode of Dasein only because it opens him to himself on the basis of the impact within him of the meaning of being: "*Die Entschloßenheit ist ein ausgezeichneter Modus der Erschloßenheit des Daseins*—Resoluteness is an eminent mode of the disclosedness of Da-sein."[62] Dasein becomes what it resolves to be, because it resolves itself to the being within it. In these two exemplary cases of phenomenology, philosophy does not consist in posing theses (assigning "theories produced by strength of thought, *erdenkliche Theorie*," says Husserl, "telling stories," says Heidegger), but in posing resolutions, or better: in exposing oneself to resolutions. There is nothing secondary or banal about this difference.

At the risk of simplifying (a risk that is sometimes necessary), one could distinguish two modes by which philosophy develops: either thinking by deduction, or thinking by resolution (or by successive decisions). Thinking by resolution and not by deduction, by decision and not by representation:

Schelling had already taken note of this capital difference of style of thought when he opposed to "negative" philosophy (Hegel, of course, but through him the whole system of *metaphysica*) a "positive" philosophy (still to come). Ill-advisedly, among the moderns, he included Descartes in "negative" philosophy, while Spinoza, Malebranche, Locke, or even Rousseau would have been more fitting.[63] And he omitted, in the other posture, Kant, without being able to foresee Kierkegaard, Nietzsche, or Bergson. Nevertheless, the cesura between the two styles is proved correct; it proposes a sure index for distinguishing the fundamentally metaphysical philosophies from those that approach or cross the boundaries of *metaphysica* (at the very least, the difference between "negative" and "positive" philosophies is more valuable than the overly superficial distinction between philosophies of the concept and of consciousness, each of which derive from metaphysics). A positive philosophy takes or would like to take its point of departure from a *positum*, from a fact of reason or more exactly from a fact *for* reason, that reason cannot think in advance, cannot foresee on the basis of itself—an *unprethinkable* (*ein Unvordenkliches*). The question remains, clearly, to identify this unprethinkable. We saw (Chapter Four) Descartes' indecision in front of the double possibility of identifying the infinite, which is diffracted in the *ego* as much as in God. It remains at least possible to pick out the primordial, even initial function of the resolution that allows us to reach the unprethinkable of the infinite.

The Discourse on the Method offers the clearest cases of the priority of resolution. Before doubt, itself a resolution ("The simple *resolution* to abandon all the opinions one has hitherto accepted...," AT VI, 15.12–14; CSM I, 118), and indeed in order to make possible the *epochē*, Descartes makes the decision to become an *I*, and thus no longer to recognize himself except in "good sense" (VI.1.18), just as Husserl speaks of a "resolution (*Enschluß*) that alone can lead me to become a philosopher (*mich zum philosophischen Werden bringen kann*)."[64] At issue is the very first resolution: "*Resolving* to seek no knowledge other than that which could be found in myself or else in the great book of the world..." (9.19–22; CSM I, 115); "But after I had spent some years pursuing these studies in the book of the world and trying to gain some experience, I *resolved* one day to undertake studies within myself too and to use all the powers of my mind in choosing the paths I should follow" (10.25–31; CSM I, 116). This original resolution (to reduce the sciences to "good sense," that is, to its unique and universal operator, the *I*) opens out into other resolutions.

First, that of holding to the four precepts of the method (clarity and distinctness, and thus evidence, as the sole criterion of truth; division of difficulties into simple natures; the principle of order, moving from the simple to the complex; enumeration); in other words, to hold to a "strong and unswerving [*beharrende!*] *resolution* never to fail to observe them" (18.14–15; CSM I, 120). Next, the point is to "always remain firm in the *resolution* I had taken to assume no principle other than the one I have just used to demonstrate the existence of God and of the soul, and to accept nothing as true which did not seem to me clearer and more certain than the demonstrations of the geometers had hitherto seemed" (41.1–7; CSM I, 131). This "principle" will be taken up literally in *Meditatio III*: "Ac proinde jam videor pro regula generali posse statuere, illud omne esse verum, quod valde clare et distincte percipio—So now I seem to be able to lay it down as a general rule that whatever I perceive very clearly and distinctly is true" (VII.35.13–15; CSM II, 24). Method and rule of truth thus cannot be understood apart from the resolutions that put them into operation, as if at stake there were merely axioms, a priori principles, or dogmatic theses. For this method must be "practiced" and can allow me "to *use* my reason, if not perfectly, at least as well as [is] in my power" (VI.21, 19–22; CSM I, 121); even in "mathematical problems," one must "practice" it (29.25; CSM I, 125); in order to know what men know and think, one must "attend to what they *practiced* rather than what they said" (23.15–17; CSM I, 122). Moreover, it may be that "practical philosophy" (62.1; CSM I, 142), which Descartes opposes to "speculative" philosophy (61.30; CSM I, 142), consists less in an application of sciences to technology (as one too often understands it) than in the recommendation of exercising a more and more supple and precise usage of the method. More generally, couldn't we reread the entire Cartesian *corpus*, and in particular the *Meditationes*, or even *The Passions of the Soul*, as the sequence of decisions taken, and thus of resolutions that, not without occasional rupture of the univocal order of reasons, orient thought according to the silent injunctions of its *positum*?

§9. *Thinking by Acts*

Provided that it proceeds by resolutions, thought as such constitutes an act; not because it could also result in an action by fixing conditions and goals, but because thought itself as pure and simple thought already constitutes an action from the outset: actual thought acts. Heidegger showed it clearly: "Thinking does not become action only because some effect issues from it or because it is applied. Thinking acts insofar as it thinks. Such action is presumably the simplest and at the same time the highest because it concerns the relation of being to humans."[65] Thinking does not lead, possibly and consequently, to action; a thought that is *engaged* has already fallen from its status as thought since it agrees that it has no efficacy in the world simply by thinking so. The slogan, outdated yet recurrent, "Join up, re-enlist [*Engagez-vous, rengagez-vous*]," misunderstands the fact that thought, by thinking, and provided of course that it does indeed think, acts more than any external actions that come without thought to the public. And since thought, in its resolutions, is accomplished in actuality, it follows that it accomplishes this action only by thinking through acts of thought. Thought as act is accomplished by acts of thought: Husserl put this forward in a rule and a method: "the phenomenological method moves entirely in *acts* of reflection."[66] Not only must we speak of "intentional experiences or acts,"[67] but "what are present as available realities (*reell vorhanden*), are the relevant acts of perceiving," such that "what for us is most certain, [is] that being-an-object consists phenomenologically in certain acts in which something appears, or is thought of [...]. The phenomenological kernel of the empirical ego [or *I*] here consists of acts which bring objects to its notice, acts in which the ego [*I*] directs itself to the appropriate object."[68] Properly speaking, there are, without the *I*, no objects that are inert and already available to knowledge (that we would have to meet up with *from the outside* through representative ideas), but rather there are acts of the *I*, which so to speak make, elicit, and render visible the objects, henceforth phenomena of themselves.[69] The objects do not precede the acts; only the acts make the objects appear.

This turnaround is in no way a mere banality, since this "method" implies proceeding neither by inference, nor by deduction, nor by the connection of representations, but by decisions and resolutions, which are put into operation by acts. Of course, this is not the place to take up the enumeration of acts according to Husserl, but here we do have the opportunity to examine whether and in what sense the *Meditationes*, radically phenomenological in this way, proceed by such acts.

The list of resolutions, which decide the discontinuous movement forward of the meditation, stands out fairly easily, and we have indicated the principal ones among them: the return to phenomena through reduction to the *modi cogitandi* (§5); the neutralization of the origin and the criteria of evidence (§6); the question of the principle of correlation (§7). Against the background of this knowledge, one can spot certain acts that, through their decision, make phenomena arise that otherwise would remain unseen. First, there is the act of doubting in general, directly provoked by the reduction of things to *cogitationes*, which the reduction puts into operation only negatively. This decision, moreover, unfolds within the frame of several other acts that are secondary, but necessary. (a) Initially the decision to doubt only in theory ("generali huic mearum opinionum eversioni vacabo—I will devote myself [...] to the general demolition of my opinions"), by setting aside concern for the practical ("hodie mentem curis omnibus exsolvi... — today I have rid my mind of all worries...").[70] (b) Next, the decision to hypertrophy doubt: whatever deceives me one time must be considered always deceptive and the doubtful assimilated to the false.[71] Secondly, relaunch doubt as far as possible, through systematic choices in its favor: (a) for the argument from dreams, decide that if I have no infallible criteria available for distinguishing waking from dreaming, it is necessary to make as if, at every opportunity, I dreamed my thoughts;[72] then, (b) when simple natures and mathematics resist, go to the point of introducing the hyperbole of divine might and even, (c) to make it more credible, if not likely, add to it the voluntary fiction of the *genius malignius*.[73]

Whence—thirdly—in inevitable conclusion from the two preceding points: to maintain and support doubt "obstinately, *obstinate*" proves to be difficult, since it has to do precisely with an extreme choice; it is not only "hard-going, *laboriosum*" but "almost (*vix*)" an unfeasible act.[74] This is why, just as one begins doubting by decision, it is also necessary to know to decide to finish a doubt; the decision to doubt implies of itself knowing how to make the decision to *no longer* doubt. And thus, just as it happens that I find myself "compelled to admit (*cogor fateri*)" that I must doubt, it is also necessary that at a certain moment (*which one?* that's the difficulty), I know to decide to no longer resist the evidence: "I must finally conclude that this proposition, *I am, I exist*, [...] is *necessarily* true."[75] Each proof implies the recognition, and therefore the decision, that the positive evidence can and *must* win out over the decision to doubt. The same goes for the existence of God ("Ideoque ex antedictis, Deum *necessario* existere, est concludendum—So from what has been said it must be concluded that God *necessarily* exists"),[76] in strict conformity with the *regula generalis*, of which the first formulation ("illud omne esse verum, quod *valde* clare et distincte percipio—whatever I perceive *very* clearly and distinctly is true") is later qualified as necessary: "atque inde collegi illa omnia, quæ clare et distincte percipio, *necessario* esse vera—and I have drawn the conclusion that everything which I clearly and distinctly perceive is of *necessity* true." But this play at reversing the line of necessity depends, yet again, on an act, on my decision, on a resolution—it is about paying close attention to the reasons for my judgment: "etiamsi non attendam amplius ad rationes propter quas istud verum esse judicavi—Accordingly, I will no longer attend to the arguments which led me to judge that this is true"; in other words, "there is some difficulty in recognizing which are the things that we distinctly conceive."[77] The act of attention to clarity and distinction decides everything, always. Thus, the issue is not a logical or formal necessity, but in the final instance a phenomenal necessity exerted on the *ego* by the thing itself. The general rule moreover proves to be itself valid only under the *temporal* condition of my attention to clarity and distinction; it leads to a necessary truth only each time and for as long as I am attentive to it (*quoties, quamdiu*).[78] In this way, not only does the truth become a question of manifestation, and thus of phenomenality, but this opening of the phenomenon in its truth depends on a decision of the will to hold scrupulously to what the understanding reveals to it, the will and the understanding thus uniting in the act of attention: "Neque profecto quicquam est in his omnibus, quod *diligenter attendenti* non sit lumine naturali *manifestum*—If one *concentrates carefully*, all this is quite *manifest* by the natural light."[79]

The examples of such acts for exercising doubt and then for admitting the evidence appear so frequently—in the dialogue of *Meditation II* with a non-existent and imagined interlocutor, but which leads to the existence of the *ego*; in the demonstration of the existence of God, that makes out of the idea of the infinite the reverse of the *ego*'s finitude; in the *experientia* of the formally infinite will located in a substance that is nevertheless finite; in the recognition of the finitude of the imagination and of the passivity of the *sensus*—that it seems neither possible to expose them here, nor perhaps necessary to return to them. One might also point out astonishing examples of imaginative variations; starting with the analysis of the piece of wax in

Meditatio II, but also as early as the arguments of skeptical origin, amplified and taken apart by *Meditatio I*; just as one could also reread the whole of the *Meditationes* as a series of performative statements, in the strict sense of *acts* of thought that produce the actual arising of phenomena that, although provoked or, perhaps, *because triggered in this way*, are imposed on finite thought.

At least a partial answer to the initial question thus becomes possible. To the question of knowing in what sense phenomenology can invoke Descartes' name, *or not*, we must answer in several stages. First, this question does not come down to asking, retrospectively, whether Descartes *anticipates* the theses of phenomenology (classic and Husserlian, or later), but, inversely, whether certain phenomenological operations take up and prolong moments of the Cartesian method. Next, it is necessary to dispel the rapprochement that Husserl privileged of his own operation of the reduction (and its method, the *epochē*) with Cartesian doubt, which, in fact, corresponds not at all. But, right away, it is fitting to note that Descartes, before and independently of doubt, had almost accomplished the gesture of the reduction, or at least had anticipated it by leading all representative content back to its status as *cogitatum*, and thus suspending the preliminary question of its ontic (*real*) status: whether it be actually so or not, this changes nothing of the fact that everything that shows itself can be of value as such (*reell*) by the name of *cogitatum*. This leading back of the thing to the rank of *cogitatum* only as related to the *mens*, and no longer as being or non-being, operates, as the reduction will do, a suspension of the natural attitude. Furthermore, it breaks with the parallelism between the *ordo et connexio idearum* and the *ordo et connexio rerum*, which is so characteristic of the metaphysical dogmatics of Spinoza and his ilk. Henceforth, philosophy no longer proceeds by the deduction of concepts, and even less by the deduction of existence (or non-existence) on the basis of concepts (as in "negative" philosophy), but instead through the decision or decisions of a thought in action: Descartes says "resolutions," which are otherwise called performative acts, voluntary doubt and necessary constraints of evidence, imaginative variations, experiences of thought, and so on, all operations that release the phenomenal manifestation of things only with the work of a *decided* thought, according to a phenomenality put into *operation*. The construction of the known clearly operates a giving of sense (*Sinngebung*), where the thing is manifested only at the price of the work of the *ego*. Nothing is shown that is not given; but what is given only succeeds in showing itself to the extent that the *ego*, a phenomenologist before phenomenology, succeeds in *willing* to do so.

What is Descartes missing for the exact anticipation of historical phenomenology? Probably this: that what appears for him as *cogitatum* is not yet called a phenomenon, but remains a *res*, an object, an idea, or even a representation. Indeed, his successors will try to follow all these byways as far as possible, but without reaching (no more, and much less) the phenomenon as such. These impasses will be the result of a too narrow conception of the *ego*, the always exclusively active operator (even for the supposed "empiricists") of a constitution of objects by representation, reproduction, or production, synthesis and concept; a conception in which the question *An sit?* always held primacy over the question *Quid sit?* Descartes would have had to make a decision about two ambiguities: how can the *ego* operate by acts not only actively but passively? And is the being of the known summed up by certitude about the object? We will finally be Cartesians if we face them.

SIX

Montaigne, or Doubt without *Ego sum, Ego existo*

§1. Without "Any Communication with Being"

Before debating subjectivity, it would be necessary to measure its equivocity—an equivocity that is not only inevitable, but above all salutary. Indeed, subjectivity's equivocity alone allows, for example, the establishment of an *ego* without forcing us to maintain a transcendental *I*. Renouncing the transcendental *I*, for that matter, does not lead back to an empirical *moi*, since the empirical *moi* always results from a more originary complicity with this transcendental *I*, which it completes. In order to move beyond the one, it is necessary to surpass the other and not, as it happens most of the time, to alternate from the one to the other without seeing that, under the cover of a radical conveyance, one has only passed from one corner to the other of the same conceptual cell; it is not a question of choosing between the transcendental *I* and the empirical *moi*, but of being freed from the apparatus that links them to one another. What thinkers ought we to question in order to guide such an inquiry? Probably Descartes himself, who, provided that we read him literally rather than giving in to metaphysical retroactivity, could offer the unexpected resources of an originally dialogical subjectivity. But Montaigne as well, from whom Descartes stems to an essential degree, directly and probably also indirectly—once again, however, on the condition that we do not immediately impose on him theses that are too banal and, moreover, are weak or vague; or plainly put, on the condition that we avoid reducing him either to prior models (stoicism, skepticism, epicureanism, etc.)

or subsequent ones (materialism, atheism, "erudite libertinage," etc.). Rather, it would be necessary to take the measure of what was his destined role: rendering possible a new beginning for philosophical speculation at the endpoint of the scholastic cycle and, through it, of the ancient cycle. Of course, he succeeded in doing so by recasting prior inheritances, but this recasting itself would have had no sense or any strength if it had not proceeded from a new beginning. It is fitting, then, to let Montaigne unfold his determination of subjectivity (which is neither transcendental nor empirical) starting from the most radical and original kernel of his thinking as a *philosopher*.

Would it be too much, and a bit naïve into the bargain, to claim to designate such a speculative event—the initial "philosophical intuition" that Bergson assigned to every genuine philosophy? Maybe, but to draw back in front of this risk would be to refrain from speaking, to the point that, in such an original case as Montaigne's, the speculative event lets itself be glimpsed fairly certainly, even fairly bluntly. We have only to consider the decision Montaigne states at the beginning: "for it is I myself that I portray [. . .] I am myself the matter of my book."[1] Clearly, taken on its own, this declaration still remains enigmatic, for many others had already taken themselves for the matter of their book (and not only the composers of elegies, or Saint Augustine), and that in itself is not enough to spot clearly the originality of Montaigne's choice; what's missing is understanding the reason, which must be imagined as strong, even radical. He does formulate the reason almost immediately: "being outside of being, we have no communication with what is" (I.3, V17; F10). One cannot underestimate this opinion, since it puts us, with Montaigne, literally outside of being, out of being, or in short, *without being* [hors de l'être, hors d'être, bref *sans l'être*].

How should we understand this? To begin, we will refer to a second text: "We have no communication with being, because every human nature is always midway between birth and death, offering only a dim semblance and shadow of itself, and an uncertain and feeble opinion." Our contingency prevents us from gaining consciousness of our proper being, because, contrary to the behests of metaphysics, it can neither last nor subsist: "And if by chance you fix your thought on trying to grasp its essence [*son être*], it will be neither more nor less than if someone tried to grasp water [. . .] all things being subject to pass from one change to another, reason, seeking a real stability [*une réelle subsistance*] in them, is baffled, being unable to apprehend anything stable [*subsistant*] and permanent" (II.12, V601; F455). In short, like every living thing, man is born and dies, and thus passes; he in no way satisfies the characteristic demand of *ousia*, that of subsisting equal to himself ("no mortal substance can be found twice in the same state," V602; F455); now, because ever since Aristotle *ousia* rules over every function of being (*to on*), that which cannot realize *ousia* cannot claim the status as a being in the strict sense. A being, but not as a substance, man truly is not, for "if he is not one and the same, he also *is* not" (V603; F456). If man and nature are not, who will be? God, and he alone. "Wherefore we must conclude that God alone *is*—not at all according to any measure of time, but according to an eternity immutable and immobile, not measured by time or subject to any decline; before whom there is nothing, nor will there be after, nor is there anything more new or more recent; but one who really is—who by one single *now* fills the *ever*; and there is nothing that really is but he alone—nor can we say 'He has been,' or 'He will be'—without beginning and without end" (V603; F457). God alone is according to the title *ontōs ōn* (following Plato here² more than the Septuagint in Exodus 3:14). Only divine being merits the title of being [*étant*] and thus has access to "what is" (I.3, V17; F10), since it is, as "being of beings, *être des êtres*" (II.12, V513; F381).

And yet, we still must make clear the essential. For we are not only separated from being (*l'étant*) ("no communication with what is," I.3, V17; F10), which is summed up by God; above all we find ourselves without access to being (*l'être*) in general: "being out of being" (V17; F10), "we have no communication with being" (II.12, V601; F455). Thought not only cannot pose the question of being in its being, but it cannot even refer itself to being as the horizon of its search. Montaigne's radicality lies in the fact that he does not limit himself to stigmatizing the contingency of my fragile beingness [*étantité*]—rehashed constantly by all the moralists—but in that he extinguishes the question of the meaning of being; for being loses all meaning for he who has no access whatsoever to it. I am, but paradoxically, I am outside of being. I *am* so little that I know of being nothing but precisely that I do not know it. Whence this unavoidable consequence: philosophy on principle becomes impossible for me, and "I am no philosopher" (III.9, V950; F725) because not only am I not (genuinely being), but I lack all access to being. In short, "being out of being," I am without being, I am precisely the being in which *being is not the issue*. The declaration that "I study myself more than any other subject. That is my metaphysics, that is my physics" (III.13, V1072; F821) does not invalidate it, but rather confirms it: henceforth, upon what "subject," upon what *subjectum* or *hypokeimenon* does this "metaphysics" bear? Precisely not on being, since I myself am precisely not a "subsistent and permanent" being (II.12, V601; F455), lacking the least "communication with what is" (I.3, V17; F10); nor does it bear on the being of beings, since, "being outside of being" (V17; F10), I have "no communication with being" (II.12, V601; F455), and thus none with its meaning. If one attempts a new "metaphysics," it will be a downgraded one, without beings or being [*sans étant ni être*], a metaphysics of this "I" that studies itself only because it is strictly speaking not—I do indeed study myself, but insofar as *I am not*. The "moi" is imposing itself on the entire stage only because genuine being and beings are disappearing from it. Philosophy, or indeed metaphysics, will remain thinkable, if they remain thinkable, only by displacing themselves (at the risk of being made into a metaphor) from being to that which becomes foreign to it, "me" outside of being, "I" without being. Metaphysics would remain only by displacing itself outside of being and without leaning on any permanent being: which is as much as to say it disappears. And in fact, named here once and for all, Montaigne will not speak of it again. Metaphysics fades away as does the question of being—one takes no notice of them; one cannot reach them and does not wish to hear tell of them.

§2. The "Being Outside of Being," or the Dying "Moi"

Thus, the point of departure already imposes a paradox:[3] unable to reach either genuine beings or being, "metaphysics" must limit itself to considering the "moi"—taken precisely as outside of being. And yet, can that which, properly speaking, *is not* still support a "metaphysics" (much less a "physics")? How could the "moi," at the same time, still give itself sufficiently so that I might study it exactly, and yet show itself as precisely "being outside of being"?

Nevertheless, Montaigne takes up this paradox brilliantly. The same sequence that, from the opening of the *Essais*, admits that "we have no communication with what is," continues in this way: "it would be better to say to Solon that man is never happy, then, since he is so only after he is no more" (I.3, V17; F10). And the fittingly titled essay "That our happiness must not be judged until after our death" will take up "the warning that Solon had once given [Cyrus]: that men, however fortune may smile on them, cannot be called happy until they have been seen to spend the last day of their lives, because of the uncertainty and variability of human affairs, which the slightest shift changes from one state to another entirely different" (I.19, V78; F54).[4] At issue is not so much a moral counsel (it is better to wait until the end of the story to judge it) than a determination in the final instance of the manner of being, or of *not being*, of the "moi" henceforth "outside of being": it discovers the process of being outside of being, and thus of *not being*, only by experiencing itself as *moribundus*, destined to die, to be no longer, at all. Not that the "moi" first is, serenely and fully, only to have to one day cease being, thus accomplishing a being that is genuine but temporally restrained; for it happens otherwise: the "moi" is (if indeed it is) only from the outset under the domination of the final non-being, which rules it in turn and determines in advance the illusion of being that we call life. The day of my death not only sanctions the end of my life, but manifests its original status—that my life, in its mode of being, stems, rather, from non-being: this day "is the master day, the day that is judge of all the others" (I.19, V80; F55). Death, or rather the process of dying that advances at every instant of what we call life, determines the mode of non-being that is proper to this "moi," "being outside of being" (V17; F10). And "metaphysics," henceforth without access to being but applied to the dying "moi," will thus have to bear on its death: "all the wisdom and reasoning in the world boils down finally to this point: to teach us not to be afraid to die"; in short, and strictly speaking, "to learn to die" constitutes the only possible act of "philosophizing" (I.20, V81; F56), with a philosophy that is not simply reduced to moral philosophy, but that is seeking the mode of [non-]being of man reduced to his dying moi [*son moi mourant*].

For Montaigne does not consider death in itself, as a moment that is actual and thus merely terminal in life; one could not in any case say anything about it since when it comes I will no longer be there to experience it, nor to say anything about it, while for as long as I will be there, it will not be there. Rather, he considers it as that which governs the effectivity of the "moi" outside of being all the more radically in that it remains a *possibility*. Indeed, death responds to properties that confer upon it the character of a paradox. Something necessary, "death [. . .] is inevitable" (I.20, V83; F57), and yet it cannot be foreseen and remains absolutely indeterminate: "It is uncertain where death awaits us; let us await it everywhere" (I.20, V87; F60). Thus, at issue is an event that is at once certain *and* unforeseeable; these two notes would contradict one another if we were dealing with an actuality, being able to be only one *or* the other; but they fit together, or even reinforce one another once the concern is a *possibility*, affirmed as certain because inevitable, confirmed as possible because unforeseeable; death *is* only by making itself awaited; it has no need to happen to invade us; on the contrary, it possesses us strictly to the extent that it has not yet swallowed us up. Henceforth it becomes useless and even impossible to oppose life and death: the one does not succeed the other, like two steady states, the clash of which obliges each in turn to occupy an exclusive actuality. On the contrary, life makes death manifest as its ultimate and original possibility (for only a living person can die, and must): "The constant work of your life is to build death. You are in death while you are in life; for you are after death when you are no longer in life. [...] during life you are dying" (I.20, V93; F65); "He who acts dead when still alive is subject to be thought alive when dying" (III.9, V979; F748); "But you do not die of being sick, you die of being alive" (III.13, V1091; F837). Reciprocally, death, as terminal event, alone shines light on the mortality of life, which is to say, its mode of being without being (for only a mortal *is without being*): "youth dies within us, which in essence and in truth is a harder death than the complete death of a languishing life"; and, "Long life and short life are made all one by death" (I.20, V91 and 91; F63 and 64); and further: "Death mingles and fuses with our life throughout. Decline anticipates death's hour and intrudes even into the course of our progress" (III.13, V1102; F846); or: "the shorter my possession of life, the deeper and fuller I must make it" (III.13, V1112; F853). Death understood as possibility allows us to conceive of how a being can nevertheless be without communication with being, precisely because death both undoes the being and upholds it at the same time. The ontological paradox of the being outside of being is accomplished in the ontic paradox of life as a dying life. These paradoxes not only render the condition of the "moi" conceivable, but also practicable; it is enough to assume the possibility as such, that is to say, to foresee it, for "Premeditation of death is premeditation of freedom" (I.20, V87; F60). Why does "premeditating give [...] a great advantage" (I.20, V90; F63)? To be sure, because it is better to anticipate necessity (dying) than to oppose it in vain; but above all because a possibility (that of life traversed by death as its manner of being) cannot be experienced as an actuality (the moment of death), but only as a possibility, and thus through the impetus and the expectation that foresees it.

In this way, Montaigne succeeds in thinking—or even in phenomenalizing—the "moi" as a "being outside of being," by determining its mode of quasi-[non-]being according to the identity within it of life and of death as a possibility, to the point of making that mode actually accessible through anticipation ("premeditation"). Dying at each instant of its life: this is how the being of the being [*l'être de l'étant*] that does not reach being [*l'être*] is defined. Of course, one could not miss comparing this dazzling determination by Montaigne of the "moi" in its [non]-being according to the possibility of death, to that made by Heidegger, of Dasein according to its being-toward-death. Without any doubt, it is the same description of the phenomenon, as a more detailed study would confirm.⁵ And yet, the results drawn in the end from this description differ and are even rigorously inverted. In *Sein und Zeit* death as possibility opens access for Dasein to its being, and indeed to being absolutely, so as to confirm Dasein in its privilege as sole being in which the question is being, while in the *Essais*, the same death as possibility attests that man is a being without communication with being, the being in whom the question is precisely not being, the being that is only inasmuch as he never ceases *not to be*. The "moi," in opposition to Dasein, does not attain itself by deciding on and through being; he finds himself only in first recognizing that in him the question is decidedly *not* that of being, because he is only inasmuch as he does not communicate with being. The "moi" appears as a Dasein without being. And as this formula already states a contradiction, we must rectify it right away by defining the "moi" as a *Da-* without *sein*, a "*here*-without being."

§3. The "Moi" without Cogitatio of Self

Does such an impossibility of gaining access to being and even to its own being forbid the "moi" from gaining access to itself? In principle, its powerlessness to occupy the figure of Dasein should not prevent it from at least gaining access to that of the *ego cogito sum*. But, in fact, it does.

Indeed, the impossibility of an access to being in general also and in particular disqualifies the ambition to infer my existence from the exercise of the act of my thought; the "moi" of Montaigne challenges in advance the "first principle" and the "first truth," of which Descartes' *ego sum* boasts. If I have no communication with being, a fortiori I will have no access to my being, nor to my existence in particular. If I cannot "really know what it is that *is*" (II.12, V603; F456), how would I be able to say "hoc pronuntiatum, *ego sum, ego existo*, quoties a me profertur, vel mente concipitur, necessario esse verum—this proposition, *I am, I exist*, is necessarily true whenever it is put forward by me or conceived in my mind"?[26] If I am ignorant of all being, all being will remain incommunicable to me, whether it is being for me (Descartes) or being in itself (Heidegger). Thus, the impossibility of establishing the existence of the *ego* of the *cogito* redoubles, or even specifies the impossibility of putting oneself into play in being, like Dasein. Might one nevertheless be able to object that, even by admitting that possible death governs life to the point of putting it outside of being, one can contest that the "moi," even outside of being, loses as well any access to its own thought, that it cannot in an indisputable immediacy find an access to this very thought, and that it loses all communication with its ipseity, in short all knowledge of self as such? That the "moi" remains "outside being" and thus does not exist (not in the ontic sense of the *ego* any more than in the ontological sense of Dasein) in no way implies that it cannot at least think of itself, know itself, and thus be individualized. However, Montaigne contests the knowledge of self of the "moi" so strongly that he had challenged its access to being. The second refusal definitively buries the first and, in advance, challenges the two stages of the Cartesian argument: the experience of my thought gives me no access to being (neither to my own, nor in general), since my thought gives me no experience of myself. The "moi" does not think itself any more than it has communication with being.

That the "moi" has no communication with itself through its own thought, and thus neither understands itself nor is individualized in that way, is established by Montaigne through at least five arguments. (a) Thought dreams more than it is awake: "Those who have compared our life to a dream were perhaps more right than they thought," since indeed "Our waking is more asleep than sleep [. . .]. Our dreams are worth more than our reasonings" (II.12, V596 and 568; F451 and 427). And yet, following Descartes one will reply, dreams also put thought into operation, and the difference between waking and dreaming in no way affects my exercise of thought: "Imo etiam hoc nihil mutat."⁷ (b) A counterargument therefore arises: when thought is put into operation, it does not therefore follow that *I* think, nor that it is me that thinks, for it can perfectly happen that I am not the author of my own thought: "My will and my reasoning are moved now in one way, now in another, and there are many of these movements that are directed *without me*" (III.8, V934, emphasis added; F713). Rather, one ought to say, the *im*proper thought that escapes me does not come from me, nor belong to me; most often I can think for myself such a thought not only without causing it, but without my even having made a decision for the least cause; for example, I throw myself into battle and its fury without any conscious cause: "What do you mean, a cause? None is needed to agitate our soul: a daydream without body or subject dominates and agitates it" (III.4, V839; F637). (c) Inversely, that a "moi" would produce and decide its thoughts is not enough to make them clearer and more distinct; on the contrary, for it may be that I lie to myself clearly by thinking confusedly. More radical than Descartes, who will limit his doubt to theory, Montaigne does not exclude morality from the question of thought, but instead begins with it; he thus contemplates from the outset the deepest disturbance that can disqualify evidence: not the error (voluntary or involuntary) of solipsistic knowledge, but the deception (involuntary or voluntary) of communicating knowledge to others; I can think in the mode of lying, which most often and at first glance becomes the essentially jumbled mode of my own thought, and which escapes others because it first escapes me myself: "Truth and falsehood are alike in face, similar in bearing, taste, and movement: we look upon them with the same eye. I find not only that we are lax in defending ourselves against deception, but that we seek and hasten to run ourselves through on it" (III.11, V1027; F785–86). Reciprocally, I can also lie to myself, and thus produce thoughts that in the end are inaccessible to myself, as well: "It is at the expense of our frankness and of the honor of our courage that we disown our thought [. . .]. We give ourselves the lie to save the lie we have given to someone else. You must not consider whether your action or your word may have another interpretation; it is your true and sincere interpretation that you must henceforth maintain, whatever it costs you" (III.10, V1019; F780). Between me and my thought, in several ways, a gulf deepens, a properly ethical or indeed a political gulf. But this gulf arises in the end from a difference between me and myself: "Myself now and myself a while ago are indeed two" (III.9, V964;

F736), whether "Life is an uneven, irregular, and multiform movement" (III.3, V819; F621), or "whether I am different myself" (III.2, V805; F611). This difference makes me *differ* from myself, because through and through my temporality alienates me from myself. Temporality affects the "moi" so radically, de-formed, and re-formed "from minute to minute" (III.2, V805; F223), that "I live from day to day" (III.3, V829; F629) and am never what I am, or rather, what I was, and which no longer will be what I am presently. Temporality no longer confirms me in what I am (in the sense of "what it was to be," *to ti ēn einai* was equivalent for Aristotle to the real essence of an individual defined in the present), but it deepens and emphasizes without stop the impassable divorce between what I was (and no longer am) and what I am (entirely other than what I was): the past (*ēn*) never coincides with the present (*einai*). Time separates me from myself, sets me behind myself, sets me apart from myself, in short *defers* the access of the "moi" to the self [*du "moi" à soi*]. In this differ*a*nce, the "moi" that I claim for myself remains always another than myself, because it first breaks with itself. I think, but my thought never attains this "moi" that I am only in already no longer being it.

Two final arguments follow, this time in the form of conclusions. (d) No definition of the essence of man (and thus of the "moi") can be conceived, because the very rules for the definition in metaphysics make it problematic: "The question is one of words, and is answered in the same way. 'A stone is a body.' But if you pressed on: 'And what is a body?'—'Substance.'—'And what is substance?' and so on, you would finally drive the respondent to the end of his lexicon. We exchange one word for another word, often more unknown. I know better what is man than I know what is animal, or mortal, or rational. To satisfy one doubt, they give me three; it is the Hydra's head" (III.13, V1069; F818–19). To give a definition, the metaphysician goes back to the first substance, which he aims at from the second substance by zeroing in on the genre and then the specific difference; but it so happens that these last terms ("animal," or "reasonable," or "mortal") would themselves require a definition, wider and even more problematic than what they were supposed to define ("man"). The supposed definition only substitutes for a name little known among other names, which are more numerous and above all even less comprehensible. Descartes will take up this critique of the supposed definition of the cogitating *ego* as "man," and then by "rational animal"; but, contrary to Montaigne, he will consider [*estimera*] that he has attained another (*res cogitans, cogito*) that is certain and evident.[8] However, since Montaigne challenged the self-transparency of the "moi" by thought (and thus its access to being, as well), there remains for him, once the Aristotelian definition has been set aside, no other resource than to conclude that the essence of man is inaccessible to the "moi." A result that another text inevitably reaches: "Let us not forget Aristotle: what naturally makes the body move is something which he calls entelechy—by as frigid an invention as any other, for he speaks of neither the essence, nor the origin, nor the nature of the soul, but merely notes its effect. Lactantius, Seneca, and the better part of the dogmatists have confessed that it was a thing they did not understand." The "frigid invention" of the soul, defined as "first entelechy of the physical body having life potentially in it,"[9] effectively takes into account only the unity of the human individual, not his humanity, and even less his ipseity, which remain indescribable. Moreover, "when we wish to pronounce ἐγώ, which means I," we have only to designate, without anything other than a deictic (a mute gesture), a part of the body: "we drop the lower jaw toward the stomach" (II.12, V543; F406, 407). Which of course marks our "marvelously corporal condition" (III.8, V930; F710), but above all our radical aporia in front of our own *ego* (or rather, in Greek, our ἐγώ). And this aporia is in no way provisional or circumstantial, since Montaigne sanctions it in the end with an explicitly theological argument drawn from Saint Bernard: "'I know by myself,' says Saint Bernard, 'how incomprehensible God is, since I cannot understand the parts of my own being'" (II.12, V543; F406), thus translating the original literally: "Ex me intelligo quam incomprehensibilis sit Deus; quoniam me ipsum intelligere non possum, quem ipse fecit."[10] From which we must conclude that, for Montaigne, the essence of man so decidedly surpasses the grasp of philosophy (of that which he inherits from Aristotle, but also of that to come from Descartes) that it comes under theology, because theology shares the incomprehensibility of God himself.

As a consequence, (e), it is necessary to give up as well on implementing the Delphic precept γνῶθι σεαυτόν. To begin with, it is "a paradoxical command that was given us of old by that god at Delphi: 'Look into yourself, know yourself, keep to yourself'"; to be sure, we know everything except ourselves and are perhaps "the fool of the farce" (III.9, V1001; F766). But is it enough to take note of this exception—only man remains unknowable to man—to remediate it? In fact, if the "advice to everyone to know himself must have an important effect, since the god of learning and light had it planted on the front of his temple, as comprising all the counsel he had to give us," this requirement to know encounters the same "Platonic subtlety" that compromises every science: the one who knows already must no longer learn and the one who is unaware will never be able to learn; whence it follows that the claim "of knowing oneself, about which everyone is seen to be so cocksure and self-satisfied, [...] signifies that everyone understands nothing about it" (III.13, V1075; F823). Indeed, how would "the knowledge of man" not be "very difficult for man" (II.12, V557; F418) once there is neither a definition of self nor any self-access by thought, nor even an immediate mastery of his own thought at his disposal?

To the question, "Let us see what human reason has taught us of herself and the soul" (II.12, V542; F405), we obtained an answer: the "moi" has no more communication with itself than it had with being. Already being without being, it also remains without *cogitatio*.

§4. "Keeping to Oneself,"[1] or the Reduction

Thus, what I am in the innermost part of myself, that is, precisely, the "moi," remains inaccessible to me, because properly speaking it is *not*, due to its lack of communication with being and mastery of its own thought. The contradiction of the moi seems unsurpassable and, at the same time, unjustifiable: how could this "moi," which I nevertheless remain, become foreign to me? And yet, this "moi," this man who in principle is inaccessible, "I tell of him, and portray a particular one, very ill-formed, whom I should really make very different from what he is if I had to fashion him over again. But now it is done" (III.2, V804; F610). It is henceforth already done: the "moi," supposedly inaccessible, nevertheless always already imposes itself here and now, as an established fact. The facticity of the "moi" in fact refutes its incomprehensibility in principle. And this contradicts the first contradiction.

How is this to be understood? By distinguishing between two hypotheses. Either it would be necessary to definitively challenge the "moi" as a pure illusion, unable to be or to think, and therefore unable to be thought as a being. Or it would be necessary to recognize that I am in reality this "moi," and that it remains at once both unreal and unknown to me only because the questions (the questions and their presuppositions) claiming to reach it fall short, have nothing to do with it, and, consequently, render it inaccessible. It could be that the two questions posed to the "moi"—is it a permanent being, is it master and possessor of its thoughts, and thus of a thought of the self [*une pensée de soi*]?—cannot receive an answer, not due to a weakness in the "moi," but because they are in no way fitting to it, at least such as it is given to be thought. It may be that these two questions not only lack answers, but to begin with, pertinence, that they speak into the void and leave aside a fact that is nevertheless massive and uncontestable, but also radically different from what they foresaw. It could be that we are dealing with badly posed questions, because, more radically, their statements are senseless. In short, there would be no more sense in asking the "moi" whether it is a permanent being and whether it masters a thought of self, than to ask it if it is green or yellow, even or odd. In this last hypothesis, it is fitting to modify radically our method of analysis: one must adapt philosophy (with the risk that the philosophers no longer recognize it as theirs) to the specific exigencies of the "moi," and no longer claim to adapt the "moi" (with the risk of losing it) to philosophy.

There is no question that Montaigne follows this new path: "We entangle our thoughts in generalities, and the causes and conduct of the universe, which conduct themselves very well without us, and we leave behind our own affairs [*notre fait*—literally, our fact, trans.] and Michel, who concerns us even more closely than man in general" (III.9, V952; F726). The "moi" is not reached from a universal, even from "man," for example, who would be specified after the fact, but instead by recognizing right away my "fact," the fact of the me that I already am—the facticity of my fact always already accomplished. To do justice to this facticity, nothing less than a new mode of philosophy is necessary. Montaigne insists on this point, taking his time: "Cicero says that to philosophize is nothing else but to prepare for death. [...] In truth, either reason is a mockery, or it must aim solely at our contentment, and the sum of its labors must tend to make us live well and at our ease, as Holy Scripture says" (I.20, V81; F56).[12] This is a mode of philosophy that inverts its usage: "An ancient who was reproached for professing philosophy, of which nevertheless in his own mind he took no great account, replied that this was being a true philosopher" (II.12, V511; F379). This inversion, which Pascal will prolong, in fact goes back through Erasmus to Saint Paul: "the wisdom of this world is foolishness with God" (1 Corinthians 3:19), quoted almost literally by the *Apology for Raymond Sebond*: "the truth [. . .] inculcates in us that our wisdom is but folly before God" (II.12, V449; F328).[13] This overturning goes to the point of a modification of the paradigm: "My philosophy is in action, in natural and present practice, little in fancy" (III.5, V842; F639–40). It must be understood that philosophy no longer consists in representing (by imagination), because it did too much of that, and to the point of absurdity: "it has so many faces and so much variety, and has said so much, that all our dreams or reveries are found in it. Human fancy cannot conceive anything good or evil that is not in it" (II.12, V546; F408). Thus, it consists, instead, in acting; but nevertheless not as understood by "political philosophy," which always aims at the universal (III.9, V952; F727), nor by "moral philosophy" (III.2, V805; F611), the "ethical laws" of which cannot truly "be framed" (III.13, V1070; F819). At stake, then, is not the establishment as first philosophy of one of the other branches of the tree of philosophy, for example the "practical," against one of the theoretical philosophies. The issue is to redefine philosophy entirely, beginning from "our affairs [*notre fait*]" (III.9, V952; F726), from facticity. The issue is first to accept, and only then to understand, that henceforward, it is done with "me [moi]," "But now it is done [meshuy c'est fait]" (III.2, V804; F610): I am in the mode of an incomprehensible facticity, foreign to my thought, differ*a*nt in time. Which means that this fact is always undone in order to be remade, in endless difference:

> Stability itself is nothing but a more languid motion. I cannot keep my subject still. It goes along befuddled and staggering, with a natural drunkenness. I take it in this condition, just as it is at the moment I give my attention to it. I do not portray being: I portray passing. Not the passing from one age to another [. . .], but from day to day, from minute to minute. My history needs to be adapted to the moment. (III.2, V805; F610–11)

The "fact [*fait*]" that has to be thought cannot remain like a permanent object, like a present being in being, and above all it must not do so. This means that it can be thought only by a thought that, like the "moi" that it concerns, also gives way to passing; for how could I who am this "moi" that is constantly passing think, and think this "moi," if not through a thought that is itself ceaselessly passing and moving, different from itself at each moment? In order to respond to this double inversion of the customary conditions of metaphysical identity (the permanence of the being, the transparency of the concept), nothing less is necessary than an inversion of philosophy into a philosophy henceforth "in action" (III.5, V842; F639). To this will correspond a "new figure: an unpremeditated and accidental philosopher" (II.12, V546; F409)—a philosopher who will try to know his own "moi" without premeditating it, without fore-seeing it in the horizon of being, without restricting it to the chance of "passage," in short without claiming to govern it by his own thought, or, to begin with, to govern his own thought.[14]

And Montaigne in fact undertook—and, I claim, accomplished—such an inversion of the philosopher and of philosophy. He did it by taking up an operation of the mind that was so ancient and so well known that it had almost lost all its power—the suspension of judgment, practiced by the skeptics: "Their expressions are: 'I establish nothing; it is no more thus than thus, or than neither way; I do not understand it; the appearances are equal on all sides; it is equally legitimate to speak for and against. Nothing seems true, which may not seem false.' Their sacramental words is *epechō*, that is to say, 'I hold back, I do not budge.' [. . .] Their effect is a pure, complete, and very perfect postponement and suspension of judgment" (II.12, V505; F373–74).[15]

Nevertheless, the difference between Montaigne and the Ancient skeptics and their revival bursts forth right away. For the latter, the point is to neutralize opinions, to hold oneself back from assuming the one or the other term of an alternative, or in short, an abstention in theory that allows "the actions of life" to take place in "the common fashion" (F374). For Montaigne, it's completely otherwise: the suspension of the accepted opinions in philosophy does not depend on theoretical indifference but, by clearing away the cast-offs of theory, instead discovers through a practical exercise a new domain of experience—myself: "Oh, what a sweet and soft and healthy pillow is ignorance and incuriosity, to rest a well-made head! [. . .] In the experience I have of myself I find enough to make me wise, if I were a good scholar" (III.13, V1073; F822). To be sure, doubt still allows for, negatively, not giving in to belief and being freed from opinions; but above all it allows, positively, for much more. First, it gives access to the experience of self; next, it brings to light this "moi" as the very instance that allows for wisdom. The suspension of opinions is not limited to neutralizing them, but is ordered to the "support" of the "moi," in which it must be "held [*se tenir*]." "Our illness *grips* us [*nous tient*] by the soul, and the soul cannot escape from itself [...]. Therefore we must *bring it back* and *withdraw* it into itself: that is the real solitude" (I.39, V240; F176); or: "Through all these I have conceived a mortal hatred of being obliged [*tenu*] either to another or by another than myself" (III.9, V969; F741); or again: "I have long been preaching to myself to *stick* [*tenir*] to myself and break away from outside things" (III.12, V1045; F800); and also: "You have quite enough to do at home; don't go away. [...] I keep [*tiens*] myself to myself" (III.10, V1004; F767–68). Thus, I must apply myself to *hold myself* [*m'en tenir*] to this "moi" that I am, because, first of all and most of the time, I precisely do not hold to myself; the opinions of the world and the doctrines of philosophers turn me away from the "moi" and take me away from myself. This is why I must suspend opinions and doctrines (like a skeptic), in order to arrive at finding myself as the "moi" that I should never have ceased to be, the place of another wisdom. The suspension labors, then, at the invention of the "moi," and the skeptical clearing out is ordered to the appropriation of the proper basis of the *ego*.

How is such an operation accomplished? Despite his undulations and variations, Montaigne does not fail to provide precise indications, or at least ones that are susceptible to precision. As we have just seen, a suspension is necessary first: all the doctrines of the philosophers, among others, on nature and the definition of the soul must be bracketed.[16] Next, one must aim resolutely at the "moi" itself amidst all the decoys, or indeed at the heart of the authentic experience made possible by the suspension: "It is many years now that I have had only myself as *target* [*visée*] of my thoughts, that I have been examining and *studying* only myself; and if I study anything else, it is in order promptly to *apply* it to myself, or rather within myself" (II.6, V378; F273). Further, it is necessary, precisely in order that this aim [*visée*] reach the "moi" exactly, that the "moi" appear as the sole target. Whence the recourse, at once both polemic and rigorous, to an exclusivity of the "moi": "If the world complains that I speak too much of myself, I complain that it does not even think of itself" (III.2, V805; F611). And: "I dare not only to speak of myself, but to speak only of myself" (III.8, V942; F720). It is necessary to hold "only" to the "moi," because it alone remains with me and remains accessible to me, while everything else, which is not "moi," nor with me, escapes me, flees me, and disappoints me. The frontier traced in this manner by the criteria of an "only" separates what goes beyond what I remain in myself, and this remaining or abiding itself—transcendence and immanence. The suspension thus no longer has anything skeptical about it, because it doesn't so much defer to theories as open the access to the absolute immanence of the "moi." About the suspension, moreover, Montaigne said, "*epechō*, that is to say, 'I hold back, *I do not budge*'" (II.12, V505; F373)—I retain my judgments, of course, but also I do not budge, I maintain myself in my state, thus I remain in myself, quite exactly in my immanence, without overflowing it, nor venturing outside, without transcending myself toward the non-"moi." Let us venture a conclusion: *epechō*, that is to say, I reduce, I carry out a reduction that frees the pure immanence of the "moi."17

Montaigne, then, does not begin with the "moi," as an overly lazy reading would leave us to think; rather, he ends by arriving there, not without labor and always provisionally, by applying to himself the difficult discipline of the reduction. Indeed, even if "I have had only myself as the target [*visée*] of my thoughts [. . .] [t]here is no description equal in difficulty, or certainly in usefulness, to the description of oneself" (I.6, V378; F273). For the immanence always remains fragile, precisely because it claims to accomplish a flawless possession: "I have nothing of my own but myself, and even there my possession is partly defective and borrowed" (III.9, V968; F740). And: "I who am king of the matter I treat, and who owe an accounting for it to no one, do not for all that believe myself in all I write" (III.8, V943; F720). The reduction must be repeated each moment, but above all it must be radicalized and perfected so that the immanence of the "moi" is not dissolved in the transcendence of the world, in its flux and in its permanence (for both belong to the world's mode of being).

§5. The "Entire Form"

In the end, what is obtained by the suspension, which I have suggested should be understood here as a reduction? Indeed, what reduction is at issue? Clearly, not a reduction that is transcendental by anticipation; not because an anachronism forbids it (are there really any anachronisms in philosophy?), but because here the possibility of the least *ego* (a fortiori transcendental) is definitively lacking, a possibility that will not be opened, even if only partially, until Descartes. Above all, every reduction would be exercised starting from an *ego*, which, depending on the reduction, would soon come to constitute objects, which the temporal flux of the "moi" does not contemplate, and even forbids. If there must be a reduction here, it will be exercised, for

Montaigne, not from the *ego* toward objects, but upon the *ego*; more exactly, it will transform the *ego* into a "moi," resulting from the reduction and itself the first to be reduced. The impossibility of constituting objects—"I cannot keep my object still"—results indeed from the more original impossibility of establishing myself as the subject of the reduction: "I am other myself" (III.2, V805; F610, 611). Henceforth, if the (non-transcendental) reduction bears on the "moi" and does not come from it, how is it defined?

I suggest that it has to do with a kind of *eidetic reduction* of the "moi." More precisely, that the ensemble of the lived experiences of consciousness indefinitely describable in the empirical realm and, for that very reason, undefinable, which Michel de Montaigne records under his proper name in the *Essais*, is found assigned to the very *eidos* of the "moi," both individualized and perfectly universal. By "reciting" himself, Montaigne attempts (it is up to the reader to decide if he succeeds) to make appear this individual—a unique individual specified as no one perhaps was before him—following a reduction that every reader can repeat and in which he or she can find him or herself.[18] This *eidos* does not lead the individual back to the abstraction of the essence "man" any more than he is dissolved in an indefinite flow of incommunicable lived experiences; he is reduced to himself, so as to appear as his ownmost "moi," revealing in this way that every other individual gains entry to the humanity in himself, likewise discovering himself as such a "moi." The "moi" remains neutral—each one himself becomes so once reduced to his own depths, deeper than any of the empirical determinations that he takes on one after the other—but with a neutrality that is nevertheless absolutely individualized—each accedes to his "moi" beginning from its incommunicable and unrepeatable characteristics. Even in as much as each one allows to appear in oneself the "moi" to which he alone can be reduced, each one makes manifest the seal of the human condition in him, namely that of not being a being (nor a living thing [*un vivant*], nor a rational or laughing living thing, nor a substance, etc.), but the facticity of a "moi," which, always temporally behind himself, ever separated from his actions and his thoughts, nevertheless ceaselessly masters himself in it and finds himself again there through a decision. This double function of the "moi" of Montaigne seems difficult to conceive, or even contradictory, to the point that the polemics often summon us to choose a camp ("nominalism" or "essentialism"), because they always spontaneously conceive the "moi" beginning from Descartes, and thus follow the double postulation that Kant and Husserl drew from it: either the "moi" constitutes objects and we must radicalize it into the transcendental *I*, or it does not constitute, and it is fitting to dissolve it into the empirical *moi*. However, it could be that Montaigne understands the "moi" precisely according to a more originary mode, anterior to this ruinous dichotomy and, in any case, powerless to conceive it. Better, it could be that the "moi" accomplishes these two functions all at once, and without standing them up against one another, because it assumes the stakes beginning from the radical ordeal of facticity: before thinking and thinking oneself (or not being able to think oneself), even before being a being (even a privileged one), the "moi" is born in view of dying, is only in the mode of what differs from self, makes up its mind only upon meeting that which cannot make up its mind, and in short, receives itself only by losing itself. When the "moi" describes to itself everything that separates it from its identity with itself (its accidents against its inaccessible essence), it says its only possible identity—that of having none other than that which one discovers after the fact, too late for an *anticipatory* resolution. Its non-identity defines its identity. And at the same time, it makes manifest the essence of all ipseity, of mine, of yours. Yet again, there is pertinence in the contrasted comparison with Dasein.

Now we can come back to a famous text, where the polemic is concentrated, and which I will read following the guiding thread of the eidetic reduction of the "moi" as such:

I set forth a humble and inglorious life; that does not matter. You can tie up all moral philosophy with a common and private life just as well as with a life of richer stuff. Each man bears the entire form of the human condition.

Authors communicate with the people by some special extrinsic mark; I am the first to do so by my universal being, as Michel de Montaigne, not as a grammarian or a poet or a jurist. If the world complains that I speak too much of myself, I complain that it does not even think of itself. (III.2, V805; F611)

These two sentences obey the same construction: starting from the particular (the "private life," the individual "Michel de Montaigne"), the point is no longer to make the particular (grammarian, poet, etc.) rise up, but instead the "universal being" or "the entire form of the human condition." One immediately notes that such a passage from the particular to the "universal," for as much as it has to do with an "entire form," defines quite exactly what an *eidetic* reduction can accomplish.[19] It remains that only polemical arguments can be raised by recognizing here, in this text that has been overly commented on in every sense, the enterprise of reading the universal in the particular, of seeing the individual as the form that makes a man. I admit that the importing of the phenomenological theme for interpreting a Renaissance text seems to add a new ambiguity to two other, more familiar discussions. Nevertheless, I will try to illuminate them thanks to the phenomenological point of view itself, which I hope in this way to render more acceptable.

The first polemic: in the sequence "each man bears the entire form of the human condition," does the term "form" imply that Montaigne is taking up the Platonic definition (Pierre-Maxime Schuhl[20]), or indeed the Thomist definition of man (M. A. Screech[21])? In order to respect the supposedly uncontestable dogma of the skepticism of Montaigne, or indeed of his supposed atheism beyond question, shouldn't we give up on such a "dogmatic" reading? Could we not interpret this (too metaphysical) "form" starting from the "condition" that it introduces—on the condition of understanding this "condition" in a strictly and exclusively juridical sense (André Tournon[22])? This argumentation is worthy of consideration, but it can only convince once several preliminaries have been accorded, all of which are debatable. First, it would be necessary to demonstrate that a juridical determination of the "condition" emancipates itself from metaphysics, and thus that the law, that is to say the political (maybe the so-called theologico-political) remains free, indemnified, and autonomous in relation to metaphysics, an assumption at the very least rather problematic, even though it seems to hold the philosophers' attention. We would also have to assure ourselves that, as a matter of fact, "condition" often, or even always, has a juridical meaning in the *Essais*; and many of these occurrences seem to come under metaphysics as much as law. Let's look at three. First, "Our own peculiar condition is that we are as fit to be laughed at as able to laugh" (I.50, V304; F221), where the allusion to what is proper to man, laughter (a metaphysical definition if there is one), goes without saying, like its reversal. Next: in order to define "our ordinary condition," namely the mortal condition (that the famous syllogism of the first figure demonstrates: "every man is mortal; Socrates is a man; therefore Socrates is mortal"), Montaigne holds that it is naturally a violent death, if one at least calls "natural what is general, common, and universal" (I.57, V326; F237); so that "condition" here takes on a universal and frankly logical meaning, and therefore a metaphysical one. Finally, "the laws of human nature, and of Venus and Bacchus" (III.13, V1109; F851), indeed define the nature, and thus the essence (metaphysical), of man. Thus, doubt of the impossibility of allowing a metaphysical sense of "condition," of "our wretched human condition," remains at least permitted (I.14, V50; F33).

In any event, in the sequence "each man bears the entire form of the human condition," it is still the case that the meaning of "condition" depends on that of "form," which bears it; "condition" therefore can only escape from metaphysics if the "form" itself escapes first from a metaphysical meaning. Now, one can hardly doubt that Montaigne holds to (at least sometimes) the most technical meaning. For example: "He who speaks true can speak as foolishly as he who speaks false; for we are concerned with the manner, not the matter, of speaking. My humor is to consider the form as much as the substance" (III.8, V928; F708)—here "matter" and "substance" are identified with one another, just as the *hylē* is assimilated, for Aristotle, to the *synolon* (taken as the compound and the substrate). We find the same terms beginning in the *Prologue*, which they structure; for "my naïve form" makes itself manifest only against the ground of "myself the matter of my book"; so that the "moi" becomes its own "subject" (V3; F23), in the double sense of the *ego*, but above all of the substrate, of the *synolon* of the "form."[23] In short, my "moi" offers the substrate (and thus the matter) on which alone the "form" of the human condition can appear. I am the material condition of the appearing of the universal "form" of man in me. Indeed, the "form" does not indicate a mere anecdotal figure but the very basis of the person, in opposition to the social or accidental appearance: "Just consider the evidence of this in our own experience. There is no one who, if he listens to himself, does not discover in himself a pattern all his own, a ruling form, which struggles against education and against the tempest of the passions that oppose it" (III.2, V811; F615). The "ruling form" thus makes me appear as the "moi" that I am in my "foundation which is all my own" (as Descartes puts it, AT VI, 15.6; CSM II, 118), and thus also as the man of the human condition. And man appears in this way even and above all in the "very ill-formed" individual, for it still allows him to be known as such, as "a particular" (III.2, V804; F610). The "form" thus makes known the essence: "It is not my deeds that I write down; it is myself, it is my essence" (II.6, V379; F274). An essence that is mine does not remain any less an essence of man; on the contrary. Aristotle makes clear that form, even as it must always come to terms with matter (as in the case of the accidents of the sublunary world), can nevertheless accomplish the universal essence and manifest it in an individual: it is enough that it puts into action this very matter through *entelecheia*.[24] Consequently, one understands that by leading back any individual from its accidental appearance to its form, and thus to its essence, it becomes in the end possible to read in it the very humanity of man: "Each man bears the entire form of the human condition" (III.2, V805; F611). But then again, Montaigne does not take the case of just any old individual. For, aside from it being "Michel de Montaigne" who is in question (III.2, V805; F611), he also chooses no one less than Socrates, because Socrates incontestably furnishes "a saintly image of the human form" (III.12, V1054; F807). How could we avoid thinking here of the custom, so constant in Aristotle, of choosing Socrates when the issue is that of defining man as such, or even of making explicit how the form of humanity appears in and against matter? "And when we have the whole, such and such a form in this flesh and in these bones, this is Callias or Socrates; and they are different in virtue of their matter (*to toinde eidos*), but the same in form (*tauto tō eidei*)."[25] The sole same form appears in the diversity of Callias and Socrates, in their bones and in their flesh—as it does in Michel de Montaigne, bearer thus to a greater degree of the form of the human condition than "as grammarian or poet or jurist" (this social flesh and bones).

Let us conclude: form here retains its Aristotelian meaning and Montaigne well and truly claims that in its most individuated figure the indefinable and passing essence of man as such comes forth and appears. His powerful originality in relation to Aristotle does not disappear, but resides simply in this appearing being accomplished of the essence in the individual, for Montaigne and contrary to Aristotle, without the least attempt at defining this "moi" (*entelecheia* provides no *horismos*). "Michel" shows "the entire form of the human condition," yet without ever defining it. What appears is not described. What shows itself is not demonstrated.

§6. "My Universal Being"

We can pass on, then, to the second polemic, which asks about the status of "my universal being": as such, is Montaigne here suggesting a metaphysical determination? How—since it has to do with what is mine ("*my* universal being")—can the universal become individual? For the difficulty lies in the fact that the universal seems to be better accomplished the more it is individualized: "I am the first to [communicate with the people] by my universal being, as Michel de Montaigne, not as a grammarian or a poet or a jurist" (III.2, V805; F611). We must understand, then, that these determinations as grammarian, poet, and jurist remain too general (not sufficiently individualized) to reach me universally in my "moi." Nevertheless, elsewhere the universal appears to be opposed to the individual, rather than freeing him: "We entangle our thoughts in generalities, and the causes and conduct of the universe [. . .], and we leave behind our own affairs and Michel, who concerns us even more closely than man in general" (III.9, V952; F726). Is the universal opposed to the individual ("Michel," "moi"), or does it make him evident? The dilemma seems to go without saying: we would have to choose between the individual or the abstract—such is the classic alternative.[26]

But perhaps it is a bit too classic, just like every question asked only half way. First, it must be admitted that "my universal form" indeed designates me the individual in my totality, since changing it would signify "my complete reformation"; my faults in fact do not stain me with a particular blemish that can be isolated, but rather with a "universal tincture with which I am stained"; I am universally imperfect, guilty, and a sinner, that is to say completely stained as an individual, through and through. Also "God sees into me, universally" (III.2, V813; F617); he sees me totally and without remainder in all my guilty and sinful individuality. But in this "Michel," taken in his totality according to this first meaning of "universal," what does the reader see? Precisely what Montaigne wants to show him: "Everyone recognizes me in my book, and my book in me" (III.5, V875; F667), for "my design [. . .] wishes to make a show only of what is my own, and of what is naturally my own" (III.12, V1055; F808). But this goal becomes realizable by anyone (in the second, most classic meaning of "universal") precisely because Montaigne was the first to realize it in its totality (according to the first meaning of "universal") and in him every reader, whoever he may be, can notice that such a description of the "moi," even without definition, can be accomplished. All at once, this realization in him of the "universal being" of the "moi," as total individual, can also become a "universal form." The "moi" of "Michel" can and must be universalized for every reader, who, in reading him, recognizes his own "moi," or the analogue of his own. For "there is no quality so universal [. . .] of things as diversity and variety" (III.13, V1065; F815), so that, in the diversity, the variety, and the irreducible individuality of this "moi" arbitrarily chosen by Montaigne as "Michel" there dawns the universal and indefinably reproducible figure of all the other possible "moi"; in short, there dawns the "entire form of the human condition" (III.2, V805; F611), the "image of the human form" (III.12, V1054; F807), or namely, "man in general, the knowledge of whom I seek" (II.10, V416; F303). Pascal and Malebranche would have been right to see here an egocentric vanity if Montaigne's "moi" described only "Michel"; but they are wrong, because this "moi," by letting itself describe in its particularities and in their "universal" enumeration (total, without remainder), makes appear that which makes the humanity of every other man—the "moi" described without definition, shown without demonstration.

Once again, we must recognize in the analytic of the "moi" an *eidetic* reduction of "Michel" to his essence, to "the entire form of the human condition," and thus to our own. This eidetic reduction could, moreover, make use of the Aristotelian doctrine of the universal. For, since Montaigne speaks of a "universal form" that precedes and surpasses the accidents (grammarian, jurist, etc.), and that responds to "what I am and to my condition" (III.2, V813; F617), one ought to think here of another Aristotelian thesis: the universal is not at first or only defined as the smallest (or widest) common denominator of several individuals, obtained by leaving out individualizing characteristics, but, more radically, as what belongs to each individual as such, through and through and by itself (*kata pantos, kath'auto, hē auto*).[27] Thus, the universal is not opposed to the individual by abstraction so much as it designates by characterization the essential that entirely constitutes it, so that it lacks nothing of that without which it would no longer be itself—in short, its ultimate form as the "*entire* form," the quiddity as "being *exactly* my own" (III.5, V875; F667). The universal, labeled as this "form" of the "human condition," stands out when each individual—Socrates or Michel—far from sinking into a foreign and alienating abstraction, attains the depths that belong to it properly, by itself and as itself. My "moi" makes visible "man" insofar as he is himself found in what he discovers of himself that is most his own, most inalienable and most irreducible. The more this "by itself" defines and realizes the universal, and the more Michel de Montaigne accedes to himself, the more he opens to us the "human condition," that is to say the "moi" in him. As a result, there is no choice to make between the individual and the universal form. And between Aristotle and Montaigne, the connivance probably surpasses what we would like to acknowledge.[28]

A confirmation of this universality of the individual as manifested by himself arises elsewhere, in Montaigne's insistence on underscoring that the access of the "moi" to the "universal form" is accomplished most often by the intermediary of the other and according to the mirror of myself that he presents to me. "I take such great pleasure in being judged and known that it is virtually indifferent to me in which of the two forms I am so" (III.8, V924; F705). Indeed, it is necessary to "[use] its own examples on all occasions as well as those of others, and [testify] frankly about itself as about a third party" (III.8, V942; F720). In this way, it is fitting to "see my own life mirrored in that of others" (III.13, V1076; F824). For my own "moi," if in the end it wants to serve the purpose of knowing "the entire form of the human condition," must not be studied exclusively in a particular individual (even my own), but in the other, as a way of particular access to the form of humanity (I make visible not me, but man); and, therefore, beginning from another gaze as well as from my own. The "moi" that I am must not only come under my gaze and my knowledge, but also be accessible to the gaze [*le regard*] and the knowledge of others. If "moi" counts for the "human condition," then all those who have a part in this same condition—that is, all other human beings—can and must take hold of it. "Nearly every man would say as much of himself, if he considered himself as I do [*s'il se regardait comme moi*]" (II.12, V566; F426). Taken in my "universal being" I dispossess myself of the "moi," which is valid for all and exposes itself to all. This plurality of gazes on the "moi" further allows us to oppose Montaigne clearly to Descartes. For Descartes, "I," as *ego cogito*, as the one who sees and who sees himself, becomes straight away the "first principle" of all vision of all things, in as much as it is the unique origin of knowledge. For Montaigne, "moi" is offered as what must be seen, and seen not only for itself, but on behalf of whoever wants to see himself by becoming the "universal form"; the "moi" becomes what all the gazes can see and lead back to their own—the universal visible, common and belonging to no one, because a phenomenon of all and for all.[29]

§7. Being and "Life"

There nevertheless remains, hidden beneath these two polemics, a more genuine difficulty. For the "entire form of the human condition" makes itself visible in "my universal being" (III.2, V805; F611); or better, the whole itinerary travelled in the *Essais* ends up in the duty to recognize that "It is an absolute perfection and virtually divine to know how to enjoy our being rightfully" (III.13, V1115; F857), and to avoid "despising our being" (V1110; F852). Now, does accomplishing our being in this way not contradict the notice made at the outset, namely that "we have no communication with being" (II.12, V601; F455)? How and by what right could being reestablish itself after it was certified as inaccessible? Should we put into question either our starting point or our point of arrival, despite the textual evidence that supports both? Unless we concede either that Montaigne cares very little for coherence or precision, or that the word "being" offers to his eyes no theoretical importance. While recourse has often been made to these sorts of evasions, we will avoid them, if only because another way opens to our reflection: it is possible that we are not dealing with the same "being" in the two terms, and that this equivocity dissolves the contradiction. In a first case, the one where we have precisely no access to it, being is defined by the pure and simple substance, the permanence and the immutability of substance (therefore the "being of beings" refers to God alone). On the contrary, in the second case, the one where we must "enjoy it rightfully," being is no longer understood as a bare position in brute permanence, but as "living well," which Aristotle called *to eu zein*, the simple conclusion of the axiom that it "is better to be than not to be."[30] For, in order to be up to the level of the human that is in him, a human being must first endeavor to be well, know how to live well; but the know-how of living well is determined in the final instance as "life." "What, have you not lived? That is not only the fundamental but the most illustrious of your occupations" (III.13, V1108; F850). Put differently, the *Essais* could very well end up in only a single result: substituting for the ambition of being (in permanence, as *ousia*), an ambition that is inaccessible and probably inhuman (uncertain and useless), the resolution (useful and possible) of a good *life*, a resolution in which the humanity of the human being is properly accomplished.

"There is nothing so beautiful and legitimate as to play the man *well* and properly, no knowledge so hard to acquire as the knowledge of how to *live this life well* and naturally; and the most barbarous of our maladies is to despise our being" (III.13, V1110; F852, emphasis added). In other words, man has to live well—being is not enough; for in order to be in the human way, it is not enough to be, it is necessary not to "despise" one's being well. Why do we have the temptation to do so? Because this being as such does not fulfill us—as neither infinite, nor permanent, nor perfect, we could certainly hate it; and the unhappiness of men does not come from elsewhere. In order to be like a human, it is therefore necessary to resist the danger and the "barbarous" temptation to despise one's being, and thus to endeavor to "*live this life well*. The philosophers' philosophy (that which it is fitting to mock) errs, because it imagines fulfilling the humanity of man by promising him (a promise that is not kept, of course) permanence, substantiality, and "the preservation of [our] being" (II.12, V456; F333). In contrast, the philosophy of the eidetic reduction to the "moi" (that which mocks philosophy) aims correctly, by renouncing the being that neither assures nor reassures man, for the life that he, man, must protect, safeguard, or in short, love: "Life is a tender thing and easy to disturb" (III.9, V950; F245). For "life is a material and corporeal movement, an action which by its very essence is imperfect and irregular; I apply myself to serving it in its own way" (III.9, V980; F756). Serving it means precisely first to live it in a soul and a body, following my "wondrously corporal condition" (III.8, V930; F710) and inasmuch as I am a decidedly material substance, and therefore moving; next, to accept it as moving and changing by definition, without laying claim to a definitively fixed *ousia*; and finally, to "serve" it, thus to protect it by respecting its demands and its limits. In order to live it is thus not enough for a "moi" (a man passed through the reduction) to be and to persist in that being; he still needs to know how to use it well; wisdom is summed up in this art of well-being, in the strict sense of living: "My trade and my art is living" (II.6, V379; F274); nothing less is required, for "it takes management to enjoy life" (III.13, V1111; F853). In this way, living is learned, each day, like a real science, the only one that allows one to "know how to enjoy our being rightfully" (V1115; F857) by way of "attention [*application*]" (F853). And, paradoxically, I wind up knowing all the better how to live (to be well) as the availability to being shrinks: "The shorter my possession of life, the deeper and fuller I must make it" (V1112; F853). I do not live in proportion to my persisting in present being, but to the extent that I raise this being to its well-being, or in other words, that I enjoy it as a life. Indeed, contrary to what common philosophy imagines about being and expects of it, life can never be taken for granted, guaranteed and guaranteeing; on the other hand, it must be managed in its very mobility; if I accept that "the world is a perennial movement; [that] [a]ll things in it are in constant motion [. . .; that] [s]tability itself is nothing but a more languid motion [. . .; and that] I cannot keep my subject still" (III.2, V804; F610), then I must live my humanity even to the extent that my being does not last and does not persist, in short I must *be* in the mode of life: "In short, we must *live among the living*, and let the river flow under the bridge, without caring, or, at the very least, without being altered by it" (III.8, V929; F709, emphasis added)—letting the passage pass by, and passing it by myself without losing myself in it, without altering myself as "moi" in it.

This returning of being into life finds an impressive confirmation in the overturning of the posture toward death. Henceforth, since there is no longer any question of assuring oneself of being nor of lasting with it, but rather of "enjoying" it as well-being, that is, as life, it is fitting to enjoy life even into the experience of death, precisely because death appears as the process of life, and no longer as the mere end of subsistent being. In short, the life to enjoy annuls the being to die by substituting for it "dying tranquilly": "In my opinion it is living happily, not, as Antisthenes said, dying happily, that constitutes human felicity" (III.2, V816; F619). More explicitly,

Philosophy orders us to have death ever before our eyes, to foresee and consider it before the time comes, and afterwards gives us the rules and precautions to provide against our being wounded by this foresight and this thought. That is what those doctors do who make us ill so that they may have something on which to employ their drugs and their art. If we have not known how to live, it is wrong to teach us how to die, and make the end inconsistent with the whole. If we have known how to live steadfastly and tranquilly, we shall know how to die in the same way. They may boast about it all they please. *Tota philosophorum vita commentatio mortis est.* But it seems to me that death is indeed the end, but not therefore the goal of life. (III.12, V1051; F805)

Now the same quotation from Cicero, which here is the subject of criticism, had already been used, but as a positive argument, at the beginning of the *Essais*: "Cicero says that to philosophize is nothing else but to prepare for death [. . .]. [A]ll the wisdom and reasoning in the world boils down finally to this point: to teach us not to be afraid to die" (I.20, V81; F56);[31] it thus presents the unquestionable marker of the overturning operated by Montaigne in the course of his journey. Death can become the goal and the summit of life only for the one who interprets both starting from subsistence, and thus in view of a present to make last; for death puts a term to this subsistence only by being consistent with its horizon and confirming it. In contrast, for the one who thinks being beginning from life, and thus this time as a "passage" without subsistence, death no longer has anything to triumph over, since there is no permanence for it to interrupt; it enters into a flux, and is swallowed up in it just like everything else. For "death mingles and fuses with our life throughout: decline anticipates death's hour and intrudes even into the course of our progress" (III.13, V1102; F846). As soon as the issue, after reduction to the "moi," is no longer that of knowing being in general and, possibly, of mastering my own being, but solely of living (well) its finitude and its constant change, philosophizing no longer concerns the end of being (death) but the fact of living and its art, to the point of encompassing even death in this know-how of living, called "dying happily." I no longer have to possess being as an assurance of subsisting; I have to receive it as given to live, possibly to live well, with art. "Have you been able to think out and manage your own life? You have done the greatest task of all," for "Our great and glorious masterpiece is to live appropriately" (V1108; F850, 851). And this philosophy doubtless surpasses metaphysics—except in the sense wherein "I study myself more than any subject. That is my metaphysics, that is my physics" (V1072; F821).

§8. To God's Grace

The art of enjoying one's being as life evidently presupposes that I renounce possessing my being as a basis that would assure me of subsisting in a provisional permanence. Enjoying one's life implies that I abandon present being so as to give myself up without reserve in passing: "I melt and slip away from myself" (III.13, V1101; F845). But how does one get to this giving up without experiencing it as a loss, a dissolution, and an anticipation of nothingness? Montaigne in fact succeeds in avoiding the plunge into an obsessive meditation on chaos and death, which gnaws at several of his contemporaries (from Jean-Baptiste Chassignet to Jean de Sponde); what is

178   *Chapter Six*

more, he envisages the passage itself as an almost unfailing enjoyment of self; he thus overturns the Stoic topic—what does not depend on me becomes the very thing that gives me to myself. How can one conceive of this serene abandonment?

Without claiming to deliver an exclusive answer here, and without fearing the contradiction of received opinions either, I will suggest a hypothesis: Montaigne succeeds in no longer possessing being, which the art of enjoyment raises to the status of a life, because he accepts to receive it as a gift: "We should neither pursue them [pleasures] nor flee from them, we should accept them [*il les faut recevoir*]" (V1106; F849). Receiving being as a gift, so as to respond to it by endeavoring to "play the man well and properly, [. . . and] to acquire [. . .] the knowledge of how to live this life well and naturally" (V1110; F852), Montaigne tries to succeed in this way by considering his life (and his being) as a gift of God's grace. This theme returns with such a clear insistence in the last of the *Essais* that one ought not to be able to ignore it. "Others feel the sweetness of some satisfaction and of prosperity; I feel it as they do, but it is not in passing and slipping by. Instead we must study it, savor it, and ruminate it, to *give proper thanks* [*en rendre grâce*] for it to him who grants it to us" (V1112; F854, emphasis added). Happiness is only worthwhile if it is received consciously, so as to give me the opportunity all the more to give thanks for it. The same goes for my being and my body: "She [my soul] measures the extent of her *debt to God* for being at peace with her conscience and free from other inner passions, for having her body in its natural condition enjoying controlledly and adequately the agreeable and pleasant functions with which he is pleased to compensate by *his grace* for the pains with which his justice chastises us in its turn" (V1112; F854, emphasis added); for even physiological well-being (as well as pain) must be received as a grace, welcomed as such. Or again, regarding my body: "There is no part unworthy of our care in *this gift that God has given us*; we are accountable for it even to a single hair"; for our "condition," "the creator has *given* it to us seriously and sternly" (V1114; F855–56, emphasis added). The same goes for my life in its totality: "As for me, then, I love life and cultivate it just as *God has been pleased to grant it to us*" (V1113; F854). In short, I can "live appropriately" (V1108; F851) only if I do not fear the change; and I can do so only if I see it as a grace and a gift (my body, its pleasures and its pains, my being and my very life); and if I take them not as the fund that I would possess but rather as a gift that I receive, I must give thanks for them; it could even be that I cannot see them as something to be received, if I do not see them first as to be given—as that reason why I must give thanks. Thanks for thanks, grace for grace.

In this context, we will attach a more precise attention to three texts, which quote literally the formulas in which Saint Paul puts forward divine grace and the man who receives it. To begin with: "I [...] stay in the position where God put me. [...] Thus *I have, by the grace of God, kept myself intact*" (II.12, V569; F428, emphasis added). Here we recognize 1 Corinthians 15:10: "Gratia autem Dei sum id quod sum—By the grace of God I am what I am." By anticipation, one might say Saint Paul and Montaigne agree here to challenge every attempt by the *ego* to come at self-identity: what I am I am of course through me (my thought, my consciousness, etc.), but by inserting God's grace between me and the self [*moi et soi*], which thus becomes more inward to me than myself. Next: "Princes give me much if they take nothing from me, and do me enough good when they do me no harm; that is all I ask of them. Oh, how much I am obliged to God that it was his pleasure *that I should receive all I have directly from his grace*, and that he has kept all my indebtedness for himself privately!" (III.9, V968; F738, emphasis added). Here we find 1 Corinthians 4:7: "Quid autem habes quod non accepisti?—What have you that you did not receive?" Moreover, Montaigne here goes further than Paul: he of course recognizes having received everything that he has, but he recognizes having received it without mediation, which is to say that his *self*, which receives everything, he also receives, and first of all (as gifted, *adonné*); what is more, he gives thanks for this gift and thus goes so far as to admit his dependance on God as a gift. Finally, in the sequence, "*the man who is presumptuous of his knowledge does not yet know what knowledge is*; and the man, who *is nothing, if he thinks he is something, seduces and deceives himself*" (II.12, V449; F328, emphasis added). Montaigne here meets up with some "pronouncements of the Holy Spirit," that is, not only one but two statements of Saint Paul, which he translates literally: first, 1 Corinthians 8:2: "Si quis existimat se aliquid scire, nondum cognoscit quomodo oportet illud scire"; and then Galatians 6:2: "Nam si quis existimat se aliquid esse, cum nihil sit, ipse se seducit."³² Here, we take a new step forward: the disqualification of self-knowledge is no longer accomplished solely from the point of view of man himself (§3), due to epistemological or metaphysical impossibilities, but by virtue of a reference to God; or more exactly, as the consequence of the relation of giving [*la relation de donation*] that the "moi" cannot fail to undertake with its own "being," which it must receive as a "life." And it can accept to receive it only to the extent that it succeeds in giving thanks for it [*en rendre grâce*], or succeeds in rendering it as a grace, and in no case at all by claiming to possess it as its own.

There is no convention, no precaution, and no hypocrisy in this finale (III.13, VIII16; F857). Having to do with his "old age," and thus the final enjoyment of his "life," beyond his "being" that is declining according to subsistence, there is nothing more coherent and serious for the "moi" than to "Let us commend it [old age] to that *God who is the protector* of health and wisdom, but gay and sociable wisdom."[33]

Thus, the initial questioning on being, by way of the complex path of a critique of self-knowledge and of a reduction of the *ego* to the "moi," ends up at the question of the gift and of its grace. Does Montaigne attain to philosophy? It may be that he moves across it and exceeds it.

SEVEN

Hobbes, or the Idea and Being as Body

§1. *The Debate about the Idea*

Following the majority of interpreters, it would seem that the debate on the *Third Set of Objections and Replies* between Hobbes and Descartes did not really take place. And for a rather clear reason: Descartes likely failed to recognize Hobbes as a serious interlocutor, since he had been warned against him as a mathematician and did not recognize him as a philosopher. Nor was he entirely wrong, as Hobbes, who had probably only cast a glance at the *Meditationes*, was in reality continuing instead his discussion on the *Discourse* and, at the time he was composing his objections, did not have at hand his own papers, nor the means for serious work. In fact, the arguments exchanged quickly became repetitive, and the discussion soon reached an impasse, where the two interlocutors were stuck— to the extent that the final remark on the ignorance of the "atheist" likely conveys an *ad hominem*[1] and counts as a dismissal.

And yet, without claiming to modify by new textual facts what is generally admitted of their respective positions, I would like to suggest, in a few remarks, that a genuine debate did indeed bring them together, and then drew them apart. First because as a general rule, when two philosophers clash, they always manage to locate each other, and not miss. Next, because Hobbes knew Descartes very well, by his firsthand reading of publications from 1637 as much as by indirect knowledge. And especially because, even if *De Corpore* would not appear until 1655, Hobbes was already in possession of his fundamental philosophical theses, as attested by the previous drafts of *De Corpore*, especially *De Principiis* (1638–39?); *The Elements of Law*, completed, if unpublished, in 1640–41; and the 1643 reply to *De Mundo*, a work published by White in 1642.[2] I will thus attempt to clarify, starting from these indications, certain arguments which remain still implicit in the public dispute, in order to better assess its genuinely metaphysical scope.

At least six of the fifteen objections of Hobbes to Descartes concern the definition of the idea. Or more exactly the definition of those ideas that Descartes claims to have and which Hobbes says he does not and which he attempts to demonstrate are strictly impossible for anyone to have: "Notavi saepius ante neque Dei [obj. V], neque animae [obj. II] dari ullam ideam; addo jam, neque substantiæ [obj. IX].—I have frequently pointed out that we do not have an idea of God, or of the soul. I will now add that we do not have an idea of substance" (AT VII, 185.5–6; CSM II, 130). In fact, Objection V affirms that "Nullam esse in nobis Dei ideam—there is no idea of God in us" (180.9; CSM II, 127), in agreement with Objection VII: "Si non detur Dei idea (non autem probatur dari)—if an idea of God has not been given (for it is not proven that one has been given)" (183.13; CSM II, 129). Objection II denies that a thinking thing could arise from the *cogitati*, operated by the *ego* and thus to the contrary "rem cogitantem esse corporeum quid—the thinking thing is something corporeal" (173.15–16). Finally, Objection IX rather simplistically identifies the substance to the substrate and substrate to prime matter, in order to then remove it from the grasp of the concept: "Substantia enim (ut quæ est materia subjecta accidentibus, et mutationibus) sola ratiocinatione evincitur, nec tamen concipitur, aut ideam ullam nobis exhibet—for substance (in so far as it is the matter which is the subject of accidental properties and of changes) is something that is established solely by reasoning; it is not something that is conceived, or that presents any idea to us" (185.6–9; CSM II, 130). Descartes should thus strike first at the definition of the idea, knowing quite well that the status of the idea decides the dimensions of the entire metaphysical field.

His response consists in drawing the sharpest possible distinction between the imagined or imagining idea (in all cases an idea of something imaginable) and the idea as such. We see this in Reply IV: "Differentiam inter imaginationem et puræ mentis conceptum—a difference between imagining and the concept in the mind" (178.19–20; CSM II, 125); as well as in the piece of wax (mentioned in 178.21), "me nequidem imaginari quid sit hæc cera, sed sola mente percipere—I did not even imagine what this wax is, but I perceived by the mind alone" (31.16–18; CSM II, 21). Or in Reply V, in contrast with Hobbes' narrow definition of ideas as "imagines rerum materialium in phantasia corporea depictas—images of material things which are depicted in the corporeal imagination," Descartes recalls that he himself, on the other hand, "nomen ideæ sumere pro omni eo quod immediate a mente percipitur—[is] taking the word 'idea' to refer to whatever is immediately perceived by the mind" (181.1–8; CSM II, 127). He thus takes up the definition already fixed by the *Second Set of Replies*:

Ideæ nomine intelligo cujuslibet cogitationis formam illam, per cujus immediatam perceptionem ipsius ejusdem cogitationis conscius sum. [. . .] Atque ita non solas imagines in phantasia depictas ideas voco; imo ipsas hic nullo modo voco ideas, quatenus sunt in phantasia corporea, hoc est in parte aliqua cerebri depictæ, sed tantum quatenus mentem ipsam in illam cerebri partem conversam informant.—I understand the term "idea" to mean the form of any given thought, immediate perception of which makes me aware of the thought [. . .] thus it is not only the images depicted in the imagination which I call "ideas." Indeed, in so far as these images are in the corporal imagination, that is, are depicted in some part of the brain, I do not call them "ideas" at all; I call them "ideas" only in so far as they give form to the mind itself, when it is directed towards that part of the brain. (161.14–162.3; CSM II, 113).

Or again: "me per ideam intelligere id omne quod forma est alicujus perceptionis—for by an 'idea' I mean whatever is in the form of a given perception"[3] (188.14–16; CSM II, 132). In doing so, Descartes is provoking and rejecting here exactly the argument that would become public in the *De Corpore*: "Eundem errorem errant, qui ideas alias in intellectu, alias in phantasia ponunt; quasi alia esset idea sive imago hominis quæ orta a sensu in memoria retinetur, alia quæ in intellectu est, quando intelligimus *hominem est animal*—This is the same error made by those who place some ideas in the understanding, and others in the imagination; as if when we understand that *man is an animal*, we had one idea or image of a man derived from senses, retained in the memory, and another idea which is in the understanding"[4] (I.V.9).

The two opponents are thus in contact; and it must be observed that Hobbes' position, even though, or *because* it remains the most cursory, is not the least convincing. For Descartes does not himself completely avoid the imaginative (or at least "imaginal") interpretation of the idea, as Hobbes does not hesitate to remind him, citing a passage of *Meditatio III* that is as famous as it is ambiguous: "Quædam ex his [*sc.* meas cogitationes] tanquam rerum *imagines* sunt, quibus solis proprie convenit ideæ nomen, ut cum hominem, vel chimeram, vel cœlum, *vel angelum, vel Deum* cogito—some of my thoughts are as it were the *images* of things, *and it is only in these cases that the term 'idea' is strictly appropriate*—for example, when I think of a man, or a chimera, or the sky, or *an angel, or God*."⁵ Who, indeed, does not immediately see that thinking by image, and thus by imagination, cannot hold for God or an angel, which, according to Descartes himself, surpass the field of the imagination, not to mention the reach of my own mind? Hobbes does not have any trouble responding first that we only have an imagined representation of angels (a flame, "beautiful children with wings," etc.), even if by it we intend the "invisible and immaterial creatures who serve God"; so that we do not have an idea of them as such, as imaginable by a precise image. Next, that we have still less *"Dei [. . .] imaginem sive ideam*—an image or idea [. . .] of God" (180.5–6; CSM II, 127); such a God remains for us by definition unimaginable, thus "*inconceptibilis*—incapable of being conceived,"⁶ since he surpasses every sensation; and so our relation to God would remain without imaginable representation, thus without idea, mediated by the causal relation alone. The reserve of Objection III, "suppositionem alicujus causæ æternæ—the supposition of some eternal cause" (180.18; CSM II, 127), anticipates the unchanging doctrine of Hobbes: "unicam et æternam rerum omnium causam, quam appelant omnes Deum—a First, and an Eternall cause of all things; which is that which men mean by the name of God."⁷ Thus Descartes is said to have not maintained his own distinction and given in to the first argument of Hobbes.

§2. Unimaginable Ideas

For Hobbes, this objection actually goes back to the pure and simple assumption of an Aristotelian principle, according to which "the soul never thinks without imagination—(*aneu phantasmatos*)":⁸ a principle that is all the more famous, as Thomas Aquinas, in order to preserve the possibility of a material soul even in the letter of Aristotle's text, had deemed it should be interpreted in a somewhat subtle way: the soul of course always thinks with a *phantasma*, and thus according to the body; yet this body does not serve as an instrument of thinking, but offers only an object to be thought: "indiget corpore, non tamen sicut instrumento, sed sicut objecto—it needs the body, not as its instrument, but only as its object."[9] We know that Pomponazzi had contested this interpretation of Aristotle, by maintaining that "in omni namque quantumcumque abstracta cognitione [sc. intellectus humanus] idolum aliquod corporale sibi format—For in all cognition, however far abstracted [the human intellect] forms some bodily idol" and thus that "Commentator, divus Thomas et quicumque sentit Aristotelem censere humanum intellectum vere esse immortalem, longe a vero distat—the Commentator [Averroes], St. Thomas, and whoever thinks that Aristotle judged the human intellect to be truly immortal are far from the truth";[10] which, incidentally, led to his condemnation by the Council of Lateran V in 1513. Returning to the debate, this clarifies the discussion of 1641: whether he intends it or not, Hobbes takes up the interpretation of Aristotle by Pomponazzi (as every idea is imaginative, the mind therefore remains material) while Descartes returns to the Thomist interpretation (the mind treats a material and imaginable object, without itself belonging to the corporal realm). And is this not the choice proclaimed explicitly in his dedicatory letter to the Faculty of Theology at the Sorbonne that opens the *Meditationes* (AT VII, 2.31–3.9; CSM II, 3–4)?

But this is not only a point about interpreting Aristotle: indeed, Descartes admitted himself in 1627 a close relation between the ideas—at least some of them, particularly that of extension—and the imagination. For example in *Regula XIV*: "Ut vero aliquid etiam tunc imaginemur, nec intellectu puro utamur, sed speciebus in phantasia depictis adjuto [. . .] illam magnitudinis speciem, quae omnium facillime et distinctissime in imaginatione nostra pingetur—if we are to imagine something now, and make use not of the pure intellect, but of the intellect aided by images depicted in the imagination [. . .] that species of magnitude which is most readily and distinctly depicted in our imagination."[11] For the *figura* indeed defines the idea: "figuras [. . .] ostensum est quomodo per illas solas rerum omnium ideae fingi possint—figures, we have already shown how they can depict by means of themselves alone the ideas of all things" (450.10–13; CSM I, 64). But, and this point makes all the difference, figure defines only the idea insofar as it is imagined, insofar as it is produced first in and by the imagination: "nihil omnino facilius [sc. extensio] ab imaginatione nostra percipitur—there is nothing more easily perceived by our imagination [than extension]" (442.18ff; CSM I, 59). And so the privilege of the imagination comes down to the (Cartesian) doctrine of science: the imagination alone can make certain ideas (those of material or mathematical things) visible, that is *imaginable* [*figurable*] by reducing sensible qualities or relations between discontinuous orders of magnitudes with continuous orders of magnitudes and imaginable figures, according to the principle that "Eadam [sc. quæstio] est ad extensionem realem corporum transferenda et tota per nudas figuras imaginationi proponenda—[the problem] should be re-expressed in terms of the real extension of bodies and should be pictured in our imagination entirely by means of bare figures" (438.9–10; CSM I, 56). The imagination allows us to give a figure to what has none, to quantitatively model the qualitative, in short to produce evidence in questions that are initially obscure and confused. And yet, if it increases the evidence for some of them (those which bear on understanding or can be reduced to it), it does not include in itself alone all possible ideas and we cannot restrict their entire field to extension, and thus, to materiality.

It is then necessary to correct the terms of the debate: it is not about imagination as such, but rather, about ideas that would possibly be exempt from an exclusively figurative and imaginative conception. It is not about proving that *some* ideas are linked to the imagination (as everyone admits, thinking of mathematicians' ideas) but rather, if and how Descartes can demonstrate the possibility of *some* unimaginable ideas. And so, we must take up the list of unimaginable, and therefore purely intellectual, ideas that are the object of dispute.

§3. Ideas of God and the Self

And first off the idea of God. Let us fix the frame of the debate by Objection VII: "Si non detur Dei idea (non autem probatur dari)—if an idea of God has not been given (for it is not proven that one has been given)" (VII 183.13; CSM II, 129). Hobbes holds that, since we have no imaginable figure, and thus no image of God, we have thus no idea at all about him, according to a forcefully precise formula:

Hobbes, or the Idea and Being as Body 187

Est autem infiniti scientia finito quæsitori inacessabilis. Quicquid homines scimus a phantasmatis nostris didicimus; phantasma autem infiniti (sive magnitudine sive tempore) nullum est; neque enim homo neque ulla alia res, præterquam quæ ipsa infinita est, infiniti conceptionem ullam habere potest—But the science of the infinite is inaccessible to a finite mind. Everything that we know, as men, we learn from our imaginations; but there is no imagination of the infinite, either by magnitude or by time; for indeed no man and no other thing, except the one who is infinite, can have the least conception of the infinite.[12]

This blunt affirmation has the appearance of being obvious common sense—a finite mind cannot have an idea of the infinite. But this appearance covers up the crux of the question, which is far more complex (see Chapter 4, §5–7), and Descartes responds to it in two arguments.

First, as *ego*, man disposes of an "infinite will within us" or, more modestly, "tantam in me [sc. voluntatem] experior, ut nullius majoris ideam apprehendam—I experience in myself such a will such that I do not apprehend the idea of any [will] which would be greater"; and so I can and must recognize a will that is at least formally infinite; in this sense, I can thus equal the infinity of God, since my will bears in it his image and likeness; for, "ratione cujus imaginem quandam et similitudinem Dei me referre intelligo—it is by virtue of the will that I understand myself to bear in some way the image and likeness of God," although, clearly, I can only imagine by figure and in extension.[13] Descartes assumes without reserve the ontic paradox of a finite *res cogitans*, endowed with an infinite mode (the will); it is a fact of experience that even Hobbes himself does not contest. Next, the epistemological impossibility of knowing the infinite by the finite seems eminently questionable to Descartes. For the idea of the infinite not only does not require adequate comprehension but excludes it explicitly: "Nec obstat quod non comprehendam infinitum, vel quod alia innumera in Deo sint, quæ nec comprehendere, nec forte etiam attingere cogitatione, ullo modo possum; est enim de ratione infiniti, ut a me, qui sum finitus, non comprehendatur—it does not matter that I do not grasp or comprehend the infinite, or that there are countless additional attributes of God which I cannot in any way comprehend, and perhaps cannot even reach in my thought; it is in the nature of the infinite not to be comprehended by a finite being like myself." In other words, "idea enim infiniti, ut sit vera, nullo modo debet comprehendi, quoniam ipsa incomprehensibilitas in ratione formali infiniti continetur—the idea of the infinite, if it is to be a true idea, cannot be comprehended at all, since the impossibility of being comprehended is contained in the formal definition of the infinite."[14] Hobbes and Descartes thus perfectly agree on the incomprehensibility of the infinite by the finite; they differ only on the conclusion they draw from it: is it possible, or thinkable, to have an idea that is neither imaginable nor representable in extension by default, but incomprehensible by privilege? It must be, since according to Descartes we have real experience of it ("ut manifestum illam [sc. ideam] dari—as it is manifest that it [the idea] is given"[15]).

Once again, we observe that the debate does not concern the idea of the infinite as such, but the status that we must concede to its incomprehensibility: does it forbid having a knowledge of it, or not? In this regard, we might risk the following characterization of the two positions. Descartes, in the posture of a critical thinker (privileging the conditions of possibility of experience, and thus finitude), recognizes incomprehensibility as the very mode of apprehension of the idea of the infinite, a mode that is positive and unique. Hobbes, on the other hand, in the situation of a pre-critical thinker (dogmatically assimilating the known and the true), concludes from incomprehensibility of the infinite (for us) its unthinkability (in itself): what cannot be understood as an object cannot be conceived of at all: "Itaque nomen Dei non usurpatur ut illum *concipiamus* (est enim *incomprehensibilis* et magnitudo potentiæque ejus *inconceptibilis*) sed ut honoremus—And therefore the Name of God is used, not to make us *conceive* him; (for he is *Incomprehensible*; and his greatenesse, and power are *unconceivable*;) but that we may honour him." As a result, the distinction between conceiving and comprehending is discarded and knowledge is reduced to comprehension.[16] It obviously follows that philosophy excludes the knowledge of God (even, of course, according to his metaphysical name, as cause): "Itaque excludit a se Philosophia Theologiam, doctrinam dico de natura et attributis Dei, aeterni, ingenerabilis, incomprehensibilis et in quo nulla compositio, nulla divisio institui, nulla generatio intelligi potest—Therefore Philosophy excludes Theology from itself, I mean the doctrine of the nature and attributes of God, eternal, ungenerable, incomprehensible, and in whom no composition or division can be established, nor any generation be conceived."[17] But this conclusion concerns less the particular case of God than the general question of finitude and its status in philosophy.

We can now verify this by proceeding to the second debate, on the idea of the self. From his second objection, Hobbes argues thus: he admits that, from what I think (I cogitate), it follows that I am, and even that I am a *res cogitans* (we need not make an anticipation of Kant's objections here); but he contests that, from the very same fact that I am insofar as I think, it follows that I am rightly a "mens, animus, intellectus, ratio—a mind, or intelligence, or intellect, or reason" (it would instead be an anticipation of Nietzsche's objection). In short, I would no more be able to deduce from the fact that I am walking (*sum ambulans*) that I am a walk (*sum ambulatio*) than I would be able to deduce from the fact that I am thinking (*sum cogitans*) and cogitating by understanding (*sum intelligens*) that I am a thought or an understanding, that *sum cogitatio* or *sum intellectus*.[18] He asks on the other hand to carefully distinguish the *subjectum* and its faculties, from which it differs: for the *subjectum* differs from its accidents, attributes or qualities, in that it must always remain "*corporeum quid*—something corporeal," for "subjecta [. . .] omnium actuum videntur intelligi solummodo sub ratione corporea, sive sub ratione materiæ—the subjects [i.e., *hypokeimena*] of any act can be understood only in terms of a body or in terms of matter." In short, every substance should be understood as material: "Substantia enim (ut quae est materia subjecta accidentibus et mutationibus)—for substance (which is the matter as subject of accidental properties and of changes)."[19] Not only does every accident and attribute require a substrate, not only must every substrate be corporeal, and thus material, but this body, as material substrate, is sufficient to define substance.[20] The radical simplicity of these equivalences suffers no exception, and *especially not* even for the thing that I am when I think. Against appearances, the difficulty for Hobbes does not in the end come from the impossibility of redoubling the thinking of the self ("omnino est impossibile cogitare se cogitare—it is quite impossible for [someone] to think that he is thinking"—a thesis that, it must again be emphasized, Descartes himself had rejected—which Hobbes did not know);[21] it comes rather from the fact that this redoubling would lead to doing without a material *subjectum* for thought. From his point of view, by saying and thinking *ego sum, ego existo*, I certainly attain my existence by thought, but not by essence, which does not require thought, but, here as elsewhere, matter—a substance, therefore a body. By a paradox that is rather blunt, but infinitely less original than that of Descartes (my existence is verified by thought), Hobbes always wants to infer from an act of thought an essence defined by a material *subjectum*: "videtur inferendum potius rem cogitantem esse materialem quam immaterialem—it seems that we must infer that the thinking thing is material rather than immaterial" (AT VII, 174.1–2; CSM II, 123). It is surprising that such a cursory conclusion of Hobbes, which ignores Aristotle as much as Descartes, should have found so many favorable echoes, from Gassendi and Regius to the present day.

The first debate led to the epistemological question of whether the idea of the infinite is an exception (or not) to the requirements of imagination. But the second leads to the ontic question of a definition of substance in general as exclusively material.

§4. *The Question of Substance*

Let us take up the third question, which underlies the prior ones: must substance always be understood as material and thus corporeal? What does a *body* really mean here?

On this difficulty (as on the difficulty of thinking by imagination), Hobbes here relies closely on Aristotle, both for the choice of sublunar *ousia* as a point of departure for the analysis of every being and for the principle that, at least in sublunar space, "All other things are predicated of *ousia*, but this is predicated of matter, *hylē*."[22] This fidelity would be worth questioning all the more when it is deployed against the backdrop of a constant and ostensibly virulent polemic against the "scholastics" and Aristotelians. It would be worth questioning it even more from the fact that it is diverted from one of the most consistent aims of Aristotle: to admit, attain, and know as much as possible separated *ousiai*—separated from every matter and potentiality and therefore united to themselves. And so the unacknowledged orthodoxy toward Aristotle's material ousiology is overturned in a militant omission of the immaterial *ousia* of the divine and its primacy. This relation to Aristotle is too ambivalent to allow clarification of Hobbes' decision about substance.

And so I will risk another hypothesis: that Hobbes, anticipating with a remarkable clairvoyance the aporias of the future Cartesian treatise on substance (*Principia philosophiæ I*, §51–54), tried a radical, even drastic solution.[23] For the thesis of Descartes indeed presents at least one weakness, found in his discussion with Hobbes in 1641. On the one hand, the *cogitatio* admits and demands a substrate: "*cogitationem non posse esse sine re cogitante*—a cogitation cannot exist without a thing that is cogitating" (VII, 175.26; CSM II, 124), therefore without a substance, anticipating as well the definition of 1644: "Per *substantiam*, nihil aliud intelligere possumus quam rem quæ ita existit, ut nulla alia re indigeat ad existendum—by *substance* we can understand nothing other than a thing which exists in such a way as to depend on no other thing for its existence" (*Principia philosophiæ I*, §51; CSM I, 210). On the other hand, this substance will differ according to whether it provides a substrate of "quite different acts or accidents—*plane diversorum*" (VII, 176.5; CSM II, 124); spiritual or material substrates must therefore be admitted according to whether the acts and accidents are this or that, thus defining two *rationes communes* of substance after two principal attributes[24] (thought and extension).

The difficulty of such a distinction between kinds of substances according to the "reasons" of accidents and attributes becomes abundantly clear. For, according to Descartes himself, substance as such is not "immediate—immediately" accessible starting from primary attributes, since it does not bear any similitude with them; ensuring that without them and as such, as pure existing substrate, substance "nos non afficit—does not affect us."[25] It is therefore necessary to bridge this gap, widened by the lack of immediacy, precisely by relying on attributes, following the principle that they should be attributed to something (=X), since nothing has no property. But, to the extent that we can admit that these attributes must refer to a substrate existing by itself (although strictly speaking this is only true of God), we cannot know it, recognize it, or identify it (as extended/material or as thought/immaterial) on the model of these attributes, precisely because they do not reach it themselves and are distinguished from it. The existence of a substance can be inferred from its attributes, *but not its essence*. What the *ego sum* has already established (I know that I am, but I do not know what I am) must now be generalized to all cases: the substance remains unknown and anonymous, even if it exists, or precisely *because it exists* purely and simply. By what right, then, can we differentiate several substances according to their different attributes, if their essences remain inaccessible, and thus undetermined? And what gain can we even expect from this fantastical imposition? To the contrary, a radical and simple solution imposes itself: admit only one substance (undifferentiated or, what comes down to the same thing, absorbing all determinations without exception) for all the primary attributes. Spinoza will choose this simple and effective path. Berkeley will offer a brilliant variant: suppressing every substance and every substrate as well, and thus all matter, since it does not affect us.[26]

In this context, the decision of Hobbes is surprising, but less by its audacity or radicality than by its timidity, or even conformism.[27] For it consists in saying quite simply, "Subjectum Philosophiæ, sive materia circa quam versatur, est corpus omne—the subject [*hypokeimenon, subjectum*] of Philosophy, or the matter it treats of, is every body"; or "Philosophia est corporum [...] acquisita cognitio—philosophy is the knowledge acquired by the body," or again, "philosophia prima, ubi agitur de corpore—first philosophy, where the body is discussed."[28] Put otherwise: starting from the Cartesian aporia stigmatized by him (and others), which wishes to establish that the (rational?) distinction of attributes or accidents does not by principle allow us to conclude a (real?) distinction of substance, Hobbes concludes that every attribute, even intellectual, relies on a substance that is always and univocally material: "materia prima est corpus universal—prime matter is a universal body."[29] But the argument is immediately overturned: by what right can we still qualify the substance as material, if the attributes say nothing about the essence of the substance? Or again: why deny intellectual attributes the faculty to define a substance by pronouncing it as immaterial, if only to grant material attributes (extension and its modes), at the same moment and without any other argument, the faculty of defining a substance and pronouncing it as material, while matter and spirit are, rigorously speaking, only attributes and accidents? If the attribute of thought does not allow us to qualify a substance as thinking, how would the attribute of extension allow us to qualify a substance as extended and thus material, or even more, to make it the only substance under the partial and biased title of an attribute of extension? Is this, for Hobbes, a masked conceptual decision or a manifest inconsistency? It hardly matters, as long as we can at least explain the reasons.

§5. *The Privilege of Simple Material Natures*

I suggest several. The first argument comes from the doctrine of science: I will thus call it *epistemological*. In his 1641 response to Hobbes, Descartes opposes (in §4) two "common reasons" of substance to distinguish two substrates (*subjecta*), and he goes back to their "acts" in two sets: on the one hand, "magnitudo, figura, motus et alia omnia quæ absque locali extensione cogitari non possunt—size, shape, motion and all others [notions] that cannot be thought of apart from local extension," and on the other, "intelligere, velle, imaginari, sentire, etc., qui omnes [sc. actus] sub ratione communi cogitationis, sive perceptionis, sive conscientiæ, conveniunt—understanding, willing, imagining, having sensory perceptions, and so on, these [acts] all fall under the common concept of thought or perception or consciousness."[30] Where do these two sets come from? Clearly, from what in 1627 Descartes meant by simple natures, and which he distinguished on the one hand as simple material natures, "quæ non nisi in corporibus esse cognoscuntur: ut sunt figura, extensio, motus etc.—which are recognized only in bodies—such as shape, extension and motion, etc.," and, on the other, by simple intellectual natures,

quæ per lumen quoddam ingenitum et absque ullius imaginationis corporeæ adjumento ab intellectu cognoscuntur: tales enim nonnullas esse certum est, nec ulla fingi potest idea corporea quæ nobis repræsentet, quid sit cognitio, quid dubium, quid ignorantia, item quid sit voluntatis actio, quam volitionem liceat appellare, et similia—which the intellect recognizes by means of a sort of light placed in us by nature and without the aid of any corporeal image. That there is a number of such things is certain: it is impossible to form any corporeal idea which makes present for us what knowledge or doubt or ignorance is, or the action of the will, which may be called "volition," and the like.[31]

This dichotomy, first instituted to define the *Mathesis universalis*, spans all his work, and it would be impossible to underestimate its architectonic importance.[32] It may be that Hobbes had taken advantage of it, if only by a reading of the *Meditationes* (or even the *Regulæ*, copies of which were circulating around Mersenne), and it would make sense to determine what he retained from it. From this we may draw a conclusion: Hobbes only retained Descartes' simple natures as material, as the *De Corpore* literally confirms: "corpus sive materia, quantitas sive extensio, motus simpliciter, denique quæ omni materiae insunt—body or matter, quantity or extension, movement understood simply (i.e. local), and finally what belongs to all matter," for "non omnia accidentia suis corporibus ita inesse, sicut inest extensio, motus, quies, aut figura; exempli causa calorem, colorem, odorem, virtutem, vitium et similia, aliter inesse et (ut dicunt) inhærere—All accidents are not [inherent] in their [respective] bodies in the same way as extension, motion, rest, or figure; for example, colour, heat, odour, virtue, vice, and the like, are in them and (as they say) *adhere* to them otherwise."[33] This reduction of simple natures to simple material natures alone goes so far that it requires transposing man's intellectual properties into a *subjectum* that is itself material, and in terms of exclusively material simple natures. Hobbes claims at the same time to recognize in man only corporeal (material) determinations *and* assume in him intellectual faculties *in these very terms*: thus the problematic juxtapositions that "homo est *corpus animatum sentiens rationale*—man is an *animated, sentient, and rational body*"; but is lining up qualifiers enough to unify them? Surely the "parts" of man are themselves "non [. . .] caput, humeros, brachia, etc., sed figuram, quantitatem, motum, *sensionem, ratiocinationem et similia*—not [. . .] his head, his shoulders, his arms, etc., but his figure, quantity, motion, *sense, reason, and the like*"; but, once again, can we enumerate without transition, or articulation, simple material natures (figure, quality) and simple intellectual natures (sense, reason)? To understand the mind, is it enough to define it as "corpus tenue—a thin body"?[34] Or, more simply, without contradiction or approximation, what is such a body, so tenuous that it provides no extension? Claiming to dispense with simple intellectual natures, or to reduce them effectively to simple material natures alone, is surely not enough to achieve it.

Let us come to a provisional conclusion. Hobbes takes up the doctrine of simple natures elaborated by the *Regulæ* (and maintained in the *Meditationes*) but chooses to use only simple material natures, and so concentrates exclusively on the study of the body; or rather to apply only simple material natures not only to bodies but also to intellectual functions, now deprived of their own simple natures. This is not only a matter of eliminating them but also of substituting them with simple material natures, even to discuss matters of thought. But Descartes, who did not even consider such a *metabasis eis allo genos*, such a grammatical error, would open another possibility in 1627 (even if he did not develop it so explicitly until 1641): he already mentioned simple intellectual natures, and even sketched a first use of them, which anticipated the first principle, *cogito, sum*. "Uniusquisque animo potest intueri se existere, se cogitare—everyone can see by the mind that he exists, that he is thinking."[35] Hobbes also takes an alternative (reducing all simple natures to simple material natures alone) that Descartes never follows, since the *Regulæ* by contrast already offer the lineaments of a specific (non-material) use of simple intellectual natures; Hobbes thus borrows his fundamental concepts (simple material natures) from the *Regulæ*, while condemning other concepts that are just as fundamental for Descartes (simple intellectual natures). Descartes also does not reproach him for his borrowing, but for the condemnation; not for following his path, but leaving it too quickly and too cheaply: "I am not worried that his philosophy resembles mine—although, like me, he wants to restrict his attention to shapes and movements. These are indeed the true principles, but if one makes mistakes in following them, the errors can be spotted very clearly by those with the modicum of understanding; so if we want to achieve success, we must not go as fast as he does."[36] Hobbes therefore does not so much critique Descartes as disregard his principles, while holding them hostage to a narrow reading of the *Regulæ*.

§6. Conceived Being, or the Body

The Hobbesian thesis thus has nothing unexpected, or new, or subtle, but results from a simplification of the Cartesian doctrine of science. And so it would seem perfectly arbitrary, if we did not assign to it its final motive, which comes down more to the theory of being—to an *ontic* decision. This thesis is formulated as follows: substance is only corporeal, thus material: "*sub ratione substantiæ* (vel etiam, si lubet, *sub ratione materiæ*, nempe Metaphysicæ)—*in terms of substance* (or even, if he insists, *in terms of matter*, i.e. metaphysical matter)"; such that "Subjectum Philosophiae [. . .] est corpus omne—the subject of Philosophy is every body."[37] Two primary arguments support this.

Originally, an opposition is established between substance, understood as a body, and accident: "Rerum autem nominatarum genera quattuor sunt, nimirum *corpora, accidentia, phantasmata et nomina ipsa*—there are four kinds of things which are named, namely, *bodies, accidents, imaginations, and names themselves*"; or again the opposition of matter, as a body, to some accident: "utrum ea res, cujus causam quærimus materia sit, sive corpus, an corporis accidens, aliquod—whether the thing whose cause is sought after is matter or body or some accident of body?"[38] These oppositions are also surprising, and for two reasons; first of all because, on the one hand, they assimilate an indisputably ontic term (accident) with two others (phantasm and names) that remain strictly noetic; next because, on the other hand, they identify terms (body, matter, even substance) that are ontically different, even incompatible between themselves. We must suppose that another difference, more radical than their (ontico-noetic) heterogeneities, assures these two groups the possibility of opposing each other. What other difference?

It is (at least it seems) a difference between two kinds of *entia*: on the one hand, beings that cannot be imagined and that thus remain incomprehensible (angels and God), and on the other, the *ens imaginabile*, imaginable and thus comprehensible: in other words,

omissa definitione *entis* quod non est imaginabile, et quod appellari solet substantia incorporea, definiemus *ens imaginabile* tantum. Est igitur *ens*, in hoc sensu id omne quod definiti spatium, sive id quod æstimari potest longitudine, latitudine et profunditate. Ex qua definitione apparet idem esse *ens et corpus*—Leaving aside the definition of *being* which is not imaginable, and which we usually call an incorporeal substance, we will define only *imaginable being*. *Being* in this sense is everything which occupies space, or everything which can be estimated [measured] in length, width, and depth. From this definition, it follows that being and body are the same.

From now on, if the body takes nothing less than the rank of being as being, it logically follows that everything which does not form a body passes to the side of non-beings (or non-imaginables). And so the *ens imaginabile*, the only thing real, is opposed even to *esse*, now paradoxically become unreal. Indeed, strictly speaking, "*esse nihil aliud sit præter accidens corporis*, quo modus ipsum concipiendi determinatur et distinguitur—*being is nothing other than the accident of a body*, by which is determined and distinguished the very way of conceiving it."[39] The distinction thus seems clear: not only is there a difference between the ontic (the real *ens*) and ontological (the irreal *esse*), but it results in privileging the ontic over being itself, as only beings succeed in being identified in and as a body. It is thus a matter of an ontico-ontological difference, which overturns the ontological difference in the modern sense, and which only operates by a simple difference between the corporeal and everything else. The body is sufficient to organize and differentiate the field of being and beings.

But where does the body draw its extraordinary privilege over this remainder? Hobbes puts forward two criteria, independence and anteriority. Independence from imagination, first: the corporeal being is "aliquid quod ab imaginatione nostra non dependet—something that does not depend on our imagination"; also independence from thought in general: "Itaque definitio corporis hujusmodi est: *corpus est quicquid non dependens a nostra cogitatione cum spatii parte aliqua coïncidit vel coextenditur*—The definition, therefore, of body may be defined as *the sort of thing which, having no dependence upon our thought, coincides with some part of space or is coextensive with it.*"[40] Yet, this independence opens as many difficulties as it resolves. First, it is only a question of an epistemological independence: the body, which does not depend on my knowledge, is that on which my knowledge depends; but is a simple independence from thought enough to define an irreducible and autonomous ontic independence? To achieve this, shouldn't Hobbes go farther and found the independence of the body in the body itself, positively and not relative to thought? But how, then, can we avoid restoring or trying to restore Aristotle's *ousia*, which alone is absolute and independent in this strict sense, because "no *ousia* is said to be of [is not numbered among] relative terms"?[41] This path, in any case, is one Hobbes has already closed. How, then, can we attain an independence that is not only epistemological, but ontic?

At this point a second difficulty arises: these two kinds of independence cannot be added to each other, but instead exclude one another. Descartes knew this and assumed it fully. In the *Regulæ*, all notions, including those that are qualified as absolute (not relative to the others, independent), only remain independent insofar as the series of knowledges begins through them, but not to the extent that they would not depend on knowledge itself. Every notion and every being depends on the *mens*, such as they must relate "ad nostrum propositum—to our project." Everything is, and especially in the domain of simple material natures, only "in quantum unae ex aliis cognosci possunt—in so far as some things can be known on the basis of others."[42] But did Hobbes not implicitly assume his Cartesian position—the universal dependence of the known on the *mens*, the universal dependence of being on knowledge—when he proposed *ens* as *imaginabile*, as *corpus*? How could what is "imaginabile tantum—only imaginable" remain also at the same time and under the same relation "non dependens a nostra cogitatione—not dependent on our thought"— except by imagining an imagination that does not think? The reduction to the being of the body therefore does not confer on it any ontic independence, since the imaginable character of the body submits it first to a radical epistemological dependence on imagination, thus on the thought of the *mens*. In other words, the privilege of the imaginability of the material body *contradicts* its independence from thought, even its claim to ontic anteriority.

And so without a doubt we reach the heart of the debate between Hobbes and Descartes, admittedly hidden at first sight: does the primacy of simple natures, even material ones, abstracted from simple intellectual natures, depend from the outset and by definition on the anteriority of the perspective of thought over the known, and thus from the primacy of the *mens*? Does the (ontic) materialism of Hobbes not contradict itself, by claiming to suppress what makes it possible—the (epistemological) primacy of the imagination, and thus of the *mens*? If one objection must ruin the enterprise of Hobbes, it would not so much be the dogmatic claim to materialism, as the transcendental conditions of science, which he himself presupposes in a confused way.

§7. *The Irreducible Privilege of the* Cogitatio

But does Hobbes precisely not admit, be it only implicitly and factually, that the body (which, for him, is the only being qua being allowed) still depends on thought, therefore on its representation and conception, so that the primacy and anteriority return to the *mens*, with a genuine independence? Despite the dogma of its independence from the imagination, many arguments tend to establish this without contest. Hobbes would therefore remain more faithful to the logical conditions of his argument than to his declared dogmatic intention. Here philosophy would ultimately prevail for him over ideology.

In a first argument: the body receives its privilege from the priority of the perspective of thought and for its conceptions: "Exempli causa, in conceptu hominis [...] primus *conceptus* est, eum aliquid esse extensum, cui rei *notandae* adhibitum nomen *corpus*—for example, in the conception of man [...] the first *concept* is, that he is something extended, a thing which is *marked* by using the word *body*." Or again,

Hobbes, or the Idea and Being as Body   199

Exempli grata cum aliquid videamus, vel visibile aliquid *animo concipiamus*, apparet illa res, vel *concipitur* non in uno puncto, sed ut habens partes a partibus distantes, id est, ut extensa per spatium aliquod; quoniam igitur *rem ita conceptam* voluimus appellari *corpus*—For example, when we see something, or *conceive by our mind* some visible thing, that thing appears to us, or is *conceived*, not as being [constricted] into one single point, but as having parts distant from one another, that is, as extended through some space. This therefore is why we wanted the *thing so conceived* [i.e. by concept] to be called *corpus*.[43]

Thus the body, too, and it first, *is conceived*, and in this alone consists its entire privilege over the non-body: it is primary because it is the first conceived, the first thing as conceived first: "actus corporis, h. e. *entis conceptibilis*—the act of a body, that is, of a *being which is conceivable* [by concept]"; in other words, when we say *corpus*, we mean *ens conceptibilis* and, when I say *essentia*, "intelligo semper *conceptibilem*—I always understand a *conceivable* [essence]."[44]

From this follows a second argument: for we understand better, in this framework, the derived status of names, of *esse* and accidents, which are still without explanation. In fact, their secondary character results from what we conceive only after, from and under the condition of *ens ut corpus*, itself conceived first, in virtue of its privilege of imaginability. They also belong to "*concipiendi* corporis modus—the mode of *conceiving* a body,"[45] but a second mode and dependent on the prior concept of body. We no longer hesitate before this nevertheless surprising conclusion from a supposed "materialist," that "the *esse* too belongs to the order of the conceivable."[46]

To this we can add a third argument, taken from the *annihilatio mundi*, since, like the analysis of the piece of wax and like every reduction, it only ends up granting validity to ideas:

Dico igitur *remensuras* illi homini, mundi et corporum omnium, quae ante sublationem eorum, oculis aspexerat vel aliis sensibus perceperat, *ideas*, id est memoriam imaginationemque magnitudinum, motuum, sonorum, colorum, etc., atque etiam eorum ordinis et partium; quae omnia, etsi *ideae tantum et phantasmata* sint, ipsi *imaginanti interne* accidentia, nihilominus *tanquam externa* et a virtute animae *minime* dependentia *apparitura* esse—I say, therefore, there would *remain* to that man *ideas* of the world, and of all bodies which before their removal he had seen with his eyes, or perceived by the other senses; that is, memory and imagination of magnitudes, motions, sounds, colours, etc, as also of their order and parts. All these things, though they be nothing *but ideas and imaginations*, of accidents internal to the one who imagines, will nevertheless *appear as if they were external*, and depending only *very little* on any virtue of the mind.[47]

We find here an exact anticipation of what contemporary thought has called transcendence in immanence: what appears as external and independent of the mind nevertheless *still* appears there, as an (imagined) idea in the mind. But what this doctrine shows negatively—the world disappears, leaving us its ideas—Hobbes also formulates positively, in his no less famous definition of the science of phenomena.

Phænomena autem appellantur quæcumque apparent sive a natura nobis sunt ostensa.
  Phænomenōn autem omnium, quae prope nos existunt, id ipsum τὸ φαίνεσθαι est admirabilissimum, nimirum, in corporibus naturalibus omnium alia fere rerum, alia nullarum in seipsis exemplaria habere; adeo ut si phaenomena principia sint *cognoscendi* caetera, sensionem *cognoscendi* ipsa principia principium esse, scientiamque omnem ab ea derivari dicendum est, et ad causarum ejus investigationem ab alio phaenomeno, praeter eam ipsam, initium sumi non posse.—
  We call phenomena whatever appears or is shown to us by nature.
  Of all the phenomena which exist near us, the most admirable is appearing itself, *to phainesthai*; certainly, in their natural bodies some have in them the exemplars of almost all things, and others of none at all. So that if phenomena are the principles for *knowing* others, sensation is the principle for *knowing* the principles themselves, and science must be said to be derived entirely from it, and in the search for causes [science] cannot begin from any other phenomenon except sense itself.[48]

If, by *sensio*, by sensation in the broadest sense (in fact the *nous* of principles according to Aristotle), we mean the principle of knowledge of principles, we must obviously conclude from this that knowledge determines every apprehension of the body, and thus all beingness [*étantité*].

If we admit these arguments, it becomes possible to read literally the definition of the object of metaphysics (or first philosophy): "*notionem* τοῦ ὄντος, id est entis, communissimam omnium esse—the *notion* of *to on*, that is, being, is the most common of all."[49] This could be surprising, since the identification of *ens* with *corpus* is missing. In fact, it is not missing, for being paradoxically takes the name of body precisely because it can just as well *be conceived*, that is, be imagined. Indeed, "Subjectum Philosophæ, sive *materia* circa quam versatur, est *corpus omne*, cujus generatio aliqua *concipi*—The subject of Philosophy, or the *matter* it treats of, is every body of which we can *conceive* some generation."[30] What Hobbes calls *corpus* anticipates a possible materialism only insofar as it first and foremost recasts the interpretation of *ens* as a *conceptus* [*entis*], as it arose from Duns Scouts to Suarez, and soon as a *cogitabile*, as Timpler, Calov, Clauberg, and Wolff christened it under the name *ontologia*.[51]

The war between Hobbes and Descartes has thus taken place. It is clear that Hobbes indeed attempted a rupture with Aristotle, but without pushing the deconstruction as far as the *Regulæ* attempted to do. First of all, because he only professes simple material natures, without recognizing the intellectual ones, or their epistemological primacy. Next because, against the *Regulæ*, which remain still metaphysically neutral and pre-ontological ("grey" ontology, confined to the only object of the *Mathesis universalis*), simple material natures could and, for Hobbes, should ensure a full ontology from the outset, in black and white, supporting the entire weight of metaphysics. Of a metaphysics, or a first philosophy? This debate, rather abstract and arbitrary, hardly matters. For a *philosophia prima*, what is essential is to determine which type of primacy it recognizes, what being it concedes that primacy to, and within what onto-theology it includes it. Descartes first recognizes primacy as knowledge and the *cogitatio*, thus assigning it to the *ego*. Spinoza recognized it as the infinite, unique, and indeterminate *substantia*, and Malebranche as the infinite and eternal understanding of order; both therefore assigned it to God. Hobbes recognizes only the primacy of the *physica*, whether that of the individual body, or that of the body politic—but does this not leave undetermined the knowledge that defines this body and establishes it in its primacy? What missing *mens* haunts this prized body?

EIGHT

Spinoza, or the Unification of the Proofs of God's Existence

§1. Delay and Divergence

Spinoza does not begin with God, any more than Descartes does. And God, for him, is not in the beginning, even if the *ego cogito* isn't, either. What opposes him to Descartes is to be found elsewhere.

Indeed, neither the *Treatise on the Emendation of the Intellect* nor, more importantly, the *Ethics* opens by demonstration of the existence of God or a determination of his essence, even if they do not set the *ego cogito* as their principle. We should, however, be a little more surprised at the eight definitions that open the first part of the *Ethics*. First of all because the definition that introduces God (I, D6) ("ens absolute infinitum, hoc est substantiam constantem infinitis attributis, quorum unumquodque æternam et infinitam essentiam exprimit—being absolutely infinite, i.e., a substance consisting [*constans*] of an infinity of attributes, of which each one expresses an eternal and infinite essence"[1]) only arises in the sixth place, just after the definitions of the finite (D2), substance (D3), attribute (D4), and even mode (D5), so that, if ontically God consists of attributes, his definition *results* above all and as well from those that logically preceded him; as a result God is not ontologically first, because he is not logically first. This first observation is all the more surprising if we consider the first definition: "Per causam sui, intelligo id, cujus essentia involvit existentiam; sive id, cujus natura non potest concipi nisi existens—by cause of itself I understand that whose essence involves existence, *or* that whose nature cannot be conceived except by existing" (I, D1). It is surprising, first of all, that the *causa sui* is not explained here by causality, but by the implication of existence in essence, following another logic, that which the subsequent tradition will name the "ontological argument"; why this shift and this collusion, right away and without explanation? It is further surprising that this title of *causa sui*, invented by Descartes not without precautions for the unique case of God, intervenes precisely without mentioning God—unless it is moving so quickly that the equivalence is taken for granted. Finally, one wonders if, in this last case (the most probable, we will see, after P11), the existence of God might not be found at the outset, and already demonstrated *by definition*, because already included in the essence. Yet this is not the case, since it will take seven more axioms and 11 propositions to finally establish the existence of God that Definition 6 brings into play: "Deus, sive substantia constans infinitis attributis, quorum unumquodque æternam et infinitam essentiam exprimit, necessario existit—God, *or* a substance consisting of infinite attributes, each of which expresses eternal and infinite essence, necessarily exists" (I, P11). And so, the existence and the essence of God arise too early and without mentioning God, but explicitly too late to claim the primacy of the concepts that, logically, make them thinkable.

This enigmatic delay cannot be explained here by the epistemological anteriority of the finite *cogitatio* over the infinite, as in the Cartesian system; for the *ego cogito* will be marginalized and finite thought will enter onto the scene only in the second part of the *Ethics*, precisely as it will be overcome by taking up the infinite point of view and the adequate idea. The delay results rather from the supposedly geometrical order of the *mos geometricus* claimed by Spinoza, precisely against Descartes and his reservations in the appendix of the *IIæ Responsiones*. Could it, then, be one of the reversals of priority that metaphysicians admit and often claim as a requirement, the priority of logic over the divine, in Hegel's sense: "Therefore, if in the expression of the absolute, or the eternal, or God (and God would have the perfectly undisputed right that the beginning be made with him), if in the intuition or the thought of them, there is more than there is in pure being, then this more should first emerge in a knowledge which is thinking and not representing"?[2] Clearly and immediately (starting from the *causa sui* and with Definition 6), it is no longer for Spinoza as for Hegel a matter of pure and simple being (*reines Sein*), but something that must be "thought" and not only "represented." However, if it is a question of thinking rather than representing, is this not precisely what Descartes sought to do (and succeeded), when he thought what we think when we think, when he thought it in act, in doubt, and brought to light in it not the uncertainty of the represented, but the certainty of the existence of the one who thinks, the *ego*? But this path will be closed by Spinoza, who degrades the *ego sum, ego existo* to the inglorious rank of the simple observation that "*Homo cogitat*" (*Ethics II*, A2). Was Hegel not thinking of Descartes, rather, when he celebrated him as the inventor of what finally pointed to the philosophical horizon of modernity, the identity between thought (in act) and being (in actuality in the concept), an identity that is accomplished in the *ego cogito*? And yet, if the supposedly geometrical order is unable to begin with the ego, it would have to begin with a principle that was absolutely first, therefore absolute; Spinoza assumes this requirement and the *Ethics* should therefore begin with God, and the title of its first book claims it. However, and this is my question, by delaying the final definition of God and the proof of his existence until P11, *Ethics I* seems to leave us with a difficulty: it is not enough for the geometrical order to renounce the primacy of the *ego* for it to succeed all at once in establishing the primacy of God.

Ethics I, P11 thus poses questions more than it provides answers.[3] First of all, as has been noted, this late demonstration that "*Deus* [. . .] *necessario existit*—God [. . .] necessarily exists" is all the more striking in that it took ten propositions and demonstrations to arrive at this conclusion. Also, this conclusion might seem useless, since it literally reiterates the prior definition of the divine essence ("ens absolute infinitum, hoc est substantiam constantem infinitis attributis, quorum unumquodque æternam et infinitam essentiam exprimit—a being absolutely infinite, i.e., a substance consisting of an infinity of attributes, of which each one expresses an eternal and infinite essence," D6 = "Deus, sive substantia constans infinitis attributis, quorum unumquodque æternam et infinitam essentiam exprimit—God, or a substance consisting of infinite attributes, each of which expresses eternal and infinite essence, necessarily exists," P11). Even further, whatever its motive, this identical reiteration of the same definition underlines the offset between essence and existence, in contradiction to their identification by the *causa sui* as "id, cujus essentia involvit existentiam—that whose essence involves existence" (D1): Spinoza does not begin with God, because God does not begin with his existence, as this existence is delayed by its own essence. God therefore lags behind himself; his beginning does not coincide with the beginning. Next, this Definition 1, while taken up in the body of P11, will no longer appear either in the demonstrations nor in the scholium that follows them, where it thus plays no role. Everything takes place as if the so-to-speak official definition of God did not allow or was not sufficient to demonstrate his existence, which nevertheless must belong immediately to the essence of the *causa sui* (D1), or, following Descartes, result from the a priori proof. Finally, this defect finds confirmation in a major fact: not only does P11 never use its own definition of God for proving his existence in its demonstrations, and thus literally does not prove the existence of the essence as defined, or in short, does not prove the existence of *this essence* supposed of God; but above all it mobilizes three demonstrations (one *demonstratio* or two *aliter*) or even four (if we add the argument of the scholium), none of which mention Definition 6, cited in P11. Each of these demonstrations relies on other definitions, different from each other, and all different from the definition nevertheless cited in P11, whose existence it was necessary to prove. Everything thus happens as if Spinoza proved the existence of *other* essences of God than the one put forward by Definition 6 and repeated by the body of P11.[4]

The divergence between the definition of God advanced in the proposition and those actually used in the demonstrations is all the more striking since P11 admits a number of demonstrations; yet the *Ethics* offers no other example of a triple (or even quadruple) demonstration of the same proposition.[5] What is the significance of this exception? At the very least this: delaying the demonstration of the existence of God until after the definition of his essence provokes in turn the multiplication of the essence of God, that is, its bursting open. Everything happens as if, in God according to Spinoza, not only does existence lag behind essence, but it lags behind *several* competing essences. But we see here, already and almost at once, how problematic it becomes to claim that the "mens humana adæquatam habet cognitionem æternæ et infinitæ essentiæ Dei—the human Mind has an adequate knowledge of God's eternal and infinite essence" (*Ethics II*, P47). For, beyond the incomprehensibility belonging to the formal reason of the infinite, and escaping (positively) by definition *every* adequate comprehension (Descartes), one will object to this delusion of presumption (to speak like Kant) that if, according to Spinoza's own theses, this essence itself can be defined by *several* meanings (or conceptual idols), it would not as a result allow for the least adequate knowledge.

§2. The Cartesian Origin of the Multiplication of Proofs

To confirm the consequences of this multiplication of definitions of God, we must first more precisely identify them, and above all understand why they should remain distinct. The hypothesis of my reading consists in identifying a Cartesian origin for each of the three (or four) demonstrations of P11.

The first demonstration neither repeats Definition 6 nor the terms of the body of P11. It introduces an argument by absurdity: it is impossible to conceive the divine essence as non-existent, because then its essence would not include its existence (following A7); or, as we already know, by P7, because "Ad naturam substantiæ pertinet existere—it pertains to the nature of a substance to exist"; therefore, as substance, God necessarily exists. On the other hand, the demonstration does not indicate if and why God is a substance, which is all the more surprising as Definition 6 (cited by the body of P11) mentions it. Moreover, one could defend this by a quicker and simpler argument: since God is defined as a substance (D6), and because it belongs to every substance to exist (P7, by D1 of the *causa sui*), God already exists, well before the first demonstration of P11. Why, then, resort to a conclusion *already* established, directly and positively, after the fact, and by reversing it negatively into an argument by absurdity? Perhaps because Spinoza appeals to *another* argument than the one we have reconstituted according to his indications. This underlying argument can be detected in the (absurd) counterargument that "[God's] essence does not involve existence—[Dei] essentia non involvit existentiam"; this phrase is almost a reversal of the formulation of the so-called ontological argument, as Spinoza's prior reading of Descartes' *Principia philosophiæ* reports it: "ab hoc solo [sequitur], quod ad Dei naturam pertinet existentia, sive, quod Dei conceptus involvit necessariam existentiam, sicut conceptus trianguli, quod ejus tres anguli sint æquæs duaobus rectis; sive, quod ejus existentia, non secus, atque ejus essentia, sit æterna veritas—on this alone [it follows]: that existence pertains to the nature of God, *or* that the concept of God involves necessary existence, as the concept of a triangle involves that its three angles are equal to two right angles, or that his existence, no less than his essence, is an eternal truth."[6] In doing this, Spinoza refers, on the one hand, to the summary in geometrical order from *IIæ Responsiones* (which he always privileged): "existentia necessaria in Dei conceptu continetur. Ergo verum est de Deo dicere, necessariam existentiam in eo esse, sive ipsum existere—necessary existence is contained in the concept of God. So, it is true to say of God that necessary existence is in him, *or* that he exists"; and, on the other, to *Mediatio V*:

Certe ejus ideam, nempe entis summe perfecti, non minus apud me invenio, quam ideam cujusvis figuræ aut numeri; nec minus clare et distincte intelligo ad ejus naturam pertinere ut semper existat, quam id quod de aliqua figura aut numero demonstro ad ejus figuræ aut numeri naturam etiam pertinere—Certainly, the idea of God, or a supremely perfect being, is one which I find within me no less than the idea of any shape or number. And I understand no less clearly and distinctly that it belongs to his nature that he always exists, than [I understand] what belongs as well to the nature of some shape or number which I demonstrate.[7]

And so, in this first demonstration of P11, Spinoza takes over the a priori argument of *Meditatio V*, with all its harmonics (priority of the geometrical order, comparison of the divine essence with mathematical truths, the inherence of perfection and properties in essence, etc.). This is why we can reasonably admit that he also assumes the Cartesian definition of God, which supports the a priori argument, God as *ens summe perfectum*.[8]

The second demonstration (*aliter*) offers two remarkable features. First, it uses redundantly the phrase "*causa sive/seu ratio*" (nine occurrences) and it invokes from the outset the principle of causality (or of reason?): "Cujuscunque rei assignari debet causa seu ratio, tam cur existit, quam cur non existit—for each thing there must be a sign of cause, or reason, as much for its existence as for its nonexistence" (P11, *aliter*). Do these features allow reconstitution of a Cartesian origin? Perhaps, if we take into consideration the fact that the phrase *cause sive ratio*, although rather rare, appears in Descartes, precisely in the *more geometrico* appendix to *IIæ Responsiones*: "Nulla res existit de qua non possit quæri quænam sit causa cur existat. Hoc enim de ipso Deo quæri potest, non quod indigeat ulla causa ut existat, quia ipsa ejus naturæ immensitas est *causa sive ratio*, propter quam nulla causa indiget ad existendum—There is no thing that exists of which it is not possible to ask the cause why it exists. For this question may even be asked concerning God, not because he needs any cause in order to exist, but because the immensity of his nature is the *cause or reason* why he needs no [other] cause in order to exist."⁹ The point of their agreement is obvious: not only must there always be a cause to produce existence as a fact, but existence is established through the mediation of casualty, which alone can justify it by right. The case of God is no exception to this requirement, since the absence of a cause of his existence already has a reason, and a good reason: the immensity of his nature; so there remains by right a reason for justifying the absence of cause. Spinoza unambiguously submits God himself to the properly metaphysical requirement of a principle that is logically and therefore ontically prior to him, the reason of the cause, and in this way follows a decision that is just as explicit in Descartes: "Dictat autem profecto lumen naturæ nullam rem existere, de qua non liceat petere cur existat, sive in ejus causam efficientem inquirere, aut, si non habet, cur illa non indigeat, postulare—For it is indeed a *diktat* of the light of nature that nothing exists that we are not allowed to ask why it exists; or, we may inquire into its efficient cause, or, if it does not have one, we may demand why it does not need one"; and again:

Atque considerationem causæ efficientis esse primum et præcipuum medium, ne dicam unicum, quod habeamus ad existentiam Dei probandam, puto omnibus esse manifestum. Illud autem accurate persequi non possumus, nisi licentiam demus animo in rerum omnium, etiam ipsius Dei, causas efficientes inquirendi: quo enim jure Deum inde exciperemus, priusquam illum existere sit probatum?—A consideration of efficient causes is the primary and principal way, if not the only way, that we have of proving the existence of God, which I think is clear to everyone. But we cannot pursue this with precision unless we grant our minds the permission to inquire into the efficient causes of all things, even God himself. For what right do we have to make God an exception, before we have proved that he exists?¹⁰

Spinoza nevertheless modifies Descartes' statement. First by an omission: he lacks the explicit mention of the *causa sui*; then by an addition: for him, the cause does not only give the reason for existence, but also for non-existence. It remains to determine whether this is an extension or a transformation of the principle of a reason of existence by the cause.

The argument that follows the statement of the principle remains rather obscure and seems unable to shed light on these two modifications. (a) The cause or reason can be found inside or outside the nature of the thing. Let us immediately note that strictly speaking only a cause can be a being inside or outside the nature of a thing, while reason is only found within the understanding that comprehends it. This confusion is confirmed in the example that follows: a square circle does not exist, for it is contradictory. Of course, but it does not in any way have to exist, since here it is only a question of a logical contradiction in the concept of its nature, not the impossibility of producing its existence outside of understanding. When Spinoza adds that the reason that a triangle or a circle "exists" does not depend on its essence, but "ex ordine universæ naturæ—from the order of universal nature" (P1, *aliter*), we do not see what he really means by the *existence* of such a triangle or circle: is it about an existence in material things (but then it is no longer a mathematical ideal) or a reality in the mathematical world (but here we are speaking only of essence, not existence)? The lack of distinction between the logical order (*ratio cur*...) and the ontic order (*causa existentiæ*) is elsewhere confirmed by the only positive case invoked, where the two orders could possibly be identified, that of substance, which exists by the simple fact of its nature: "quia scilicet existentiam involvit—because it clearly involves existence," and refers, once again, to P7, which clearly mentions this inclusion. Yet the demonstration of P7 identifies the substance as the preeminent case of the *causa sui*: "Substantia non potest produci ab alio [...]; erit itaque causa sui—substance cannot be produced by anything else [...]; therefore it will be the cause of itself." We thus find here an indirect confirmation that the second demonstration (*aliter*) responds to the *causa sui* inaugurated by Descartes: "videtur non nimis improprie dici posse [Deus] causa sui—it seems not too inappropriate to call him [God] 'the cause of himself'"; or "Deum dici quodammodo posse sui causam—God can in a sense be called the cause of himself."[11] But it is surprising that the same text that constantly employs *ratio seu causa* nonetheless fails to ever explicitly mention the *causa sui*.

Does the second part of the second demonstration (b) allow us to understand this? For it develops what Descartes never mentions and Spinoza alone upholds: the necessity of a *ratio sive causa* (a Spinozist formula that inverts the Cartesian *causa sive ratio*) not only relates to the possibility or necessity of existence, but also to the impossibility of non-existence. In other words, "Ex quibus sequitur, id necessario existere, cujus nulla ratio nec causa datur, quæ impedit quominus existat—from which it follows that a thing necessarily exists if there is no reason or cause which prevents it from existing"; in short, if nothing stops God from existing, he therefore exists necessarily. For either this obstacle would be something other than God—but a substance cannot be limited by another substance, since they cannot have anything in common (at least P2 should have proven this), and thus, no external *ratio sive causa* stops God from existing—or, this obstacle would be internal to the very nature of God, which would be absurd in the case of an *"ens absolute infinitum et summe perfectum*—a being absolutely infinite and supremely perfect." We see that in the extended meaning of *ratio siva causa*, the argument no longer positively rests on the *causa sui*, but negatively on the impossibility for a substance, perfect, infinite, and by itself, to be limited by anything at all. For a direct demonstration of existence by the (exterior, or, in the case of God, interior) cause there is substituted an indirect demonstration of the non-existence of a cause of non-existence. This double negation is certainly not taken from any theological apophasis, but from a purely logicist interpretation of the *causa sive ratio*, which, for Descartes, rightly had for its function to *pass beyond* the logical interpretation of existence. It nevertheless becomes logical that the *causa sui* moves aside, in the second part of the second demonstration, to the benefit of the supremely perfect and unique substance. But the fact nevertheless that the *causa sui* still covertly governs this extension (essentially useless since P7) of the *ratio sive causa*.

The third demonstration (*aliter* again) offers a particularity: it is the only one to be glossed by a scholium, which secures its status and which must be explained. In itself, it only seems to repeat the second, since it interprets existence as a *potentia* or *impotentia*. However, it is no longer a matter of radicalizing the power of the *causa*, but, as indicated in the beginning of the scholia, of providing (curiously) an a posteriori demonstration: "In hac ultima demonstratione Dei existentiam a posteriori ostendere volui, ut demonstratio facilius perciperetur—in this last demonstration I want to show God's existence a posteriori, so that the demonstration would be perceived more easily" (scholium). Knowing the reluctance of the principle of *mos geometricus* for a posteriori reasoning, this improvised and unnatural argument is not surprising: if only finite beings existed necessarily, they would be more powerful than the absolutely infinite being (*potentiora Ente absolute infinito*), which is absurd; therefore either nothing exists necessarily, or only *Ens absolute infinitum* exists necessarily. Whether this is an a posteriori demonstration can be disputed; no effect would lead back to a cause here (the two terms are missing); but we can also admit a reference to the a posteriori proof of *Meditatio III*, since we rely on the relationship of the finite to the infinite, and the fact that the identification of God as *Ens absolute infinitum* (three times) obviously echoes Descartes: "summum aliquem Deum—some supreme God," "substantiam quandam infinitam—a substance that is infinite," or "perceptionem infiniti [. . .] hoc est Dei—perception of the infinite, that is God."[12]

The determination of God by the infinite even takes on such importance that Spinoza does not hesitate as well to maintain the formulation, albeit a priori, of the scholium that immediately follows: "Non autem propterea, quod ex eodem fundamento Dei existentia a priori non sequatur—but not because God's existence does not follow a priori from the same foundation"; the privilege of the infinite remains, and is reinforced since it is supposed to be exercised as both a priori and a posteriori. Of course, this is a certain speculative naiveté; for Descartes himself knew that the infinite, by definition and according to the rigor of things, could not be comprehended as such a priori, but must only be conceived through its effects, strictly and exclusively a posteriori. He thus took care to distinguish two points from the beginning: for the a posteriori demonstration, the infinite is known by its effects; for the a priori demonstration, the *ens summe perfectum* is known by its essence.[13] In fact, the difference between the third demonstration and its scholium comes not so much from the problematic reversal of the infinite a posteriori and the infinite a priori than from the absolute infinity of the supreme being, or rather from its interpretation as the *potentia* of existing, or more exactly as the *potentia* of the substance that exists by itself and in virtue of its essence. The infinite becomes an active power of existing, which almost returns to a phrase from Descartes: "Deum autem ita judico esse *actu* infinitum, ut nihil ejus perfectioni addi possit—God, on the other hand, I judge to be infinite in act, so that nothing can be added to his perfection."[14]

We can now present a conclusion: together with its scholia, the *four* (not three) demonstrations of the one P_{11} can be explained as the recovery of the three principal proofs of the existence of God proposed by Descartes. *Ens summe perfectum* in the first demonstration takes up the definition of God in the a priori proof of *Meditatio V. Causa sui* in the second demonstration responds to the definition of God in the *Responsiones I* and *IV*. Finally, the *infinitum* is divided, first a posteriori in the third demonstration, then, curiously, a priori in the final scholium.

§3. The Irreducible Plurality of Definitions

The multiplication of demonstrations of God's existence in P11 is thus explained as the reworking of different proofs of God's existence in Descartes, or rather, of the three definitions of God that support them in the *Meditationes*: *infinitum*, *ens perfectissimum*, and *causa sui*. This result clarifies the formal structure of P11, but it also and above all reveals a substantive difficulty. For, as I have at least tried to establish elsewhere, the Cartesian proofs are not entirely compatible with each other, since they rest on three determinations of God that do not quite overlap, or even contradict each other. If these determinations of God do not overlap, and do not agree, it is no concern for revealed theology, because the divine names certainly do not claim to make a system, nor aim at some unified essence of God; rather, their reciprocal play and incessant circulation guarantee what remains essential to spiritual contemplation: all the divine names apply under some relation to God, because none defines him adequately or comprehends his immanent transcendence. Anonymous and therefore also polyonymous? Of course, since God is not spoken of so that we understand him, but so that we praise him. It works entirely differently in the domain of metaphysics, especially when it tends towards the shape of a system: it requires that the determinations of God, if they remain plural, must at least prove to be coherent, if not unified into one single definition, and ensure a precise function—of grounding, of supreme perfection, of *causa sui*, etc.—in its accomplished system. The originality of Descartes, on this point as well as the other, resides in his *indecision*: he conceived at least three proofs of the existence of God (and in a sense was the first to conceive them strictly speaking). But he was no doubt aware that these proofs did not exactly overlap in their conclusions, or even contradicted each other in their presuppositions; and so he did not try force them into a unified system, either; in fact, he bequeathed them, floating, to his successors, who, one by one, privileged one or the other, until finally renouncing all three[15] (say, with Kant). In this debate, where does Spinoza fall? Does he try to unify the plurality of definitions of the divine essence by implementing the (three or four) demonstrations of the *Ethics I*, P11? If so, does he succeed?

As, curiously enough, the plurality of these definitions in P11 (and elsewhere) has not attracted much attention from Spinozist commentators, it is also not surprising that the response to this question also remains fallow.

We could not, for example, reunite them all under the single title of *ens realissimum*, a term absent from the *Ethics* and all of Spinoza's work.[16] And so, before directly confronting this question, it is fitting to verify how far Spinoza assumes the Cartesian definitions of God and how he changes them; we will thus be able to fine-tune the question of their consistency and compatibility.

We have interpreted the first demonstration of P11 as a recovery of the so-called ontological argument that Descartes backs up with the determination of God as *ens summe perfectum*. One fact seems to contradict this hypothesis, however: if P11 uses the phrase *ens summe perfectum*, it is in the second demonstration and its scholia, not in the first. To which we could respond that Spinoza confirms this phrase everywhere, although with some imprecision. (a) At least once he mentions perfection as an old and well-known thesis, and thus questionable; for example, when he admits that his own thesis, "substantiam extensam unum ex infinitis Dei attributis esse—extended substance is one of God's infinite attributes," may be opposed by "argumentum petitu[m] etiam a summa Dei perfectione. Deum enim, *inquiunt*, cum sit ens summe perfectum, pati non potest—an argument which is also drawn from God's supreme perfection. For God, *they say*, since he is a supremely perfect being, cannot but be passive" (I, P15S). Now, a divisible extended substance is passive, and so the extension does not belong to the essence of God. We see that the determination of perfection is unstable and general enough at times to play *against* the doctrine of Spinoza as well. (b) He must qualify and overdetermine perfection for it to be able to take on a positive meaning as well; this is confirmed in phrases like *summa Dei perfectio* (I, P33), or *summa perfectio* and *Dei perfectio*, which evaluate perfection by the power of its nature ("rerum perfectio ex sola earum natura et potentia æstimanda—the perfection of things is to be judged solely from their nature and power").[17] In fact, perfection ends up becoming a synonym of reality: *realitatis aut perfectionis idea*,[18] to the point of being reduced to a property of substance in general, only profiting from a positive sense in relation to substance, which alone has the privilege of existence: "Contra quicquid substantia perfectionis habet, nulli causæ externæ debetur; quare ejus etiam existentia ex sola ejus natura sequi debet, quæ proinde nihil aliud est, quam ejus essentia—on the other hand, whatever perfection substance has is not owed to any external cause. So its existence must follow from its nature alone; hence its existence is nothing but its essence" (I, P11S). In other words, perfection only attains its full meaning by being identified with substance, to which rightfully belongs its existence (I, P7: "Ad naturam substantiæ pertinet existere—it pertains to the nature of a substance to exist"); yet the inclusion of existence in the essence (and this in virtue of P7) is precisely the crux of the so-called ontological argument, taken up by the first demonstration; we can thus assign to the latter the phrase *ens summe perfectum* of the former.

We have interpreted the second demonstration of P11 as a return to the Cartesian proof of God's existence by causality as *causa sui*; which calls for several clarifications. (a) Arguably, God in the *Ethics* is submitted to the same requirement as the one imposed on him in the *Responsiones*: "Cujuscunque rei assignari debet causa sive ratio tam cur existit, quam cur non existit—for each thing there must be assigned a cause, or reason, as much for its existence as for its non-existence" (P11, *aliter* 1). And in God alone the cause or reason does not come from the exterior, but from his very essence, which is enough to ensure his existence: "Per causam sui, intelligo, id cujus essentia involvit existentiam—by cause of itself I understand that whose essence involves existence" (I, D1). (b) Yet the divergence from Descartes soon appears. For the latter (as was said elsewhere), the *causa sui* remains a logically and temporally contradictory concept, which we can only assume with reservation (*quodammodo, per analogiam*) and in order to maintain even in God, be it only negatively, the principle of existence as the effect of a [quasi] cause; in short, it is a passage to the limit, tolerated for the case of God, but which remains exceptional, even under the rule of the *causa sive ratio*.[19] The same cannot be said for Spinoza. First of all, the concept of *causa sui* is never examined for its own sake nor in its own difficulty; when Spinoza mentions it for the first time, he takes it as already well known and simply a synonym of being in itself: "si res sit in se, sive, *ut vulgo dicitur, causa sui*, tum per solam suam essentiam debebit intelligi—if the thing is in itself, or, *as is commonly said, is the cause of itself,* then it must be understood through its essence alone."[20] Far from this circularity of cause with itself (without effect different than itself) constituting a limit case and a frontier, so to speak, it becomes the rule of *every* causality, producing every existence starting from and on the model of the divine *causa sui*, supposedly clear and distinct. Far from being limited to God, it presides over the production of all things, including modes: "eo sensu, quo Deus dicitur causa sui, etiam omnium rerum causa dicendus est—God must be called the cause of all things in the same sense in which he is called the cause of himself" (I, P25S). Spinoza's originality does not consist in including essences as well as existences in divine causality,[21] but in wiping out the distinction between the causality of the *causa sui* immanent to itself and that of a cause distinct from its effects, by conflating them (without any real explanation) in the univocity of an "omnium rerum causa immanens, non vero transiens—imminent, not transitive, cause of all things" (I, P18). We can even read all of *Ethics I* as the effort to generalize the initial *causa sui* (D1) into a universal *causa essendi rerum* (P2, demonstration and corollary).

Set up by Spinoza in the paradigm of the *ratio sive causa*, the *causa sui* offers nothing less than a patent difficulty: the second demonstration of P11, which validates this extension, never mentions *causa sui*, while it cites at once the two other formulations, "de Ente absolute infinito et summe perfecto." Yet it is here that, according to the very text of P34 (demonstration), the *causa sui* should appear: "Ex sola enim necessitate Dei essentiæ sequitur Deus esse causam sui (per P11)—for from the necessity alone of God's essence it follows that God is the cause of himself (by P11)." Another absence is added to the first: prior to P11, no explanation comes to clarify D1's brutal and enigmatic assimilation of the *causa sui* to what, for Descartes, defines the so-called ontological argument, that is, that the essence includes existence, *essentia involvit existentiam*: the only intermediary mention (to P7, demonstration) repeats D1 without comment; after P11, the mode of causality of the *causa sui* is never elaborated in a way that justifies what also extends to "all things" (as in the scholium of P25). How can we explain not only this silence on the *causa sui* in P11, but its indetermination in the other occurrences, while it opens and dominates the whole first part of the *Ethics*? The most common response of the commentaries—the religious invocation of P25—is worth nothing.

I can hardly see any other possible answer: Spinoza universalizes, without further explanation and against the Cartesian restriction, the domain of the *causa sui* not only because he wrongly holds that it is well known and widely accepted, but because he thinks he can apply it less to the cause of existence than to the cause of non-existence, or even to the non-cause of inexistence, less to the positive cause of existence (of God) than to the non-cause of the inexistence of God *and of all things*: "nulla ratio nec causa dari possit, quæ impedit quominus Deus existat—if there is no reason or cause which prevents God from existing" (P11 *aliter* 1, second demonstration). Hence it follows that "eo sensu, quo Deus dicitur causa sui, etiam omnium rerum causa dicendus est—God must be called the cause of all things in the same sense in which he is called the cause of himself" (P25). The *causa sui* was not explicitly mentioned in P11 (even though P34 assigns it to P11 explicitly in its demonstration) because in fact it is not so much a question of only proving an existence (God's) by a cause as of already proving by causality the non-existence of a cause of non-existence in general. The universalization of the *causa sui* does not mention it as such, precisely because it universalizes it. This curious situation testifies perhaps as well to an unresolved dilemma, which Descartes had himself settled. For either we understand the *causa sui* as an absence of any other cause than the exceptional essence of God, interpreted as *potentiæ immensitas*, thus negatively; in which case, like Descartes, we fall back on a variant of the *aseitas*, which is only applied to God. Or, as Spinoza clearly understands it, we try to think an *aseitas* that is not only positive by effective causality, but by an effective causality which coincides with a logical necessity and which allows us to formally deduce modes from the essence of the divine substance; in this case it is necessary to dissolve it into its very accomplishment—the *causa [sui]* is extended to everything that the *self* of the unique substance expresses and becomes *omnium rerum causa immanens* (P18). Perhaps it would be therefore necessary to consider the first definition of *Ethics I* as provisional and having to disappear as soon as possible (from P17) into universal causality, of which it is still only a particular case. We would almost have to say, in a reversal of the famous thesis of P25, that God is *causa sui* in the very way that he is the cause of all other things.

We have interpreted the third demonstration of P11 as a repetition of the a posteriori proof of the existence of God in *Meditatio III*. Indeed, Spinoza takes up again without reservation the determination of God by the infinite. First, directly: "Per Deum, intelligo ens absolute infinitum—By God I understand a being absolutely infinite" (D6); and: "Cum Deus sit ens absolute infinitum—since God is an absolutely infinite being" (P14, demonstration); or: "de Deo, ente scilicet absolute infinitum—of God, viz. of being absolutely infinite" (P15S). It is then found in P11, "Ens absolute infinitum" (P11D3, three times), "Ens absolute infinitum sive Deum" (P11S). Indirectly as well. Whether indirectly by the intermediary of substance: "Omnis substantia est necessario infinita—every substance is necessarily infinite" (P8, see P13S); or through attributes or essence: "Per Deum intelligo ens absolute infinitum, hoc est, substantiam constantem infinitis attributis, quorum unumquodque æternam et infinitam essentiam exprimit—By God I understand a being absolutely infinite, i.e., a substance consisting of an infinity of attributes, of which each one expresses an eternal and infinite essence."[22] So that the infinity of substance is redoubled in power by the infinity of attributes, themselves infinite in number. But it would perhaps be this frequency of *infinitus* that should alert the interpreter. For infinity always keeps the status of an adjective, which qualifies not only God, but being, substance, essence, attributes, and finally certain modes, quantity, and corporal substance (P5). These adjectival uses can be multiplied and expanded precisely because it is no longer a matter of the substantive use of *infinitum*, which Descartes reserves exclusively for God.[23] This downgrading of the infinite from the rank of substantive to an adjective, and a widely distributed one at that, would explain as well why the a posteriori proof is itself relativized, and why the adjective "infinite" is sometimes made a characteristic determination of the a priori proof, perfection: "existentia entis absolute infiniti seu perfecti, hoc est Dei—existence of a being absolutely infinite or perfect—that is, of God" (P11S).

And so we arrive at a result and retrieve a prior question. A result: the three proofs of P11 not only correspond to the three primary Cartesian proofs of the existence of God, but take from them, in a modified order, the three determinations of God (*ens summe perfectum, causa sui,* and *[ens absolute] infinitum*). Above all, they put into play the three paradigmatic determinations of God that, intertwined and yet distinguished, weave through the whole of *Ethics I*. P11 is not an exception; or rather, it reveals with exceptional clarity the difficulty of unifying these three determinations and showing by three different ways the single proposition that God necessarily exists. For the genuine and ultimate difficulty is not found in the existence of God (the question *an sit?*), but in the identification of the essence of this X = "God" (the question *quid sit?*). However easily and overabundantly Spinoza responds to the first, the scattered rivalry between the three (or four) demonstrations attests that he does not succeed in responding to the second.

This result leads back to the question already posed earlier: what coherence can we recognize in the demonstrations of the existence of God, and therefore, in the definitions of the essence of God that support them in P11? Does Spinoza succeed, here or elsewhere, and to what degree, in maintaining the coherence indispensable to a system of metaphysics, and which the *mos geometricus* dominating the entire construction of the *Ethics* requires? Or does the diversity remain, irreducible, because in the final instance these supposed definitions of divine essence, at least to reduce them to their conceptual idols, remain only darkened phantoms of divine names that, themselves, cannot and must never form a system?

§4. Perfection and Cause

Did Spinoza admit, or even explain these possible tensions between the different determinations of the essence of God? It seems that at least two texts suggest a disparity between God as perfection (*ens summe perfectum*) and God as cause (and *causa sui*).

In the *Cogitata metaphysica* (the appendix to *Principia philosophiæ cartesianæ*, namely, in his closest debate with Descartes), Spinoza seems to privilege the definition of God by causality, as "omnium rerum causa," and thus "vi causæ Dei, nempe omnium rerum creatoris—by the power of their cause, God, the creator of all things," or "vi causæ omnia creantis, scilicet Dei—by the power of the cause who creates all things, namely God."[24] And yet the same text also maintains another definition, by perfection: "Deum infinitam perfectionem habere, hoc est infinitam essentiam, seu infinitum esse—God has infinite perfection, that is, infinite essence *or* infinite being" (since here perfection determines infinity); or: "Deum ens perfectissimum esse—God is a supremely perfect being"; and: "Deus, ens nempe perfectissimum, nulla perfectione carere debet—God, as a supremely perfect being, must lack no perfection."[25] How are these two determinations articulated here? More clearly than in *Ethics I*, P11, and perhaps because they are closer to the Cartesian thematic, the *Cogitata metaphysica* do not attempt to disguise their disparity. They even expose it without ambiguity: "solus Deus dicendus absolute infinitum, nimirum quatenus reperimus ipsum revera constare infinita perfectione—only God is to be called absolutely infinite, insofar as we find that he really consists of infinite perfection"; here infinity always follows from perfection. But the same cannot be said of divine immensity, which, itself, does not come from God's perfection, even if infinite; nor does it constitute one of his internal perfections. And this is why we can establish it by appeal to another determination of his essence, causality: "Immensitas vero Deo tantum respective tribuitur; non enim pertinet ad Deum, quatenus absolute tanquam *ens perfectissimum*, sed quatenus ut *prima causa* consideratur; quæ quamvis non esset perfectissima, nisi respectu entium secundarium, nihilominus tamen esset immensa—But immensity is only described to God in a certain respect. For it does not pertain to God insofar as he is considered absolutely, *as a most perfect being*, but only insofar as he is considered as the *first cause*, which, even if it were only most perfect in respect to secondary beings, would still be no less immense."[26] Keeping to the first meaning of immensity (the property of being incapable of being measured, incommensurability, the meaning as used by Descartes since the *Regulæ*), Spinoza deduced from this (correctly) that it cannot be conceived except in relation with measure (be it the unit of measurement, or other measurable things); in contrast to infinity, it therefore implies more than the internal perfection of the divine essence, but depends on the relation to created (or derived) things. This external relation can only come from the determination of God as first cause, which then relates, as immense, to measurable effects. Of course, the *Cogitata metaphysica* still acknowledges a relation of creation between God and "all things," which the *Ethics* will replace by a relation of expression. Nonetheless, the difference between God as *ens perfectissimum* and God as *causa* [*sui*] is marked, even more clearly than between the two first determinations of P11.

This early text does not stand alone, but finds a confirmation in the later Letter to Tschirnhaus. In it, Spinoza clarifies the difference between a true and an adequate idea, in terms parallel to the doctrine of the *Ethics* (II, P43S): the first implies, according to the supposedly classical doctrine of similitude with the *res*, a relation (*respectus*) to its *ideatum*; the second remains absolute, without relation, true in its own evidence, "veritas norma sui et falsi"; and so the adequate idea of the circle implements its genetic definition, which produces it starting from itself and from which all its properties can be deduced. And what about the definitions of God: can we qualify them all as adequate ideas? We must make a distinction, following the same Letter 60: the determination of God by perfection provides a true idea, but not yet an adequate one; and so we must rely on another determination, causality, to attain a true and adequate idea:

Sic quoque, cum Deum definio esse Ens summe perfectum, cumque ea definitio non exprimat causam efficientem (intelligo enim causam efficientem tam internam quam externam), non potero inde omnes Dei proprietates expromere; at quidem cum definio Deum esse *Ens* etc. (vide Definitio VI, *Ethica I*)—Similarly, when I define God as a supremely perfect Being, since that definition doesn't express the efficient cause (for I understand the efficient cause to be both internal and external), I won't be able to derive all God's properties from it, but when I define God to be a Being [*absolutely infinite, that is, a substance constituted of an infinity of attributes, of which each expresses an eternal and infinite essence*], etc. (see *Ethics I*, D6).[27]

From this abbreviated explanation, let us take note of several clear points. First, the definition of God as *Ens summe perfectum* (that of D1 in P11, which takes up the so-called ontological argument of *Mediatio V*) is true, but it does not yet offer an adequate idea. Second, to gain an adequate idea, one must pass to causality (as does the second demonstration of P11). Third, Letter 60 repeats the distinction introduced by the *Cogitata metaphysica*, which allows us to conclude there is a clear-cut difference, if not an opposition, between God as perfection and God as cause in P11 of *Ethics I*.

Yet we can be amazed that Letter 60, at the very moment where it enshrines the superiority of causality over perfection in the definition of God, refers not to Definition 1 (that of the *causa sui*), for example, but to Definition 6, which precisely does not mention causality, but establishes the *substantia constans infinitis attributis*. What, then, is the status of the infinite?

§5. Perfection and the Infinite

On the status of the infinite, the *Cogitata metaphysica* fixed the principle of its subordination to perfection quite early on: "Eatenus ipsum [sc. Deum] infinitum esse dicimus, quatenus ad ejus essentiam sive summam perfectionem attendimus—we call him infinite in so far as we are tending to his essence, *or* supreme perfection."[28] Infinity is deduced from perfection, as one of those perfections that defines *Ens summe perfectum*. The confirmations of the primacy of perfection are not lacking elsewhere in the *Principia philosophiæ cartesianæ*, which reach "in naturam Entis perfectissimi—into the nature of the most perfect being" (235) in the "Dei, sive entis summe perfecti conceptu—God, or a supremely perfect Being" (243) as "ens summe perfectum, seu Deum—a supremely perfect being, or God" (252) who is "quid summe perfectum, ac proinde (per D8) Deus—something supremely perfect, and therefore (by D8) God." In short, it holds without exception that "quicquid perfectionis in Deo reperitur, a Deo est—whatever perfection is found in God, is from God [himself]."[29] This position nevertheless meets with an objection: in the final position of the *Ethics*, perfection appears neither in Definition 6, nor in any other, nor in the axioms, or even before P11 and its demonstrations. On the contrary, it is the infinite that governs Definition 6 ("ens absolute infinitum, hoc est substantiam constantem infinitis attributis—a being absolutely infinite, i.e., a substance consisting of an infinity of attributes") and that of the substance *unius attributi* ("Omnis substantia est necessario infinita—every substance is necessarily infinite," P8). Between these two texts, could Spinoza have changed his position at the expense of perfection and for the benefit of the infinite?

One can maintain that this is not the case. First a word of precaution: the definition of God, given by the *Principia philosophiæ cartesianæ*, I, §8, as the "Substantia, quam per se summe perfectam esse intelligimus, et in qua nihil plane concipimus, quod aliquem defectum sive perfectionis limitationem involvat—the substance which we understand to be through itself supremely perfect, and in which we can see nothing which involves any defect or limitation of perfection," repeats word for word a definition from Descartes, not of course in the *Principia philosophiæ*, but, as is often the case, in the *more geometrico* appendix of the *IIæ Responsiones* (AT VII, 162.4–7; CSM II, 114). Could we induce from this that the primacy of perfection, in the early period, reflects a thesis that is more Cartesian than authentically Spinozist? But the opposition may be only apparent, and—a second precaution—it may be that by reading this Definition 6 more carefully, the apparent privilege of the infinite disappears. For it does not define God as infinite, but as *"absolute infinitum*—absolutely infinite." The difference is not trivial, since the absolute infinite, according to the explanation that immediately follows, conflicts with the infinite *in suo genere*. In this latter instance, one cannot deny that there were attributes of "quicquid [. . .] *est in sua genere tantum infinitum*—something [which] is only infinite *in its own kind*" (I, D6): each attribute unfolds in its kind, a kind of infinity, for example the infinite of thought or the infinity of understanding, each infinity excluding the other. But in the first case, it comes back to the *absolutely* infinite and includes "quicquid essentiam exprimit et negationem nullam involvit—whatever expresses essence and involves no negation pertains to its essence" (I, D6); in other words, the *absolute infinitum* expresses without negation all the infinities in their respective kind. God is not infinite in his kind like each of his attributes are, but infinite without negation or limitation, *absolute*. In the first sense, the infinite now concerns the attribute and not yet the substance, which includes all the infinites of attributes in an infinity of infinites. The substance (or God), on the other hand, is characterized by an infinity of infinites, or rather by infinitely more than their infinities—by the *causa sui* (Definition 1) and supreme perfection (P11).

This distinction is confirmed. First from before the *Ethics*, in a letter to Oldenburg: "unumquodque attributum est infinitum, sive summe perfectum, in suo genere—each of which attributes is infinite, or supremely perfect in its kind." And in the *Short Treatise*: "[God] is a being [*wezen*] of which all, or infinite, attributes [*oneyndelyke eygenschappen*], are predicated, each of which is infinitely perfect [*oneyndelyk vollmaakt*] in its own kind."³⁰ Next in *Ethics I*: "infinitis attributis, quorum unumquodque æternam et infinitam essentiam exprimit—of infinite attributes, each of which expresses eternal and infinite essence" (P11) and: "aliquod Dei attributum, quatenus idem concipitur infinitatem et necessitatem essentiæ sive æternitatem exprimere—some attribute of God, in so far as that attribute is conceived to express infinity and necessity of existence, *or* [...] eternity" (P23, demonstration); or: "a Deo, non quatenus substantia absolute infinita est, sed quatenus attributum habet, quod infinitam et æternam cognitionis essentiam exprimit—by God, not insofar as he is an absolutely infinite substance, but insofar as he has an attribute that expresses the infinite and eternal essence of thought" (P32, demonstration). All these propositions are in fact limited to citing Definition 6.

Downgrading the infinity of substance to attributes, so to speak, and even to certain modes (see P23ff) allows us not only to eliminate the hypothesis of a supposed substance to its only attribute (in P8), but above all to correctly translate the phrase that is so ambiguous in Definition 6: *substantia constans infinitis attributis*. Should we understand this to mean *infinite attributes*, or *an infinity of attributes*? In fact, it must be understood to mean both at once:

each attribute is infinite *in its kind*; thus, there are *kinds of infinity*. This multiplication of the infinite results in a twofold consequence: on the one hand, there can be an infinity of attributes, each one infinite (even though we only really use two); on the other hand, the infinite is not sufficient to define God, who, however infinite as the *absolutely* infinite, deepens this infinity of infinite[s] as the *Ens [summe] perfectissimum*. We can better understand, then, why the third demonstration of P11, meant to proceed a posteriori, and so starting from the infinite, is soon corrected by the recovery of the "same ground" on an a priori mode, by converting the infinite either into power ("Ens absolute infinitum sive Deum, infinitam *potentiam* existendi in se habere—an absolutely infinite Being, or God, has, of himself, an absolutely infinite *power* of existing"), or perfection ("quicquid substantia *perfectionis* habet, nulli causæ externæ debetur—whatever *perfection* substance has is not owed to any external cause") (P11S). We can better understand why it is only after P10, which introduces between substance and attributes a relation not only of constitution (*constans infinitis attributis*), but expression (unumquodque [*sc.* attributum] realitatem sive esse substantiæ *exprimit*), and thus allows us to unify by reference (*pros hen*) the plurality of attributive infinites into the single substance, that P11 can attempt to establish in its three (or four) demonstrations a certain primacy of perfection, and then attempt to reunite in an (almost) coherent whole the three possible determinations of the essence of God.

One conclusion seems likely: between the infinite and perfection, Spinoza chose the second, on substantive grounds. It alone can establish the hierarchy between the attributes (even certain modes) and substance, all the while maintaining their irrefutable unity by substituting the relation of expression for the simple inherence of an attribute in a substance. Descartes had left undecided the question that has become crucial for Spinoza: if substance does not affect us immediately as such but only by an attribute, must it summon a substance for each attribute? But then there would be at least two substances *cogitantes* between the *ego* and God, one finite, the other infinite; there would then also be one single extended substance (infinite or indefinite?) for all bodies, whose individuation would become (and indeed will become) problematic; there would even be two (finite) substances for the same *meum corpus* (which nevertheless does not constitute a third substance). The Spinozist response comes down not only to distinguishing the one substance from infinite (in all its meanings) attributes, but, in order to achieve this, submits infinity to perfection. Which immediately leads to other difficulties.

§6. The Unification of Metaphysical Names

Descartes had faced the speculative task of proving the existence of God by pure reason, and in a sense was the first to do so. He had mobilized to this end proofs that assumed many definitions, or rather conceptual determinations of God: the idea of the infinite (with or without the support of a substance), the perfection of essence and the *causa sui*. But he had not recognized it as a necessary task to unify these determinations into only one, or even to coordinate them into a system. This was for two reasons. First, Descartes did not try to constitute his philosophy into a system—the very duality of two onto-theo-logies (of the *cogitatio* and of the *causa*) offer the best indication of this—and for this reason it was not wholly inscribed in the destiny of *metaphyisica*. Next, and confirming the first point, he never tried or even aspired to arrive at a single definition of God, precisely because his highest determination of the divine, the infinite, forbids by principle such a definition: the *in*finite, by nature, constitutes an *in*definition and is limited to allowing a radically a posteriori approach, by and in its finite effects. Thinking God as infinite does not promise and does not allow "any way of being grasped by thought—*quocunque modo cogitatione attingere* poss[e]" (AT VII, 52.5ff; CSM II, 35), but forbids the comprehension of the incomprehensible.

Incomprehensibility, which does not contradict knowledge of the infinite but designates its *ratio*, had freed Descartes from the task that Spinoza could not and perhaps above all did not want to avoid: attaining an "adæquatam [. . .] cognitionem æternæ et infinitæ essentiæ divinæ—adequate [. . .] knowledge of God's eternal infinite essence" (*Ethics II*, P47). This would require unifying the definition of God and above all claiming that their single result would allow us to grasp at once the essence of God, or, which amounts to the same thing, that God has an essence. By claiming to such a knowledge, Spinoza would be affiliated with the systematic project of *metaphysica*: deducing it a priori and following an absolute logic. To thus reduce all the proofs (Cartesian, incompatible among themselves) to one alone: such was the task of *Ethics I*, P11.

We have seen that P11 only manages to accomplish it confusedly and approximately, as attested by the multiplication of demonstrations and the correction of the third by its scholium. We will thus not be surprised that, at the very end of the *Ethics*, Spinoza should find himself obliged to repeat the juxtaposition of the very determinations of God that I, P11, was responsible for unifying, without success. Even at this summit of the whole *Ethics*, when the intellectual love of God should allow human beings to be "suæ Mentis æternitatis esse quidem conscios—indeed conscious of the eternity of their Mind" (V, P34S), there appears, still unresolved, the juxtaposition of the three terms of P11 without unification:

Deus est absolute *infinitus* (per DVI, p. 1), hoc est (per DVI, p. 2), Dei natura gaudet infinita *perfectione*, idque (per P2, p. 2) concomitante idea sui, hoc est (per P11 & DI, p. 1) idea *suæ causæ*; et hoc est, quod, in coroll. P32, hujus amorem intellectualem esse diximus—God is absolutely *infinite* (by I, D6), i.e. (by II, D6), the nature of God enjoys infinite *perfection*, accompanied (by II, P3) by the idea of himself, i.e. (by I, P11 and D1), by the idea of *his cause*. And this is what we have said (P23C) intellectual Love is. (V, P35)

The metaphysical determinations of God derived from (Cartesian) proofs thus do not succeed in forming a system, even for Spinoza. Moreover, his successors will either no longer risk it, or never succeed in it (even if some believed they did). And it is perhaps his unexpected greatness that he dared to try to reduce them and *did not succeed*. He did not succeed, but for one good and sufficient reason: the real divine names come from revealed theology, where they never aim to secure the knowledge of the essence of God but rather to celebrate its essential unknowing.

NINE

Spinoza: Adequacy and Vision

§1. *The Construction of Inadequacy*

I have argued, somewhat paradoxically, that even in the first book, the *Ethics* does not begin with God. I will argue here that it perhaps finds its real but concealed beginning in the second book, *De mente*, where, as in the *Treatise on the Emendation of the Intellect*, it contends with thought in its most common and least avoidable form, error. Where Descartes begins by doubt, Spinoza begins by trying to understand why we do not understand, why thought begins by its inadequacy to the thing that must be thought.

It is at the innermost level, at the connection between the body and mind, that inadequacy lies: each thinking mode feels in its body the inadequacy of its idea of modes to these same modes as extended, which are what the thinking mode nevertheless calls the body. "Mens humana partium corpus humanum componentium adæquatam cognitionem non involuit—The human mind does not involve adequate knowledge of the parts composing the human body" (*Ethica II*, P24). Indeed, the affections of my body through an indefinite number of other bodies all refer, according to the laws of the communication of movements, to other modes, outside of this body. Of course, in God, the idea of my body implies, in a single infinite deduction, the idea of every other mode of extension acting on it; and so an *alia et prior* idea of a singular thing, in God, precedes the idea of myself, that is, my body. If God can have the (obviously adequate) idea of my body, it is because, far from having the idea that I have of it, he has the idea that I do not have; knowledge of the parts that make up my body (and the modes that affect it) are only found in God, but in God "quatenus plurimis rerum ideis affectus est, et non quatenus Corporis humani tantum habet ideam— in so far as he is affected with a great many ideas of things, and not in so far as he has only the idea of the human body" (P24D). God has the adequate idea of my body, because he does not have it on its own, but linked to many others; he has this idea, because he does not have it only through what my mind thinks of it. I, on the other hand, who can only think to the extent of my mind, have no idea of my body except to the extent of what this mind perceives of it (P19), that is, "*certus* extensionis modus actu existens, et *nihil aliud*—a *certain* mode of Extension which actually exists, and *nothing else*" (P13, emphasis added). Not knowing what my mind knows, I thus do not have adequate knowledge of my own body, whose causal connections with other bodies infinitely surpasses the limits of my mind: "Corpus humanum componitur ex plurimis diversis naturæ individuis, quorum unumquodque valde compositum est—the human Body is composed of a great many individuals of different natures, each of which is highly composite" (postulate I after P13). Hence the inevitable consequence: since my mind is and has only the idea of its own body, it does not have an adequate idea of it; God, on the other hand, because he has the idea of other bodies and is not limited to knowing the idea of my body, alone has the adequate idea of this body, though mine. My mind does not adequately know its own body, precisely because it has only its idea. God adequately knows my own body, because he knows all the other bodies.

Let us analyze this paradox. "Idea cujuscunque affectionis corporis humani adæquatam corporis externi cognitionem non involuit—the idea of any affection of the human Body does not involve adequate knowledge of an external body" (P25). The idea of an effect experienced by one's own body does not include adequate knowledge of this effect's cause, since it represents a body external to my own; for if the idea of affection experienced by body A included the idea of body B affecting it, this body B remains external, other, and *prior natura* (P25D), and thus unknown to the idea of body A (my mind). God knows the body affecting B only by "*alterius* rei idea—the idea of something *other*" than that of body A, my own; which remains impossible to me, since "Mens humana nullum corpus externum ut actu existens percipit, nisi per ideas affectionum sui Corporis—the human Mind does not perceive any external body as existing in act, only through the ideas of the affections [experienced] of its own Body" (P26). Yet the idea of another body affecting mine remains that of an effect that does not yet know its cause, at best presumed indirectly, therefore incorrectly. Here we see deployed the full consequence of a principle stated earlier: "ideæ, quas corporum externorum habemus, magis nostri corporis constitutionem quam corporum externorum naturam indicant—the ideas which we have of external bodies must involve the nature of our [own] Body and at the same time the nature of the external Body" (P16C2); and so, when Paul experiences the idea of Peter, he knows the constitution of his own body more than the nature of Peter's body (P17S). Even if I know the other and thus avoid a strict solipsism, the conditions of my knowledge impact my knowledge of this other so much that I recognize myself in him more than I recognize him. Hence a quasi-solipsism is still brought about, resulting from the general doctrine of perception by imagination: to know by the senses is to suffer more than to know: "Quatenus mens humana corpus externum imaginatur, eatenus adæquatam eius cognitionem non habet—Insofar as the human Mind imagines an external body, it does not have adequate knowledge of it" (P26C).[1] It would be fitting, on another occasion, to reflect on the choice made here by Spinoza never to consider the *mens* that *in se sola considerata* (P28S): this restriction, this atomism of mind without door or window, directly contradicts not only any intentionality, but even the definition that the entire tradition took from Aristotle: the human mind has proper to it "[to be] in a manner potentially all beings, but is actually none of them until it thinks—δυνάμει πώς ἐστι τὰ νοητὰ ὁ νοῦς, ἀλλ' ἐντελεχείᾳ οὐδέν, πρὶν ἂν νοῇ." Descartes himself had remembered it, when he opened the *Regulæ* by affirming that "scientiæ omnes nihil aliud sint quam humana sapientia, quæ semper una et eadem manet quantumvis differentibus subjectis applicata—for the sciences are nothing other than human wisdom, which always remains one and the same, however different the subjects to which it is applied."[2] In contrast to intentional consciousness, always conscious of something, that is, of something other than itself, the Spinozist *mens* is not conscious of anything other than itself. And this is still to say too much, since it has consciousness of itself only by the idea of its body; or still less: the affections of its body alone: "Mens se ipsam non cognoscit, nisi quatenus corporis affectionum ideas percipit—the Mind does not know itself, except insofar as it perceives the ideas of the affections of the body" (P23). Yet it is absolutely not able to know them adequately, since "Ideæ affectionum corporis humani, quatenus ad humanam mentem tantum referuntur, non sunt claræ et distinctæ, sed confusæ—the ideas of the affections of the human Body, in so far as they are related only to the human Mind, are not clear and distinct, but confused" (P28); the mind therefore has adequate knowledge neither of its body, nor of itself: "mentem humanam [. . .] nec sui ipsius, nec sui corporis, nec corporam externorum adæquatam, sed confusam tantum et mutilatam habere cognitionem—the human mind [. . .] does not have an adequate, but only a confused and mutilated knowledge of itself" (P29C). Knowledge by inadequate idea, stigmatized first concerning (imaginative) knowledge of exterior bodies, flows back unchecked and unbounded over the entire epistemic field, until it invades knowledge of the body itself, but above all until it disqualifies the indubitable par excellence: the supposedly rational knowledge of the self by itself, the *ego sum, ego existo*. We must then return to Descartes, to see if the "first principle" is indeed known by an adequate idea, or not.

§2. The Conditions of Adequacy: Spinoza's Agreement with Descartes

Indeed, the interrogation of the possibility of an adequate knowledge of self and body arises first in Descartes. To be more exact, on the occasion of the always very pertinent objection addressed to Descartes by Arnauld: how is it that the *ego*, which discovers itself existing as a *res cogitans*, can claim from *Mediatio II* to be actually distinguished from the *res extensa* and exist without relying on it?[3] For, Arnauld continues, "quod de corpore dubitem, vel corpus esse negem, non efficitur nullum esse corpus—the fact that I have doubts about the body, or deny that it exists, does not bring it about that no body exists" (198.20–23; CMS II, 139). Of course, once the hyperbolic doubt is removed, Descartes has established the modalities of equivalence between the distinction of reason and real distinction, for example relying on the correspondence between the ego "capax percipiendi" and God "capax efficiendi"[4] (71.13–20; CSM II, 50); but he precisely only establishes it after removing the hyperbolic doubt and therefore could not claim it from *Mediatio II*. Even in *Meditatio VI*, in order to affirm absolutely that "certum est me a corpore meo revera esse distinctum, et absque illo posse existere—it is certain that I am really distinct from my body, and cannot exist without it"

(78.19–20; CSM II, 54), it would have been necessary to first elaborate an explicit theory of distinctions, which is lacking.

Yet it is precisely at the point where Descartes sketched this theory that a serious aporia appears. Indeed, Arnauld subtly remarks that in the response to Caterus, who is already concerned about the real distinction between *res cogitans* and *res extensa*, Descartes had opposed the formal (and also modal) distinction, which operates "per abstractionem intellectus rem *inadæquate* concipientis—by an abstraction of the intellect which conceives the thing *inadequately*" and therefore only frees up *entia incompleta* ("incomplete entities"),[5] to the real distinction, which leads to terms understood as *complete*, to a *res completa* ("complete thing"; 220.8 = 221.7; 220.10; CMS II, 155). But, asks Arnauld, since complete knowledge is equivalent to adequate knowledge,[6] does this completeness not demand an adequacy (*cognitio adæquata rei*, 200.6; CMS II, 144), and does it not exclude every inadequacy (*inadæquata tantum [sui] conceptione*, 200.21; CSM II, 141)? But Descartes never produced, nor even claimed to produce, this adequate knowledge of self, which is nevertheless required for his own definition of the real distinction; from the fact that the ego can observe his existence starting from the knowledge of the body, it follows *aliqua [sui] notitia*, but that "notitiam illam esse completam et adæquatam [. . .] mihi nondum plane perspicuum est—it is not yet transparently clear to me that this knowledge is complete and adequate" (201.19 and 20–23; CMS II, 141). And indeed, many serious arguments rose up against the possibility of such an adequacy.[7] Thus, Arnauld anticipates, at least approximately, the augmentation that Spinoza will use to oppose Descartes: the *res cogitans* does not have adequate knowledge of itself, because it does not have adequate knowledge of its real distinction from its body; this distinction in turn is lacking because it lacks the adequate idea of its own body.

How can Descartes reply? In refuting Arnauld's objection, will he claim an adequate knowledge of self and its body? Will he renounce the distinction between my extended body and my thought because of the still inadequate knowledge of them? Neither of these. But, in fact, the analysis of this response offers a twofold interest: it defines the doctrine of Descartes, but above all it frees up the horizon where Spinoza's thesis on this same point will unfold. By way of anticipation, let us summarize the Cartesian thesis: true knowledge does not demand adequacy, but requires completeness: the *res cogitans* of *Meditatio II* did not lack adequacy, precisely because it did not suppose it; it did not suppose it, because it did not need it to know itself in truth; moreover, true knowledge remains within finitude and is sufficient for a regulated and formalized non-adequacy, which no more equals inadequacy than it aspires for adequacy.

More precisely, Descartes argues as follows: the question is not to know if the consequence holds for clear and distinct knowledge to reality (*revera*)—for it holds indisputably in the regime of evidence guaranteed by God; the question is to determine under which conditions knowledge itself is true.[8] In the case of the *res cogitans*, it suffices (*sufficit*[9]) that it exist on its own for it to be an actually distinct substance, since subsisting defines substance in general.[10] This sufficiency defines it as a *res completa*;[11] it is therefore not required, in order to attain a substance as a complete thing, to attain adequate knowledge of it: "Neque enim existimo adæquatam rei cognitionem hic requiri—I do not [. . .] think that adequate knowledge of a thing is required here."[12] To understand how adequate knowledge could be *not* required, let us first note the space between completion and adequacy: in order for knowledge to be adequate, it is first necessary, according to Descartes, that "in ea contineri omnes omnino proprietates quæ sunt in re cognita—it must contain absolutely all the properties which are in the thing which is the object of knowledge" (220.8–10; CSM II, 155); if it were only a question of "equaling, *adequare*" the reality of the thing by factual knowledge, surely the human mind would arrive at adequate knowledge: "Ad hoc enim ut habeat [i.e. the human mind] adæquatam alicujus rei cognitionem, requiritur tantum ut vis cognoscendi quæ in ipso est adæquet istam rem; quod facile fieri potest—In order [for the human mind] to have adequate knowledge of a thing all that is required is that the power of knowing possessed by the intellect is equal to the thing in question, and this can easily occur" (220, 14–17; CSM II, 155). But this facility of being equal to the thing is not sufficient to obtain adequacy; it would require, in addition to this, the reflexive knowledge of this first de facto adequacy; to know adequately, once reality is equaled by science, one must also adequately know this adequacy. But only God succeeds at such adequacy to the second degree: "solus est Deus, qui novit se habere cognitiones rerum omnium adæquatas—Only God can know that he has adequate knowledge of all things" (220.10–11; CSM II, 155). Created understanding, if it can "easily" equal one or many things,[13] nevertheless cannot know it reflexively, because to achieve this, one must know that "Deum nihil amplius posuisse in illa re, quam id quod cognoscit, [...] ut sua vi cognoscendi adæquet infinitam Dei potestatem, quod fieri plane repugnat—God put nothing in that thing beyond what it is aware of, so that its power of knowing would have to equal the infinite power of God, and this would plainly be contradictory" (220.17–21; CSM II, 155). In a word, knowing adequately requires not only equaling the essence of the thing, but above all equaling the divine power that establishes it. Yet, as the distance from infinite to finite is widened between the divine *immensa potentia* and the human mind,[14] we must conclude that "solus est Deus qui novit se habere cognitiones rerum omnium adæquatas—only God can know that he has adequate knowledge of all things" (220.10–11; CSM II, 155), and that "Intellectus autem creatus [...] numquam tamen potest scire se habere [sc. cognitiones adæquatas rerum], nisi peculiariter ipsi Deus revelet—a created intellect, by contrast [...] can never know it has such knowledge [i.e. adequate knowledge of things] unless God grants it a special revelation of the fact."[15] From this arises a clear alternative: on the one hand, the human mind remains limited to its own power of knowing and does not arrive at truly adequate knowledge; on the other hand, this adequate knowledge is only possible in God or by assimilation to the divine point of view.

This Cartesian alternative essentially occurs in the determination of the conditions of adequate knowledge in the *Ethics II*. Spinoza distinguishes, on the one hand, the (finite) human knowledge that remains by definition inadequate: "Dico expresse, quod Mens nec sui ipsius, nec sui Corporis, nec corporum externorum adæquatam, sed confusam tantum cognitionem habeat, quoties ex communi naturæ ordine res percipit—I say expressly that the Mind has, not an adequate, but only a confused and mutilated knowledge, of itself, its own Body, and of external bodies, so long as it perceives things from the common order of nature" (P29S). To be sure, the common order of Spinozist Nature, made from stochastic gatherings, does not correspond exactly to the Cartesian order of thoughts, made from methodical series; yet these two orders nevertheless converge on the essential point: the only concern is always the finite mind and its mode of knowledge. Spinoza, on the other hand, opposes the fact that "omnes ideæ, quatenus ad Deum referuntur, veræ sunt—all ideas, insofar as they are related to God, are true" (P32). In other words, here, too, adequate knowledge returns to God alone, in whatever sense that we understand God. And so Spinoza takes up as essential an alternative constructed by Descartes himself, and resulting in the same conclusion: between finitude of human understanding and adequacy of knowledge, one must make a choice.

§3. Divine Knowledge and Adequacy: Spinoza's Disagreement with Descartes

Spinoza and Descartes thus agree on the terms of the question; they are therefore able to oppose each other all the more on the solution they provide.

Descartes, having recognized the de facto impossibility of adequate knowledge for an *intellectus creatus* (220.12; CSM II, 155), concludes from this that it is not necessary ("non requiritur," 220.26). He therefore substitutes for it, in conformity with this admitted finitude, a merely complete knowledge, which is reduced to having "cognitionem, quam nos ipsi per abstractionem intellectus non redderemus inadæquatam—knowledge that we have not ourselves made inadequate by an abstraction of the intellect" (221.4–5; CSM II, 156). For, if in the regime of finitude, we cannot ever be wholly assured of the adequacy of our knowledge with a thing (by knowledge adequate to the creative power of God concerning this very thing), if therefore knowledge *plane adæquata* (221.6; CSM II, 156) remains impossible for us, it remains legitimate to aim at a knowledge "eousque adæquatam, ut a nobis per abstractionem intellectus, inadæquatam non reddi percipiamus—adequate enough to enable us to perceive that we have not rendered it inadequate by an abstraction of the intellect" (221.9–10; CSM II, 156). Indeed, if the verification of adequacy surpasses our finite comprehension, non-inadequacy can be validated *until proven otherwise*; when we develop the implications of a notion, it is enough that we do not end with contradictions or imprecisions—which are so many clues that the concept remains inadequate to what is being conceived.

In the same Letter to Gibieuf of 1642, Descartes clearly explains his doctrine: "To tell whether my idea has been made incomplete or *inadæquata* by an abstraction of my mind, I merely look to see whether I have derived it, not from some thing outside myself which is more complete, but by an intellectual abstraction (*per abstractionem intellectus*) from some other, richer or more complete idea which I have in myself. This intellectual abstraction consists in my turning my thought away from one part of the contents of this richer idea the better to apply it to the other part with greater attention."[16] Two cases are presented here. In the first, abstraction separates one idea from another which it cannot actually be separated from. For example, considering the idea of shape starting from the idea of substance or extension comes from abstraction, because in reality the simple nature of the shape presupposes simple natures of understanding and substantiality (or existence). And so the idea of shape will prove itself to be inadequate, according to theoretical usage, since it is incapable of taking into account the attributes that it nevertheless entails. Its separation was only abstraction, it will be provisional or even false by incompleteness. In the second case, one idea can be separated from another and, in this very distinction, take into account all its implications. For example, "the idea of a substance with extension and shape is a complete idea, because I can conceive it entirely on its own, and deny of it everything else of which I have an idea"; or in the same way, "the idea which I have of a thinking substance is complete in this sense."[17] The idea is found to be complete not by an adequacy of principle founded in God, but in use and under the ongoing surveillance of procedures of falsification, which, in the best of cases, ensure that it is not yet inadequate. Admitting the finitude of human understanding, renouncing the adequacy reserved for an infinite understanding, Descartes exempts finite rationality from the requirement of making itself adequate to the power of God or infinite understanding; finitude, in its limited recognition, can thus be deployed without reference to absolute science, but by self-verification and self-validation. Descartes attempts or at least sketches, with the paradigm of the complete notion, the very modern determination of scientific truth: certain, even if not absolute, verified because provisional.

Spinoza, also recognizing the de facto impossibility of adequate knowledge for a finite "human mind," infers from this the contrary, that finite understanding must, by procedures yet to be won, be made adequate to infinite understanding, in order to achieve by itself an adequate knowledge of things. This approach rests on an unquestioned postulate: knowledge could be only false or adequate. At no moment does Spinoza appear to suspect that theoretical fecundity of the middle position brilliantly introduced by Descartes: knowledge is finite, but complete and thus true. Above all, the thesis chosen by Spinoza requires, against that of Descartes, considerable conceptual trappings: for it is a question of establishing not one, but *two* adequacies. The first, between ideas and their ideates, inevitably implies a second, between the "human mind" and God. The famous II, P32 ("Omnes ideæ, quatenus ad Deum referuntur, veræ sunt—all ideas, insofar as they are related to God, are true"), already grounds the truth of ideas on their deferral to God; but this deferral necessarily presupposes the finite mind's access to God, that is to his adequate knowledge; whence the extraordinary but inevitable audacity of II, P47: "Mens humana adæquatam habet cognitionem æternæ et infinitæ essentiæ Dei—The human Mind has an adequate knowledge of God's eternal and infinite essence." In short, to ensure epistemological adequacy, Spinoza must accomplish, by perfect univocity, a theological adequacy.

§4. The Conquest and the Aporia of Adequacy

Establishing the possibility of adequacy involves two stages: first that of epistemological adequacy in the strict sense, concerning all the ideas of the finite human mind; next that of theological adequacy, allowing univocal knowledge of the essence of God. We must examine if Spinoza succeeds in mastering them.

"Omnes ideæ, quatenus ad Deum referantur, veræ sunt—all ideas, insofar as they are related to God, are true" (II, P32). The explicit demonstration establishes that in God ideas correspond to their respective ideates (in virtue of the "parallelism" declared by P7) and that this correspondence establishes their truth (following the definition of truth fixed by axiom 6 of *Ethica I*). But, besides the fact that it curiously prefers the extrinsic definition of the truth to the intrinsic definition that Spinoza had nevertheless worked hard to privilege,[18] this demonstration passes in silence over the essential difficulty: it is not a question of proving that the "ideæ, quæ in Deo sunt" are true, therefore also adequate (since no one reasonably doubts it, and it is the least that one can expect of God); the real question bears on an entirely different point: can we hold the ideas *in Deo* as identical to the ideas *in nobis*?[19] Or again: if truth results from the reference of ideas to God, is it only possible to refer the ideas of a *mens humana*, or a finite understanding, to God? Inversely, if "nullæ [ideæ] adæquatæ nec confusæ sunt, nisi quatenus ad singularem alicujus mentem referuntur—there are no inadequate or confused ideas except insofar as they are related to the singular Mind of someone" (P36D), is it only conceivable that a new reference to God could simply come take up the reference to the human mind? Can the same ideas then change reference, without changing nature? In any case, the indetermination of the formula "*in mente*" (P39 and 49) is not enough to either explain or justify the reference of the finite mind to infinite understanding.[20] In order to remove this ambiguity, we can turn to the argument that supports P34: to demonstrate that the adequate idea *in nobis* is also true (which incidentally calls for no demonstration), Spinoza specifies what the givenness of an adequate idea *in nobis* would mean: it would be equivalent to an adequate and perfect idea being given "in Deo, quatenus nostræ mentis essentiam constituit—in God, insofar as he constitutes the essence of our Mind." But precisely, could God, if limited to constituting the essence of our mind alone, have the slightest adequate idea, since, limited to himself, this mind does not attain any (see Chapter 9, §1)? It suffices to refer to the corollary of P11 to respond in the negative: to say that the *mens humana* perceives some object amounts to saying that God "non quatenus est infinitus, sed quatenus per naturam humanæ entis explicatur—not insofar as he is infinite, but insofar as he is explained through the nature of the human Mind," has some *finite* idea; as a result, God limited to the finitude of the *mens humana* cannot adequately conceive the least idea, since this would clearly imply many others, known inadequately and by imagination. By contrast, if God, in order to adequately conceive an idea, were understood as infinite, then the *mens humana*, reduced to itself, could again only understand him inadequately. "Et cum dicimus Deum hanc vel illam ideam habere, non tantum quatenus naturam humanæ Mentis constituit, sed quatenus simul cum Mente humana alterius rei etiam habet ideam, tum dicimus mentem humanam rem ex parte, siue inadæquate percipere—and when we say that God has this or that idea, not only insofar as he constitutes the nature of the human Mind, but insofar as he also has the idea of another thing together with the human Mind, then we say that the human Mind perceives the thing only partially, or inadequately" (P11C). And so the gap is widened between God as constituting the *mens humana* and God as infinite, a gap that is destined to reproduce, under another name, the gap between finite understanding and divine understanding, which Descartes had recognized and delineated.[21] How does shifting the abyss from the finite to the infinite in God himself, rather than between human understanding and infinite understanding, allow one to cross it? Spinoza, in juxtaposing two uses of *quatenus* with regard to God, no more explains that the idea passes from one to the other, than he proved that the idea, adequate *in Deo*, also becomes so *in nobis*, or that the reference of our ideas to God are simply possible, that is, thinkable. In short, the impossibility of adequacy remains for Spinoza just as for Descartes. Only one difference sets them apart: Descartes acknowledges the impossibility that Spinoza merely conceals. We can conclude that the first adequacy, the epistemological adequacy, however asserted and claimed, remains inaccessible to the *mens humana*.

What about the second adequacy, the theological adequacy? "Mens humana adæquatam habet cognitionem æternæ et infinitæ essentæ Dei—the human Mind has an adequate knowledge of God's eternal and infinite essence" (P47). The staggering audacity of the statement merits examination of its demonstration. It consists of three moments, encumbered by at least as many flaws in logic. (a) "Mens humana ideas habet (per P22) ex quibus (per P23)—the human mind has ideas (by P22) from which (by P23)": of course, the human mind has ideas that give some access to other things; however, according to these same propositions 22–23, these ideas are in fact only affections of the body perceiving in a confused way the ideas of other external modes, referring less to the latter than first to the perceiving body; they shut the *mens humana* in on itself more than they open to objective knowledge; without rectifying them from the outset, they will not be able to allow any progress. (b) "[E]x quibus (per P23) se suumque corpus (per P19) et (per cor. P16 et per P17) corpora externa, ut actu existentia, percipit—from which it perceives (by P23) itself (by P19), its own body, (by P16 cor. 1 and P17) and external bodies as actually existing": the argument bears witness to a surprising duplicity, though likely unintentional; for P19 invoked here indicates definitively that all these ideas—even and above all the idea of self—depends on ideas of affections, in other words (according to P24, P25, P26, and again P27), they are inadequate. P29C, as we have seen, even explicitly contradicts the demonstration of P47: "mens humana, quoties ex communi naturæ ordine res percipit, *nec sui ipsius, nec sui corporis, nec corporum externorum* adæquatam, sed confusam tantum et mutilatam habere cognitionem—the human Mind perceives things from the common order of nature, it does not have an adequate, but only a confused and mutilated knowledge *of itself, of its*

238 *Chapter Nine*

own body, and of external bodies." Thus, starting from these ideas, it is impossible to pass to the slightest adequate knowledge unless, instead of relying on them, Spinoza began by making them adequate. We can perhaps admit the possibility that even inadequate ideas reveal a still implicit core of adequacy, which a Cartesian-style analysis could free up; but never once does Spinoza here proceed to either analyze or correct the inadequate ideas into adequate ideas; one must then conclude that every subsequent argument lacks a firm bedrock. (c) "[A]deoque (per P45 et 46) cognitionem æternæ et infinitæ essentiæ Dei habet adæquatam—and so (by P45 and 46) it has an adequate knowledge of God's eternal and infinite essence": this concerns, in P45–46, the necessary implication of the idea of a mode in the idea of substance, as is shown by the references made in props. 15–16 of *Ethica I*. Spinoza thus recalls that "res singulares non possunt sine Deo concipi—singular things cannot be conceived without God" (II, P45, citing I, P15), that is, that everything follows from the necessity of divine nature—at least everything that an infinite intellect can conceive, "hoc est omnia, quæ sub intellectum infinitum cadere possunt—i.e., everything which can fall under an infinite intellect" (I, P16). But precisely here, in *Ethica II*, P47, it is no longer a question of demonstrating that an infinite understanding conceives everything adequately (which any well-disposed reader will readily admit), but in fact, the reverse, that a finite human mind can conceive adequately the idea of the infinite essence of God. These two questions remain wholly different. Nevertheless, Spinoza demonstrates with care what goes without saying (that infinite understanding adequately conceives everything that proceeds from divine essence), and says not a word on the real issue—that the *mens humana*, too, can first conceive adequately what infinite understanding conceives, then conceive adequately the infinite essence of God. Why does Spinoza commit the quasi-sophism of conflating these two questions? Undoubtedly because he does not have any specific demonstration of the point of contention.[22] We thus conclude that theological adequacy, while expressly asserted, remains inaccessible.

§5. *The First Challenge of the Recourse to Adequacy*

Spinoza thus assumes adequate knowledge is acquired more than he demonstrates it—the boldness, not to say insolence, of such a judgment cannot escape us, even if the reading of the text imposes it on us. It remains to correctly appreciate this paradox, and not, in any case, to stigmatize with hasty, slapdash presumption who knows what error or inconstancy of Spinoza. Great thinkers remain great even in their inconsistencies and violent excesses, for which they have their reasons. We must thus reformulate the question and ask, not so much whether adequate knowledge is demonstrated (because it arguably never is),[23] but why Spinoza claims it, despite its lack of theoretical foundation. In short, for what reason does Spinoza postulate adequate knowledge of all things and the infinite essence of God by the finite *mens humana*, when he does not succeed in demonstrating them?

Let us take as guiding principle a proven fact: even before *Ethica II*, Spinoza had developed a doctrine of the adequate idea. It appears in *De Intellectus Emendatione*, §§69–76. A fundamental thesis introduces it: formally considered, true knowledge differs from false knowledge "non tantum per denominationem extrinsecam, sed maxime per intrinsecam—not only by an extrinsic, but chiefly by an intrinsic denomination" (§69, p. 31); thus, when an architect conceives a building according to (correct) order, when even this building would not yet have been carried out to the end (existence), it remains no less already (in essence) a *"cogitatio vera"*; on the contrary, the statement of an essence endowed with existence (for example "Peter exists"), in order to remain true simply as thought, must formally imply this existence outside of thought. As a result, the truth consists *aliquid reale* in the idea (§70). *Ethica II* will make itself in part an echo of this thesis by defining the truth as *a norma sui et falsi*.[24] Knowledge henceforth consists in deducing from an idea—whose coherent deployment becomes the evidence of its truth—what it already *objectively* comprehends in it, according to the double meaning of comprehending: what it encompasses by representation as well as what it makes understood as a principle and cause, presumably itself (§71).

The truth "sine relatione" (§70) is deployed following two examples. (a) §71 first of all presumes some *intellectus*, then divine understanding before the creation of the world ("sicut aliqui Dei intellectum concipunt—as some conceive God's intellect"); if it conceives some new being ("ens aliquod novum"), which does not yet exist outside of thought, and if from this thought it correctly deduces (*deducere*) other thoughts, the truth of the whole will not rest in any externally existing object, but in the power of understanding alone. (b) §72 then generalizes this result, which holds not only for divine understanding but also for us, provided that "ideam aliquam veram ob oculos ponamus—we place before our eyes some true idea" independent of any object of nature. Thus, even without generating any sphere in nature, we can generate its concept based on its cause and its true idea alone: a semi-circle rotating around its "center" (in fact around its axis); in contrast, the idea of a semi-circle taken "nuda" (nude, in nature) would lead to an "affirmatio falsa," if it were not joined to those of movement and sphere.[25] The deduction is only correct to the extent that true ideas are reciprocally implied; falsehood consists only in what "aliquid de aliqua re affirmetur, quod in ipsius, quem formavimus, conceptu non continetur—something is affirmed of a thing that is not contained in the concept we have formed of the thing": a deduction must only affirm of a thing what its idea understands already or deduces from it. These two examples of ideas that are adequate by their intrinsic characteristics call for a rapprochement with the traits of an intrinsically adequate idea, and faithfully reproduce the traits of a true idea according to Descartes. (a) First, the thesis that "simplices cogitationes non posse non esse veras—simple thoughts cannot but be true" (§72, p. 32) responds to a constant thesis of the *Regulæ* concerning simple natures: "naturas illas simplices esse omnes per se notas, et nunquam ullam falsitatem continere—the simple natures are all self-evident and never contain any falsity."[26] (b) The example of the sphere generated by its semi-circle responds quite well to the examples of objects known by *intuitus*: "Ita uniusquisque animo potest intueri [...] triangulum terminari tribus lineis tantum, globum unica superficie, et similia—everyone can see by his mind [...] that a triangle is bounded by just three lines, and a sphere by a single surface, and the like."[27] (c) Spinoza determines the falsehood of deduction by a criterion that is also intrinsic to it: it results in truncated and mangled ideas, ideas without causes, or properties without reason. The error results, then, from a "nimis abstracte" conception, which separates objects by abstraction instead of linking them together (§75); in this way abstract universals also arise (§76). Yet, we have seen, Descartes uses the same criterion.[28]

From this point, if the *De Intellectus Emendatione* treats the adequate idea in strictly Cartesian terms, how can we explain the ultimate disagreement with Descartes in the *Ethica*? Or must we situate it between *De Intellectus Emendatione* and the *Ethica*? I will suggest that the two ruptures take place successively. Of course, in a first move, the *De Intellectus Emendatione* retrieves the Cartesian corollary of the true idea, that is, the finitude of the human mind; the two examples thus place in parallel the deduction of a true idea by divine understanding (§71) and its deduction by *nos*, the finite understanding (§72). But immediately a difference opposes them: we must fix "qua potentia mens nostra eas [sc. ideas] formare possit—by what power our mind can form these [simple ideas]," and thus recognize that this power "se non extendere in infinitum—does not extend to infinity"; this "defectus nostræ perceptionis—defect of our perception" makes it inevitable that at one moment or another our deduction gets stuck in abstractly truncated ideas. Our thought, in its finitude, does not succeed in adequately producing all ideas and in deducing all their properties, for inadequacy results from finitude and indicates by contrast another thinking being. "Certum est, ideas inadæquatas ex eo tantum in nobis oriri, quod pars sumus alicuius entis cogitantis, cuius quædam cogitationes ex toto, quædam ex parte tantum nostram mentem constituunt.—It is certain that inadequate ideas arise in us only from the fact that we are a part of a thinking being, of which some thoughts wholly constitute our mind, while others do so only in part" (§73, p. 33). This recognition could be at most extended, then, to what Descartes thought of it, as the profession "of intellectual nature in general, the idea of which, if considered without limitation, is that which presents God to us, and if limited, is that of an angel or a human soul" (AT I, 353.22–26; CSMK, 55). But, far from admitting this limitation received from Descartes, *De Intellectus Emendatione* also immediately proceeds to subvert it. Already §49 had clarified that, if the investigation must begin "ad normam datæ cuiuscumque veræ ideæ—taking as a standard any given true idea" (p. 22), the perfect method requires having an *idea Entis perfectissimi*, thus attaining "quanto occius—as quickly as possible" the knowledge of this being, and no longer of any particular being. The same urgency punctuates the whole treatise, with ever greater insistence the more it develops. We must begin with the first elements, thus "a fonte et origine Naturæ, quam primum fieri potest—from the source and origin of Nature, if we proceed as far as we can" (§75, p. 33); to order our perfections and unify them (by deduction of adequate ideas) "requiritur ut, quamprimum fieri potest et ratio postulat, inquiramus an detur quoddam Ens et simul quale, quod sit omnium rerum causa, ut ejus essentia objectiva sit etiam causa omnium nostrarum idearum—it is required, and reason demands, that we ask, as soon as possible, whether there is a certain Being, and at the same time, what sort it is, which is the cause of all things, so that its objective essence may also be the cause of all our ideas" (§99). The break with Descartes thus arises clearly: if our finite understanding necessarily results in ideas made inadequate by abstraction (Cartesian observation), we must not admit this limit, but transgress it by going back to the true idea of God, such that from it an always adequate deduction of all ideas becomes infinitely possible. Indeed, as early as the *De Intellectus Emendatione*, Spinoza postulates that adequate knowledge of nature, to attain the required apodicticity, implies adequate knowledge of God: "nihil nos de Natura posse intelligere, quin simul cognitionem primæ causæ, sive Dei, ampliorem reddamus—we cannot understand anything of Nature without at the same time rendering our knowledge of the first cause, *or* God, more ample" (§92, note, p. 39). The final break of finite and infinite, which played out as a transcendental determination for Descartes, no longer appears to Spinoza except as an epistemological obstacle, and thus can be overcome.

Here is where the second rupture intervenes, this time between *De Intellectus Emendatione* and the *Ethica*. Their common ground comes from the fact that, according to the former, "pars sumus alicujus entis cogitantis, cujus quædam cogitationes ex toto, quædam ex parte tantum nostram mentem constituunt—we are a part of a thinking being, of which some thoughts wholly constitute our mind, while others do so only in part" (§73, p. 33), and, according to the latter,

mentem humanam partem esse infiniti intellectus Dei; ac proinde [. . .] cum dicimus Deum hanc vel illam ideam habere non tantum quatenus naturam humanæ mentis constituit sed quatenus simul cum mente humana alterius rei etiam habet ideam, tum dicimus mentem humanam rem ex parte sive inadæquate percipere.— the human mind is a part of the infinite intellect of God. Therefore, when we say [. . .] that God has this or that idea, not only in so far as he constitutes the nature of the human mind, but in so far as he also has the idea of another thing together with the human mind, then we say that the human mind perceives a thing only partially, or inadequately. (II, P11C)

But the *De Intellectus Emendatione* does not yet overcome this gap, because it never reaches the absolutely true idea of the supremely perfect being, by deducing "ad normam datæ cujuscunque veræ ideæ—to the standard of any given true idea"; and thus it remains incomplete.[29] The *Ethica*, on the other hand, claims to attain adequate knowledge of God's infinite essence

(II, P47), thus adequate knowledge of all ideas by referring them to God (II, P32); and indeed the true ideas of the *causa sui, substantia*, and God are in fact given from the initial definitions. It is thus no longer a question of going back from some true idea to the true idea of the supremely perfect being (a posteriori), but of deducing from the only true infinite and perfect idea all its properties, namely the infinite substance of all the modes (a priori).

It is not necessary to consider here the procedures or the absence of procedures that allow such a transition; what is important is simply to determine if the adequacy preserves, from one work to the other, the same features. Clearly, this is not the case, on a number of points. (a) The true idea is defined in the *Treatise* by an intrinsic adequacy (§69), thus absolutely "sine relatione ad alias—without reference to others" (§71), "nullo alio signo—no other sign" (§35, p. 18). Certainly the *Ethica* maintains the self-sufficiency of the true ("sine relatione ad objectum [. . .] denominationes intrinsecas habet—without relation to an object, has [. . .] intrinsic denominations of a true idea," II, D4); but it prefaces this definition by the traditional extrinsic definition "Idea vera debet cum suo ideato convenire—a true idea must agree with its object" (I, A6); it is precisely this that it relies on to establish the possibility of a reference for all our ideas of God: "Omnes enim ideæ quæ in Deo sunt, cum suis ideatis omnino conveniunt (per cor. P7) adeoque (per A6, I) omnes veræ sunt—For all ideas which are in God agree entirely with their objects (by P7), and so (by I, A6) they are all true" (II, P32D). How can we fail to be surprised that, at the precise moment that the aporia which had stopped *De Intellectus Emendatione* first caves in, Spinoza uses precisely the definition of the truth that he had fought against? How could we not take seriously the conjunction of these two innovations—our ideas becoming the very ideas of God, while the truth changes from intrinsic to extrinsic? In short, how can we avoid the suspicion that the loss of self-sustaining adequacy would be the price to pay for attaining epistemological univocity? The *De Intellectus Emendatione* concluded from the intrinsic definition of the true idea that "in ideis dari aliquid reale, per quod veræ a falsis distinguuntur—something real is given in ideas, through which the true are distinguished from the false" (§70, p. 31); how can we admit from this that *Ethica* declares just after having acquired epistemological univocity, that "Nihil in ideis positivum est propter quod falsæ dicuntur—there is nothing positive in ideas on account of which they are called false" (II, P33)? Of course, we could say that falsehood does not constitute a positive reality; this is a banality taken up by the tradition and to which Spinoza adds nothing; but, from the point of view of the adequate idea in the strict sense, falsehood is indeed indicated by *aliquid positivum*: the apparition of mangled, abstract, contradictory ideas. How to reconcile the criteria of an *aliquid reale* between the true and false idea, with the *nihil positivum* that signals (or rather does not signal) the false idea? Without prejudice to other arguments, we conclude that the *Ethica* only accomplishes the program of the *De Intellectus Emendatione* by abandoning it, even by inverting its method.

And the reason for this is evident: this method, particularly that of the adequate idea as intrinsically true, owes too much to the Cartesian thematic and the transcendental role of the abyss between the finite and infinite, which precisely the *Ethica* has as its goal to fill. For it claims to accomplish rationally and exactly what Descartes considered to remain inaccessible to the finitude of our *mens humana* except by divine intervention—"nisi peculiariter [. . .] Deus revelet—unless God grants a special revelation," "nisi a Deo reveletur—unless it is revealed by God," in short except for "quelque extraordinaire assistance du ciel, et [. . .] être plus qu'homme—some extraordinary aid from heaven and to be more than a mere man."[30] In the light of this convergence a strange hypothesis thus arises: does the Spinozist doctrine of the adequate idea aspire to accomplish at the strict "level of reason" what the appeal to grace and revelations would have allowed in the domain of theology?

§6. The Second Challenge of the Recourse to Adequacy

Once he links these two possibilities of adequate knowledge (of the essence of God and ideas of singular things), Spinoza takes up in a negative mode two questions that, for example, Suarez joined by a common denial: "Nam, si termini intelligantur, est per se evidens, non posse nos in hac vita cognoscere quidditative illas substantias [i.e. separatas] [. . .]. Est autem evidens non posse nos Deum in hac vita quidditative cognoscere—If we understand the terms, it is self-evident that we cannot in this life understand separated substances in their quiddity [. . .]. It is just as evident that we cannot in this life understand God in his quiddity." These two prohibitions are not only juxtaposed, they are interconnected: "Non possunt illa divina exemplaria in *se conscipi, nisi Deus in se ipso videatur*—These divine exemplars cannot be contemplated in themselves, unless God can [also] be seen in himself."[31] From the common medieval vantage point, we cannot know originary ideas of the essence of particular things (making our ideas of modes adequate, as *Ethica II* would say) except by knowing God himself, that is, either that God reveals himself (as again Descartes will say, in an echo of Suarez), or that we attain the adequate idea of the essence of God (according to the formula of *Ethica II*, P47). The two questions are bound together by a joint denial for Suarez (and Descartes) and by an equal affirmation for Spinoza.

It remains, then, to examine how Suarez asked these two questions and justified his double denial; in contrast, we could measure more precisely the scope of the Spinozist inversion. In fact, Suarez does not conflict with Spinoza head on. The knowledge that he refuses *in hac vita* to human beings he nevertheless accords to the *beati*, the blessed; with two minor reservations that must be laid out, Suarez recovers in the beatific vision the characteristics that Spinoza grants in this life to readers of the *Ethica* who reach adequate knowledge. The beatific vision would thus anticipate adequate knowledge and transpose it from theology to metaphysics—at least this is the thesis that I would like to sketch out.

The *beati* know the essence (the quiddity) and the divine substance that men do not yet know *in via* and thus prefigure the Spinozist ambition. Suarez states without equivocation that the "*objectum proximum et immediatum visionis beatæ esse Deum ipsum per essentiam et substantiam suam absque ulla creatura seu imagine creata*—the closest and immediate object of the beatific vision is God himself seen by his essence and his substance, without any creature or created images."[32] Further, this knowledge of God results directly from the finally adequate knowledge *in patria* of the object already recognized *in via* by our mind, the concept of infinite being: "*Deum, absolute loquendo, contineri sub objecto adæquato intellectus, quod est ens, in quantum ens*—Speaking absolutely, God is contained under the *adequate* object of understanding, which is being as being"; for God, infinite being, appears as the "*adæquata* ratio objecti intellectus nostri—the *adequate* reason of the object of our understanding," remaining confused and indeterminate *in via*.[33] This adequate knowledge is also *intuitiva*.[34] Nevertheless, a restriction comes to weaken the anticipation of *Ethica II* and maintain the opposition between Spinoza and Suarez (together with Descartes): for

Suarez, even in the beatific vision, intuitive and adequate knowledge of the divine essence does not attain exhaustive comprehension: "visio beatifica non est comprehensio Dei, nimirum, quia de ratione comprehensionis est, ita uidere totum quod est in se formaliter et intrinsece, ut ex vi talis visionis etiam cognoscatur quidquid ex tali re consequi potest, vel ab ea pendere— the beatific vision is not a comprehension of God, namely, because it belongs to the definition of comprehension to see everything that is formally and intrinsically in itself, such that by the power of such a vision everything that can follow such a thing or depend on it is also known"; even Suarez retreats before this consequence, which Spinoza nevertheless takes on: "visio creata hoc non habet, neque habere potest, ideo comprehensio non est—created vision does not have this and cannot have it—therefore it is not comprehension."[35] For Suarez, despite the adequacy of beatific vision, it is never an adequacy to the very infinity of God, for "impossibile est ut comprehendat [sc. intellectus creatus] rem intelligibilem simpliciter infinitam, ut est Deus. Patet consequentia, quia *comprehensio* requirit *adæquationem* quandam inter capacitatem intelligentis, intellectionem et intelligibile, quam adæquationem impossibile est invenire inter finitum et infinitum.—It is impossible that [a created intellect] comprehend a thing that is purely and simply infinite, like God is. The consequence is clear, because a *comprehension* requires a certain *adequacy* between the capacity of the one who understands the understanding, and the understandable, an *adequacy* which is impossible to find between the finite and the infinite."[36] It is thus once again necessary to distinguish carefully between two adequacies: God, as a being, is thus grasped or comprehended under the adequate object of the concept of *ens*, yet without God in his infinity falling under any equality with finite understanding. In this sense, even the beatific vision of Suarez does not promise *in patria* what the adequate knowledge of Spinoza ensures from the second kind and even for a finite understanding: "Intellectus, actu *finitus* aut actu infinitus nihil, præter Dei attributa ejusque affectiones, *comprehendit*."[37] Such a Suarezian point of departure therefore clearly situates the Spinozist enterprise, but by accentuating all the more its exceptional audacity.

This starting point can be described by recourse to Suarez, but it in fact concerns common debates, as is illustrated as well by Thomas Aquinas, for whom "simpliciter concedendum est, quod beati Dei essentiam uideant— Hence it must be absolutely granted that the blessed see the essence of

God."³⁸ They can only do so as a consequence of natural desire for God, for the ambiguity of the objective concept of *ens* does not yet intervene and leaves the field to God's gratuitous initiative. "Oportet, si Dei essentia videatur, quod per ipsammet essentiam diuinam intellectus ipsam videat, ut sic in tali visione divina essentia sit et quod videtur et quo videtur—if God's essence be seen at all, it is necessary that the intellect see it by the divine essence itself, so that in such a vision the divine essence is both what is seen and that by which it is seen"; the vision would remain impossible if God himself did not make it, "nisi Deo hoc faciente—unless God himself bring this about," "nisi per actionem diuinam—except through the divine agency."³⁹ As a result, it is fitting that "ipsa diuina essentia copuletur intellectui [sc. humani] ut forma intelligibilis—the divine essence itself must be united to the [human] intellect as an intelligible form," which immediately becomes the form actively informing the passive intellect;⁴⁰ whence its extraordinary intervention as *lux gloriæ* provoking a *lumen gloriæ*.⁴¹ For the disproportion between the intelligible form, which is in this case exceptional, and understanding, which is always finite, prohibits it from reaching comprehension and adequacy, precisely because vision ultimately takes place.

Virtus finita non potest *adæquare* in sua operatione obiectum infinitum. Substantia autem divina est quoddam infinitum per comparationem ad omnem intellectum creatum, cum omnis intellectus creatus sub certa specie terminetur. Impossibile est ergo quod visio alicuius intellectus creatus *adæquet* in videndo divinam substantiam; scilicet ita perfecte ipsam videndo, sicut visibilis est. Nullus igitur intellectus creatus ipsam *comprehendit*—A finite power cannot in its operation *equal* an infinite object. Now the divine substance is something infinite in comparison with every created intellect, since every created intellect is confined to a certain species. Therefore, the vision of a created intellect cannot possibly *equal* the divine substance in seeing it, namely, in seeing the divine substance as perfectly as it is visible. Therefore, no created intellect *comprehends* it.⁴²

We must go back at least as far as Thomas Aquinas to lay out the scope of the Spinozist assertion of adequate knowledge of divine essence. Its originality does not consist in declaring it has obtained such a knowledge (since, until Descartes, all Christian thinkers admitted this), but in its claim to have obtained it *before* the beatific vision, by means of simple rationality, now responsible for salvation. To question the possibility or impossibility of such success becomes all the more legitimate when the now explicit ambition to naturalize divination is declared openly. For in Spinoza, it is no longer knowledge which, by the grace of the vision, results from divinization, it is adequate knowledge which, alone and by its own means, must ensure divinization. The possible impasse of *Ethica II*, P47, would, in this context, become an irremediable failure.

We can now take up, this time starting from Thomas Aquinas, the second question opened by the beatific vision: what do the *beati* see when they see the divine essence? Although they cannot comprehend all the consequences of the creative principle, they know, in the known essence of the creator, the essences (species) of things created: "Intellectus igitur qui per lumen divinum elevatur ad videndam Dei substantiam, multo magis eodem lumino perficitur ad omnia alia intelligenda quæ sunt in rerum natura—Consequently, the intellect which, by the divine light, is raised to see the substance of God is all the more perfected by the same light so as to see all other intelligibles in the universe."[43] Seeing the essence of God by the direct action of God's essence on the finite understanding allows it not only to see God (if inadequately) as God himself is seen and is known, but also to see, in his essence, the created things as he sees them even before creating them. Without yet qualifying these two kinds of knowledge as adequacy, Suarez reproduces the strict Thomist connection. "Per visionem Dei possunt videri creaturæ in Deo tanquam in causa et medio cognito per quod et in quo alia simplici intuitu et sine discursu videntur—By the vision of God, creatures can be seen in God, as in their cause and the means by which other things are seen by looking and without discursivity."[44] Suarez' contribution to the Thomist doctrine, which he maintains in its structure (the connection between the vision of divine essence and that of the essence of created things), lies in the introduction of the possible: even in the beatific vision, it is under the original metaphysical category of the possible that the *beati* see creatures in the Word. If we think that Spinoza also defines the *ens* as that which can exist, and that in a way he transposes the Word into an attribute of thought in the *intellectus absolute infinitus*, we must pay attention to the surprising coincidence between his definition of the medial infinite mode in the attribute of extension as *facies totius Universi* and what according to Suarez the *beati* see in the Word: "omnes beatos visuros in Verbo totam universi machinam, compositionem

Spinoza: Adequacy and Vision 249

et ordinem—all the blessed will see in the Word, the entire frame, composition and order of the universe."[45]

Could Spinoza retrieve the theme of the beatific vision? At the very least, his stubborn but fragile effort in *Ethica II* can be read within this horizon. Adequate knowledge of the eternal and infinite essence of God (P47) would replicate the intuition of the divine essence according to the beatific vision by transposing it into the knowledge of the second kind (without even waiting for the third). The adequate knowledge of ideas of finite modes (P32–34) would replicate the vision of essences of creatures by transposing it into that of the essence of the creator—with one key difference: the order of the two kinds of adequate knowledge would be inverted, for a fundamental reason; while for Thomas Aquinas (and to a lesser extent for Suarez) it is the beatific vision that commands knowledge, for Spinoza it is knowledge that commands beatitude. Finally, radicalizing these two kinds of theological knowledge into resolutely adequate sciences would also result from a fundamental reason: rejecting divine transcendence in effect lifts the hypothesis of an incommensurability of the infinite and the finite.

From now on, nothing is opposed to a reconciliation that, far from minimizing Spinoza's originality, opens the horizon where it stands out and can be evaluated more precisely. With the doctrine of adequate ideas, *Ethica II* would try within the limits of metaphysics alone to reach the extreme position of human knowledge that had been attained by Christian theology, and that Descartes' metaphysics had given up recapturing, ever aware of its theological finitude.

§7. Spinozist Thought and the Beatific Vision

This reconciliation, within the current state of the analysis, could only claim the dignity of a reflective judgment, not a decisive one. Be that as it may, can it be reinforced by arguments of fact, which would establish, if only partially, a relation between Spinoza and the theological problematic of the beatific vision?

The direct lines between Spinoza, on the one hand, and Thomas Aquinas or Suarez, on the other, have not been definitively established. The similarities or allusions that have been already revealed, although quite numerous, do not yet substantiate any genuine reading.[46] I will confine myself to depositing in the unresolved file of this question one new piece of evidence. The theses of Suarez were violently disputed and thus carefully presented to Spinoza in a lively way by a Protestant author, Jacobus Revius, who published a *Suarez repurgatus. Sive Syllabus Disputationum Metaphysicarum Franscisci Suarez societatis Jesu theologi* from Leiden in 1643.[47] Spinoza had had at least a good reason to comment: several years later in *Statera Philosophiæ Cartesianæ,* Jacobus Revius would attack Adriaan Heereboord, whose *Meletemata Philosophicæ* he knew well.[48] Yet, one of the "purified" passages of Spinoza precisely concerns the beatific vision; without speculating on the authenticity of a Spinozist reading of this dispute, its main arguments may be enlightening.

Suarez maintained that the *beati,* seeing God, also form a mental word:

Vere enim conspiciunt Deum prout in se est, et ita formant in se conceptum formalem, quo sibi repræsentant Deum prout est in se; et ille conceptus est verbum et non aliud. [. . .] Addo præterea, beatum videndo Deum et creaturam in Deo, etiam uidere ideam quam Deus habet de creaturis, et ideo ipsummet conceptum formalem Dei posse quodammodo subire rationem ideæ.—For they truly behold God as he is in himself, and thus they form in themselves a formal concept, by which they represent God as he is in himself; and so this concept is a word and nothing else. [. . .] I add, in addition to this, that the blessed seeing God and the creature in God, sees also the idea that God has of creatures, and therefore in a certain way the very formal concept of God will be able to fall under the definition of the idea.[49]

Underneath the scholastic appearances, profound theoretical stakes are being decided: does the beatific vision always come down to representation, taken in its metaphysical sense? Do the *beati* see the divine essence by itself (as Thomas Aquinas held) or by a distinct formal concept, thus by an instrument proper to finite understanding? Does finite understanding thus also dispose of the same formal concept that God would use to know creatures, as would then be logical? In short, does finite understanding see creatures by the same concepts as God, to the point that these concepts can, perhaps, become the *exemplaria* for its own actions and finite operations? The audacity and imprudence of Suarez seem patent enough for Revius to feel justified in stigmatizing *multa monstra* in the Jesuit's text.

Let us therefore identify these three "monsters." (a) If vision takes place by a formal (human) concept, and not directly by divine essence, then this concept will be finite, before an infinite; representation would not be possible: "nam conceptus ille finitus est tam quoad esse reale quam intellectuale, itaque Deum ut in se est et consequenter ut infinitus est, repræsentare nullo modo potest—for this concept is finite, with respect to both its real being and its intellectual being, thus it cannot in any way represent God, since he is in himself and consequently infinite." Descartes will face this difficulty against Gassendi (Chapter 4, §5–6), and he will only overcome it by admitting that infinity remains incommensurable (incomprehensible) to the finite idea that is conceived by a finite mind; but it is not certain that Spinoza avoided a similar aporia of the infinite. (b) If the *beati*, seeing God, see "etiam [. . .] ideam quam Deus habet de creaturis—as well [. . .] the idea that God has of creatures," it follows that they are "omniscient"; indeed, if they know the divine essence, and by his very idea, the essence of things, there is no longer anything more to God that outstrips the science that the *beati* already have: "nihil Deo reliquit quo ipsum hac in parte exuperet—[Suarez] leaves nothing to God, by which he surpasses [man] in this domain." It is clear that Spinoza will consciously try to arrive at exactly this similar result: that science remains univocal, that it is deployed starting from finite modes or from an infinite mode (*Ethica I*, P16 and P30; *II*, P32–P34 and P43). (c) Finally, if the *beati* in their vision have a genuinely formal concept, they can appropriate it and use it as exemplary for their possible actions; supposing they receive a corresponding practical power, nothing is to stop their "omniscience" from doubling: "Hinc sequitur beatos omnipotens esse posse—hence it follows that the blessed can be all-powerful." But doesn't Spinoza also seek this power by assuring an activity of the spirit with respect to all the ideas by their adequate knowledge in God (*Ethica V*, P3–P15)? When Revius concludes by denouncing in Suarez an "anthropolatry by which the blessed are equal to God,"[30] is he not also critiquing in advance the Spinozist identity of a consciousness equally "sui et Dei et rerum—of himself, of God, and of things" (*Ethica* V, P42S, 617)? But we do not even have to decide on these questions to observe that the very terms of the polemic that Revius directs against Suarez largely overlap the lexicon and concepts of the *Ethica*, and therefore it is not absurd to read it starting from the debate on the beatific vision.

One last question remains: why would Spinoza risk intervening in a theological debate that his whole enterprise only aims, in a sense, to render useless and inane? First, one might argue, to critique the common theses on the beatific vision, and, extending the evolution of Suarez, to transpose them within the limits of strict metaphysics. Next and above all because he had presupposed from the outset that the human mind must have, in this life, an idea, and thus knowledge, of God. The *Cogitata Metaphysica I*, §2, had posed a constraining dilemma: "Quæri adhuc possest, quomodo nos, nondum intellecta natura Dei, rerum essentias intelligimus; cum illæ, ut modo diximus, a sola Dei natura pendeant—still, it could be asked how we understand the essences of things, when the nature of God is not yet understood. For these essences, as we have just said, depend on the nature of God alone"; the response, still barely Spinozist, examines two hypotheses: (a) either, since "res jam creatæ sunt—things have already been created," we can thus know their essences a posteriori; (b) or, they are not, and then "prorsus concederem, id impossibile fore nisi *post* naturæ Dei *adæquatam* cognitionem—I should concede fully that it would be impossible to understand [them] except *after* an *adequate* knowledge of the nature of God":[51] if one ignores (or rejects) creation, (adequate) knowledge of finite things is no longer possible, except by having an a priori idea, which depends in the last analysis on nothing less than the adequate knowledge of the eternal essence of God. As soon as the hypothesis of creation is rejected, Spinoza will thus limit himself to presupposing adequate knowledge of this sole and first idea. Indeed, affirmations are not lacking: "Habemus enim ideam Dei—we indeed have the idea of God"; or: "Maar de mensch heeft een Idea van God. *Ergo*.—But man has an Idea of God. Therefore"; and all the *De Intellectus Emendatione* will be punctuated by the dependence of adequate knowledge of things on adequate knowledge of God.[52] I thus suggest a hypothesis: because by the refusal of all creation he forbids himself a posteriori access to ideas of both particular things and God, Spinoza limits himself to an exclusive a priori knowledge of both; he must therefore take up, whether he wants to or not, the theological model of the beatific vision, which alone allows him to envisage the necessary relation between these two kinds of knowledge.

Perhaps, besides, one must ascribe to the powerful fascination of this model the fact that Spinoza was imperturbably able to pursue the course of the demonstrations of *Ethica II* despite the patent aporias that by all appearances should have stopped him.

CONCLUSION

The Descartes to Come

This final journey may disconcert or even disappoint the reader, since it ceaselessly corrects, complicates, and indirectly rereads the Cartesian texts. As if these very texts furnished only indications that are always subject to revision by other texts of Descartes or by reference to other authors, sustaining their attacks, or aiming at them by adapting themselves. Henri Gouhier demanded that the Cartesian corpus be put under a microscope, but Jean Beaufret added that it was just as necessary to look at it through an astronomical telescope's magnification. Having practiced both, we often end up, it seems, with distortions of the doctrine, which take away the evidence and the cohesion that we usually presuppose it has. But there are explanations that justify this result. Unlike his great successors (up to but not including Kant), Descartes did not defend any doctrine or aim at any system. He proceeded from "battle" to battle, advancing at the pace of those conflicts "where [he] had fortune on [his] side" (AT VI, 67.24; CSM I, 145), registering them, in whatever region they might be, as they came, with tactics that were different each time, in a sense without a preconceived strategic plan. He did not want to establish an empire but instead secure strongholds. These battles depended on issues debated in his time, by his contemporaries and his predecessors, and each time, he adapted his weapons, taking up the arms of his adversary and occupying his terrain, so as finally to make his breakthroughs there and redefine everything.

254 Conclusion

Order does not consist in organizing in advance a space of conquest and possession, but in following a single procedure in active confrontations according to the actions to be engaged. Order does not proceed from a system and does not aim at one; it even tends to free itself from systems so as to better mobilize its forces by adjusting them to the situations it faces. Order follows a method, not an architectonics. It always remains at the origin, far from disappearing into an appendix (as in Malebranche) or dissolving into the system (as in Spinoza). Descartes in this sense illustrates fairly well what Husserl defined as the order that phenomenology must follow when it enquires into the status of the "European sciences":

> Thus we find ourselves in a sort of *circle*. The understanding of the beginnings is to be gained fully only by starting with science as given in its present-day form, looking back at its development. But in the absence of an understanding of the *beginnings* the development is mute as a *development of meaning*. Thus we have no other choice than to proceed forward and backward in a zigzag pattern; the one must help the other in an interplay. Relative clarification on one side brings some elucidation on the other, which in turn casts light back on the former.[1]

I have tried to apply to the very texts of Descartes what Husserl carried out in order to understand the origins of the Galilean and Cartesian science of nature. Each time what Descartes advances—like one army advancing against another—he moves forward by entering into the opposing line, by turning back its thrust and, overcoming it, imposing on it his new order. The originally dialogical nature of Cartesian thought implies combat and the reorganization of the defeated forces. Cartesian theses can only be understood by reconstituting the history and the itinerary of his victories, which he never masks, and whose losses and wounds he retains (once again, unlike Spinoza and Malebranche). Thus, he must not be read as a system, but as a list of names of victories inscribed on a triumphal arch. This is why Descartes' polemics against his adversaries and partners (including against the Cartesians) constitute the architecture of his thought and the proofs of its good order.

This order without system now confirmed, it becomes possible, as we have already noted at several points, to conceive that the order of the meditation and of the research proceeds by acts, and thus by decisions. Husserl saw this in Descartes quite perfectly:

This reflection is one that originally occurs in the *will*. Indeed, in defining himself as philosophical, the subject makes a resolution of the will (*Willensentschluß*) directed at his entire future cognitive life. From that point on, he no longer wants to know things in general and in just any manner at all, no longer wants to know things as he previously has known them (whether prescientifically or scientifically), but instead defines himself willingly (*willentlich*) as one who perpetually desires (*Wollenden*) nothing but absolutely justified cognition, and cognition that is systematic [?] and universal—a philosophy. Out of this reflective will (*reflektiven Willen*) arise meditations on the sense of this ambition and the possibilities of its realization. The contents of these latter meditations [. . .] constitute the necessary first beginning (*Anfang*) on the path to philosophy. They form the site of the method [. . .]. If, accordingly, the philosophizing *Ego* must become for itself the focus of its own will (*Willen*), if it is to arrive at a philosophy, then it falls to it also, but only later on, to become for itself its first cognitive theme: it must grasp itself, on the basis of a certain methodological apperception, as a transcendental or pure *Ego*.[2]

If the order comes under the philosophical decision, and thus a will, the theses that each time it advances (like a line of attack advances on the field of battle) do not consist in statements, in theses and doctrines, but in acts of thought actually carried out, as much as in physical acts:

The Cartesian *Meditationes* do not purport to be accidental subjective musings on Descartes's part, let alone a literary-artistic device for the transmission of the author's thoughts. Rather, they clearly present themselves as meditations which are necessary in respect of the manner and order of their motivations, as meditations that the radically philosophizing subject as such *must necessarily pass through. It must do so* as a subject that has chosen the idea of philosophy as the guiding purposive idea of its life and that therefore is to become a genuine philosopher precisely *by realizing* this idea in its cognitive life through its own activity.[3]

The *Meditationes* must be read as a succession of decisions and thus of acts of thought; they do not develop a doctrine through demonstrations (like Spinoza's *Ethics* or Malebranche's *The Search After Truth*), but venture theses that, if they are actually accomplished, restart the advance of thought as far as the things themselves will allow.

In this way, perhaps, the unquestionable ruptures in the order of material and even of reasons in the *Meditationes* are best explained: they point more deeply to revivals of thought through the advance of a new hypothesis and through the act each time of thinking it, as if fresh troops came to reinforce the spirit of the struggle. It is as if the meditating *ego* asked itself, when a resistance stops it, "What would happen if I thought with new hypotheses, new tools? What acts of thought would then become possible? And how far?" The patent examples of such restarts are not lacking. Let us take note of the most striking examples.

In *Meditationes I–II*, the resistance of common skeptical doubt finds itself carried away by the hyperbole of the God who can do everything, but who, for that very reason, must presuppose an *ego sum* that responds to him. The *cogitatio* is inaugurated in the mode of doubt, since doubt itself appears as an act of thought.

In *Meditatio II*, the *res cogitans*, operating in the mode of the *intellectus*, observes that it knows with certainty its existence even if it does not know its essence; the bracketing of the essence of the *ego* (*res* rather than *essentia*) identifies it certainly as an act of principal attribute without an identified *substantia*, one of *unknown substance*.

In *Meditatio III*, the assimilation of the ideas in general to *modi cogitandi* manifests their univocity in the actual immanence, by a genuine reduction to (and through) the *cogitatio* undifferentiated as such. Then the consideration of these same immanent lived experiences as intentional and the introduction of the criteria of their distinctions (substance / accidents, finite / infinite substances, the principle of causality) allows for comparison of the intentional meanings of the different *cogitata*. This rupture in the order of reasons triggers a phenomenological revival and the conquest of the existence of God.

In *Meditatio IV*, the variation in the modes of *cogitatio* begins. By repeating (re-executing) the *ego cogito* in another mode than the *intellectus* (privileged in *Meditationes II–III*), the will also allows the repetition of the relation of immanent transcendence of the *ego* with the infinite (already confirmed at the end of *Meditatio III*) through the infinity of the will of a *mens finita*.

In *Meditatio V*, identifying the proper place for the mathematical truths by assigning them to the *cogitatio*'s imaginative mode allows us, by going backwards and against the grain, to prove once again the existence of God, but this time at the level of this imaginative mode of the *cogitatio*.

In *Meditatio VI*, the restart happens in two stages. First, the proof of the existence of material things is gained through the reinforcement of the *cogitatio* as imagination (the essence of material things is reduced to mathematical ideas) and the new hypothesis of sensation as the passive mode of the *cogitatio* as sensation; this passivity attests to the external existence of things running counter to their essence, which is imagined. Next, a final restart (the observation of the *meum corpus* as *arctissime conjunctum et quasi permixtum* [*menti*], not as the objectifiable extended body) authorizes the rational observation of the union of the soul and the body and thus a *limited* validation of the *cogitatio* in the mode of the *sensus*. Thus, the *ego* is freed from the ontico-ontological determinations (existence, essence) so as to reach that which, for lack of a better term, we will characterize as *ethical* determinations—passivity and also activity, generosity and freedom, decision and recognition of the infinite.

At each stage, the order of the reasons advances only by reinforcing and modifying itself, by venturing new hypotheses that, in fact, are only new acts of thought, each time more complex and difficult than the simpler ones that preceded them. What goes for the course of the *Meditationes* goes as well for the whole Cartesian uptake of *metaphysica*, such that in its era, it will be irreversibly constituted in a system. Such a Cartesian renewal of philosophy was interrupted, starting from the *ego*, by Montaigne, and categorically affirmed, starting from the *logos*, by Suarez. Descartes thus found himself at the confluence of the two possible routes. The one toward *metaphysica*, through onto-theo-logy, or indeed the redoubling of onto-theologies, a path that will be followed by Spinoza, Malebranche, and Leibniz. The other toward an abandoning of philosophy, by the refusal of the system of metaphysics: the route followed by Pascal, and perhaps also by Fénelon and Rousseau. *Metaphysica* was nevertheless the successful attempt (and the whole problem lies in that success) to conjoin in a single system, that of metaphysics, the *logos* and the *ego*, to make the *cogitatio* exercise the sufficiency of reason or, if you prefer, to sanction the *cogitatio* by the authority of the principle of reason, or finally, to identify *Denken* and *Sein* (Hegel).

It was the singular and unprecedented greatness of Descartes to have seen these possibilities, to have been the first to test them all, but, unlike those who invoked his name to put that greatness into operation (Clauberg, Spinoza, Malebranche and others), to have abandoned them. Kant, Schelling, and Nietzsche tried their best, but long after him. Husserl, Heidegger, and Levinas attempted it, but in constant reference precisely to the Cartesian *ego*. All of them believed it necessary to criticize Descartes in their attempt to depose *metaphysica*; but, in order to succeed, all of them very wisely depended on him.

The ambiguities, the modifications, and the alternative paths of Descartes are as important as his most visible breakthroughs, for they too delineate our history and our provenance, our wanderings as well as the possibilities that remain for us.

Appendix: Montaigne, or the Proper Usage of the Skepticism of Saint Augustine

Among the myriad authors quoted by Montaigne, Saint Augustine does not seem, at first glance, to require a privileged treatment. And yet, even without going so far as to follow Andrée Comparot, who judges that the *Essais* could contain some 370 references or allusions to the Augustinian corpus,[1] and by instead confining oneself to the restrictive hypothesis of Pierre Villey[2] of a late reading of St. Augustine by Montaigne (essentially in the 1595 edition, beginning with the translation of the *City of God* by Gentian Hervet, commented upon by Juan Luis Vivès[3]), one must at least take note of about one hundred explicit mentions of the name of St. Augustine, with a dozen identifiable quotations according to the *Concordance* of the *Essais*.[4] A somewhat detailed examination of these occurrences will perhaps allow us to avoid restricting ourselves to the imprecise appreciations that generally dominate interpretation. For example, when a scholar concludes: "we see clearly that he [Montaigne] thinks, more than once and in important matters, like St. Augustine. Is that enough to make of him, from the very first edition of his essay, an Augustinian? Probably not. But would it not be more correct to call him a fideist?"[5] All the commonplaces and imprecisions are found here in a single false question. Indeed, no one thinks of making Montaigne into a pure "Augustinian," a term that, moreover, has no precise meaning; but no one would prefer the term "fideist," which is even less precise (at best it would have to do with a theological heresy); and as to the dating of Montaigne's reading, it would change almost nothing. If in the end Montaigne thinks like St. Augustine, one must be able to show when and how he does or does not do so (what does "more than once" mean here?), and if "important matters" are at issue, they should be identified.

Without claiming to make more than an outline, I would like to undertake here a conceptual reading of the texts in which Montaigne seems to think *with* St. Augustine, in order to decide whether, in each case, he thinks *like* St. Augustine.

1/ *Essais* I.14 [1580]: "it [pain] occupies in us only as much room as we give it. *Tantum doluerunt*, says Saint Augustine, *quantum doloribus se inseruerunt* [They have suffered just so much as they have given into pain]. We feel a surgeon's cut with the razor more than ten sword strokes in the heat of combat" (V58; F39).

The quotation is from *City of God* I.10.1, "Bibliothèque Augustinienne" (cited as BA going forward), vol. 33, p. 224.[6] But a sharp difference here opposes Montaigne, for whom the matter is physical suffering, to Saint Augustine, for whom the matter was only moral suffering provoked by the loss of material goods; moreover, he argued that such loss affects only those of the faithful who are not yet sufficiently detached from them, following 1 Timothy 6:6–10 (quoted just earlier, p. 222): "For we brought nothing into the world, just as we shall not be able to take anything out of it. If we have food and clothing, we shall be content with that." Let us note that here Montaigne, by extending pain's control of thought from the solely moral domain to the properly physical one, thus goes further than Saint Augustine in the positive appreciation of the power of the mind.

2/ *Essais* I.21 [1588]: "Saint Augustine names another who whenever he heard lamentable and plaintive cries would suddenly go into a trance and get so carried away that it was no use to shake him and shout at him, to pinch him and burn him, until he had come to; then he would say that he had heard voices, but as if coming from afar, and he would notice his burns and bruises. And that this was no feigned resistance to his senses was shown by the fact that while in this state he had neither pulse nor breath" (V99; F69–70).

Montaigne quotes almost word for word from *City of God*, XIV, 24, BA 35: 452–53:

Quando ei [a priest named Restitutus, of Calama in Numidia] placebat (rogabatur autem ut hoc faceret ab eis, qui rem mirabilem coram scire cupiebant), ad imitatas quasi lamentantis cujuslibet hominis voces ita se auferebat a sensibus et jacebat simillimus mortuo, ut non solum vellicantes atque pugentes minime sentiret, sed aliquando etiam igne uteretur admoto sine ullo doloris sensu, nisi postmodum ex vulnere; non autem obnitendo, sed non sentiendo non movere corpus eo probabatur, quod tanquam in defuncto nullus inveniebatur anhelitus; hominum tamen voces, si clarius loquerentur, tanquam de longinquo se audire postea referebat.

While he does indeed take up the literal Augustinian description of this case, Montaigne does not hold on to the theological value of the argument that Saint Augustine clearly assigned to it. Augustine included it within a more complex argument: since, even today, the body can obey the will with precision despite our being in the state of sin, how can we not admit that this was even more clearly the case before sin, and thus that procreation could therefore take place without involuntary desire? "Quid causae est, ut non credamus ante inoboedientiae peccatorum corruptionisque supplicium ad propagandam prolem sine ulla libidine servire voluntati humanae humana membra potuisse?—What reason, then, is there for us to believe that, before the sin of disobedience and its punishment of corruptibility, the members of the human body could have been the servants of the human will without any lust, for the procreation of offspring?" (ibid., 454; Dyson, 627). Nevertheless, there is a point of agreement between the two authors regarding the common example: the power of the imagination surpasses what plausibility usually admits.

3/ *Essais* I.21 [1588]:

The organs that serve to discharge the stomach have their own dilatations and compressions, beyond and against our plans, just like those that are destined to discharge the kidneys. To vindicate the omnipotence of our will, Saint Augustine alleges that he knew a man who commanded his behind to produce as many farts as he wanted, and his commentator Vives goes him one better with another example of his own time, of farts arranged to suit the tone of verses pronounced to their accompaniment; but all this does not really argue any pure obedience in this organ; for is there any that is ordinarily more indiscreet or tumultuous? (V102–103; F72–73)

A simple allusion, without an explicit quotation, because it has to do with what is almost a tracing of *City of God* XIV.24.2, BA 35: 452: "Nonnulli ab imo sine paedore ullo ita numerosos pro arbitrio sonitus edunt, ut ex illa etiam parte cantare videantur." Or, in Hervet's translation: "Some make from below, without any shame [if one reads *pudore*] / without filth or stench [if one reads *paedore*], such loud sounds at their pleasure, such that it even seems that they are singing through that place" (*Cité de Dieu*, trans Hervet, 411). Which seems to make an allusion to another case added by Vives: "Within my memory, there was such a man in this city, German by nationality, following the Emperor Maximilian and his son Philip. And he would have rehearsed any verse whatsoever with distinct noise from his rear" (ibid., p. 411). This time, the case is indeed used by Montaigne for the benefit of the same theological argument as that of Saint Augustine, but the stakes are nevertheless not the same. For Saint Augustine, these cases (this one and the preceding one, which both come from the same text) confirm the hypothesis of a prelapsarian and thus also eschatologically possible order of things, where the mind controls the body, in contrast to the order *in via* where sin prevents it—while for Montaigne, the point is to establish "the omnipotence of our will" in this life, without reference, as for Saint Augustine, to its status in the theological economy of salvation. And so, Montaigne would instead anticipate Descartes here.

4/ *Essais* I.27 [1580]:

But to condemn wholesale all similar stories seems to me a singular impudence. The great Saint Augustine testifies that he saw a blind child recover his sight upon the relics of Saint Gervase and Saint Protasius at Milan; a woman at Carthage cured of a cancer by the sign of the cross that a newly baptized woman made over her; Hesperius, a close friend of his, cast out the spirits that infested his house with a little earth from the sepulcher of our Lord, and a paralytic promptly cured by this earth, later, when it had been carried to church; a woman in a procession, having touched Saint Stephen's shrine with a bouquet, and rubbed her eyes with this bouquet, recover her long-lost sight; and he reports many other miracles at which he says he himself was present. Of what shall we accuse both him and two holy bishops, Aurelius and Maximinus, whom he calls upon as his witnesses? Shall it be of ignorance, simplicity, and credulity, or of knavery and imposture? Is there any man in our time so impudent that he thinks himself comparable to them, either in virtue and piety, or in learning, judgment, and ability? (V181; F134)

This is the literal repetition of several developments by Saint Augustine on contemporary miracles from *City of God* XXII.8.37, respectively n. 2, p. 561 (the blind child in Milan), n. 4, p. 568 (cancer), n. 7, p. 572 (Hesperius), n. 11, p. 578 (woman with flowers). Here one notes a perfect agreement between the two authors about attesting the omnipotence of God. Montaigne begins with, "but reason has taught me that to condemn a thing thus, resolutely, as false and impossible, is to assume the advantage of knowing the bounds and limits of God's will and of the power of our mother nature" (I.27, V179; F132). This is a fundamental and recurrent thesis in the *Essais*: our finite and fallible reason cannot and thus must not proclaim impossibilities on the power of God.[7] Saint Augustine finishes with, "Fiunt ergo etiam nunc multa miracula eodem Deo faciente per nos quod vult et ad quem modum vult, qui et illa quae legimus fecit—Even now, therefore, many miracles are wrought by the same God Who wrought those of which we read, acting by whom He wills and as He wills" (XXII.8, ibid., p. 588; Dyson, 1131). Or: "Ecce qualibus argumentis omnipotentiae Dei humana contradicit infirmitas, quam possidet vanitas—Behold the kind of arguments by which human infirmity, consumed with vanity, speaks against the omnipotence of God!" (XXII.11, ibid., p. 602; Dyson, 1137). The skepticism, if there is indeed any to see here, bears on the reach of human understanding and, on the contrary, reinforces the recognition of divine omnipotence. For the two thinkers, the miracles thus become not the objects of skepticism, but of arguments against it.

5/ *Essais* I.32 [1588]:

God, wishing to teach us that the good have something else to hope for, and the wicked something else to fear, than the fortunes and misfortunes of this world, handles and allots these according to his occult disposition, and deprives us of the means of foolishly making our profit of them. And those people delude themselves who try to take advantage of them by human reason. They never score one hit but they receive two. Saint Augustine gives a fine proof of this against his adversaries. It is a conflict that is decided by the weapons of memory more than by those of reason. (V216; F161)

This is a development of *City of God* I.8, BA 33: 210; Dyson, 12:

Placuit quippe divinae providentiae praeparare in posterum bona justis, quibus non fruentur injusti, et mala impiis, quibus non excruciabantur boni; ista vero temporalia bona et mala utriusque voluit esse communia, ut nec bona cupidius adpetantur, quae mali quoque habere cernuntur; nec mala turpiter evitentur, quibus et boni plerumque adficuntur—It has pleased the divine providence to prepare for the righteous in the world to come good things which will not be enjoyed by the unrighteous, and punishments for the ungodly with which the good will not be tormented. He has, however, willed that the good and evil things of this world should be common to both, so that we may neither grasp too eagerly after those goods which are seen to be possessed by the wicked also, nor dishonourably flee those evils with which even the good are generally afflicted.

Augustine and Montaigne agree in underlining that the distinction between goods and ills does not coincide with the distinction between the good and the wicked, nor does it contradict it. To the extent that these goods and these ills refer to things of the world, the righteous must not worry themselves with them, while only the unjust can see in them a criterion for their happiness or unhappiness. For the distinction between the goods and the ills *according to the world* has no pertinence in relation to the distinction between the good and the wicked *from God's point of view*. To the good, therefore, God teaches indifference toward the goods and the ills of the world by distributing them arbitrarily. But here, Montaigne seems more theological than Saint Augustine, who remains a moralist, since Montaigne uses this argument first of all to mark the omnipotence of providence: "In short, it is difficult to bring down divine things to our scale without their suffering loss" (ibid.; F160).

6/ *Essais* II.8 [1580]: "It would perhaps be impiety in Saint Augustine, for example—if it were proposed to him on the one hand to bury his writings, from which our religion receives such great fruit, or else to bury his children, in case he had any—if he did not prefer to bury his children" (V401; F292).

There is probably an allusion here to the fact that Saint Augustine did have a child: "puerum Adeodatum, ex me natum carnaliter de peccato meo" (*Confessions* IX.vi.14, BA 14: 94). But there is no obvious proof that Montaigne had read this text, although it seems unlikely that he was ignorant of the *Confessions* (our modern ignorance cannot serve as paradigm for those of the past).[8]

7/ *Essais* II.12 [1588]: "For Saint Augustine, arguing against these people, has good cause to reproach them for their injustice in that they hold those parts of our belief to be false which our reason fails to establish. And to show that there can be and can have been plenty of things whose nature and causes our reason cannot possibly establish, he puts before his adversaries certain known and indubitable experiences into which man confesses he has no insight; and this he does, like all other things, with careful and ingenious research" (V449; F328).

This is a clear reference to *City of God* XXI.5.1, BA 37: 388; Dyson, 1052:

Verum tamen homines infideles, qui, cum divina vel praeterita vel futura miracula praedicamus, quae illis experienda non valemus ostendere, rationem a nobis earum flagitant rerum, quam quoniam non possumus reddere (excedunt enim vires mentis humanae), existimant falsa esse quae dicimus, ipsi de tot mirabilibus rebus, quas vel videre possumus vel videmus, debent reddere rationem. Quod si fieri ab homine non posse perviderint, fatendum est eis non ideo aliquid non fuisse vel non futurum esse, quia ratio inde non potest reddi, quando quidem sunt ista, de quibus similiter non potest—Despite all this, when we proclaim the miracles which the divine power has performed in the past and will perform in the future, but which we cannot make available to the experience of men who lack faith, they demand that we give a rational explanation of these things. And when we cannot do so, precisely because such things surpass the powers of the human mind, they conclude that what we say is false. Let them, then, give a rational account of all those wondrous things which we can or do see. And if they see that this is beyond what a man can do, let them admit that the fact that a rational explanation cannot be given for something does not entail that it could not have happened in the past or that it cannot happen in the future, seeing that there are these things in the present which are similarly inexplicable.

This quotation calls for several remarks. First, it occurs in a massively Pauline context of the edition of 1580,[9] which mobilizes several quotations from the Epistles: (a) "flee worldly philosophy" (= Colossians 2:8); (b) "our wisdom is but folly before God" (= 1 Corinthians 3:19); (c) "the man who is presumptuous of his knowledge does not yet know what knowledge is" (= 1 Corinthians 8:2); (d) "man, who is nothing, if he thinks he is something, seduces and deceives himself" (= Galatians 6:3). Now, all these Pauline references develop the paradox of wisdom and folly (which is inverted between God and the world), a paradox that has a function that is skeptical *because* biblical, as in Erasmus (and, moreover, Luther). Here, Montaigne thus takes a position in favor of Christian skepticism. But it is necessary to note right away that the purpose of the Christian skepticism is to refute atheism, for "this incipient malady [namely, Luther] would easily degenerate into an execrable atheism" (V439; F320); or: "he [that is, Sebond] undertakes by human and natural reasons to establish and prove against the atheists all the articles of the Christian religion" (V440; F320); or further: "And as for what Plato says, that there are few men so firm in their atheism that a pressing danger will not bring them back to recognition of the divine power" (V445; F324); and: "Atheism being a proposition as it were unnatural and monstrous, difficult too and not easy to establish in the human mind, however insolent and unruly it may be" (V446; F325); and finally: "an atheist flatters himself by reducing all authors to atheism" (V448; F327). Descartes' inheritance from Montaigne, above all in the Letters of 1630 and the "Letter to the Faculty of Theology" of the Sorbonne in 1641, appears clearly here.

Above all, the whole question that Saint Augustine poses in the text quoted by Montaigne concerns the possibility (and the legitimacy) of postulating a *reddere rationem* [rational account] (*City of God* XXI.5.1, p. 388; 5.2, p. 392 and 394; and finally, 7.2, p. 408), inaccessible to the human mind in making recourse to divine omnipotence: "fixam tamen apud nos esse rationem: non sine ratione omnipotentem facere, unde animus infirmus rationem non potest reddere—our reason is persuaded that the Almighty does nothing without a cause, even though the frail human mind cannot explain what that cause is" (5.2, p. 394; Dyson, 1054); "omnipotentem Deum" (7.2, p. 408); "Portentum ergo non fit contra naturam, sed contra quam est nota natura—A portent, therefore, is an occurrence contrary not to nature, but to nature as we know it" (8.2, p. 412; Dyson, 1061); "Sicut ergo non fuit impossibile Deo, quas voluit instituere, sic non est ei impossibile, in quidquid voluerit, quas instituit, mutare naturas—Therefore, just as it was not impossible for God to create whatever natures He chose, so it is not impossible for Him to change those natures which He has created in whatever way He chooses" (8.4, p. 418; Dyson, 1063). Finally, we must underscore that all these questions come under what Augustine calls the things *quae non videntur*, that for Descartes will become the domain of the incomprehensible, which is nevertheless perfectly knowable without any help from the imagination to the understanding.

8/ *Essais* II.12 [1588]:

In truth we are nothing. Our powers are so far from conceiving the sublimity of God, that of the works of our creator those bear his stamp most clearly, and are most his, that we understand least. To Christians it is an occasion for belief to encounter something incredible. It is the more according to reason as it is contrary to human reason. If it were according to reason, it would no longer be a miracle; and if it were according to some example, it would no longer be singular. "Melius scitur Deus nesciendo [God is better known by not knowing]," says Saint Augustine; and Tacitus, "Sanctius est ac reverentius de actis deorum credere quam scire [It is more holy and reverent to believe in the works of the gods than to know them]" [*De moribus Germanorum*, 24]. (V499; F368–69)

For once, this quotation does not refer to *City of God*, but to *De Ordine* II.16.44, BA 4: 438, through the intermediary of Juste Lipse, *Politiques* I-2,[10] a translation that would indeed explain why a quotation does not come from the habitually used source up to this point: "Quisquis ergo ita nesciens, non dico de summo illo Deo, qui scitur Melius nesciendo, sed de anima ipsa sua quaerere ac disputare voluerit, tantum errabit quantum errari plurimum potest." Which is confirmed by *De Trinitate* VIII.1.3: "Non enim parvae notitiae pars est, cum de profundo isto in illam summitatem respiramus, si antequam scire possimus quid sit Deus, possumus jam scire quid non sit—For it is no small part of knowledge, when we emerge from these depths to breathe in that sublime atmosphere, if before we can know what God is, we are at least able to know what he is not" (BA 16: 30).[11] We note that quite clearly, the entire passage bears on the unknowableness of God: "We say indeed 'power,' 'truth,' 'justice'; they are words that mean something great; but that something we neither see nor conceive at all" (V499; F369). In other words,

It is not by reasoning or by our understanding that we have received our religion; it is by external authority and command. The weakness of our judgment helps us more in this than its strength, and our blindness more than our clear-sightedness. It is by the mediation of our ignorance more than of our knowledge that we are learned with that divine learning. It is no wonder if our natural and earthly powers cannot conceive that supernatural and heavenly knowledge; let us bring to it nothing of our own but obedience and submission. For, as it is written, "I will destroy the wisdom of the wise, and will bring to nothing the understanding of the prudent. Where is the wise? Where is the scribe?" (Isaiah 29:14 and 19:12); "Where is the disputer of this world? Hath not God made foolish the wisdom of this world? For after that the world by wisdom knew not God, it pleased God by the foolishness of preaching to save them that believe" (1 Corinthians 1:19–21). (V500; F369–70)

"Ignorance that knows itself, that judges itself and condemns itself, is not complete ignorance: to be that, it must be ignorant of itself" (V502; F372). The consideration of the omnipotence of God, dominant to this point, thus implies just as directly that of his unknowability. The relation to Descartes ("ipsa incomprehensibilitas in ratione formali infiniti continetur—incomprehensibility itself is contained in the formal definition of the infinite," AT VII, 368: 3–4; CSM II, 253) here goes without saying.

9/ *Essais* II.12 [1588]: "Here is the excuse that is given us, upon consideration of this matter, by Scaevola, a great pontiff, and Varro, a great theologian, in their day: that it is necessary for the people to be ignorant of many true things and to believe many false ones: 'cum veritatem qua liberetur inquirat, credatur ei expedire, quod fallitur [Since he seeks the truth whereby he may be free, let us believe that it is expedient for him to be deceived]'" (V535; F399).

This is a direct quotation, but without a reference, of *De Civitate Dei* IV.27, BA 33: 614.[12] Pascal will also quote this text, very likely picking it up from Montaigne: "That is why the wisest of legislators used to say that men must often be deceived for their own good, and another sound politician, *Cum veritatem qua liberetur ignoret, expedit quod fallitur* [When he does not know the truth that is to bring him freedom, it is a good thing that he should be deceived]" (*Pensées*, L. §60).[13] But Pascal was not aware that this doctrine is not that of Saint Augustine, who quotes Varron and Scaevola only in order to refute them soon after:

Ergo ista conjicere putari debui, nisi evidenter alio loco ipse [*sc.* ipse Varro] disceret de religionibus loquens, multa esse vera quae non modo vulgo scire non sit utile, sed etiam tametsi falsa sunt, aliter existimare populum expediat [. . .]. Haec tamen fallacia miris modis maligni daemones delectantur, qui et deceptores et deceptos pariter possident, a quorum dominatione non liberat nisi gratia Dei per Jesum Christum Dominum nostrum—I should be suspected of conjecture here had he himself [Varro], speaking of religious observances in another place, not plainly said that there are many truths which it is not useful for the common people to know, and, moreover, that there are many false views which it is expedient that the people should take to be true. [. . .] But malignant demons are wonderfully delighted by such deceit, for, by it, they possess deceivers and deceived alike, and nothing sets men free from their dominion save the grace of God through our Lord Jesus Christ. (*De Civitate Dei* IV.31, BA 33: 628; Dyson, 182)[14]

10/ *Essais* II.12 [1588]:

At one object the stomach rises; at another, a certain part lower down. But how a spiritual impression can cut such a swath in a massive and solid object, and the nature of the relation and connection between these wonderful springs of action, no man has ever known. "Omnis incerta ratione et in naturae majestate abdita—All those things are indeterminable by reason and concealed in the majesty of nature," says Pliny; and Saint Augustine: "Modus quo corporibus adhaerent spiritus, omnino mirus est, nec comprehendi ab homine potest: et hoc ipse homo est—The way in which souls cling to bodies is completely wonderful, and cannot be understood by man; and this is man himself." (V539; F402–403)

This text quotes and modifies *The City of God* XXI.10.1, BA 37: 426; Dyson, 1067:

Sed, ut dixi, miris et ineffabilibus modis adhaerendo, accipientes ex ignibus poenam, non dantes ignibus vitam; quia et iste alius modus, quo corporibus adhaerent spiritus *et animalia fiunt*, omnino mirus est nec comprehendi ab homine potest, et hoc ipse homo est—Rather, as I have said, this connection will be brought about in a wondrous and ineffable way, so that the devils receive pain from the flames, but give no life to them. It is by a different mode of union that bodies and spirits are bound together *and become animate creatures*: the mode, entirely marvelous and beyond the understanding of man, by which man himself is made. (emphasis added)

We note that the incomprehensibility of the union of the spirit (the soul) with the body refers to man's unknowability to himself. And thus that this reproduces the incomprehensibility of God, following the well-known theme of Gregory of Nyssa, *On the Creation of Man*, XI, *Patrologia Graeca* 44, col. 156b.[15]

11/ *Essais* II.12 [1580]:

The diversity of idioms and languages [. . .], what else is it but that infinite and perpetual altercation and discordance of opinions and reasons, which accompanies and embroils the vain construction of human knowledge? [1588] And embroils it usefully. What would hold us in, if we had one grain of knowledge? This saint [namely, Augustine] gave me great pleasure: "Ipsa utilitatis occultatio aut humilitatis exercitatio est, aut elationis attritio—This very concealment of what is useful is either an exercise in humility or an attrition of pride." To what point of presumption and insolence do we not carry our blindness and our stupidity? (V553–54; F415)

This text from *The City of God* XI.22, BA 35: 98, quoted without the author's name, absolutely confirms that skepticism, bearing on the entire extent of human knowledge, serves a theological design, that of the recognition of divine omnipotence.

12/ *Essais* III.5 [1582]: "In honor of the Huguenots, who condemn our private and auricular confession, I confess myself in public, religiously and purely. Saint Augustine, Origen, and Hippocrates have published the errors of their opinions; I, besides, those of my conduct. I am hungry to make myself known, and I care not to how many, provided it be truly. Or to put it better, I am hungry for nothing, but I have a mortal fear of being taken to be other than I am by those who come to know my name" (V846–47; F642).

Is there an allusion, for the erroneous "opinions" recognized as such, to the *Confessiones* and above all the *Retractiones*? In any case, this indication contradicts the common interpretation according to which Montaigne would have absolutely impugned the confession of faults. In fact, "Du repentir" [Of Repentance] does not support a negative but rather a positive thesis on the confession of faults: "I do not teach, I tell" without taking back or regretting anything, because "if I had to live over again, I would live as I have lived; I have neither tears for the past nor fears for the future" (III.3, V806 and 816; F612 and 620). Or how about: "As for me, I may desire in a general way to be different; I may condemn and dislike my universal form, and implore God to reform me completely and to pardon my natural weakness. But this I ought not to call repentance, it seems to me, any more than my displeasure at being neither an angel nor Cato" (ibid., V813; F617). The repentance impugned would not so much be opposed to confession (auricular or public, in short the sacrament of forgiveness) as to the illusion of being able to remake the past, or of regretting it in vain, or in short, to ressentiment— at once the denial of the irremediable past and self-hatred for not having surmounted it (in some way, Nietzsche). "Reform" and "excuse," which define the sacrament of reconciliation, are above all not to be confused with ressentiment.

13/ *Essais* III.5 [1588]: "But those men of whom Saint Augustine tells us attributed to nudity a wonderful power of temptation by doubting whether at the universal judgment women will rise again in their own sex and not rather in ours, lest they tempt us still in that holy state" (V860; F654).

This text copies from *The City of God* XXII.17, BA 37: 620 and following; Dyson, 1144–45:

Nonnulli propter hoc, quod dictum est "Donec occurramus omnes in unitatem fidei, in virum perfectum, in mensuram aetatis plenitudinis Christi" (Ephesians 4:13) and "Conformes imaginis filli Dei" (Romans 8:29), nec in sexu femineo resurrecturas feminas credunt, sed virili omnes aiunt, quoniam Deus solum virum fecit ex limo, feminam ex viro. Sed mihi Melius sapere videntur, qui utrumque sexum resurrecturum esse non dubitant. Non enim libido ibi erit, quae confusionis est causa. Nam priusquem peccassent, nudi erant et non confundebantur vir et femina. Corporibus ergo illis vitia detrahentur, natura servabitur. Non est autem vitium sexus femineus, sed natura—In view of the words, "Till we all come to a perfect man, to the measure of the age of the fullness of Christ", and "Conformed to the image of the Son of God", not a few people believe that women will not be resurrected as female in sex, but that all are to be men, because God made only man of earth, and the woman from the man. But it seems to me that the better opinion is that of those who do not doubt that both sexes are to rise. For then there will be no lust, which is now the cause of confusion. For before they sinned, the man and the woman were naked, and were not ashamed. Vice will be taken away from those bodies, therefore, and nature preserved. And the sex of a woman is not a vice, but nature.

Let us note that Augustine here opposes Jerome, *Commentary on the Epistle to the Ephesians*, V.29, and *Adversus Jovinianum*, I.36 (and his response to Rufin, *Apologia*, I.29), which are closer to Montaigne's position.

14/ *Essais* III.11 [1582]: "It seems to me that we may be pardoned for disbelieving a marvel, at least as long as we can turn aside and avoid the supernatural explanation by nonmarvelous means. And I follow Saint Augustine's opinion, that it is better to lean toward doubt than toward assurance in things difficult to prove and dangerous to believe" (V1032; F789–90).

Montaigne here is commenting on *The City of God* XIX.18, BA 37: 132–34:

Credit [scientia] etiam scripturis sanctis et veteribus et novis, quas canonicas appellamus, unde fides ipsa concepta est, ex qua justus vivit; per quam sine dubitatione ambulamus, quamdiu perigrinamur a Domino; qua salva atque certa de quibusdam rebus, quas neque sensu, neque ratione percepimus, neque nobis per scripturam canonicam claruerunt, nec per testes, quibus non credere absurdum est, in nostram notitiam pervenerunt, sine justa reprehensione dubitamus—It believes also in the Holy Scriptures, the Old Testament and the New, which we call canonical, from which comes the faith by which the just live, and by which we walk without doubting while we are pilgrims journeying towards the Lord. For as long as this faith is whole and certain, however, we may without just reproach have doubts regarding certain things: things which we have not perceived either by sense or reason, and which have not been revealed to us by the canonical Scriptures, nor become known to us through witnesses whom it would be absurd not to believe.

We can doubt that we are dealing here with the same argument in the two authors. Indeed, Montaigne seems to want to say that one can be pardoned for not believing as a marvel what one can explain naturally, and that doubt is better than belief in the case of difficult or dangerous things. Saint Augustine said rather that if the faith is safe and if the other things proposed to belief offer no verification (sensation, reasoning, Scripture, or trustworthy witnesses), doubt is permitted. But both of them accept that doubt can remain, including in religious matters, a wise solution.

What should we conclude from this rapid review? First, that Saint Augustine constitutes a source and a significant (and for certain people, doubtless unexpected) reading for Montaigne. Next, that it is not simply a matter of the *De Civitate Dei*, but also of the *De Ordine* and probably of the *Confessiones*, and that this is not only the case for the edition of 1588, but first for that of 1580. And also that Saint Augustine is understood as a skeptical author, less because of the *Contra Academicos*, the *Soliloquia*, or another philosophical dialogue, than because of the positive and assertoric testimonies concerning phenomena that common understanding would more readily consider as impossible: the issue, then, is a skepticism by excess of incomprehensible observations, nevertheless assured by trustworthy testimonies—in short, a *positive* skepticism.

One then conceives fairly easily that this skepticism credits this positivity to the account of an incomprehensibility that is itself positive, that of divine omnipotence, which actually accomplishes what the possibility of the philosophers cannot conceive legitimately. This positive skepticism, by excess of incomprehensible divine omnipotence, will have a radical heir: Descartes. Contemporary historians of modern philosophy are beginning to accept this evidence. But what is not yet realized and certainly requires other verifications is that this Cartesian doctrine had a background drawn by Saint Augustine, through the construal of Montaigne. Certain banalities must therefore be refined and specified. In this sense, Richard Popkin is not wrong, *wholesale*, to conclude that, "The *Apologie* unfolds in Montaigne's inimitable rambling style as a series of waves of scepticism, with occasional pauses to consider and digest various levels of doubt, but with the overriding theme an advocacy of a new form of fideism—Catholic Pyrrhonism."[16] Without a doubt, we must also see the question *item by item*.

Notes

Foreword

1. Descartes: "Ut comœdi, moniti ne in fronte appareat pudor, personam induunt: sic ego, hoc mundi theatrum conscensurus, in quo hactenus spectator exstiti, larvatus prodeo" (*Cogitationes Privatæ*, ed. Charles Adam and Paul Tannery, *Œuvres de Descartes*, new presentation by Bernard Rochot and Pierre Costabel [Paris: Vrin, 1964–1974], vol. X, p. 213, lines 4–7, henceforth abbreviated AT X, 213, 4–7). For this text, I've used the translation and interpretation found in the edition of Vincent Carraud and Gilles Olivo: René Descartes, *Étude du bon sens. La Recherche de la verité, et autres écrits de jeunesse (1616–1631)* (Paris: PUF, 2013), 64 and 81–83. *Larvatus prodeo* could also be translated, *I perform, I make myself public, I publish myself masked, I publish anonymously*. [Translators' note: English translations of the works of Descartes throughout this book will refer to *The Philosophical Writings of Descartes*, 3 volumes, trans. John Cottingham, Robert Stoothoff, Dugald Murdoch, plus, in vol. 3, Anthony Kenny (Cambridge: Cambridge University Press, 1984–1991). They will be indicated by the shortened title CSM or CSMK, volume number, and page number, with the tacit understanding that modifications will often have been made where necessary in order to stay close to Marion's French translations of Descartes' Latin writings.]

2. See my study *On Descartes' Passive Thought: The Myth of Cartesian Dualism*, trans. Christina M. Gschwandtner (Chicago: University of Chicago Press, 2018).

3. See François Azouvi, *Descartes et la France. Histoire d'une passion nationale* (Paris: Fayard, 2002).

4. Which Denis Kambouchner has, moreover, begun to do: see *Descartes n'a pas dit [. . .]. Un répertoire des fausses idées sur l'auteur du Discours de la méthode, avec les éléments utiles et une esquisse d'apologie* (Paris: Les Belles Lettres, 2015).

5. Following the model of Ferdinand Alquié in *Le Cartésianisme de Malebranche* (Paris: Vrin, 1974), it would have been possible and highly desirable to add further confrontations, for example regarding the relation of infinite freedom to the theological tradition (particularly St. Bernard of Clairvaux), the radicalization of hyperbolic doubt and Fénélon's idea of the infinite, the return to the *ego* starting from passivity according to Rousseau, or even the closing, among all the Cartesians, of the horizon opened by the doctrine of the creation of the eternal truths. For lack of time, I will leave such attempts to others.

6. Maurice Merleau-Ponty, *Notes de cours 1959–1961* (Paris: Gallimard, 1996), 264.

7. Edmund Husserl, *First Philosophy: Lectures 1923/24 and Related Texts from the Manuscripts (1920–1925)*, trans. Sebastian Luft and Thane M. Naberhaus (Dordrecht: Springer, 2019), I, §10, p. 66.

Chapter One

1. Nicolas Malebranche, *Recherche de la vérité*, II, "De l'imagination," III, chap. 5, "Du livre de Montaigne," in *Œuvres complètes*, vol. 1, ed. Geneviève Rodis-Lewis (Paris: Vrin, 1962), pp. 359–69.

2. Vincent Carraud, "Première Méditation," in Dan Arbib, ed., *Les* Méditations métaphysiques, Objections *et* Réponses *de Descartes. Un commentaire* (Paris: Vrin, 2019), 72.

3. This formula, "si vel minimum quid invenero, quod certum sit et inconcussum" (AT VII, 24.12–13), does not contain the term *principium* (contrary to the reading of Heidegger), but echoes St. Augustine: the wise man "non modo perceptum habere debet id quod tuetur ac sequitur, verum etiam inconcussum tenere" (*Contra Academicos* I.VII.19).

4. These modes lead to the suspension of assent to a statement according to the following distinctions: 1) the variety of animals, 2) the difference between human beings, 3) the differences among the sense organs (*tōn aisthētēriōn*), 4) the circumstances (*peristaseis*), 5) positions, distances, and locations, 6) admixtures, 7) the quantity and the constitution of substrata, 8) relativity (*to pros ti*), 9) the continuity or the rupture of occurrence, 10) usages, customs, mythic beliefs, and dogmatic convictions—see *Outlines of Pyrrhonism* I.14, §§36–38; English translation: *The Skeptic Way: Sextus Empiricus's* Outlines of Pyrrhonism, trans. with Introduction and Commentary by Benson Mates (Oxford: Oxford University Press, 1996), 94.

5. Sextus Empiricus, *Outlines of Pyrrhonism* I.14, §135, §136, §138, and then §139 (in *Esquisses pyrrhoniennes*, ed. and trans. Pierre Pellegrin [Paris: Seuil, 1997], 128–30), in opposition to Aristotle, who grants to relation only a derivative rank among the categories, to the point of removing from it all relation to *ousia*: "It is true to affirm that no *ousia* is relative" (*Categories* VII, 8b21, in Aristotle, *Categories: On*

Interpretation: Prior Analytics, trans. H. P. Cooke and Hugh Tredennick, Loeb Classical Library 325 [Cambridge, MA: Harvard University Press, 1938], 63).

6. Sextus Empiricus, *Outlines of Pyrrhonism* I.23, §197 (*Esquisses*, 162; *The Skeptic Way*, 115). Whence the definitive *aoristia* of the wise man (I.24, §198; *Esquisses*, 162).

7. *Conversation with Burman*, AT V, 165. And: "Finis autem meus optimus fuit, [. . .] ut melius everterem Scepticismum atque Atheismum—Now my purpose was excellent, [. . .] for the better overthrow of Skepticism and Atheism" ("To the Curators of Leiden University," 4 May 1647, AT V, 9.8–10; CSMK, 316–17). Descartes had certainly read "Montaigne and Charron" ("To the Marquess of Newcastle," 23 November 1646, AT IV, 575.3). See, among others, Geneviève Rodis-Lewis, *L'Œuvre de Descartes* (Paris: Vrin, 1971), 80, 465, and "Montaigne, Charron, Descartes et le doute," in Emmanuel Faye, ed., *Descartes et la Renaissance. Actes du colloque international de Tours des 22 au 24 mars 1996* (Paris: Champion, 1999). During his stay in Neuburg an der Donau, Descartes had even received from J. B. Molitor, SJ, a copy of Charron's treatise *De la Sagesse* (see Frédéric de Buzon, "Un exemplaire de la Sagesse de Pierre Charron offert à Descartes en 1619," *Bulletin cartésien XX, Archives de Philosophie* 55, 1992/1).

8. Taking up the alternative posed in *The Search for Truth*, AT X, 369; CSM II, 408 (going forward I will follow the text provided in Descartes, *Étude du bon sens. La recherche de la verité et autres écrits de jeunesse (1616–1631)*, ed. Vincent Carraud and Gilles Olivo, 260).

9. Sextus Empiricus, *Outlines of Pyrrhonism* I.7, §15 (*Esquisses*, 62; *The Skeptic Way*, 91).

10. Descartes, "To Hyperaspistes," August 1641, AT III, 434.1–5; CSMK, 196–97. See also: "Quippe omnes hordierni Sceptici non dubitant quidem in praxi, quin habeant caput, quin 2 & 3 faciant 5, et talia; sed dicunt se tantum iis uti tanquam veris, quia sic apparent, non autem certo credere, quia nullis certis rationibus ad id impelluntur—No sceptic nowadays has any doubt in practice about whether he has a head, or whether two and three make five, and so on. What the sceptics say is that they merely treat such claims as true because they appear to be so, but they do not accept them as certain, because no reliable arguments require them to do so" (*VIIæ Responsiones*, AT VII, 549.10–15; CSM II, 375).

11. Vincent Carraud, in Arbib, ed., *Les Meditations, Un commentaire*, 72.

12. Diogenes Laertius, *Lives of Eminent Philosophers* IX, §62, trans. R. D. Hicks (London: William Heinemann; New York: G.P. Putnam's Sons, 1925), vol. 2, pp. 474–75. See also Cicero: "Quare qui aut visum aut adsensum tollit, is omnem actionem tollit et vita—therefore one who abolishes either presentation or assent abolishes all action out of life" (Cicero, *Academica* II.13, §39, in Cicero, *De Natura Deorum. Academica*, trans. H. Rackham [Cambridge, MA: Harvard University Press, 1972], 516, 517).

13. Sextus Empiricus, *Esquisses pyrrhoniennes* I.8, §17, p. 63; *The Skeptic Way*, 91.

14. Pierre Charron, *De la Sagesse*, Bk. II, chap. II, ed. Barbara de Negroni (Paris: Fayard, 1986), 386.

15. Sextus Empiricus, *Esquisses pyrrhoniennes* I.11, §21, p. 66; *The Skeptic Way*, 92.

16. Pierre Charron, *Petit traité de Sagesse*, chap. IV (Paris, 1606), taken up in *De la Sagesse*, 858.

17. There remains a final characteristic to make note of: doubt, restrained to theory, must be exercised in a situation free of *"curis omnibus*, all cares" (AT VII, 17.13; AT IX, 1.13), leaving aside the *commoda / incommoda* (*Meditatio VI*, AT VII, 74.21 and following; 83.18; *Principia philosophiæ I*, §71; *Discourse on the Method*, VI, 31.11, etc.), forbidding, at least at this moment in the order of reasons, the taking into consideration first of my own body, and then of the world that surrounds me and gives myself to me, and thus every existential analytic of Dasein (see Marion, *On the Passive Thought of Descartes*, §10, pp. 61–71).

18. Emphasis added in all the preceding quotations. Cicero had already mentioned this argument: "Si unus sensus *semel* in vita mentitus sit, *nulli unquam* esse credendum—if one sense has told a lie once in a man's life, no sense must ever be believed" (*Academica* II.25, §79, in Rackham, pp. 566 and 567, and also II.32, p. 596). Descartes, however, sometimes allows an attenuation: "I held as *well-nigh* false everything that was merely probable" (*Discourse on the Method*, AT VI, 8.28–29; CSM I, 115 = *fere*, AT VII, 19.21).

19. See Sextus Empiricus, *The Skeptic Way* I.10–11, §19–24, pp. 91–92. On the ambivalence of this "criterion," see Jacques Brunschwig, "Le problème de l'héritage conceptuel dans le scepticisme: Sextus Empiricus et la notion de *kritêrion*," chap. 11 in his *Études sur les philosophies hellénistiques. Épicurisme, stoïcisme, scepticisme* (Paris: PUF, 1995), 289–319.

20. See, as well, "Tandem cogor fateri nihil esse ex iis quæ olim vera putabam, de quo non liceat dubitari [. . .]; ideoque etiam ab iisdem, non minus quam ab aperte falsis, accurate deinceps assentionem esse cohibendam—I am finally compelled to admit that there is not one of my former beliefs about which a doubt many not properly be raised; [. . .] I must withhold my assent from these former beliefs just as carefully as I would from obvious falsehoods, if I want to discover any certainty" (AT VII, 21.27–22.1; CSM II, 14–15). And: "illa omnia quæ prius ut vera quammaxime credideram, propter hoc unum quod de iis *aliquo modo posse dubitari* deprehendissem, plane falsa esse supposui—the mere fact that I found that all my previous beliefs *were in some sense open to doubt* was enough to turn my absolutely confident belief in their truth into the supposition that they were wholly false" (*Meditatio IV*, AT VII, 59.24–27; CSM II, 41). Or, finally, "quibus [pre-conceived opinions] non aliter videmur posse liberari, quam si semel in vita de iis omnibus studeamus dubitare, in quibus *vel minimam incertitudinis suspicionem* reperiemus—It seems that the only way of freeing ourselves from these opinions is to make the effort, once in

the course of our life, to doubt everything which we find to contain *even the smallest suspicion of uncertainty*" (*Principia philosophiæ I*, §1; CSM I, 193).

21. A point confirmed by *Principia philosophiæ I*, §6: "In nobis libertatem esse experimur, ut semper ab iis credendis, quæ non plane certa sunt et explorata, possimus abstinere—We experience freedom in ourselves, enabling us to withhold our assent in doubtful matters and hence avoid error" (CMS I, 194).

22. A law voted by the Convention in September 1793, and then in March/April 1794. Hegel brilliantly gives it a theoretical bearing: "*Becoming a suspect* thus takes the place of *being guilty*, or it has the same significance and effect as being guilty"; for, "after it [absolute freedom] has finished eliminating the real organization and is now stably existing for itself, this is its sole object—an object that no longer has any other content, possession, existence, and external extension but is rather only this knowing of itself as an absolutely pure and free singular self" (G.W.F. Hegel, *The Phenomenology of Spirit*, trans. Terry Pinkard [Cambridge: Cambridge University Press, 2018], §591 and §592, pp. 344 and 343). We see that, once the radical definition of doubt is established, the question is no longer whether it will lead to the *ego*, but if, in this negation, it will even be able to stop and hold tight there. Descartes' strength will consist in holding to the *ego*, and not allowing it to commit suicide. But it will be necessary to accept that the idea of the infinite precedes and grounds it.

23. *IIæ Responsiones* (AT VII, 130.21–22; CMS II, 94), literally, "reheat this old cabbage, *krambē*." The same reserve occurs in the *IIIæ Responsiones*: "Dubitandi rationes, quæ hìc a Philosopho [namely, Hobbes] admittuntur ut veræ, non a me nisi *tanquam verisimiles* fuere propositæ; iisque usus sum, non ut pro novis venditarem, sed partim ut lectorum animos præpararem ad res intellectuales considerandas, illasque a corporeis distinguendas, ad quod omnino necessariæ mihi videntur; partim ut ad ipsas in sequentibus Meditationibus responderem; et partim etiam ut ostenderem quam firmæ sint veritates quas postea propono—The arguments for doubting, which the philosopher here accepts as valid, are ones that I was presenting as *merely plausible*. I was not trying to see them as novelties, but had a threefold aim in mind when I used them. Partly I wanted to prepare my readers' minds for the study of the things which are related to the intellect, and help them to distinguish these things from corporeal things; and such arguments seem to be wholly necessary for this purpose. Partly I introduced the arguments so that I could reply to them in the subsequent Meditations. And partly I wanted to show the firmness of the truths which I propound later on" (AT VII, 171.18–172.5; CSM II, 121, emphasis added).

24. *Meditatio VI*, AT VII, 76.22–24 = AT IX-1, 61; CSM II, 53. See the stars, small or large, and the towers, square or round, in *Optics*, AT VI, 146.26–147.2; CSM I, 175; and Sextus Empiricus, *The Skeptic Way: Outlines of Pyrrhonism* I.13, §32, p. 93; I.14, §118, p. 104; II.6, §55, p. 134. See as well, "I am well aware that the senses are sometimes deceptive [. . .] if their objects are too far away, as when we

look at the stars, which never appear so large to us as they really are" (*The Search for Truth*, AT X, 510; CSM II, 407).

25. *Première méditation*, AT IX-1, 14.26–27; the original Latin does not mention gold, but adds "caput habere fictile [they have heads of clay]" (AT VII, 19.3–4). The mistaken translation of *cucubitas* (gourds) by "des cruches (pitchers)" (AT IX-1, 4.28 for VII, 19.4) perhaps suffers from the attraction of *The Search for Truth*: "those melancholic individuals who think themselves to be vases [*des cruches*]" (AT X, 511; CSM II, 407).

26. Miguel de Cervantes, *Exemplary Stories*, first published 1613, translated into French in 1615. I here follow A. Redondo, "La folie du Cervantin licencié de verre," in Augustin Redondo and André Rochon, ed., *Visages de la folie (1500–1650)* (Paris: Publications de la Sorbonne, 1981), 33–44; Jacques Darriulat, "Descartes et la mélancolie," *Revue philosophique de la France et de l'étranger*, 1996/4: 465–86; and Ettore Lojacono, in Descartes, *La Recherche de la vérité par la lumière naturelle de René Descartes*, ed. E. Lojacono et al. (Milan: FrancoAngeli, 2002), xxiv and following.

27. The same attitude is found in the *VIIæ Responsiones* (AT VII, 460.7–12), and above all in *The Search for Truth*: "To be sure, a good man would be indignant if you told him that his beliefs cannot have any more rational basis than theirs [the madmen's], since he relies, like them, on what the senses and imagination represent to him" (AT X, 511; CSM II, 407). The debate about this text arises from claims by Michel Foucault, *L'Histoire de la folie à l'âge classique* (Paris, 1961, 1972), which were contested by Jacques Derrida, *L'Écriture et la différance* (Paris, 1967), and concluded by Jean-Marie Beyssade, "'Mais quoi, ce sont des fous'. Sur un passage controversé de la *Première Méditation*," *Revue de Métaphysique et de Morale*, 1973. The origin of the argument may be found in Cicero: "At enim ipse sapiens sustinet se in furore ne adprobet falsa pro veris. [. . .] Sed ex hoc genere toto perspici potest levitas orationis eorum, qui omnia cupiunt confundere. [. . .] Non enim proferremus vino aut somno oppressos aut mente captos tam absurde ut tum diceremus interesse inter vigilantium visa et sobriorum et sanorum et eorum qui essent aliter adfecti, tum nihil interesse. Ne hoc quidem cernunt, omnia se reddere incerta [. . .] si enim res se ita habeant ut nihil intersit utrum ita cui videantur ut insano an sano, cui possit exploratum esse de sua sanitate? Quod velle efficere non mediocris insaniæ est—But you will say that the wise man in an attack of madness restrains himself from accepting false presentations as true. [. . .] But out of all this what is 'perspicuous' is the lack of substance in the case put by these thinkers, who aspire to introduce universal confusion. [. . .] We should not bring forward people who are tipsy or fast asleep or out of their minds in such a ridiculous fashion as at one moment to say that there is a difference between the presentations of the waking and sober and sane and of those in other conditions, and at another moment to say that there is no difference. Do they not even see that they make everything uncertain— [. . .] for if objects are so constituted that it makes no difference whether they appear to anybody as they do

to a madman or as they do to a sane person, who can be satisfied of his own sanity? To desire to produce this state of affairs is in itself no inconsiderable mark of insanity" (*Academica* II.17, §53–54, in Cicero, *De Natura Deorum. Academica*, trans. H. Rackham, pp. 534–37).

28. *Meditatio I*, AT VII, 19.20; CSM II, 13; see: "Lastly, considering that the very thoughts we have while awake may also occur while we sleep without any of them being at that time true, I resolved to pretend that all the things that had ever entered my mind were not more true than the illusions of my dreams" (*Discourse on the Method*, AT VI, 32.9–15; CSM I, 125). Descartes' argument is all the more relevant because it takes up a major argument of the skeptics against the Stoic "dogmatism," which claims the absence of any criteria allowing the distinction between a true and a false *phantasia katakēptikē* (see Cicero, *Academica* II.27, §88, in Rackham, 570 and following, and Saint Augustine, *Contra Academicos* III.5, 11–12, BA 4, ed. R. Jolivet (Paris: Desclée de Brouwer, 1948), 78–82.

29. Michel de Montaigne, *Essais* II.12, ed. Pierre Villey and Louis Saulnier (Paris: PUF, 1965), 596; English translation: *The Complete Essays of Montaigne*, trans. Donald Frame (Stanford, CA: Stanford University Press, 1965), 451. Subsequent references to Montaigne's *Essais* will list the Book in Roman numerals, the essay in Arabic numerals, and either V or F followed by the page number to indicate pages in the Villey edition and the Frame translation, respectively.

30. Jean-Baptiste Chassignet, sonnet 263, in *Le Mépris de la vie et consolation contre la mort* (Besançon, 1594).

31. Pedro Calderón de la Barca, *La vida es sueño*, published since 1636 in the *Primera Parte de Comedias*, here lines 1683, 2152–60, and 2186–87; English translation: *Life Is a Dream, and Other Spanish Classics*, ed. Eric Bentley, trans. Roy Campbell (New York: Applause, 1959, 1985), 267–68. See Robert Garnier, "What fight is this? Ho, God, what have I undertaken, / Am I awake or asleep?" (*Bradamante* [1592], III.v); and Jean de Rotrou: "Am I awake or asleep? I feel myself, I touch myself, / Here I find neither my sheets nor my bed" (*Les Occasions perdues* [Paris, 1653], II, iii, and *Les Sosies* [1635], IV, iv). On this tradition, see Jean Rousset, *La littérature de l'âge baroque en France. Circé et le Paon* (Paris: Librairie José Corti, 1953), 26 and 268 and following; Geneviève Rodis-Lewis, *L'Œuvre de Descartes*, 220–25 and 519n, and *Le Développement de la pensée de Descartes* (Paris: Vrin, 1997), 221, mentioning Honoré d'Urfé; and Vincent Carraud and Gilles Olivo, *Descartes: Étude du bon sens*, 393–96, mentioning Plautus/Hermolaus Barbarus. Descartes, moreover, himself confirms the theatrical origin of the theme: "Have you never heard this expression of astonishment in comedies: 'Am I awake or asleep?' How can you be certain that your life is not a continuous dream, and that everything you think you learn through your senses is not false now, just as much as when you are asleep?" (*The Search for Truth*, AT XI, 511; CSM II, 408).

32. *To Balzac*, 15 April 1631, AT I, 198; CSMK, 30. Regarding this text and others, it has been possible to speak of a "Cartesian derealization of the world" (Ferdinand Alquié, *La Découverte métaphysique de l'homme chez Descartes* [Paris: PUF, 1991], 97).

33. AT X, 184, emphasis added. On the self-interpretation of the three dreams and Descartes' discovery of the indifference of the *cogitatio* toward the difference between waking and dreaming, see my study in *Cartesian Questions: Method and Metaphysics* (Chicago: University of Chicago Press, 1999), chap. 1.

34. *The Discourse on the Method*, AT VI, 39.11–17; CSM II, 130. The argument goes back to Plato, *Theaetetus* 190b; Cicero, *Academica* II.14, §47–48 (in Rackham, 526); and Saint Augustine, *Contra Academicos* III.11, §25, BA 4: 160, or *De Immortalitate animæ* XIV, §23, BA 5, ed. Pierre de Labriolle (Paris: Desclée de Brouwer, 1939), 212. On this thesis, see *Cartesian Questions: Method and Metaphysics*, chap. 1, §3, 14–19. Confirmations can be found in *Meditationes I* and *V*, AT VII, 20.27–31 and 70.28 and following.

35. *Optics, IV*, AT VI, 112.5–114.11; CSM I, 165. To be sure, Descartes does not make an exception for doubt of the "real colors"; these serve only as a simple example to explain the relation of sensible perception to its conceptual presuppositions (contrary to the mistaken interpretation of Jean Laporte, *Le Rationalisme de Descartes* [Paris, 1945], 103, which was followed by Martial Gueroult, *Descartes selon l'ordre des raisons* [Paris, 1953], vol. 1, p. 34 and following; see Jean-Luc Marion, *Sur la théologie blanche de Descartes* [Paris: PUF, 1991], 319 and following). On the role of the *naturæ simplicissimæ* in the *Meditationes*, see my study in *Cartesian Questions: Method and Metaphysics*, chap. 3, 53–66.

36. On the essential device of encoding / decoding [*codage / décodage*], see my *Sur la théologie blanche de Descartes*, II, chap. 1, §12–14, p. 231ff.

37. This story is reported by Descartes' friend Guez de Balzac (*Socrate chrétien* [Rouen/Paris, 1661], 255 and following), but well after the fact (the Prince died in 1625) and without naming the author. Molière will take it up in 1665 for his *Dom Juan* (Act III, scene i). On the history of this theme, see Charles Adam, *Vie et œuvre de Descartes*, AT XII, 41; Geneviève Rodis-Lewis, *L'Œuvre de Descartes*, 82 and 466; and Mariafranca Spallanzani, "'Bis bina quatttuor,'" *Rivista di filosofia*, 83/2, 1991: 301–17.

38. AT VII, 6.7; 8.21; 8.10. On the context of the undertaking to refute the atheists, see Jean-Robert Armogathe, "Pour une étude des textes luminaires, l'*Épître dédicatoire*, la *Préface au lecteur, Le Libraire au lecteur*," in Dan Arbib, *Les* Méditations métaphysiques, Objections *et* Réponses *de Descartes : Un commentaire*, 31 and following.

39. Let us note that Sextus himself maintains and relies on the principle of non-contradiction: "It is not possible that the same thing be (*hyparchein*) a being

and a non-being" (*Contre les mathématiciens* [the professors], §1, ed. Pierre Pellegrin [Paris: Seuil, 2002], 72).

40. Except if we consider the Letters to Mersenne of 1630, in particular the passage, "Please do not hesitate to assert and proclaim everywhere that it is God who has laid down these laws [namely, the mathematical truths, which *you* call eternal] in nature just as a king lays down laws in his kingdom. [. . .] I hope to put this in writing, within the next fortnight, in my treatise on physics; but I do not want you to keep it secret. On the contrary I beg you to tell people as often as the occasion demands, provided you do not mention my name. I should be glad to know the objections which can be made against this view; and I want people to get used to speaking of God in a manner worthier, I think, than the common and almost universal way of imagining him as a finite being" (15 April 1630, AT I, 145.13–16 and 146.10–19; CSMK, 23, emphasis added).

41. See Heinrich Denzinger, *Enchiridion symbolorum definitionum et declarationum de rebus fidei et morum / Compendium of Creeds, Definitions, and Declarations on Matters of Faith and Morals*, ed. Peter Hünermann, 43rd ed. (San Francisco: Ignatius Press, 2012), no. 6 and 54.

42. Michel de Montaigne, *Essais* II.12, V513, 528; F380, 393. Charron says the same: "The other contrary vice is a strong and audacious temerity to condemn and reject as false all the things that one does not understand and which do not please and do not amount to taste. It is proper to those who have a good opinion of themselves, and who are the clever and the knowing, especially heretics, sophists, pedants; for in feeling themselves to have a certain wit and believing that they see a bit more clearly than the vulgar, they give themselves license and authority to decide and resolve all things. This vice is much greater and nastier than the first [namely, credulity], for *it is mad folly to think that you know how far possibility extends*, the extent and the limit of nature, the reach of *God's power and will*, and to want to sort for oneself and one's self-satisfaction the true and the false of things; which is required in order thus, and with such pride and assurance, to resolve and define them. And how many things are there, which for a time we have rejected with ridicule *as impossible*, that we have been forced to avow later, and again pass beyond to others that are stranger. And how many others have been quoted to us as articles of faith, and then as vain lies?" (*De la Sagesse* I.40, p. 277, emphasis added). And also: "But the highest question here is about the will of God. [. . .] To which it is easy to reply briefly, that *there is no why, that it is the pure, first and eternal will of God, that has no cause*" (Charron, *Discours chrétien* in *La Sagesse*, ed. Barbara de Negroni, 887). It is not only the rose that is without *why*.

43. See William of Ockham, *Quodlibet* VI, q. 6, and the *Commentary on the Sentences. Prologue*, q. 1; but see also Pierre d'Auriol and Gregory of Rimini. References in Tullio Gregory, "Dio ingannatore e genio malignio," *Giornale critico della filosfia italiana*, 53/4, Rome, 1974 (French trans. M. Raiola, *Genèse de la raison classique de*

Charron à Descartes [Paris: PUF, 2000], chap. X, which is indispensable). And see as well my analyses in Jean-Luc Marion, *Sur la théologie blanche de Descartes*, 332 and following.

44. "To Buitendijck, 1643," AT IV, 64; CSMK, 229–30. See also on this point the discussion with Burman, AT V, 150 and 177.

45. See Henri Gouhier, *La Pensée métaphysique de Descartes* (Paris: Vrin, 1962), chap. V, 1.

46. See Richard Kennigton, "Finitude of Descartes' Evil Genius," *Journal of the History of Ideas*, 32, 1971, republished in Willis Doney, ed., *Eternal Truths and the Cartesian Circle. A Collection of Studies* (New York & London: Garland, 1987). Once again, one should never speak of a "great deceiver" ("grand trompeur") (AT IX-1, 19.10), as Martial Gueroult so often does (*Descartes selon l'ordre des raisons* [Paris: Aubier, 1968], vol. 1, chap. 2, *passim*); this is an unfortunate translation by the Duc de Luynes for "iste deceptor" (AT VII, 2323.7). For a deceiver, even a powerful one, can become neither "great" nor "all-powerful," nor therefore merit the title of "God," precisely because he remains deceptive and thus imperfect.

47. Descartes to Mersenne, 6 May 1630, AT I, 150; CSMK, 24. This point was demonstrated by Geneviève Rodis-Lewis, *L'Œuvre de Descartes*, 134 and following, against the prohibition of Martial Gueroult ("there is no common measure between the theory of the eternal truths [*of the creation* of the eternal truths is what should have been said] and the hypothesis of the evil genius [*of the almighty God* is what should have been said]" (Gueroult, *Descartes selon l'ordre des raisons*, vol. I, p. 43). The point thus authorizes us to see much more than a "family resemblance" between the two doctrines (Denis Kambouchner, *Les* Méditations métaphysiques *de Descartes. Introduction Générale. Première Méditation* [Paris: PUF, 2005], 327, a work that one nevertheless always benefits from consulting).

48. See Chapter Three.

49. Descartes to Mersenne, 15 April 1630, AT I, 146.4; and 6 May 1630, AT I, 150.22; and *Iæ Responsiones*, AT VII, 110.26 and following.

50. Sextus Empiricus, *Esquisses pyrrhoniens* I.20–28, §192–207, pp. 158–70; *The Skeptic Way*, 114–17. See what he attributes to Anaxarchus: "He said that no one even knew that he did not know." We find the same awkward imprecision in others, for example La Mothe le Vayer: "When we say that there is nothing true or certain, this voice is not simply nor absolutely affirmative, but contains tacitly [?] an exception to oneself [. . .]. In this way our axiom stating that there is nothing certain comprehends itself and envelopes itself, *seipsum symperigraphei*, so that it pronounces nothing against anyone who does not understand himself. [. . .] For if it sometimes seems that, carried away by ordinary ways of saying things, we pronounce something affirmatively, that nevertheless is only taken by us as doubtful" (François de La Mothe le Vayer, *Dialogues faits à l'imitation des Anciens*, I. *Dialogue traitant de la philosophie sceptique* [1630–?], ed. André Pessel

[Paris: Fayard, 1988], 27 and following). See as well: "This voice or proposition, that there is nothing certain, is not so absolutely affirmative that it does not contain in itself a tacit [?] exception to itself; [. . .] while this proposition admits no exception, one can nevertheless say that it comprehends itself and envelopes itself with all the others that it condemns with incertitude, pronouncing nothing against the general that still has its particular effect against itself. [. . .] [O]rdinary language obliged them [the skeptics] to speak more dogmatically than they had wished" (La Mothe le Vayer, *De la vertu des païens*, 1641, ed. Jacques Prévot and Thierry Bedouelle, *Les Libertins du XVIIe siècle* [Paris: Gallimard, Pléiade, 2004], vol. 2, p. 127). To my knowledge, Gassendi holds to the "unicum propositum [. . .] *Nihil sciri*"; and in response to the objection that this still has to do with a dogmatic knowledge, he invokes the right to employ the "familiarem, vulgaremque loquendi morem" and to answer once again, "scire nos nihil sciri" (Gassendi, *Exercitationes Paradxicæ Adversus Aristoteleos* [Paris, 1624], ed. and trans. B. Rochot [Paris: Vrin, 1959], 495 and 499). But Nietzsche, Wittgenstein, and others have insisted that freeing oneself from common grammar often constitutes the first duty of the philosopher.

51. Sextus Empiricus, *Esquisses pyrrhoniennes* I.28, §206, p. 170; *The Skeptic Way*, 117, mod.

52. Diogenes Laertius, *Lives of Eminent Philosophers* IX, §62, trans. R. D. Hicks, vol. 2, p. 489.

53. La Mothe le Vayer, *Dialogues faits à l'imitation des Anciens*, I. *Dialogue traitant de la philosophie sceptique*, p. 20; here he quotes, successively, *Phaedrus* (230a2–4) and the word that Diogenes Laertius attributes to Anaxarchus: "The one who says that he knows nothing does not even know it himself" (*Lives of Eminent Philosophers* IX, §58, trans. R. D. Hicks, vol. 2, p. 471).

54. Pierre Charron, *De la Sagesse* II.2, p. 386. Charron's contradictions pile up: not only does he affirm not to know, and thus not to be able to affirm, but he affirms as well being opposed to the principle of not affirming, so as to authorize himself to affirm that one cannot affirm. We find the same confusion in the nevertheless solemn definition of the suspension of judgment: "In short, it is the doctrine and the practice of all the greatest wise men and the most noble Philosophers, who made *explicit profession* of not knowing, and of doubting, inquiring, and seeking" (II.2, p. 400, emphasis added). See as well: "human reason is made of lead; it bends, turns, and accommodates itself to everything one wants, and thus all the Wise men and the most noteworthy Philosophers made the *express profession* to doubt, inquire, seek: to be Wise is to be an inquisitor of truth" (Charron, *Petit traité de sagesse*, op. cit., p. 839, emphasis added).

55. Nicolas Malebranche, *Recherche de la vérité*, II, III, ch. 5; English translation: *The Search after Truth*, ed. and trans. Thomas M. Lennon and Paul J. Olscamp (Cambridge: Cambridge University Press, 1997), 189.

56. Montaigne, *Essais* II.12, V527, F392, 393. In passing, he challenges the confused but traditional excuse offered ever since Sextus Empiricus (see note 51): "Thus they have been constrained to take refuge in this comparison from medicine, without which their attitude would be inexplicable: when they declare 'I do not know' or 'I doubt,' they say that this proposition carries itself away with the rest, no more nor less than rhubarb, which expels evil humors and carries itself off with them" (ibid., F392–93).

57. In contrast to Pierre Villey, commenting strangely on the "What do I know?": "The excessive importance given to this saying by Mlle de Gournay in her edition of 1635 has greatly contributed to making Montaigne wrongly pass as a skeptic" (Montaigne, *Essais* V1286).

58. Blaise Pascal, *Entretien avec Monsieur de Sacy*, in *Pensées and Other Writings*, trans. Honor Levi (Oxford: Oxford University Press, 1995), 183, 184. Without truly denouncing it, Descartes evoked this indecision in skepticism when he constructed his first theory of knowledge: "Ex. gr. si Socrates dicit se dubitare de omnibus, hinc necessario sequitur: ergo hoc saltem intelligit, quod dubitat; item, ergo cognoscit aliquid posse esse verum vel falsum—If, for example, Socrates says that he doubts everything, it necessarily follows that he understands at least that he is doubting, and hence that he knows that something can be true or false" (*Regula XII*, AT X, 421.19–22; CSM I, 46). And "de ipsa etiam ignorantia, sive potius dubitatione Socratis quæstio fuit, cum primum ad illam conversus Socrates cœpit inquirere, an verum esset se de omnibus dubitare, atque hoc ipsum asseruit—Socrates posed a problem about his own ignorance, or rather doubt: when he became aware of his doubt, he began to ask whether it was true that he was in doubt about everything, and his answer was affirmative" (*Regula XIII*, 432.24–29; CSM I, 53).

59. Montaigne, *Essais* V3, F2.

60. See Chapter Six.

61. See my *On the Ego and on God: Further Cartesian Questions*, trans. Christina M. Gschwandtner (New York: Fordham University Press, 2007), chap. 1, "The Originary Otherness of the Ego," 3–29.

62. On the relation and the difference between *ego* (Descartes up to Kant) and *moi* (Montaigne) and "le moi" (Pascal), see the authoritative study by Vincent Carraud, *L'Invention du moi* (Paris: PUF, 2010).

63. Descartes, Letter to Arnauld, 4 June 1648 (AT V, 193.3–6; CSMK, 355, emphasis added). See: "taking the word 'thought' as I do, to cover all the *operations* of the soul" (Letter to Reneri for Pollot, April or May 1638, AT II, 36.4–7; CSMK, 97). See also: "alii actus, quos vocamus *cogitativos*, ut intelligere, velle, imaginari, sentire, etc.—There are other acts which we call 'acts of thought,' such as understanding, willing, imagining, having sensory perceptions, and so on" (*IIIæ Responsiones*, AT VII, 176, 16–17; CSM II, 124). Sometimes Descartes surmounts his reticence at using an Aristotelian lexicon, which he elsewhere strictly avoids (see for example

his criticism of the definition of change as *actus entis in potentia, prout est in potentia, Regula XII*, AT X, 426.16–427.2), when it is a matter of showing the "extreme strength of the *cogito* that holds to the continual possibility of reducing to nothing the distance between the proposition and experience" (Jean-Marie Beyssade, *Descartes. Le temps et la cohérence de la métaphysique* [Paris: Flammarion, 1979], 253). Fénelon was one of the few to understand correctly the Cartesian argument: "I know clearly that to think is to act, to do, to have something," for "thought is a way of being and of acting" (*Démonstration de l'existence de Dieu*, II, 1, §7, in François de Salignac de la Mothe-Fénelon, *Œuvres*, ed. Jacques Le Brun [Paris: Gallimard, Pléiade, 1997], 2: 600). More generally: "Actual thought is actual existence. [. . .] The being whose nature it is to think thus actually exists only in as much as it actually thinks, since it has no other existence than its thought. In this way possible thinking makes its essence and actual thinking makes its existence" (Fénelon, *La Nature de l'homme expliquée par les simples notions de l'être en général*, in *Œuvres*, 2: 849); see: "This actual thinking, which is always a true action" (ibid., 2: 865). One thinks of Kant: "der Aktus, Ich denke—the act I think" (*Kritik der reinen Vernunft*, B 423; *Critique of Pure Reason*, ed. and trans. Paul Guyer and Allen W. Wood [Cambridge: Cambridge University Press, 1998], 453).

64. See "hoc est proprie quod in me sentire appellatur; atque hoc præcise sic sumptum nihil aliud est quam cogitare—this is what in me is called 'sensing.' But this, precisely so taken, is nothing other than thinking" (*Meditatio II*, AT VII, 29.15–18; CSM II, 19). For a phenomenological reading, in the wake of Michel Henry, of the *cogitatio* as feeing and auto-affection, see my *Cartesian Questions: Method and Metaphysics*, chap. 5, 96–117, and *On Descartes' Passive Thought*, chap. 3, §16, pp. 104–18.

65. Respectively, *The Search for Truth* (AT X, 521; CSM II, 415) and *Principles of Philosophy I*, §10 (CSM I, 195–96). And: "Cum autem advertimus nos esse res cogitantes, prima quædam notio est, quæ ex nullo syllogismo concluditur; neque etiam cum quis dicit, *ego cogito, ergo sum, sive existo*, existentiam ex cogitatione per syllogismum deducit, sed tanquam rem per se notam simplici mentis intuitu agnoscit [. . .] ex eo quod apud se experiatur, fieri non posse ut cogitet, nisi existat—And when we become aware that we are thinking things, this is a primary notion which is not derived by means of any syllogism. When someone says 'I am thinking, therefore I am, or I exist', he does not deduce existence from thought by means of a syllogism, but recognizes it as something self-evident by a simple intuition of the mind. [. . .] in fact he learns it from experiencing in his own case that it is impossible that he should think without existing" (*IIæ Responsiones*, AT VII, 140.18–28; CSM II, 100).

66. We must underline that the statement *ego sum, ego existo*, as act and fact, must therefore be accomplished temporally, according to the discontinuous time of existence and of the event. Let us point out certain indicators of this temporalization:

Quoties: AT VII, 25.12; 26.2; 36.12. *Quamdiu*: 22.8; 25.9; 27.9; 36.16; 69.16, 30 (see "ad ea attendit, *quamdiu* autem id facit, certus est se non falli," *Conversation with Burman*, AT V, 148). *Dum*: 19.19; 30.15; 39.13; 51.23; 54.2; 55.14; 73.15; 145.24; *Principia philosophiæ I*, §49: *dum cogitat*. And *"while* I was trying thus to think everything false, it was necessary that I, who was thinking this, was something" (*Discourse*, AT VI, 32.15–18; CSM I, 127). Or again, "repugnet enim, ut putemus id quod cogitat, *eo ipso tempore quo cogitat,* non existere" (*Principia philosophiæ I*, §7); *Per momentum* (*La Recherche de la vérité*, AT X, 522 and op. cit., 336).

67. In this sense we can follow Jocelyn Benoist and consider Montaigne as one of the "anti-transcendental thinkers" ("Montaigne penseur de l'empirisme radical: une phénoménologie non-transcendantale?", in Vincent Carraud and Jean-Luc Marion, eds., *Montaigne: scepticisme, métaphysique, théologie* [Paris: PUF, 2004], 211–28).

68. AT X, 518, and *La Recherche de la vérité*, 332. Vincent Carraud sees in *The Search for Truth* a "significant step that was certainly necessary for Descartes, since 'universal doubt' there has the status of a principle" (Carraud, *L'Invention du moi*, 235).

69. *Principia philosophiæ I*, §49. Here I follow Édouard Mehl, "La question du premier principe dans *La Recherche de la vérité*," *Nouvelles de la République des Lettres*, 1991/1: 77–97, who very clearly located and exposed this difficulty; he identifies the opponents, both ancient (G. Voetius and C. Lentulus) and modern (Jean-Claud Pariente, "Problèmes logiques du *cogito*," in Nicolas Grimaldi and Jean-Luc Marion, eds., *Le Discours et sa méthode* [Paris: PUF, 1987]). His inquiry into the status of first principle claimed (or refused) for the *cogito* is completed by that of Roger Ariew, *Descartes and the Last Scholastics* (Ithaca: Cornell University Press, 1999), chap. 10.

70. *The Search for Truth*, AT X, 522, and *La Recherche de la verité*, 336; CSM II, 415–16.

71. Édouard Mehl: "Ever present, the *dubitatio* here takes the place and the role devolved elsewhere to the *cogitatio*" (Mehl, "La question du premier principe," 83). The *cogitatio* is deduced (if you like) from the *dubitatio*, and not the reverse: "Sum tamen, et quid sim scio, atque ea propter scio, quia dubito, hoc est *proinde* quia cogito—But I am, and I know what I am, and I know these facts *because* I am doubting, i.e. because I am thinking" (*The Search for Truth*, AT X, 521, and *La Recherche*, 336; CSM II, 415).

72. Descartes, *The Search for Truth*, AT X, 515, and *La Recherche*, 329–30; CSM II, 409–10.

73. *The Search for Truth*, AT X, 524, and *La Recherche*, 339; CSM II, 418.

74. As Mersenne remarks, "If you doubt further that you are doubting, I will hold you to admit infinite progression; which you yourself reject, in such a way that wherever you turn, you must confess that there is something true in this, and you must say an eternal adieu to your Pyrrhonism" (*La Vérité des*

sciences contre les sceptiques et les pyrrhoniens [Paris: Toussaint du Bray, 1625], 204/ [Stuttgart: Frommann, 1969], quoted by Édouard Mehl, "La question du premier principe," 89).

75. *Notæ in programma*, AT VIII-2, 354.18–21; CSM I, 301. Heidegger comments on exactly this: "We have to ask more precisely: *What* is it *actually* [eigentlich] that Descartes has *found*, and what is it that he himself actually means to have found with the *cogito ergo sum*? Is what is found a certum and [if so,] in what sense? What is found is an aliquid [something] not qua res; not the dubitare as such is what is found and not the esse of the dubitare. Instead what is found is: me dubitare, me esse, that for me to doubt is my being. Not found is aliquid qua res, but instead *aliquid qua state of affairs [Sachverhalt]*. The basic finding of the search is a *veritas*, a *proposition* articulated in relation to what is objectively the case [*Gegenständliche*]: an object as such, the dubitare or the ego, is not found but instead a *standing* is found, the standing of a state of affairs, that the me dubitare is in the me esse, the co-givenness of the esse in the dubitare" (*Einführung in die phänomenologische Forschung*, WS 1923/24, GA 17 [Frankfurt a/M.: Klostermann, 1994], 244; English translation: *Introduction to Phenomenological Research*, trans. Daniel O. Dahlstrom [Bloomington, IN: Indiana University Press, 2005], 188).

Chapter Two

1. A list of these formulations was made by Henri Gouhier, *Essais sur Descartes* (Paris: Vrin, 1937, 1973), 118, 127, 269, and following. On the differences between these formulations and the privilege according by the majority to "*(ego) cogito, (ergo) sum*" to the detriment of those in *Meditatio II*, see my *On the Ego and on God: Further Cartesian Questions*, chap. I, §3–4, pp. 8–19.

2. Respectively, AT VII, 25.11–13 and 27.8–9; CSM II, 17 and 18.

3. Sometimes the formula *I think therefore I am* assumed to be in *Meditatio II* is made "the shortcut" of the one found in the *Discourse* and the *Principia*, when in fact the opposite is true (Geneviève Rodis-Lewis, *L'Œuvre de Descartes*, 239). There are several exceptions to this inattention: Ferdinand Alquié: "So the formula 'I think, there I am' is not encountered here [*Meditatio II*]" (*La Découverte métaphysique de l'homme chez Descartes*, 185, and see 198); Jean-Marie Beyssade: "The proposition *I am, I exist* seems indeed to constitute, in the *Second Meditation*, the fixed and assured point on which the whole of the first philosophy is built" (*La Philosophie première de Descartes*, 217, but these lines appear in chap. V, entitled "I think, therefore I am"); or Jean-Luc Nancy: "the *cogito* first takes, as a matter of principle, the form [...] *ego sum, ego existo*" (*Ego sum: Corpus, Anima, Fabula*, trans. Marie-Eve Morin [New York: Fordham University Press, 2016], 91).

4. See *On the Ego and on God: Further Cartesian Questions*, chap. I, as well as Chapter One, §5.

290 *Notes to Chapter Two*

5. In other words: "I utter, I am. I utter *I*, I *am* uttering I" (Nancy, *Ego sum: Corpus, Anima, Fabula*, 84). It is a "self-performation" (85).

6. Martin Heidegger: "Descartes hat den metaphysischen Grund der Neuzeit vorausgedacht, was nicht besagt, daß alle nachkommende Philosophie nur Cartesianismus sei" ("Der europäische Nihilismus" [1940], included in *Nietzsche*, G.A., 6.2 [Frankfurt a/M., 1997], 148); English translation: *Nietzsche, Volume III: The Will to Power as Knowledge and as Metaphysics, Volume IV: Nihilism*, ed. David Farrell Krell, trans. Joan Stambaugh, David Farrell Krell, Frank A. Capuzzi [San Francisco: Harper Collins, 1991] vol. 4, p. 102).

7. Immanuel Kant, *Critique of Pure Reason*, A350–51, 416, 417.

8. See Chapter Seven, §4.

9. See *quoties*: AT VII, 25.12; 26.2; 62.6.

10. AT VII, 27.9–12; CSM II, 18. See *quamdiu*: AT VII, 25.9; 27.9 and 10; and 36.16. And also: "quod ego, *dum* cogito, existam" (VII, 145.24 and following), or "is qui cogitat, non potest non existere, *dum* cogitat—He who thinks cannot but exist *while* he thinks" (*Principia philosophiæ I*, §49; CSM I, 209). And "repugnat enim, ut putemus id quod cogitat, *eo ipso tempore* quo cogitat, non existere—For it is a contradiction to suppose that what thinks does not, *at the very time* when it is thinking, exist" (*Principia philosophiæ I*, §7; CSM I, 195) or "it is impossible for us ever to think of anything without *at the same time* having the idea of our soul as a thing capable of thinking of whatever we think" (To Mersenne, July 1641, AT III, 394.16–19; CSMK, 186). And further: "*while* I was trying thus to think everything false, it was necessary that I, who was thinking this, was something" (*Discourse on the Method*, AT VI, 32.16–18; CSM I, 127). See above, Chapter 1, note 60.

11. Friedrich Wilhelm Joseph Schelling, *On the History of Modern Philosophy*, translation and introduction by Andrew Bowie (Cambridge: Cambridge University Press, 1994), 47; see Schelling, *Sämmliche Werke* (Stuttgart: Cotta, 1861), I/10, p. 10; republication: *Schriften von 1813–1830* (Darmstadt: Wissentschaftliche Buchgesellschaft, 1976), 292. Nevertheless, Schelling sees a weakness in the Cartesian argument precisely where one of its strongest characteristics lies, which is proof that he misses what is essential.

12. Edmund Husserl, respectively, *Die parisianer Vorträge*, Hua. I, p. 9; English translation: *The Paris Lectures*, trans. Peter Koestenbaum (The Hague: Martinus Nijhoff, 1967), 9; and *Cartesianische Meditationen*, §11, Hua. III, p. 64; English translation: *The Cartesian Meditations*, trans. Dorion Cairns (Dordrecht: Kluwer Academic Publishers, 1993), 25.

13. Descartes, *Meditationes*, AT VII, 45.7; see also, "ex eo ipso quod sim substantia" (AT VII, 45.20).

14. Note that, in the case of the analysis of the piece of wax, it is Gassendi who, through a false quotation, introduces *substantia* into a passage from *Meditatio II*, where it does not exist: "Adfers deinde *exemplum ceræ*, ac circa illud plurima habes,

ut significes '*aliud esse, quæ vocant accidentia ceræ, aliud ipsam ceram ejusve substantiam*; ac opus esse solius metis sive intellectus, non vero sensus aut imaginationis, ipsam ceram ejusve substantiam distincte percipere'—Next you introduce the *example of the wax*, and you spend some time explaining that *the so-called accidents of the wax are one thing, and the wax itself, or substance of the wax, is another*. You say that in order to have a distinct perception of the wax or its substance we need only the mind or intellect, and not sensation or imagination" (AT VII, 271.16–21; CSM II, 189). On this point, many commentators on Descartes will follow the false direction of Gassendi rather than the text of Descartes.

15. The term appears only after the demonstration of the existence of the *ego*, respectively in *Meditatio III* (AT VII, 43.20 and following) and *Principia I* (§11, AT VIII-1, 8.21 and following). Of course, the *Synopsis* of the *Meditationes* does mention "omnes omnino substantias, sive res quae a Deo creari possunt ut existant" (AT VII, 14.1–2) within the frame of its summary of *Meditatio II*, but it anticipates, precisely, the comparison between the thinking substance and the extended substance, which, according to the order of reasons, can come up only in *Meditationes V–VI*. On this "perversion of the order of reasons," see the remarks of Jean-Robert Armogathe on the *Synopsis* (in Dan Arbib, ed., *Les* Méditations métaphysiques, Objections et Réponses. *Un commentaire*, 61).

16. AT VI, 32.23; CSM I, 127.

17. Ferdinand Alquié speaks of a "passing of the *cogito* toward substance" (*La Découverte*, 197) and assures us that "thought [. . .] derives from being as its substance" (182). Martial Gueroult confirms this opinion: "The order of reasons thus authorizes Descartes to draw, starting in the *Second Meditation*, from the thinking I affirmed as substance all the consequences required for the working of science" (*Descartes selon l'ordre des raisons*, 1: 54; see as well 76–78). Similarly, Jean-Marie Beyssade: "As a result [. . .] the first truth is always joined by the condition that makes it known: substance" (*La Philosophie première*, 223). Gueroult however will end up in a more correct position by opposing the "authentic and first substantiality" of God to the "secondary substantiality" of the *cogito* (ibid., 230), a substantiality only constituting itself "epistemologically" (223). Jean-Luc Nancy, in contrast, underscores the "nonconsecution from the thinking *I*-substance to the *I*-subject of the uttering existence" (*Ego sum: Corpus, Anima, Fabula*, 97).

18. Vincent Carraud (*L'Invention du moi*, 240 and following), whose analysis I follow and results I accept and pursue. It is right to "disqualify the substantiality" of the *moi* by challenging "responses [to the question *quis sum?*] that are unjustified and prematurely substantialist" (ibid., 242 and 260). On the difficulties that Descartes encounters and attempts to surmount in the concept of substance, see my study in *On the Ego, and on God*, chap. III, and, more recently, Dan Arbib, *Descartes, la métaphysique et l'infini* (Paris: PUF, 2017), §58–60. These difficulties will become so strong in moral philosophy that, in order to think the union of soul and

body, Descartes will end up abandoning the concept of substance completely (see my *On Descartes' Passive Thought*, chap. V). In this sense, one can already attribute to Descartes what Vincent Carraud sees in Pascal: "not so much a *philosophical refutation* as a *disqualification* of the fundamental concepts and theses of metaphysics" (*L'Invention du moi*, 37). I have already spoken of *destitution* in Pascal (*On Descartes' Metaphysical Prism*, §18, pp. 234–44), and of a *suspension* and an *advance* in Descartes (*On Descartes' Passive Thought*, §21, p. 159, and §32, pp. 242–49).

19. "quisnam sim ego ille, qui jam necessario sum—what am I, who now necessarily exist" and "quis sim ego ille quem novi—who is this 'I' whom I know" (*Meditatio II*, AT VII, 25.14–15 and 27.28–29; CSM II, 17, 18).

20. "I noticed that while I was trying thus to think everything false, it was necessary that I, who was thinking this, was something"; and "this 'I'—that is, the soul by which I am what I am" (*Discourse on the Method*, AT VI, 32.15; CSM I, 127: we note here the clear distinction between the thought *cogito* and the *cogito* thinking in actuality; and 33.9; CSM I, 127). Contrary to Saint Augustine, who aims at "a certain likeness of the Trinity [...]. I, on the other hand, use the argument to show that this *I* which is thinking, is *an immaterial substance*" (To Colvius, 14 November 1640, AT III, 247.5–11; CSMK, 159).

21. Étienne Gilson says it well: "Descartes assures himself the benefits of substantialist realism, while expelling from the notion of substance what it could harbor that is obscure or impermeable to distinct thought," so that we must consider "his substantialism as a simple realism of thought" (*Discours de la méthode. Texte et commentaire* [Paris: Vrin, 1925, 1967], 304 and 303). It may be that Heidegger's reproach—"With regard to the ontological development of the problem [namely, the analogy of substance], Descartes is far behind the scholastics" (*Being and Time*, trans. Joan Stambaugh [Albany: State University of New York Press, 1996], §20, p. 87)—means, without his suspecting it, the same thing: Descartes, indeed, does not take *substantia* into consideration because he has no use for it, nor any need, at least for the *ego*.

22. *IIIæ Responsiones*, AT VII, 174.20–23; CSM II, 123.

23. I am pleased that this conclusion connects with that of Renaud Barbaras: "Contrary to what Husserl and Heidegger assumed, namely the fact that the sense of being of that which escapes negation (consciousness) is identical to that which was negated (the world), the sense of the existence that is revealed to me in doubt cannot be that of the existence that was denied by it. Far from existence's sense of being remaining indeterminate, as Heidegger affirmed, it is on the contrary fully in its singularity [...]. This existence that arises straight from negation, that is presence of doubt to itself, remains a negative existence. [...] This thing that thinks is therefore exactly not a thing, that is, a being entirely positive and self-sufficient" ("Qu'est-ce qu'une chose qui pense?", in Dominique Pradelle and Camille Riquier, eds., *Descartes et la phénoménologie* [Paris: Hermann, 2018], 22, and see 17 and 20).

And with Claude Romano's conclusion as well: "And since all being has been put out of action, this ego possesses only a 'pre-being' (*Vorsein*), and occupies no specific ontic region, being the *Urregion* in which they are all constituted": Husserl thus finds himself "in an ambivalent proximity to the Cartesian problematic" (*At the Heart of Reason*, trans. Michael B. Smith and Claude Romano [Evanston, IL: Northwestern University Press, 2015], 283; see my similar conclusion, as far back as *Reduction and Givenness*, trans. Thomas Carlson [Evanston, IL: Northwestern University Press, 1998], chap. V, §7).

24. On the comparative role of the *naturæ simplicissimæ* in 1627 and 1641, see *Cartesian Questions: Method and Metaphysics*, Chapter 3, in particular §1 and 4.

25. AT VII, 45.7; CSM II, 31. This is confirmed in the *Principia philosophiæ II*, §9: "Others may disagree, but I do not think they have any alternative perception of the matter. When they make a distinction between substance and extension or quantity, either they do not understand anything by the term 'substance' (*vel nihil par nomen substantiæ intelligunt*), or else they simply have a confused idea of incorporeal substance (*vel confusam tantum substantiæ incorporæ ideam habent*), which they falsely attach (*quam falso tribuunt*) to corporeal substance; and they relegate the true idea of corporeal substance to the category of extension, which, however, they term an accident. There is thus no correspondence between their verbal expressions and what they grasp in their minds" (CSM I, 226–27).

26. Nietzsche, *Nachgelassene Fragmente*, 10 [59], in *Werke* VIII/2, ed. Colli and Montinari (Berlin: de Gruyter, 1970), 131 = *Wille zur Macht*, §485; English translation: *Will to Power*, trans. Walter Kaufman (New York: Random House, 1967), 268. Heidegger here comments on Descartes (*Wegmarken*, GA 9, p. 89, correcting the objections of *Sein und Zeit*, §10 and §20, pp. 46 and 93), following Leibniz: "However, since necessarily in corporeal nature there must be genuine unities, without which there would be neither multitude nor collection, it must be that what makes the corporeal substance is something that responds to what is called *I* in us" (Leibniz, *Système nouveau pour expliquer la nature des substances et leur communication entre elles, aussi bien que l'union de l'âme avec le corps*, in C. I. Gerhardt, ed., *Die philosophischen Schriften* [Hildesheim: G. Olms, 1965], vol. 4, p. 473). At times, Kant comes close to this view: "And since we are not acquainted with any absolutely inner determinations except through our inner sense, this substratum would be not only simple, but also (according to the analogy with our inner sense) determined through *representations*, i.e., all things would really be *monads*, or simple beings endowed with representations" (*Critique of Pure Reason*, A 283/B 339, p. 378). On this egological deduction of substance, see my *On Descartes' Metaphysical Prism*, §13, pp. 150–69.

27. According to Vincent Carraud's felicitous formula: "Cartesian quasi-substantivization, Pascalian substantivization, and in both cases, substantivization without substantialization" (*L'Invention du moi*, 62).

28. *Regulæ ad directionem ingenii*, AT X, 360.9 and 5; CSM I, 9.

29. *Regula I*, AT X, 374.9 and 378.3; CSM I, 17, 19. See René Descartes, *Règles utiles et claires pour la direction de l'esprit dans la recherche de la vérité*, trans. and annotations by Jean-Luc Marion and mathematical notes by Pierre Costabel (The Hague: Nijhoff, 1977), 141.

30. AT VI, 19.30–20.7; CSM I, 120–21. The other occurrences of *subject* in the *Discourse* concern either that of which one speaks (a substantive: 38.4; 43.20; 52.1; 69.1; 77.9), or that to which one submits oneself (an adjective: 3.28; 7.8; 32.6; 66.15; 68.20; 76.30).

31. *Regula VIII*, AT X, 398.14–17; CSM I, 31.

32. It already appeared in the *Regulæ* with regard to the Aristotelian doctrine of place: "id quod concipimus, nempe *subjectum* aliquod occupare locum, quia extensum est" (AT X, 443.22–23); and: "semper eamdem [*sc.* unitas] esse *subjectum* omnimode extensum et infinitarum dimensionum capax" (453.14–15); "subjectum aliquod per multas unitates mensurabile" (445.23–24); "*subjectum ver extensum*" (452.20); "concipimus subjectum sub ratione lineæ, sive sub ratione magnitudinis extensæ" (464.17–18). The term occurs only once, in this same Aristotelian sense, in the *Principia philosophiæ IV*, §86.

33. Here I am correcting my mistaken reading of this same text, in Jean-Luc Marion, "Descartes hors sujet," *Les Études philosophiques*, 2009/1, 54 and following and agreeing with the critique made by Emmanuel Faye, *Descartes. La Recherche de la verité par la lumière naturelle. Essai introductif: L'invention cartésienne de la conscience* (Paris: Livre de Poche, 2010), 43n1.

34. "allen Gedanken als Substratum zum Grunde liegt," *Kritik der reinen Vernunft*, A 350; trans. Guyer and Wood, *Critique of Pure Reason*, 417.

35. *Objectiones IIIæ*, AT VII, 172.25 and following; 173.2–3; CSM II, 122. Above all, see the surprising argument: "subjecta enim omnium actuum videntur intelligi solummodo sub ratione corporea, sive sub ratione materiæ, ut ostendit ipse [*sc.* Descartes] in exemplo ceræ—the subject of any act can be understood only in terms of something corporeal or in terms of matter, as the author himself [Descartes] shows later in his example of the wax" (173.16–18; CSM II, 122). The mistake is two-fold: first, nothing proves that the *subjectum* of the acts must always come from a body, nor even perhaps that a body is defined as nothing more than a piece of matter; and then, the analysis of the piece of wax (where, as Jean-Marie Beyssade recognizes, "the *substance* is not named a single time," *Descartes au fil de l'ordre* [Paris: PUF, 2011], 56) concludes precisely *against* the ontic materiality of its *subjectum*, but the fact depends on the *solius mentis inspectio*, by definition immaterial. It is understandable that Descartes would be irritated by these misinterpretations or this bad faith; it is also surprising that so many critics still take the objections of Hobbes absolutely seriously—see M. Pécharman, "Troisièmes objections et Réponses," in Dan Arbib, ed., *Les* Méditations, *Un commentaire*, 251–81, and my study, "Hobbes et

Descartes: l'étant comme corps," in Dominique Weber, ed., *Hobbes, Descartes et la métaphysique* (Paris: Vrin, 2005), revised and corrected in Chapter Seven.

36. Respectively: "dicat unam cogitationem non posse esse *subjectum* alterius cogitationis. Quis enim unquam, præater ipsum, hoc finxit?—he says that one thought cannot be the subject of another thought. Who, apart from him, ever supposed that it could be?" (AT VII, 175.22–24; CSM II, 124). And then: "certum est cogitationem non posse esse sine re cogitante, nec omnino ullum actum, sive ullum accidens, sine substantia cui insit—it is certain that a thought cannot exist without a thing that is thinking; and in general no act or accident can exist without a substance for it to belong to" (175.25–176.1; CSM II, 124). And finally: "ipsam substantiam non immediate per ipsam cognoscamus, sed per hoc tantum quod sit *subjectum* quorundam actuum—we do not come to know a substance immediately, but through its being the subject of certain acts" (176.1–3; CSM II, 124). The same relation between *substantia* and *subjectum* is found in the *IIæ Responsiones* (AT VII, 161.15–17).

37. The same is true in the appendix to the *IIæ Responsiones*, where both the general definition of *substantia* and that of the extended *substantia* mention the *subjectum* (AT VII, 161.14 and 23), while that of the "substantia cui inest immediate cogitatio—substance in which thought immediately resides" omits it (AT VII, 161.24).

38. Note that Pascal sometimes uses the word "subject," most often in the political sense (*Pensées*, L. §25, pp. 136, 148, 484, 838), but sometimes also in the ontic sense: "Every time that the cause by which an effect is possible is present and subject to the *subject* where it must be produced, there is the relation of possibility to power; that is to say that the effect is to the power of this *subject*, and not otherwise" (Blaise Pascal, *Écrits sur la grâce*, II, in *Œuvres completes* [Paris: Seuil, 1963], 341). He is following Montaigne: "As much as I can, I employ myself entirely upon myself; and even in that subject I would still fain bridle my affection and keep it from plunging in too entirely, since this is a subject that I possess at the mercy of others, and over which fortune has more right than I have" (*Essais* F766–67, V1003). We must note that here, indeed, the *subject* is not identified with the *moi*, and thus has absolutely no relation to the modern meaning.

39. Jean-Luc Nancy states perfectly, "The human subject has never been a figure that appeared and then disappeared within history, for the unique reason that he has never conquered his figure of subject" (*Ego sum: Corpus, Anima, Fabula*, 105, against the final conclusion of Foucault, *Les Mots et les Choses* [Paris: Gallimard, 1966]).

40. "Descartes gebraucht an wichtigen Stellen für *cogitare* das Wort *percipere* (*per-capio*)—etwas in Besitz nehmen, einer Sache sich bemächtigen, und zwar hier im Sinne des Sich-zu-Stellens von der Art des Vor-sich-stellens, des '*Vor-stellens*'—In important passages, Descartes substitutes for *cogitare* the word *percipere*

(*per-capio*)—to take possession of a thing, to seize something, in the sense of presenting-to-oneself by way of presenting-before-oneself, *representing*" (Martin Heidegger, Gesamtausgabe 6.2, *Nietzsche II*, 151; English translation: Martin Heidegger, *Nietzsche, Volumes III and IV*, IV: 104–105). Moreover, this interpretation takes up a remark made by Nietzsche: "Das Denken ist uns kein Mittel zu 'erkennen', sondern das Geschehen zu bezeichnen, zu ordnen, für unsern Gebrauch handlich zu machen—For us, thought is not a means to 'know,' but to designate what happens, to put it in order, to put it into our hands for our use" (Nietzsche, *Nachgelassene Fragmente*, August-September 1885, 40 [20], *Werke* VII/3, p. 369).

41. See *Regula III*, AT X, 368.13–26 and my note (*cogitatio* comes from *co-agere*, to gather together, to lead before oneself, to keep), as well as the *Annexe I*, "Traduction d'*intuitus* et utilisation de *regard*," in *Règles utiles et claires*, 93–95 and 295–302.

42. *Discourse on the Method*, respectively AT VI, 61.29; 62.1 and 8; and 57.9; CSM I, 142–43, 140.

43. Heidegger, GA 6.2, p. 152; English: *Nietzsche IV*: 106; and respectively, 152/105 ("Das cogitare ist ein Sich-*zu*-stellen des Vor-stellbaren—*Cogitare* is the presenting *to* oneself of what is representable") and 157/110 ("das Vorstellen ist ein Sich-mit-vorstellen—representing is a co-representing of oneself").

44. Respectively, *Meditatio II* (AT VII, 28.21; CSM II, 19; and see 34.18–19), and *The Search for Truth* (AT X, 521; CSM II, 415; this point was established in Chapter One, §6).

45. Heidegger, *Nietzsche IV*: 108 ("Das Vorstellen und der Vor-stellende sind im menschlichen Vor-stellen *mit*-vorgestellt," GA 6.2, 155) and 110 ("das Vorstellen ist ein Sich-mit-vorstellen," GA 6.2, 157). See also: "Das vorstellende Ich ist vielmehr in jedem 'ich stelle vor' weit *wesentlicher* und notwendiger *mit*vorgestellt, nämlich als dasjenige, auf das zu und auf das zurück und *vor* das jedes Vor-gestellte hingestellt wird—Rather, the representing I is far more *essentially* and necessarily *co*-represented in every 'I represent,' namely as something toward which, back to which, and *before* which every represented thing is placed" (GA 6.2, 154; English, 107).

46. Heidegger: "cogito ist cogito me cogitarem" (GA 6.2, 155–56; English: *Nietzsche IV*: 108–109), relying on "etiam sentire, idem est quod cogitare," *Principia philosophiæ I*, §9. *Sein und Zeit* had already said "cogito me cogitare *rem*" (*Sein und Zeit* [Tübingen: Max Niemeyer Verlag, 2006], §83, p. 433, emphasis added). On this rather complex dossier, see my successive clarifications in Jean-Luc Marion, "Heidegger et la situation métaphysique de Descartes," *Bulletin Cartésien IV*, *Archives de Philosophie* 38/4, 1975, *Cartesian Questions: Method and Metaphysics*, chap. 5, §1, pp. 96–103, and *On the Ego and on God*, chap. 1, §3, pp. 8–11.

47. Heidegger: "Der vermeintliche Obersatz—*is qui cogitat, est*—kann niemals der Grund sein für das *cogito-sum*, weil jener Obersatz erst dem *cogito-sum* entnommen ist, und zwar in einer Weise, daß dadurch das *cogito-sum* in seinem wesentlichen Gehalt verunstaltet wiedergegeben wird. Das 'Ich bin' wird aus dem 'Ich stelle

vor' nicht erst gefolgert, sondern das 'Ich stelle vor' ist seinem *Wesen* nach jenes, was mir das 'Ich bin'—nämlich der Vor-stellende—schon zugestellt hat.—The supposed major premise—*Is qui cogitat, est*—can never be the ground for the *cogito sum*, because that premise is first derived from the *cogito sum*, indeed in such a way that the *cogito sum* is thereby reproduced in its essential import, although in an altered form. The 'I am' is not first deduced from the 'I represent'; rather, the 'I represent,' according to its *essence*, is what the 'I am'—that is, the one representing—has already presented to me" (GA 6.2, 160–61; English: *Nietzsche IV*: 113).

48. Kant: "Das *Ich denke* muß alle meine Vorstellungen *begleiten* können; den sonst würde etwas in *mir* vorgestellt werden, was gar nicht gedacht werden könnte, welches ebensoviel heißt, als die Vorstellung würde entweder unmöglich, oder wenigstens für mich nichts sein" (*Critique of Pure Reason*, §16, B 132; English translation: Guyer and Wood, 246). Perhaps Nietzsche makes use of this relay: "Der Wille bewegt nichts mehr, erklärt folglich auch nichts mehr—er *begleitet* bloß Vorgänge, er kann auch fehlen.—The will does not do anything any more, and so it does not explain anything any more either—it just accompanies processes, but it can be absent as well" (*Götzen-Dämmerung*, "Die vier grossen Irrthümer," §3, *Friedrich Nietzsche Digitale Faksimile Gesamtausgabe*, www.nietzschesource.org/#eKGWB/GD-Irrthuemer-3; English translation: *The Anti-Christ, Ecce Homo, Twilight of the Idols, and Other Writings*, ed. Aaron Ridley and Judith Norman, trans. Judith Norman [Cambridge: Cambridge University Press, 2005], 178).

49. Nietzsche: "*Grundgewißheit.* 'Ich stelle vor, also giebt es ein Sein' *cogito, ergo est*.—Daß *ich* dieses Vorstellende Sein bin, daß Vorstellen eine *Thätigkeit des Ich* ist, ist nicht mehr gewiß: ebenso wenig alles *was* ich vorstelle.—Das einzige Sein, welches wir kennen, ist das *vorstellende Sein*. [. . .] Dem Vorstellen ist der *Wechsel* zu eigen, *nicht die Bewegung*: wohl Vergehen und Entstehen, und im Vorstellen selber fehlt alles Beharrende; dagegen stellt es zwei Beharrende hin, es *glaubt* an das Beharren 1) eines Ich 2) eines Inhaltes: dieser Glaube an das Beharrende der Substanz d.h. an das *Gleich* bleiben Desselben mit sich ist ein Gegensatz gegen den Vorgang der Vorstellung selber. [. . .] das *Sein* also, welches uns einzig verbürgt ist, ist *wechselnd, nicht-mit-sich identisch* [. . .]. Dies ist die *Grundgewißheit vom Sein*. Nun *behauptet* das Vorstellen gerade das Gegentheil vom Sein!" *Nachgelassene Fragmente*, Autumn 1881, 11 [330], vol. V, pp. 467–68.

50. Heidegger: "das Vor-stellen, das sich selbst wesenhaft vor-gestellt ist, setzt das Sein als Vor-gestelltheit und die Wahrheit als Gewißheit—The principle says that representation, which is essentially represented to itself, posits Being as representedness and truth as certitude" (GA 6.2, 162, see also 164, 171; English: *Nietzsche IV*: 114).

51. Likewise in 1637: "nothing that I could represent more distinctly to my imagination and senses" (*Discourse on the Method*, AT VI, 20.17ff), for example "material things" (41.28). Dreams also "represent" (39.18), but it can so happen that the

ideas coming from the sensible "nihil extra cogitationem positum repræsentant" (*Principia philosophiæ I*, §71, and see §68), while the imagination, through *figura*, "repræsentat" (*III*, §25, §57; and *IV*, §42; see as well §84, §92, §179). In 1641, we find also two depreciative uses: "Nihil unquam extitisse eorum quæ mendax memoria repræsentat—none of the things that my lying memory reports ever happened" (AT VII, 24.15ff; CSM II, 16), "somnia verius evidentiusque repræsentant—so that my dreams may provide a truer and clearer representation" (28.14; CSM II, 19), albeit sometimes *confused* (AT VII, 72.17, 19).

52. AT VI, 26.1ff; 28.8. In a similar sense, see: "unum et idem nomen omnibus rebus per idea istam [one of the universals] repræsentatis imponimus—we apply one and the same term to all the things which are represented by the idea in question" (*Principia philosophiæ I*, §59; CSM I, 212).

53. As in AT VII, 40.15; 43.3ff; 44.7; and 44.11.

54. *VIae Resp.*, AT VII, 559.3–7; CSM II, 382; Clerselier translates *cogitet se cogitare* not by *thinks that he thinks*, but by introducing *consciousness* (see below). On this text, see my commentary in *Cartesian Questions: Method and Metaphysics*, 100–101. On Bourdin and the *VIIae Objectiones*, see Roger Ariew, "Pierre Bourdin and the *Seventh Objections*," in Marjorie Grene and Roger Ariew, ed., *Descartes and His Contemporaries: Meditations, Objections, and Replies* (Chicago: University of Chicago Press, 1995), 208–25, and Édouard Mehl, "Septièmes Objections et Réponses," in Dan Arbib, *Les* Méditations, *Un commentaire*, 373–93.

55. *VIæ Resp.*, AT VII, 422.8–18; CSM II, 285, emphasis added. In other words, *ego sum, ego existo* is performed by a *cogito* that is non-reflective and non-representative, but that "*experimur*, we experience" through "*mentis intuitu*, a gaze of the mind" (*IIæ Responsiones*, AT VII, 140.21–22, 27; CSM II, 100).

56. [Translators' note: *Conscientia* (Latin) and *conscience* (French) (and related terms) signify with one term what in English is expressed with two: consciousness, in the sense of awareness, and the moral conscience.]

57. *IIæ Responsiones*, AT VII, 160.7–10 and 14–16; CSM II, 113; emphases added. We find an exact parallel in *Principia philosophiæ I*, §9. And, in *I*, §66, we are "*intime conscii*, intimately conscious" of the perception of the sensible; the same goes for *corpus nostrum*, of which we are "*intime conscii*, intimately conscious" (*II*, §26, we recall that the *sensus* are *modi cogitandi* as primordial as the others). The term is rare. The hapax of the *Discourse* refers to the moral sense [conscience] (AT VI, 25.16). The hapax of the *Meditationes* underscores that, if I am "conscious, *conscius*" of my "force, *vis*" in making myself subsist into the future, I "experience, *experior*" its narrow limits (*Meditatio III*, 49.18, to be compared with "ego tenuitatis meæ conscius," *Regula IV*, AT X, 378.26); but to all evidence this consciousness remains immediate.—We could compare this immediacy of *conscientia* in Descartes to a definition by Thomas Aquinas: "Nomen enim conscientiæ significat applicationem scientiæ ad aliquid; unde conscire dicitur quasi *simul* scire. Quælibet autem scientia

ad aliquid applicari potest; unde conscientia non potest nominare *aliquem* [*sc.* alium] habitum specialem, vel *aliquam* [*sc.* aliam] potentiam, sed nominat *ipsum actum*—The term conscience signifies the application of knowledge to something, hence to 'know with' [*conscire*] means, as it were, to know *at the same time*. But any science can be applied to something, so conscience cannot name *any* [other] special habit or *any* [other] power, but it names *the act itself*" (*De Veritate*, q. 17, a.1, *resp.*; English translation: Thomas Aquinas, *Selected Writings*, trans. Ralph McInerny [London: Penguin, 1998], 221–22).

58. To Gibieuf, 19 January 1642, AT III, 474.12–15; CSMK, 201. This is confirmed by *conscientia vel internum testimonum* (*Search for the Truth*, AT X, 524, and *Étude du bon sens*, ed. V. Carraud and G. Olivo, 338).

59. *Væ Responsiones*, AT VII, 352.11–13; CSM II, 244. See *To Reneri for Pollot*, March (April–May?) 1638, §3, AT II, 37.26–38.21; in particular, "To say 'I am breathing, therefore I exist', in this sense, is simply to say 'I am thinking, therefore I exist'" (38.8–10; CSMK, 98).

60. *Conversation with Burman*, AT V, 149, and moving between 148 and 149 for the quotations to come; CSMK, 335, 334, and 335. As to another text that presents some difficulty, "Experimur [. . .] generaliter quæcumque ad intellectum nostrum, vel aliunde perveniunt, vel ex sui ipsius contemplatione reflexa" (*Regula XII*, AT X, 422.25–423.1), one will note that it has to do with the knowledge of simple natures, which, being innate, do not come under reflection in the habitual sense (see *Règles utiles et claires*, n32 sub loc., p. 244ff).

61. *Regula XI*, AT X, 408.16–17; CSM I, 38. See in *Règles utiles et claires*, n6 ad loc, p. 220ff.

62. It is surprising that J.-M. Beyssade, in order to justify the usage of *reflectare* (Beyssade, 26n3), quotes two texts, one drawn, of course, from Descartes' *VIIæ Responsiones* (AT VII, 559.6–7), but in which Descartes denounces a "hallucination" of Bourdin; the other drawn from the *VIIæ Objections* of Bourdin himself, against Descartes (AT VII, 553). The very passage that Descartes critiques is attributed to him! (see p. 76). This is probably not by chance, since the same interpreter elsewhere claims, "Every thought is thus doubled by an idea that represents it to me and of which I have, if you like, a real knowledge: this formula means that I can, by reflecting on a thought, become conscious of it, and make note of it, and not that I actually accomplish this action" (*La Philosophie première de Descartes*, 248). No, not "every thought" is "doubled," since the idea is immediate to its thought; no, the idea does not represent the thought, but the thought thing.

63. *Principia philosophiæ I*, §9; CSM I, 195. Heidegger quotes this text without drawing from it the consequences opposed to his thesis (*Nietzsche II*, GA 6.2, 156).

64. Ibid. We find the same argument elsewhere: "the truth of this proposition: *I am thinking, therefore I am* [. . .], your mind sees it, feels it and handles it" (*To Newcastle (?)*, March–April (?) 1648, AT V, 138; CSMK, 331).

300 *Notes to Chapter Two*

65. Here I am following Michel Henry's analysis of *videre video*, AT VII, 29.14 and following (Michel Henry, *Généalogie de la psychanalyse* [Paris, 1985], chap. 1; see *Cartesian Questions: Method and Metaphysics*, chap. V, §2–3, pp. 103–109). Jean-Marie Beyssade is correct in remarking, "What is indubitable in thought is pure appearing, insofar as it puts aside every construction, every distance between two terms, every position by the judgment of a reality separated from the appearing. [...] For example, when it seems to me that I am seeing, it is this very doubling that is properly called feeling. It is distinguished from judgment [...]. It is distinguished also from reflection, which would be expressed by the formula *it is the soul that sees*" (*La Philosophie première de Descartes*, 235).

66. At least when he brings intentionality back to the *ego* of the *cogito* (as in *Cartesianische Meditationen*, §18, Hua. I, p. 85).

67. Heidegger: "Der Satz, daß die leblose Natur *res extensa* sei, ist nur die Wesensfolge des ersten Satzes. Sum res cogitans ist der Grund, das zum Grunde Liegende, das *subiectum für die Bestimmung der stofflichen Welt als* res extensa" (GA 6.2, 166, emphasis added; English translation: *Nietzsche IV*: 117).

68. Jean-Luc Nancy poses the point clearly: "The whole history of the *cogito* [...] has only ever been that of the various, even contradictory, ways of denouncing, avoiding, reflecting, suspending, or mediating the *im*mediacy of the *cogito*" (*Ego Sum: Corpus, Anima, Fabula*, 119n34). I will provide an example of only one case, which, it is true, is exemplary and recognized as such: Martial Gueroult, *Descartes selon l'ordre des raisons*, vol. I. (a) As we have seen, he argues that, "starting from the *Second Meditation*," the *cogito* is a substance (p. 54 and following, and see 77, 157). (b) Decidedly, he defines it by reflection, or indeed as a "reflection on my first reflection" (64 and following) by basing his claim on a single quotation, one that is moreover inaccurate: "Through a reflection of the human mind on itself. . ." (the original says: "the human mind, making a reflection on itself," in Descartes, *Œuvres philosophiques*, ed. Ferdinand Alquié, vol. 2 [Paris: Garnier, 1967], 391, text omitted in AT VII), from a passage in the *Præfatio ad lectorem*, which precisely *does not* mention the term *reflexio*: "ex eo quod mens humana in se conversa non percipit aliud esse quam rem cogiantem" (AT VII, 20). (c) The same false quotation allows him next to assure us that "this process ends in the *cogito* as reflected knowledge, *mens in se conversa*" (94 and 101). But reflection remains ("reflection is enveloped by the process that is constitutive of the *Cogito*" [60], to the point of becoming "reflection on the self" [80], "the reflexive consciousness of the *cogito*" [95, and see 99]). (d) Clearly, the absence of textual support allows for anything, to the point of basing oneself on *representation*: "I represent myself as free when I doubt [...] I know in all certainty that it is enough that I represent it [the *cogito*?] to myself, that is to say that I think, in order to exist" (75, and see 82 and 87). (e) We wind up at "a representation: that of a 'spiritual thing,' by which 'I represent myself to myself'" (155), allegedly supported solely by the French translation of the

Méditations, AT IX-1, 34; this non-directly Cartesian text provides only (and this is already too much!): "Now then among these ideas, the one that *represents me to myself*, about which there can be no difficulty"; the Latin text, the one written by Descartes, says only: "Ex his autem meis ideis, præter illam quæ *me ipsum mihi exhibet*, de qua hic nulla difficultas esse potest . . ." (AT VII, 42.29 and following); it omits nothing less than *représenter* and furnishes no textual support at all to the thesis of Gueroult. Let us emphasize once again that the concern for establishing a system does not exempt us from respect for the texts, and does not authorize just anything.

69. Nietzsche: "Die Konzeption eines Bewußtseins ('Geistes') als Ursache und später noch die des Ich (des 'Subjekts') als Ursache sind bloß nachgeboren, nachdem vom Willen die Ursächlichkeit als gegeben festand, als *Empirie*. . .," in *Götzen-Dämmerung*, "Die vier grossen Irrthümer," §3, English translation, 178.

70. Immanuel Kant, *Critique of Practical Reason*, Preface, Ak. V: 9, in *Practical Philosophy*, trans. and ed. Mary J. Gregor (Cambridge: Cambridge University Press, 1996), 144. See also Kant, *Critique of Judgment*, Introduction III, note, Ak. V: 177.

71. Kant, *Kritik der reinen Vernunft* A195-6/ B240-1; *Critique of Pure Reason*, 308–309.

72. Descartes, *Meditatio V*: "Ejus etiam sum naturæ ut non possim obtutum mentis in eandem rem semper defigere ad illam clare percipiendam" (AT VII, 69.18–20; see also 62.2). And: "the nature of the soul is such that it hardly attends for more than a moment to a single thing" (To Mesland, 2 May 1644, AT IV, 116.6–8; CSMK, 233). Or: "We cannot continually pay attention to the same thing" (To Princess Elizabeth, 15 September 1645, AT IV, 295.24–26; CSMK, 267). The failure of attention constitutes an infallible mark of finitude.

73. Nietzsche: "so enthält auch jenes erste 'es denkt' noch einen Glauben: nämlich, daß 'denken' eine Thätigkeit sei, zu der ein Subjekt, zum mindesten ein '*es*' gedacht werden müsse" (*Nachgelassene Fragmente*, Autumn 1885, 40 [23], VII, 3, p. 371). Schelling had already put it forward: "It thinks in me, thinking goes on in me (*Es denkt in mir, es wird in mir gedacht*), is the pure fact, in the same way as I can say with equal justification: 'I dreamed', and 'It dreamed in me' (*Es träumte mir*). The certainty which Descartes attributes to the *Cogito ergo sum* cannot be sustained even by thinking; if there is a certainty, then it is blind and devoid of thought" (*On the History of Modern Thought*, 48).

74. *Ethica* II, P11C and A2; and I, P25. In *The Collected Works of Spinoza*, vol. 1, ed. Edwin Curley (Princeton, NJ: Princeton University Press, 1985), 456.

75. Malebranche, *Recherche de la verité*, III, 2, 3; *The Search after Truth*, 225. See also: "Man wills, but his volitions are impotent in themselves; they produce nothing; they do not preclude God's doing everything [. . .]. I deny that my will is the

true cause of my arm's movement, of my mind's ideas, and of other things accompanying my volitions" (*Recherche de la verité, Éclaircissement XV*; *The Search after Truth*, 669). One could even argue that Leibniz opposes Descartes in the same sense and on the same point: if perceptions (or ideas) follow from the complete notion of a subject, that does not imply that the subject is the cause, since, as "it belongs only to God" to know the cause completely, it is up to him, and not to the *ego* that really thinks (me), to bring about or indeed cause my perceptions or ideas (Leibniz, *Discours de métaphysique*, §8, and see §13).

76. Nietzsche, *Nachgelassene Fragmente*, Autumn 1885, 40 [20], VII, 3, p. 369.

77. Nietzsche, *Nachgelassene Fragmente*, Spring 1888, 14 [98], www.nietzschesource.org/#eKGWB/NF-1888,14[98]; *Writings from the Late Notebooks*, ed. Rüdiger Bittner, trans. Kate Sturge (Cambridge: Cambridge University Press, 2003), 251, 252.

78. Descartes, *Discourse on the Method*, AT VII, 76.4–22; CSM I, 150. See the detailed commentary: "but I do not agree that it is circular to explain effects by a cause, and then prove the cause by the effects; because there is a big difference between *proving* and *explaining*. I should add that the word 'demonstrate' can be used to signify either, if it is used according to common usage and not in the technical philosophical sense. I should add also that there is nothing circular in proving a cause by several effects which are independently known, and then proving certain other effects from this cause" (*To Morin*, 13 July 1638, AT II, 197.25 and following; here 198.1–11 is quoted).

79. See my book *On Descartes' Metaphysical Prism*, chap. 2, §7–10. It is necessary to do this justice to Martial Gueroult, who was one of the very few among the commentators to see that "two grounds of certitude, two principles of order here seem to run up against one another" (*Descartes selon l'ordre des raisons*, I: 227, and see 226), and that "the problem of the two first principles" or "the reciprocal independence of the series of the *Cogito* and the series of God" (242) constitute not only "a rupture in the unilinear sequence of reasons" (237) and a "characteristic violation of the cardinal principle of order" (238), but institute "a sudden break" (236), "a schism" (223). It would have also been necessary to say that this rupture does not play out between two series of (epistemological) reasons, but between two metaphysical (onto-theological) figures.

Chapter Three

1. According to Geneviève Rodis-Lewis' expression, in *Le Développement de la pensée de Descartes*, 191.

2. My emphases throughout this chapter, except when noted. Thus we should not affirm too quickly that "the word *valeur* is not in Descartes," nor above all that for him as for Malebranche, "things have more value the more being they have" (Ferdinand Alquié, "Expérience ontologique et déduction systématique dans la

constitution de la métaphysique de Descartes," in *Cahiers de Royaumont. Philosophie*, no. 11, *Descartes* [Paris: Minuit, 1957, reprinted New York/London: Garland Publishing, 1987], 20). On the other hand, Jean Beaufret correctly notes the site and the meaning of this concept: "Indeed, perhaps it is not by chance that the word value begins to become a technical term in philosophy only with Descartes. [. . .] Descartes makes philosophy culminate in the determination of the 'true value' of goods whose acquisition can depend on us [. . .]. From where and how can we determine the 'true value of goods'? From where, if not from this unique center of precise determinations that is the *ego cogito*? How, if not by attaching ourselves to make *sub cogitatione cadere* all the goods of which we can have an idea? The philosophical appearance of the notion of value thus goes historically hand in hand with the cogitative interpretation, which is the Cartesian interpretation, of thought" (*Dialogue avec Heidegger* [Paris: Minuit, 1973], vol. 2, p. 186).

3. See *The Passions of the Soul*, §154, 446.13 (CSM I, 384); §156, 447.24; §159, 450.4, and To Christina, 20 November 1647, AT V, 85.22. And see my remarks in *On Descartes' Passive Thought*, §31, pp. 231–41.

4. [Translators' note: "a great light in the intellect was followed by a great inclination in the will," CSM II, 42.]

5. For indeed, "reason dictates" (*Discourse on the Method*, AT VI, 40.6, 8, 16; To Elizabeth, 4 August 1648, AT IV, 266.4–5), as does "true reason" (To Reneri for Pollot, April-May 1638, AT II, 37.28; CSMK, 98), and above all the stating of the principle of causality by the *Iæ Responsiones* (AT VII, 108.15, 18). To speak of a dictate of reason is thus in no way an exaggeration, as some have objected (see my *On Descartes' Metaphysical Prism*, 109).

6. *Discourse on the Method*, AT VI, 14.1; CSM I, 117. In Descartes' language, this "level" refers to the carpenter's or mason's tool that allows one (better than a plumb line) to be sure of the true vertical or horizontal position of a strut or a wall, through the balance of a bubble of air in the water in a tube. Certainly a skillful and experienced craftsman can *approach* such a determination, without an instrument and by estimation, like a good sailor can, if necessary, navigate by estimation (without a compass or sextant, or even the stars), but this remains a last resort. In the same way, esteem thinks without an instrument, the light of understanding, order, measure, or method, and yet it thinks and is not always wrong.

7. To Mersenne, 15 April 1630, AT I, 145.21–24; CSMK, 23. See: "the greater we *deem* [*estimons*] the works of God to be, the better we observe the infinity of his power" (To Elizabeth, 6 October 1645, AT IV, 315.19–21; CSMK, 273). And further: "when we love God and through him unite ourselves willingly to all the things he has created, then the more great, noble and perfect we *reckon* [*estimons*-nous] them, the more highly we esteem ourselves as being parts of a more perfect whole, and the more grounds we have for praising God on account of the immensity of his works" (To Chanut, 6 June 1647, V, 56.2–9; CSMK, 322).

8. To Christina, 20 November 1647: "we should not *consider* (*estimer*) anything as good, in relation to ourselves, unless we either possess it or have the power to acquire it" (AT V, 82.22–24; CSMK, 324).

9. Montaigne may have inspired Descartes' practice of esteem. (a) On the false sciences: "I see some who study and comment on their almanacs and cite their authority in current events. [...] I think none the better of them [Je ne les *estime rien de mieux*] to see them sometimes happen to hit the truth; there would be more certainty in it, if it were the rule and the truth that they always lied" (*Essais* I.11, V43, F29). (b) Against the historians: "Let them deliver history to us more as they receive it than as they see fit [que selon qu'ils *estiment*]" (*Essais* III.8, V943, F720).

10. This is why, moreover, Descartes' *Geometry* calls the unknown a "value." See: "if, in all of these 4 positions, the value of y were found to be null..." (*Géométrie II*, AT VI, 399.2) and "the value of x or of y..." (418.12).

11. *The Search for Truth*, AT X, 498; CSM II, 401. Montaigne in contrast does not make the value of money depend on its nominal value, but on the wealth of the one who gives: "It is all too easy to impress liberality on a man who has the means to practice it all he wants at the expense of others. And since its value is reckoned not by the measure of the gift, but by the measure of the giver's means, it amounts to nothing in such powerful hands" (*Essais* III.6, V903; F689).

12. To Chanut, 1 November 1646, AT VI, 534.2; CSMK, 298. Montaigne had already subjected science to esteem: "In truth, knowledge is a great and very useful quality; those who *despise* it give evidence enough of their stupidity. But yet I do not set its value [je n'*estime* pas pourtant *sa valeur*] at that extreme measure that some attribute to it, like Herillus the philosopher [...]" (*Essais* II.12, V438, F319).

13. *Discourse on the Method*, AT VI, 66.20–21; CSM I, 145. Montaigne had already said, "If man were wise, he would set the true price of each thing according as it was most useful and appropriate for his life" (*Essais* II.12, V487, F359). There is an echo in Descartes: "For I assure you that I am indifferent as to being *esteemed* or scorned by those who could be persuaded by such reasons" (Letter on the *Instances* to Gassendi, AT IX-1, 203.1–4).

14. Montaigne, *Essais* III.9, V994, F760. And what follows: "there are natures like that [...] who will think the better of me [*m'en estimeront mieux*] because they will not know what I mean" (ibid., V995, F762).

15. To Elizabeth, 1 September 1645, AT IV, 284.24–27; CSMK, 264.

16. To Elizabeth, 1 September 1645, AT IV, 286.25–27; CSMK, 265.

17. To Chanut, 1 November 1646, AT IV, 536.27–537.3; CSMK, 299.

18. *Passions of the Soul*, §52, 372.12–19; CSM I, 349. See also: "the utility of all the passions consists simply in the fact that they strengthen and prolong thoughts in the soul which it is *good* for the soul to preserve" (§74, 383.17–19; CSM I, 354); and: "Love is an emotion of the soul [...] which impels the soul to join itself willingly to

objects that appear *to be aggregable* to it" (§79, 387.3–6; CSM I, 356 = §81, 388.13–14; §85, 391.21–22); or: "The passion of desire is an agitation of the soul caused by the spirits, which disposes the soul to wish, in the future, for the things it represents to itself as *agreeable*" (§86, 392.22–24; CSM I, 358); or further: "most of the things we enjoy are *good for us* only for a time, and afterwards become *disagreeable*" (§208, 484.13–16; CSM I, 402).

19. *Meditatio VI*: "corpus illud, quod speciali quodam jure meum appellabam" (AT VII, 75.30–76.1). The *Passions of the Soul* often makes an explicit reference to this union, for example in §94, 399.15–20; §136 ("I shall content myself with repeating the principle which underlies everything I have written about them [the causes of the passions]—namely, that our soul and body are so linked that once we have joined some bodily action with a certain thought, the one does not occur thereafter without the other occurring too," 428.20–25; CSM II, 375); and §137 ("Regarding this [the five primitive passions], it must be observed that they are all ordained by nature to relate to the body, and to belong to the soul only in so far as it is joined with the body," 430.1–4; CSM II, 376).

20. See Jean-Luc Marion, *On Descartes' Passive Thought*, §10, pp. 61–71.

21. To Elizabeth, 15 September 1645, AT IV, 294.27–295.2; CSMK, 267. See: "The same is true of the other passions. They all represent the goods to which they tend with greater splendour than they deserve, and they make us imagine pleasures to be much greater, before we possess them, than our subsequent experiences show them to be" (To Elizabeth, 1 September 1645, IV, 285.23–27; CSMK, 264).

22 To Christina, 20 November 1647, AT V, 84.30–85.8; CSMK, 325–26. Montaigne remains in the background: "And what will you say of pain, which Aristippus, Hieronymus, and most of the sages have thought the ultimate evil? [. . .] Furthermore, this should console us, that in the course of nature, if the pain is violent, it is short; if it is long, it is light. [. . .] The pains of childbirth, considered great [*estimées grandes*] by the doctors and by God himself, and which we surround with so many ceremonies: there are whole nations that take no account of them" (Montaigne, *Essais* I.14, V55, 57, 58; F37, 38, 39).

23 .To Elizabeth, 20 November 1647, AT V, 91.24–25.

24. Montaigne, *Essais* II.20, V674, F511. See: "physical deformity, a constant, irremediable defect, and, according to us who greatly esteem beauty [*grands estimateurs de la beauté*], a very harmful one" (II.8, V398, F289). To which there is a response in Descartes: "a man, very virtuous and great admirer [*grand estimateur*] of persons of merit [namely, Chanut]" (To Chanut, 20 November 1647, AT V, 91.24–25). The Nietzschean accent is patent: "Humans first placed values into things, in order to preserve themselves—they first created meaning for things, a human meaning! That is why they call themselves 'human,' that is: the esteemer (*der Schätzende*). Esteeming is creating (*Schätzen ist Schaffen*): hear me, you creators! Esteeming itself is the treasure and jewel (*Schatz und Kleinod*) of all esteemed things"

(Nietzsche, *Thus Spoke Zarathustra*, I, §14, "On a Thousand and One Goals", trans. Adrian Del Caro [Cambridge: Cambridge University Press, 2006], 43). Or: "man designated himself as the being *(Wesen)* who estimates values, who evaluates and measures, as *the* 'estimating animal *(abschätzende)*'" (*The Genealogy of Morals*, II, §8, trans. Douglas Smith [Oxford: Oxford University Press, 1996], 51). Above all, if one thinks of Heidegger's interpretation of the *cogitatio* (see Chapter Two, §5).

25. To Elizabeth, 6 October 1645, AT IV, 306.13–20.

26. *Regula II*, AT X, 365.16–18. See my analysis in the "Annexe I. Traduction d'*intuitus* et utilisation de *regard*" in my edition of the *Règles utiles et claires pour la direction de l'esprit dans la recherche de la vérité*, 295ff.

27. *Discourse on the Method*, AT VI, 3.15 and 26.17, respectively; CSM I, 112, and 124.

28. All of these arguments are developed in *The Passions of the Soul*, §142, AT XI, 434–35; CSM I, 378–79.

29. To Elizabeth, 18 May 1645, AT IV, 202, 7–27.

30. *The Passions of the Soul*, §203, AT XI, 481.20–24; CSM I, 401.

31. Montaigne, *Essais* I.25, V135, F98; and I.26, V157, F116.

32. *Essais* II.12, V545, F408.

33. *Essais* II.12, V448, F327. That "knowledge and wisdom" belong to God clearly quotes Colossians 2:2–3: "the mystery of God, Christ, in whom are hidden all the treasures of wisdom and knowledge," as we find in Descartes, *Meditatio IV*, AT VII, 53.19–21 (see Vincent Carraud and Jean-Luc Marion, "De quelques citations cartésiennes de l'Écriture sainte," *Bulletin cartésien XXIV*, *Archives de philosophie*, 59, 1996/1: 2; to be completed with Vincent Carraud, "Les références scripturaires du corpus cartésien," *Bulletin cartésien XVII*, *Archives de philosophie*, 53, 1990/1).

34. Montaigne, *Essais* II.17, V656, F498.

35. *Essais* III.9, V955, F729.

36. Respectively, *Essais* III.5, V862, F656; II.7, V382, F275; and II.12, V584, F440.

37. Respectively, *Essais* II.5, V861, F655; and III.9, V965, F737 (here, regarding the quality of published books).

38. *Essais* I.42, V259, F189, 190. This is the very probable source (along with the *substantia* of Descartes) for Pascal, *Pensées*, L. §688, "What is the self [*le moi*]?" See also Montaigne: "it [nobility] is well below virtue in *esteem*. It is a virtue, if indeed it is one, that is artificial and visible" (III.5, V850, F646). And: "We owe subjection and obedience equally to all kings, for that concerns their office; but we do not owe *esteem*, any more than affection, except to their virtue" (I.3, V16, F9).

39. *Essais* II.6, V379, F274.

40. *Essais* II.17, F633, F480.

41. *Essais* II.17, V658. For example: "Not because Socrates said it, but because it is really my feeling, and perhaps excessively so, I *esteem* all men my compatriots, and embrace a Pole as I do a Frenchman" (III.9, V973, F743).

42. *Essais* III.9, V947, F722.

43. *Essais* II.17, V635, F481.

44. *Essais* II.20, V674, F511.

45. *Essais* II.12, V499, F368. This is of course a quasi-quotation of Saint Paul: "Nam si quis *existimat* se aliquid esse, cum nihil sit, ipse se seducit, *ei gar dokei tis einia*—For if any man think himself to be some thing, whereas he is nothing, he deceiveth himself" (Galatians 6:3), which also evokes esteem.

46. *Essais* II.6, V380, F275.

47. See Saint Augustine, *Confessiones* X.37.61–66, in *Les Confessions*, Aimé Solignac et al., eds., Bibliothèque augustinienne, vol. 14 (Paris: Desclée de Brouwer, 1996), here p. 254. See my analysis, *In the Self's Place: The Approach of Saint Augustine*, trans. Jeffrey L. Kosky (Stanford: Stanford University Press, 2012), §24, pp. 152–59.

48. *Essais* III.8, V922, F703, emphasis added.

49. Several texts establish their relation, but esteem seems to govern love, and not love esteem: "If he does not love such a person, he does better, he *esteems* him" (*Essais* III.1, V793, F602, emphasis added); and: "she [Mademoiselle de Gournay] loved me and wanted my friendship for a long time, simply through the *esteem* she formed for me" (II.17, V662, F502, emphasis added). See also: "I do not at all seek to be better loved and *esteemed* dead than alive" (II.37, V783, F595, emphasis added).

50. As I had the tendency to believe, not without hesitations, in *Cartesian Questions: Method and Metaphysics*, chap. V, §5 (111–14). In moral philosophy, self-esteem (generosity) certainly remains equivalent in theory to the thought of self, but in addition it also introduces the consideration of others as the criterion of balance.

51. To Chanut, 1 February 1647 (AT IV, 610.29–611.4; CSMK, 310). This thesis of the univocity of love (in its formal definition), taken up again in *The Passions of the Soul*, §81 and, especially, §82 (388.2–389.24), is also found, among other authors, in Saint Francis de Sales, and comes directly from Saint Augustine (see my *In the Self's Place*, §42, pp. 270–82).

52. *The Passions of the Soul*, §82, 389.15 (CSM I, 357), and see §90, 395.20–21 (CSM I, 360). Is this a retrieval of the *alios homines mei similes* of *Meditatio III* (AT VII, 43.4)?

53. See To Chanut, 1 February 1647: "It is not at all the case that the love which we have for objects above us is less than that which we have for other objects. I think that by nature such love is more perfect, and makes one embrace with greater ardour the interests of that which one loves" (AT IV, 611.20–25; CSMK, 311).

54. To Elizabeth, 15 September 1645, AT IV, 293.17 and 19; CSMK, 266.

55. To Chanut, 1 February 1647, AT IV, 612.14–15; CSMK, 311.

56. *The Passions of the Soul*, §83, 390.26–391.1, can be read as a commentary on St. Augustine's *De Civitate Dei* XIV.28, ed. A. Kalb, B. Dombart, Bibliothèque augustinienne (Paris: Institut d'études augustiniennes, 1993), vol. 35, p. 464.

57. To Mersenne, 15 April 1630, AT I, 145.24; CSMK, 23.

58. To Chanut, 1 February 1647, AT IV, 610.20–22; CSMK, 310. We show them "respect, veneration and admiration" (ibid., 611.10; CSMK, 310). See: "the persons that I honor and esteem" (To Elizabeth, July 1647, AT V, 66.17).

59. To Newcastle, March–April 1648, AT V, 136.19–27; CSMK, 331.

60. Respectively: To Mersenne, 15 April 1630, AT I, 150.5–6; CSMK, 25; *Epistula ad Voetium*, AT VIII-2, 57.3 and 103.21; and ibid., 206.2–4 or 207.3 (I owe these remarks to Dan Arbib, *Descartes, la métaphysique et l'infini*, 123 and following).

61. *The Passions of the Soul*, respectively: §53 and §54 (AT XI, 373.5–6, 10–11, and 21–23; CSM I, 373).

62. *The Passions of the Soul*, §204, XI, 482.13–14; CSM I, 401. A certain indecision remains in effect regarding self-esteem in relation to the self alone: "As for free will, I agree that if we think only of ourselves we cannot help regarding ourselves as independent; but when we think of the infinite power of God, we cannot help believing that all things depend on him, and hence that our free will is not exempt from his dependence" (To Elizabeth, 3 November 1645, AT IV, 332.12–18; CSMK, 277).

63. Blaise Pascal, *Pensées*, L. 628 (*Pensées*, trans. Krailsheimer, 208). The reversal of perspective is very clearly noted by the inversion of gaze between, on the one hand for Descartes, the *ego* watching pass in the street under its gaze the raincoats and hats of merely possible humans (*Meditatio II*, AT VII, 32.6–10), and, on the other hand, for Pascal, the *ego* that passes under a gaze, about which he asks himself whether "he went there to see me" (L. 688, trans. Krailsheimer, 217). On this contrast, see my *Cartesian Questions: Method and Metaphysics*, chap. 6, §2.

64. To Chanut, 1 October 1646, AT IV, 536.27–28; CSMK, 299.

65. Let us note that this inversion of the certain and the doubtful does not function only from theory to practical life (to consider that what is doubtful in theory must be held as certain in the practical realm), but also from the practical realm to theory (to consider what is doubtful in practical life as certain in theory): thus, to walk straight ahead, while having no certainty of going in the right direction, constitutes a doubtful practice; but, if one considers the reason for this decision (not knowing the right direction, I arbitrarily choose one in order to avoid remaining immobilized by indecision), it becomes, from the point of view of theory, the only rational solution for overcoming uncertainty: "Even when no opinions appear more probable than any others, we must still adopt some; and having done so we must then regard them not as doubtful, from a practical point of view, but as most true and certain, on the grounds that the reason which made us adopt them is itself true and certain" (*Discourse on the Method*, AT VI, 25.6–13; CSM II, 123).

66. *Principia philosophiæ I*, §3: "dubitatio ad solam contemplationem veritatis est restringenda. Nam quantum ad *usum* vitæ, quia persæpe rerum agendarum occasio

præteriret, antequam nos dubiis nostris exsolvere possemus, non raro quod tantum est verisimile cogimur amplecti" (AT VIII-1, 5.15–19; CSM I, 193).

67. *Principia philosophiæ I*, §2, AT VIII-1, 5.12–14; CSM I, 193. And there is even a *summa utilitas* of doubt (AT VII, 12.13).

68. On the detail of this weakness of the arguments, see *On the Ego and on God*, chap. 2, and *On Descartes' Passive Thought*, §13.

69. See AT VII, 22.23, 24.14, and VI, 32.2.

70. *Principia philosophiæ I*, §6, AT VIII-1, 6.27–29. Or: "And since making or not making a judgement is an act of will, [. . .] it is evident that it is something in our power" (Letter on Gassendi's *Counter-Objections*, AT IX-1, 204.7–10; CSM II, 270).

71. *Meditatio II*, AT VII, 25.10–13 and IX-1, 19; CSM II, 17. [Translators' note: The author here is quoting first from the original Latin text and then the French translation approved by Descartes.]

72. See: "mens nostra est talis naturæ, ut non *possit* clare intellectis non assentiri—our mind is of such a nature that it cannot help assenting to what it clearly understands" (To Regius, 24 May 1640, AT III, 64.24–25; CSMK, 147); and: "we cannot prevent ourselves from believing that this proposition, *I think, therefore I exist* is true" (*Principles of Philosophy I*, §7, AT VIIIA, 7, French translation, AT IX-2, 27), where the Latin is limited to invoking a logical contradiction ("*repugnat enim, ut putemus. . .*" AT VIIIA, 7.5–6), just as I, §43 (AT VIIIA, 21.18–19; CSM I, 207), evokes a simple powerlessness: "ei [the rule of truth] sponte assentiamur, et *nullo modo possimus* dubitare quin sit verum—we spontaneously give our assent to it and are quite unable to doubt its truth"; and see also the "Conversation with Burman": "*non possimus* de iis dubitare. . .—we *cannot be in* any doubts about them" (AT V, 178; CSMK, 353).

73. Jean Laporte rightly insists on the inversion of this relation of force, citing several textual arguments that, nevertheless, are rather imprecise (*Le Rationalisme de Descartes* [Paris: PUF, 1988], 149).

74. AT VII, 4.24–25; CSM II, 5. See: "At least I think that I have found how to prove metaphysical truths in a manner which is more evident than the proofs of geometry—*in my own opinion, that is*: I do not know if I shall be able to convince others of it" (To Mersenne, 15 April 1630, AT I, 144.13–18; CSMK, 22). The *more* than mathematical evidence for the demonstration of the existence of God does not rest on mathematical or assimilated arguments (this will be Spinoza's unfortunate choice); thus it does not forgo owing its validation to my *esteem*, or to my *judgment*. I can convince myself with this thinking by esteem, but I cannot claim to convince others of it (by arguments) if they do not exercise their own esteem on this evidence, which is patent though mute. Each one must learn to make an estimation of the evidence: some never succeed in doing so (Hobbes, Gassendi, Voet, Bourdin, even Regius, etc.), while others do (Arnauld, Mersenne *in fine*, etc.).

75. Fénelon, *Démonstration de l'existence de Dieu*, II, chap. 1, §4, 7 and 8, respectively, in *Œuvres*, ed. Jacques Le Brun (Paris: Gallimard, Pléiade, 1997), vol. 2, pp. 598 and 600. See also: "that reduces man to not being able to doubt, despite whatever effort he makes to put himself into a real doubt" (II, chap. 2, §33, p. 620).

76. Fénelon, *Démonstration de l'existence de Dieu*, II, chap. 1, §8 and 9; and then chap. 2, §32; respectively, pp. 600 and 619.

77. Here, in a more thoroughly argued form, is a thesis I already put forward in *Cartesian Questions: Method and Metaphysics*, chap. 5, §6, pp. 114–17.

78. To Elizabeth, 15 September 1645, AT IV, 295.20–21; CSMK, 267.

79. Thomas Aquinas, see respectively *Summa theologiæ*, Ia, q. 79, a. 12, *resp.*, and 13, *resp.*; then *De Veritate*, q. 16, a. 1, *resp.*, *ad* 12. See Odon Lottin, "La syndérèse chez Albert le Grand et saint Thomas d'Aquin," *Revue néo-scolastique de philosophie*, 30/17, 1928: 18–44.

80. Thomas Aquinas, *Summa theologiæ*, IIa IIæ, q. 47, a. 6, *resp.* And see also *De Veritate*, q. 16, a.1, *resp.*, *ad* 12, a. 2, *resp.*, and a.3, *resp.*

81. Thomas Aquinas, *Summa theologiæ*, Ia, q. 78, a. 4, *resp.* This *æstimatio* can fail, when for example I judge [*estime*] as due to me a good that comes from another, or I judge [*estime*] an evil (fornication) to be a good, etc. (*Summa theologiæ*, IIa IIæ, q. 162, a.4, *resp.* and *ad*1m). See Christian Trottman, "La syndérèse," in Iñigo Atucha, Dragos Calma, Catherine König-Pralong, Irene Zavattero, eds., *Mots médiévaux offerts à Ruedi Imbach* (Porto, 2011); and Maximilian Forschner, "Synderesis und *conscientia*. Zur Vorgeschichte des neuzeitlichen Gewissensbegriffs," in Sara Di Giulio and Alberto Frigo, eds., *Kasuistik und Theorie des Gewissens. Von Pascal bis Kant* (Berlin: de Gruyter, 2020).

Chapter Four

1. AT VII, 90.15–16 = IX-1, 72; CSM II, 62; or see the next-to-last words of the *Principia philosophiæ IV*, §207: "At nihilominus, memor meæ tenuitatis, nihil affirmo—Nevertheless, mindful of my own weakness, I make no firm pronouncements here" (VIII-1, 329.8–9; CSM I, 291). See as well: "tenuitatis meæ conscius—aware how slender my powers are" (*Regula III*, AT X, 378.26; CSM I, 20), or: "For my part, I have never presumed my mind to be in any way more perfect than that of the ordinary man" (*Discourse on the Method*, AT VI, 2.20–21; CSM I, 111); and also: "my weak reasonings" (8.14; CSM I, 114).

2. Taking up a formula I put forth previously in my *Reprise du donné* (Paris: PUF, 2016), §32, p. 186.

3. Emmanuel Levinas, "The Idea of the Infinite in Us," first published in Nicolas Grimaldi and Jean-Luc Marion, eds., *La Passion de la raison* (Paris: PUF, 1983), reprinted in Levinas, *Entre nous: Thinking-of-the-Other*, trans. Michael B. Smith and Barbara Harshav (New York: Columbia University Press, 1998), 220. Or: "the

affection of the finite by the infinite [. . .], beyond the pure contradiction which would oppose and separate them" (ibid.).

4. Respectively: Ludwig Wittgenstein, *Tractatus Logico-Philosophicus*, "Preface," in *Schriften* I (Frankfurt: Suhrkamp, 1980), 9; English translation: *Tractatus Logico-Philosophicus*, trans. David Pears and Brian McGuinness (London: Routledge, 1961), 3; and Immanuel Kant, *Reflexionen zur Metaphysik* §4958, Ak., vol. XVIII, p. 41.

5. Which, besides, could be contested: sunlight receives a differentiation from each of the objects that it shines on, since their surface modifies the wavelength on each occasion, so that, for the sensing eye, this modification of the wave makes it appear no longer white, but colored. Descartes does accept the distinction between "the sort of light which can be seen in transparent bodies, which philosophers call *lumen* in Latin in order to distinguish this from the light which can be seen in luminous bodies, which they call *lucem*" (To Morin, 13 July 1638, AT II, 203.30–204.1; CSMK, 108–109).

6. Here I follow my translation ("bornes" [translated earlier by "boundaries"], *Règles utiles et claires*, 2), following *Discourse*, VI, 26.22: "Through constant reflection upon the boundaries [*bornes*] prescribed for them [the Stoics] by nature"; the Kantian distinction between *limit* and *bound* [*Schranke* and *Grenze*, which in French are *limite* and *borne*, respectively—Trans.] is not, to my knowledge, common in the Cartesian lexicon.

7. See Pierre Costabel's clarification, "L'anaclastique et la loi des sinus pour la réfraction de la lumière," *Annexe IV*, in *Règles utiles et claires*, 313–22.

8. Comparable uses are found in the *Discourse on the Method*: "an infinity of devices" (VI, 62.9; CSM I, 143), "an infinity of others [forms or species]" (64.18; CSM I, 144), "an infinity of observations" (75.3; CSM I, 149).

9. Kant, *Critique of Pure Reason*, "Transcendental Theory of the Method," chap. 2, A758/B786, trans. Guyer and Wood, 652–53, emphasis original.

10. To Mersenne, 28 January 1641, AT III, 293.20–27; CSMK, 172. The capitalization of the I in "Infinite" constitutes, to my knowledge (according to Adam and Tannery and Giulia Belgioioso et al., René Descartes, *Tutte le lettere 1619–1650* [Milan: Bompiani, 2005], 1390, following the Clerselier edition, *Lettres de M. Descartes* [Paris, 1666], vol. 2, p. 289, reprint G. Belgioioso and Jean-Robert Armogathe [Lecce: Conte, 2005]), a *hapax* of Descartes (but J.-R. Armogathe retains the lower case i, in René Descartes, *Correspondance* [Paris: Gallimard, 2013], vol. I, p. 446).

11. I will not take up the dossier here. See, besides *Sur la théologie blanche de Descartes*, in particular §1–2, §9–11, my outline on "La création des vérités éternelles: le réseau d'une 'question'," in Jean-Robert Armogathe, Giulia Belgioioso, and Carlo Vinti, eds., *La biografia intelletuale di René Descartes, attraverso la* Correspondance (Naples: Vivarium, 1999).

12. The *Meditationes* will, moreover, institute this distinction: "Deus [...] habens omnes perfectiones, quas ego non comprehendere, sed quocumque modo attingere cogitatione possum—God [...] the possessor of all the perfections which I cannot comprehend, but can somehow touch in my thought" (VII, 52.2–6; CSM II, 35), even going to the point of shrinking back sometimes from such a touch: "nec comprehendere, nec forte etiam attingere cogitatione, ullo modo possum—I cannot in any way comprehend him, and perhaps cannot even touch him with thought in any way" (VII, 46.20–21; CSM II, 32).

13. *Letter to Clerselier on the* Instances *of Gassendi*, 12 January 1646 (AT IX-1, 210.10–16; CSM II, 273–74). The example of the "mountain" (in the Letters to Mersenne, at AT I, 152.14) will sometimes be replaced by that of the "sea" (*Iæ Responsiones*, AT VII, 113.18).

14. We will find this reference to infinite number as a case of the infinite (and not of the indefinite) as late as 1641: "me istam vim concipiendi majorem numerum esse cogitabilem quam a me unquam possit cogitari, non a me ipso, sed ab aliquo alio ente me perfectiore accepisse—I have the power of conceiving that there is a thinkable number which is larger than any number that I can ever think of, and hence that this power is something which I have received not from myself but from some other being which is more perfect than I am" (*IIæ Responsiones*, AT VII, 139.19–22; CSM II, 100).

15. Here we ought to remain more prudent than Dan Arbib: "The *Discourse on the Method* thus confers on the divine being no genuine infinity at all" (*Descartes, la métaphysique et l'infini*, 43, and see 103).

16. On this decisive caesura, see my analysis in *On Descartes' Metaphysical Prism*, chap. II, and Chapter Two, §3. On the linked delay of *substantia* and of the infinite until 1641, see Dan Arbib, *Descartes, la métaphysique et l'infini*, 31 and 41.

17. Gassendi interprets this restriction "a certain substance, *quandam substantiam*" as the tacit acknowledgement that Descartes admits not truly having the idea of God as substance: "bene quidem dicis *quondam*" (*Disquisitio metaphysica*, Instance 3 against the *Meditatio III*, 307, twice). As we saw earlier (Chapter Two, §3), there is a contradiction in believing that for Descartes the issue is one of respecting the non-univocal attribution of substantiality to God and to creatures, and thus of attenuating the idea of an *infinite* substance. For Descartes, however, it is precisely because it is infinite that, in God, the substance remains a *certain* substance, *approximately* in the sense of other beings, created and thus finite (to the point that with the *Principia philosophiæ* substance is no longer said *univocally* of God and of creatures, and can apply to the two *or to neither of the two*). Following a general rule, Gassendi's objections are largely overestimated by critics, those of the past as much as contemporaries.

18. And the determination by perfection becomes, from this moment on (46.19), the sole determination used in all the *Meditationes* that follow, in fact in

Meditatio V (*ens summe perfectum*, 54.13; 65.21; 66.13; and 67.9) and already in the *Præfatio* (VII, 14.25). It happens also, in the contemplative conclusion of *Meditatio III*, that immensity is substituted for infinity: "immensi hujus luminis pulchritudinem" (52.13). Igor Agostini (*L'idea di Dio in Descartes. Dalle* Meditationes *alle* Responsiones [Florence: Le Monnier, 2010], 62) shows that the objective reality of the idea of God "is never qualified as infinite," but simply contains "plus realitas" (VII, 40.19; 46.9). However, it remains that the difference, here as often in the same learned reader, seems forced: the formula "plus realitas esse in substantia *infinita* quam in finita" (45.26) indeed lets us see that the infinity of the substance explicitly implies the excess of reality that, in turn, characterizes it. The same goes for the declaration that "Descartes never qualified the objective reality of the idea of God as infinite, but [. . .] limited himself to designating it simply as greater than that contained in the idea of a finite substance" (ibid., 10); in fact and in principle, if one cannot comprehend the infinite, one can *never* qualify an objective reality (a content of thought) assertorically as infinite, but it remains only to observe that it is always greater that everything that can be thought (see VII, 139.5–22). Once again, the aporias of the interpreter reflect less Descartes' limits than his own.

19. Dan Arbib, *Descartes, la métaphysique et l'infini*, 211.

20. Thomas Aquinas, *Summa theologiæ*, Ia, q. 7, *resp*. For infinity is measured according to the perfection of the act (*IIIa*, q. 10, a.3). See: "Deus autem est actus purus absque omni potentia [. . .]. Est igitur infinitus—Now God is pure act without any potency [. . .]. Therefore, he is infinite" (*Contra Gentes*, I, § 43).

21. John Duns Scotus, *Ordinatio I*, d. 3, *pars prima*, in *Opera omnia*, ed. Carolus Balić, vol. III (Vatican City: Typis Polyglottis Vaticanis, 1954), respectively: q. 2, §25, p. 16; q. 2, §27, p. 18; q. 2, §39, p. 27; q. 3, §118, p. 73; English translation: John Duns Scotus, *On Being and Cognition: Ordinatio 1.3*, ed. and trans. John van den Bercken (New York: Fordham University Press, 2016), respectively, 51, 52, 56, and 85.

22. John Duns Scotus, *Ordinatio I*, d. 3, *pars prima*, respectively q. 1, §58, p. 43; q. 3, §139, p. 87; van den Bercken, 65, 93. See: "Deus non intelligitur nisi sub ratione entis—God is only understood under the notion of being" (§126, p. 79; van den Bercken, 88–89); and: "Quod si ens ponatur æquivocum creato et increato, substantiæ et accidenti, cum ista omnia sint per se intelligibilia a nobis, nullum videtur posse poni primum objectum intellectui nostri [. . .]. Sed ponendo illam positionem [. . .] de univocatione entis, potest aliquo modo salvari aliquod esse primum objectum intellectus nostri—Now, if being is held to be equivocal to the created and the uncreated, to substance and accident, then, since all of these are *per se* intelligible for us, it does not seem possible to propose any first object of our intellect [. . .]. But by holding the position I took [. . .] about the univocity of being, it is somehow possible to save the proposal that something is the first object of our intellect" (§129, p. 80; van den Bercken, 89). See also *Questions sur la métaphysique* [*Quæstiones super*

Metaphysicam], II, §151–52, ed. Olivier Boulnois and Dan Arbib, vol. 1 (Paris: PUF, 2017), pp. 548–51.

23. Francisco Suarez, *Disputationes Metaphysicæ XXVIII*, sect. 3, §20, in C. Berton, ed., *Opera omnia* (Paris: Vivès, 1861), vol. 26, p. 20; English translation: *The Metaphysical Demonstration of the Existence of God: Metaphysical Disputations 28–29*, trans. and ed. John P. Doyle (South Bend, IN: St. Augustine's Press, 2004), 48. On this point, see *Sur la théologie blanche de Descartes*, §6–7; Jean-François Courtine, *Suarez et le système de la métaphysique*, III, chap. 1, §7 (Paris: PUF, 1990), 394–401; and Olivier Boulnois, *Être et représentation*, chap. V and chap. VI, §4 (Paris: PUF, 1999), 223–91 and 314–25.

24. Respectively: Descartes, *Principia philosophiæ I*, §51 (and the title) (CSM I, 210); *IIæ Responsiones*, AT VII, 137.24 (CSM II, 98); *VIæ Responsiones*, VII, 433.5–6 (CSM II, 292); To H. More, 15 April 1649, AT V, 347.16–17 (CSMK, 375).

25. See perhaps, "Deum [. . .] judico esse actu infinitum," if one translates: "an infinite in actuality" (47.19). In contrast with the *Discourse*: "a being that is perfect and infinite" (VI, 39.4), and of *ens perfecti et infiniti* (VIII, 14.25; 46.12). Elsewhere, *God* is substituted for the *ens* in order to shoulder the infinite, *Deus infinitus* (9.16–17; 40.17; and 47.19).

26. Jean-Baptiste Morin, *Quod Deus sit, mundusque ab ipso creatus fuerit in tempore, ejusque providentia gubernetur. Selecta aliquot theoremata adversus Atheos* (Paris: J. Libert, 1635), quoted according to the edition of Jean-Robert Armogathe and M. Martinet, eds., "Aurifodina philosophica" (Lecce: Conte, 1996; anastatic reproduction of the edition of 1625), 10–11. Morin treats in this way only the undefined, which he confuses with the infinite (Dan Arbib, *Descartes, la métaphysique et l'infini*, §45, p. 182 and following).

27. "Ibi [*sc.* in the *Meditationes*, contrary to the *Discourse*], ergo cognovit [*sc.* the author] suam imperfectionem per Dei perfectionem. Et quamvis hoc non fecerit explicite, fecit tamen implicite. Nam explicite possumus prius cognoscere nostram imperfectionem, quam Dei perfectionem, quia possumus prius ad nos attendere quam ad Deum, et prius concludere nostram finitatem, quam illius infinitatem; sed tamen implicite semper præcedere debet cognitio Dei et ejus perfectionum, quam nostri et nostrarum imperfectionum. Nam in re ipsa prior est Dei infinita perfectio, quam notra imperfectio, quoniam nostra imperfectio est defectus et negatio perfectionis Dei; omnis autem defectus et negatio præsupponit eam rem a qua deficit, et quam negat" (*Conversation with Burman*, 16 April 1648, AT V, 153.22–33; CSMK, 338).

28. *The Search for Truth*, AT X, 515.17 and 20; CSM II, 410 (see Chapter One, §6, and Chapter Three, §7).

29. [See the translation of this Latin quotation several lines earlier.—Trans.] Luynes renders the substantivization of the terms nicely but adds, probably less felicitously, "notion": "and hence [. . .] I have in some way in me the notion of the

infinite, prior to the finite" (IX-1, 36). Sometimes the *Principia* also erase the reference to the *substantia* in order to say the pure relation of the finite to the infinite: "Deum authorem rerum esse infinitum, et nos omnino finitos—God, the creator of all things, is infinite, and we are altogether finite" (I, §24, AT VIII-A, 14; CSM I, 201); as already seen in the *Præfatio* of the *Meditationes*: "mentes nostras considerandas esse ut finitas, Deum autem ut incomprehensibilem et infinitum—our minds must be regarded as finite, while God is infinite and beyond our comprehension" (VII, 9.15–17; CSM II, 8).

30. Luynes translates, "It is the *nature* of the infinite, that my nature, which is finite and limited, cannot comprehend" (IX-1, 37), wrongly replacing *ratio infinita* with *nature*, which remains in the ontic register of *substantia*. But the same ambiguity is sometimes found in Descartes' hand: "est de *natura* infiniti, ut a nobis, qui summus finite, non comprehendatur" (*Principia philosophiæ I*, §19).

31. *IIæ Responsiones*: "Et contendo ex hoc solo quod *attingam quomodolibet* cogitatione sive intellectu perfectionem aliquam quæ supra me est [. . .], me istam vim concipiendi majorem numerum esse cogitabilem quam a me unquam possit cogitari, non a meipso, sed ab aliquo alio ente me perfectiore accepisse—Now in my thought or intellect I can *somehow come upon* a perfection that is above me [. . .], I have the power of conceiving that there is a thinkable number which is larger than any number that I can ever think of, and hence that this power is something which I have received not from myself but from some other being which is more perfect than I am" (AT VII, 139.11–22; CSM II, 100).

32. Perhaps Descartes finds in this way to the letter the negative determination of God according to Saint Anselm, when he evokes, in passing, "this power that I have of comprehending that there is a thinkable number which is larger than any number that I can ever think of—vim concipiendi *majorem* numerum esse *cogitabilem quam* a me unquam *possit cogitari*," and referring it to a being that is more perfect than I am, "alio ente a me perfectiore" (VII, 139.19–22 = IX-1 110.4–8; CSM II, 100).

33. Saint Augustine, *Confessiones* XI.4.6, ed. Solignac, vol. 14, p. 280.

34. Dan Arbib has remarkably noted the transcendental function of the infinite: the truest and the most clear and distinct idea marks "for Descartes less the representational intensity of an idea than its transcendental function" (*Descartes, la métaphysique et l'infini*, 320, and see 322). "If the *ego cogito* is the condition of the *idea infiniti*, the *idea infiniti* becomes in reverse the condition of the *idea mei ipsius*, and thus of the *ego cogito*. The privilege of the *ego* is overturned: by cogitating the infinite, it cogitates the very condition of its cogitation"; or: "The idea of the infinite, of an object for a *cogito*, becomes the condition of the *cogito* itself, the implicit of the implicit" (ibid., respectively 309 and 317). But this transcendental plays counter to the *ego*: at first transcendental with regard to the objects that it made possible, it uncovers itself going forward as non-transcendental with regard to the infinite that

makes it possible. Thus, everything is reversed and the "*idea infiniti* imposes itself as a *counter*-transcendental" (ibid., 318, and see 323).

35. Kant, *Critique of Pure Reason*, Introduction, VII, B 25; English trans. Guyer and Wood, 149, emphasis added.

36. Among others: To Mersenne, 15 April 1630: "The greatness of God, on the other hand, is something which we cannot comprehend even though we know it" (AT I, 145.21–24; CSMK, 23); To Mersenne, 25 May 1630: "I say that I know this, not that I conceive it or grasp it; because it is possible to know that God is infinite and all powerful although our soul, being finite, cannot comprehend or conceive him" (I, 152. 9–13; CSMK, 25); To Mersenne, 11 November 1640: "our soul, being finite, cannot comprehend the infinite" (III, 234.1–2; CSMK, 157).

37. "So let me say first of all that the infinite, *qua* infinite, can in no way be comprehended. But it can still be understood, in so far as we can clearly and distinctly understand that something is such that no limitations can be found in it, and this amounts to understanding clearly that it is infinite" (CSM II, 81).

38. William of Saint-Thierry, *Exposé sur le Cantique des cantiques*, §80, ed. Jean-Marie Déchanet, "Sources chrétiennes," no. 82 (Paris: Cerf, 1962), 190, which refers to his *Commentary on the Epistle to the Romans* (*Patrologia Latina*, 180, c. 638, following from Gregory the Great, among others). Did Descartes know the origins of this formula? In any case, it refers explicitly to a knowledge that is no longer philosophical but theological, such that it "needs to have some extraordinary aid from heaven" (*Discourse on the Method*, AT VI, 8.16–17; CSM I, 114), either, to speak like Charron, "an extraordinary touch from heaven" (*De la sagesse* II.3, p. 436), or, like Montaigne, a "particular and supernatural grace and favor" (*Essais* II.12, V564, F424). Dan Arbib picks out this implicit quotation and quite rightly comments on it as the taking of a position that is resolutely theological: "This failure of common knowledge (of the *intellectus humanus*) imposes as the sole mode of knowledge of God the mystical opening where the subject and the object are inverted" (*Descartes, la métaphysique et l'infini*, §71, p. 303). In any event, this text should lead to some degree of reevaluation of the end of *Meditatio III*, which is rarely taken seriously.

39. Pierre Gassendi, *Disquisitio metaphysica seu Dubitationes et Instantiæ adversus Renati Cartesii Metaphysicam et Responsa* (Amsterdam: J. Blaeu, 1644), Med. III, Dub. 4, Inst. 4, 126.

40. Gassendi, *Disquisitio metaphysica*, Med. III, Dub. VII, Inst. 3, 151.

41. Gassendi, *Disquisitio metaphysica*, Med. III, Dub. VII, Inst. 5, 156, 157.

42. AT VII, 368.2–4; CSM II, 253. See *Principia philosophiæ I*, §19: "Est de natura infiniti ut a nobis qui sunt finiti, non comprehendatur—it is in the nature of an infinite being not to be fully comprehended by us, who are finite" (CSM I, 199).

43. "Letter from M. Descartes to M. Clerselier Serving as a Reply to a Selection of the Principal Counter-Objections Produced by M. Gassendi Against the

Preceding [Fifth Set of] Replies," AT IX-1, 210.10–15; CSM II, 273–74 (the same image of the mountain appears in AT I, 152.14).

44. To Elizabeth, 3 November 1645, AT IV, 332.12–333.7; CSMK, 277 (already in 1641, "a nulla vi externa nos [. . .] determinari *sentiamus*," VII, 57.27). The similarity of the vocabulary with the claim of Spinoza, "*sentimus experimurque*, nos æternos esse" (*Ethica* V, P23, schol.), only accentuates the contrast between their doctrines.

45. See: "Talia enim sunt ut ipsa quilibet *apud se* debeat *experiri*, potius quam rationibus persuaderi—They are such that each of us ought to know by experience in his own case, rather than having to be convinced of them by rational argument" (VII, 377.19–20; CSM II, 259); which we can gloss in this way: the things that one cannot understand through rational argument are better experienced in oneself, which any thinking mind with good sense can or should be able to do (provided that he is not an "empiricist"). The same recourse to experience in order to validate freedom had already occurred against the objections of Hobbes: "Nihil autem de libertate hic assumpsi, nisi quod omnes *experimur in nobis*. [. . .] Etsi vero forte multi sint qui, cum ad præordinationem Dei respiciunt, *capere* non possunt quomodo cum ipsa consistat nostra libertas, *nemo* tamen, cum seipsum tantum respicit, *non experitur* unum et idem esse voluntarium et liberum—On the question of our freedom, I made no assumptions beyond what we all experience within ourselves. [. . .] There may indeed be many people who, when they consider the fact that God pre-ordains all things, cannot grasp how this is consistent with our freedom. But if we simply consider ourselves, we will all realize in the light of our own experience that voluntariness and freedom are one and the same thing" (191.12; CSM II, 134). And again, in response to Burman: "Sed male de hisce ita disputatur: descendant modo unusquisque in semetipsum et *experiatur* annon perfectam et absolutam habeat voluntatem, et an possit quicquam concipere quod voluntatis libertate se antecellat. Nemo sane aliter *experturus* est—But there is no point in arguing like this on these matters. Let everyone just go down deep into himself and *experience* whether or not he has a perfect and absolute will, and whether he can conceive of anything which surpasses him in freedom of the will. Of course, no one will experience it differently" (AT V, 159.1–8; CSMK, 342).

46. For example, Jean Laporte (*Le Rationalisme de Descartes* [Paris, PUF, 1945, 1988], 267 and following); Ferdinand Alquié: "These two infinite liberties that are the infinite divine liberty and the infinite human liberty" (*La Découverte métaphysique de l'homme chez Descartes*, 294); Martial Gueroult (*Descartes selon l'orde des raisons*, vol. 1, p. 325 and following); Geneviève Rodis-Lewis (*L'Œuvre de Descartes* [Paris, Vrin, 1970], 312); and myself, with some nuances and distinctions (*Sur la théologie blanche de Descartes*, §17, and p. 411).

47. Nicolas Grimaldi was one of the first to take note of it, in *Six études sur la volonté et la liberté chez Descartes* (Paris: Vrin, 1988), 25; and then in *Études*

cartésiennes. Dieu, le temps, la liberté (Paris: Vrin, 1996), 180. Since these studies, see Denis Kambouchner (*Descartes n'a pas dit*, chap. 10).

48. To Mersenne, 25 December 1638, AT II, 628.4–9.

49. See my *Sur la théologie blanche de Descartes*, §9, in particular pp. 161–68.

50. Furthermore, see: "atque adeo sit *quodammodo* sui causa—so that it is, in a sense, its own cause" (VII, 109.6–7; CSM II, 78); and: "nobis *omnino licet* cogitare illum [*sc.* Deum] *quodammodo* idem præstare respectu sui ipsius quod causa efficiens respectu sui effectus—we are quite entitled to think that in a sense he [God] stands in the same relation to himself as an efficient cause does to its effect" (VII, 111.5–7; CSM II, 80).

51. Respectively, *The Passions of the Soul*, §152, AT XI, 445.19 and following; CSM I, 384; and To Christina, 20 November 1647, AT V, 85.12 and following; CSMK, 326. On the interpretation of these texts, one must challenge the analyses of Dan Arbib, for whom these exaggerations are not necessary in order to be right in the end (Arbib, *Descartes, la métaphysique et l'infini*, §77, p. 329 and following).

52. To Mersenne, 28 January 1641, AT III, 295.22–24; CSMK, 172. See the reciprocal in *The Passions of the Soul*, §19 (AT XI, 343.15–25).

Chapter Five

1. Hegel, *Leçons sur l'histoire de la philosophie*, translation, annotation, reconstitution of the 1825–26 course by P. Garniron, vol. 6 (Paris: Vrin, 1985), p. 1384.

2. See the excellent historical investigation by François Azouvi, *Descartes et la France. Histoire d'une passion nationale* (Paris: Fayard, 2002). One can claim to be "Cartesian" while at the same moment rejecting the fundamental theses—see my study, "Creation of the Eternal Truths: The Principle of Reason—Spinoza, Malebranche, Leibniz," in *On the Ego and on God: Further Cartesian Questions*, chap. 5, 116–38, and the demonstration of Vincent Carraud, *Causa sive ratio* (Paris: PUF, 2002). Inversely, one can also prolong the theses while believing one is criticizing them ("Constantes de la raison critique. Descartes et Kant," in Jean-Luc Marion, *Questions cartésiennes II: Sur l'ego et sur Dieu* [Paris: PUF, 1996, 2002], chap. VIII, 283–316).

3. So true is it that "phenomenology is, as it were, the secret longing of all modern philosophy—*die geheime Sehnsucht der ganzen neuzeitlichen Philosophie*" (Edmund Husserl, *Ideen zu einer reinen Phänomenologie und phänomenologischen Philosophie, I: Allgemeine Einführung in die reine Phänomenologie*, Hua. III/I [The Hague: Martinus Nijhoff, 1950], §62, p. 148; English translation: *Ideas for a Pure Phenomenology and Phenomenological Philosophy: First Book: General Introduction to Pure Phenomenology*, trans. Daniel O. Dahlstrom [Indianapolis: Hackett, 2014], 114).

4. Husserl, *First Philosophy: Lectures 1923/24 and Related Texts from the Manuscripts (1920–1925)*, trans. Sebastian Luft and Thane M. Naberhaus (Dordrecht: Springer Nature B.V., 2019), §28, p. 208.

5. The discussion with Descartes begins at least as early as the *Logical Investigations*, for example in I, §18, on the distinction between imagination and understanding (*Logische Untersuchungen*, II/1 [Tübingen: Niemeyer, 1901, 1913], p. 64 and following) and above all in the appendix, "External and internal perception: physical and psychical phenomena" (ibid., III, 222–24), where the issue is nothing less than to define "the equivocations of the term 'phenomenon.'" On Husserl's evolution regarding Descartes, see F. W. von Hermann, *Husserl und die Meditationen Descartes* (Frankfurt, 1971), and "Husserl et Descartes," *Revue de métaphysique et de morale*, 92/1, 1987. Very early, this encounter became a required theme, for example in O. Becker, "Husserl und Descartes," in C.A. Emge, ed., *Gedächtnis an René Descartes (300 Jahre des Discours de la Méthode)* (Berlin, 1937), and A. de Waelhens, "Descartes et la pensée phénoménologique," *Revue néo-scholastique de philosophie*, 41, 1938 (republished in H. Noack, ed., *Husserl. Wege der Forschung* [Darmstadt, 1973]). The Cartesian horizon of Husserl was all the stronger due to the French translation of the *Méditations cartésiennes. Introduction à la phénoménologie*, appearing in 1931 in Paris through the work of Gabrielle Pfeiffer and Emmanuel Levinas (first published by Collin, then Vrin in 1947), while the German original of the *Cartesianische Meditationen und Pariser Vorträge* had to wait until 1950 to appear in volume I of the *Husserliana*.

6. Husserl, *Cartesian Meditations*, §1, Hua. I, p. 43; English trans. Dorion Cairns, 1.

7. *Cartesian Meditations*, §10, Hua. I, p. 63; Cairns, 24.

8. Ibid., 63–64; Cairns, 23–24.

9. As, moreover, the works of Koyré and Gilson, cited by Husserl, attest, and which conclude in opposing ways. Since then, the question of these relations has appeared much more complex (see Joël Biard and Roshdi Rashed, eds., *Descartes et le Moyen Âge* [Paris: Vrin, 1997], but also Emmanuel Faye, ed., *Descartes et la Renaissance*, and Roger Ariew, *Descartes and the Last Scholastics*).

10. See my *On Descartes' Grey Ontology: Cartesian Science and Aristotelian Thought in the Regulæ* (South Bend, IN: St. Augustine's Press, 2022), §11, and René Descartes, *Règles utiles et claires pour la direction de l'esprit et la Recherche de la vérité*, Annexe II, 302–309.

11. Substantiality enters in order to examine the case of God and not that of the *ego*, in conformity, moreover, with the fact that, *stricto sensu*, only God fulfills the conditions of substantiality (being without the help of any other being) and that, consequently, *substantia* is not said *univocally* of creatures (*Principia philosophiæ I*, §51). See *On the Ego and on God: Further Cartesian Questions*, chap. 1, "The Originary Otherness of the Ego," and *supra*, "*Ego Sum*, Outside the Subject," §2–3.

12. See the excellent summary by Massimo Ferrari, "Les *Regulæ* et l'interprétation néo-kantienne," *Revue internationale de philosophie*, "Modernité des *Règles pour la direction de l'esprit* de René Descartes," ed. Alain Séguy-Duclos, 2019–4,

vol. 73, no. 290, and my sketch "L'Interprétation criticiste de Descartes et Leibniz: critique d'une critique," in Jean Seidengart, ed., *Ernst Cassirer. De Marbourg à New York* (Paris: Cerf, 1990). This tendency was also represented in France by Louis Liard and Léon Brunschvicg (and *a contrario*, one might add, by Étienne Gilson or Jacques Maritain et al.).

13. "Per *substantiam* nihil aliud intelligere possumus, quam rem quæ ita existit, ut nulla alia re indigeat ad existendum. Et quidem substantia quæ nulla plane re indigeat, unica tantum potest intelligi, nempe Deus. Alias vero omnes, non nisi ope concursus Dei existere posse percipimus. Atque ideo nomen substantiæ non convenit Deo et illis *univoce*—By *substance* we can understand nothing other than a thing which exists in such a way as to depend on no other for its existence. And there is only one substance which can be understood to depend on no other thing whatsoever, namely God. In the case of all other substances, we perceive that they can exist only with the help of God's concurrence. Hence the term 'substance' does not apply *univocally* [...] to God and to other things" (*Principia philosophiæ I*, §51; CSM I, 210; see *VIæ Responsiones*, AT VII, 433.5–6; or *IIæ Responsiones*, 137.19–22; To More, 15 April 1649, V, 347). On these points, see my *On the Ego and on God: Further Cartesian Questions*, chap. 5, "Substance and Subsistence: Suárez and the Treatise on *Substantia* in the *Principles of Philosophy* 1, §51–§54," and *supra*, Chapter Two, §2–3.

14. Under the name of *commoda / incommoda*. See *Sein und Zeit*, §21 (Tübingen: Max Niemeyer, 2006), 99–101, and my discussion in *On Descartes' Passive Thought*, 66–71.

15. Respectively: *Meditatio II*, AT VII.225.12 and 27.9; the refutation of Bourdin in *VIIæ Responsiones*, AT VII, 559.7 and following; the formula privileged by Heidegger in *Sein und Zeit*, §82, p. 433 (and in *Nietzsche: der europäische Nihilismus*, §18, GA 48, p. 87 and following), according perhaps to Kant, *Critique of Pure Reason*, Transcendental Deduction, §16, B 132 and following (see *Cartesian Questions: Method and Metaphysics*, chap. V, §1, pp. 99–101, *On the Ego and on God: Further Cartesian Questions*, §3, pp. 8–9, and *supra*, Chapter Two, §5–6).

16. See my *Reduction and Givenness. Investigations of Husserl, Heidegger, and Phenomenology*, trans. Thomas A. Carlson (Evanston: Northwestern University Press, 1998), chap. III, 77–107, and my remarks on "L'*ego* cartesiano e le sue interpretazioni fenomenologiche: al di là della rappresentazione," in Jean-Robert Armogathe and Giulia Belgioioso, eds., *Descartes metafisico. Interpretazioni del Novocento* (Rome: Istituto della Enciclopedia Italiana, 1994), 179–93.

17. As Christophe Perrin recently demonstrated, in his *Entendre la métaphysique. Les significations de la pensée de Descartes dans l'œuvre de Heidegger* (Louvain—Paris: Peeters, 2013), developing in great style the indications that I sketched in "Heidegger et la situation métaphysique de Descartes," *Bulletin cartésien IV, Archives de philosophie* 38/2, 1975.

18. See my *Reduction and Givenness*, chap. 6, 167–86.

19. On this point, see my *On Descartes' Metaphysical Prism*, §7, pp. 86–90, as well as *On the Ego and on God*, chap. 8, 139 and following. One could make a similar analysis with regard to the invention of *ontologia*: if the term appears in the Calvinist milieu (from before 1613, with Jacobus Lorhardus and Rudolph Goclenius), it only stands out, beginning in 1646 (and not 1647), with a Cartesian of the strict obedience, Clauberg, who is of course under the influence of Jacobus Fontialis—see Michäel Devaux and Marco Lamanna, "The Rise and Early History of the Term 'Ontology' (1606–1730)," in Costantino Esposito, ed., *Quaestio 9*, "Origini e sviluppi dell'ontologia secoli XVI-XXI" (Turnhout/Bari: Brepols/Pagina, 2009), 173–208; and Massimiliano Savini, *Johannes Clauberg. Methodus cartesiana et ontologie* (Paris: Vrin, 2011).

20. This will be, moreover, Kant's argument in the *Refutation of Idealism*. Like Husserl, Heidegger here undergoes the influence of the Marburgian interpretation of Descartes, as witnessed by his reading of the *Regulæ* (in GA 17 and up to *What is a Thing?*), which is essentially determined, if only negatively, by Cassirer.

21. One can compare the *Études cartésiennes* (vols. I–III of the *Travaux du IXe Congrès international de philosophie* [Paris, 1937]) to the contributions of *Descartes. Cahiers de Royaumont* (Paris: Minuit, 1957, republished in W. Doney, ed., New York/London: Garland, 1987). In this context, Ferdinand Alquié's thesis remains a remarkable exception.

22. See, among many examples, Michael Hooker, ed., *Descartes: Critical and Interpretive Essays* (Baltimore/London: Johns Hopkins University Press, 1978).

23. Even Jean Beaufret leans in this direction in his "Remarques sur Descartes," *Dialogue avec Heidegger, vol. II: Philosophie modern* (Paris: Minuit, 1973), 28 and following, as well as in "Philosophie et science," ibid., vol. III: *Approche de Heidegger*, 1974, p. 28 and following, and in his "Notes sur Descartes" (*Leçons de philosophie*, vol. I, II, chap. 1, in P. Fouillaron, ed. [Paris: Seuil, 1998], p. 151 and following). This criticism also applies to a certain extent to my own work, *On Descartes' Grey Ontology*: it too easily opposes Cartesian *science* to Aristotelian knowing, while wishing to show something *else*—namely, that this science initiates only *another* ontology, in fact the *ontologia* soon to come, that of the *metaphysica generalis* of the *ens* as *cogitatum*.

24. See my *Cartesian Questions: Method and Metaphysics*, chap. VI, §2, pp. 121–29.

25. See my *Reprise du donné*, chap. I, §4–6, pp. 29–42.

26. See, among the first to become aware of these examples, Nicolas Grimaldi, "Sartre et la liberté cartésienne," and Jean-François Lavigne, "L'idée d'infini: Descartes dans la pensée d'Emmanuel Levinas," *Revue de métaphysique et de morale*, 92/1, 1987: 67–88, and 54–66, respectively; and then Jean Greisch, "Descartes selon

l'ordre de la raison herméneutique. Le 'moment cartésien' chez Michel Henry, Martin Heidegger et Paul Ricœur," *Revue des sciences philosophiques et théologiques*, 73/4, 1989: 529–48.

27. This was Friedrich-Wilhelm von Hermann's intention in his commentary on *Descartes' Meditationen* (Frankfurt am Main: Klostermann, 2011), which he defined in this way: "Against the common thesis of Descartes' rationalism, I attempt to present the perspective that the *Meditationes de prima philosophia* possess a strong phenomenological potential, which I attempt to set free. Thus my efforts move on this side of the current critique of Heidegger, but also on this side of that of Husserl, bearing on the objectivism and the proof of God. Therefore, my commentary goes much further than my appreciation of Descartes in my inaugural lecture of 1975" (personal correspondence with the author, 30 September 2011).

28. *Meditatio III*, AT VII, 34.21–35.2; CSM II, 24. Luynes develops the Latin: "Although the things that I sense and that I imagine are perhaps nothing at all outside of me and in themselves, I am nevertheless assured that these *ways of thinking*, that I call sentiments or imaginings, insofar as they are simply *ways of thinking*, certainly reside and are encountered within me" (AT IX-1, 27).

29. Edmund Husserl, *Cartesian Meditations*, §15, Hua. I, p. 75; Cairns, 36. In a certain way, Descartes anticipates this bracketing of the actuality of the object of representation when he insists on the anteriority of the question *quid sit?* to the question *an sit?* (see *Iæ Responsiones*, AT VII, 107.27–108.1, and To Mersenne, 31 December 1640, AT III, 272.25–273.3).

30. *Cartesian Meditations*, §8, Hua. I, p. 60; Cairns, 20. And: "The whole world, when one is in the phenomenological attitude, is not accepted as actuality, but only as an actuality-phenomenon" (ibid., §14, p. 71; Cairns, 32).

31. Husserl, *The Crisis of European Sciences and Transcendental Phenomenology: An Introduction to Phenomenological Philosophy*, §41, Hua. VI, p. 155; English trans. David Carr (Evanston: Northwestern University Press, 1970), 152.

32. Ibid., §53, p. 185; Carr, 181. See also: "Through the reduction, this world [. . .] becomes a pure and simple phenomenon for him [the observer]" (§71, p. 257; Carr, 254).

33. Descartes, *Meditatio III*, AT VII, 36.26; CSM II, 25.

34. "Quamvis illa quæ sentio vel imaginor extra me fortasse nihil sint, illos tamen cogitandi modos, quos sensus et imaginationes appello, quatenus cogitandi quidam modi tantum sunt, in me esse sum certus" (VII, 34.21–35.2; CSM II, 24).

35. See *supra*, note 29.

36. *Olympica*, AT X, 184, emphases added; English translation in Lawrence Lipking, *What Galileo Saw: Imagining the Scientific Revolution* (Ithaca and London: Cornell University Press, 2014), 227–28. For a detailed edition with commentary,

see Vincent Carraud and Gilles Olivo, eds., *René Descartes. Étude du bon sens. La recherche de la verité. Et autres écrits de jeunesse*, 104. It may be that the mention of the "treasures of all the sciences," discovered by the "Spirit of Truth," is an implicit allusion to St. Paul (Col. 2:2–3: "agnitionem mysterii Dei Patris et Christi Jesu, in quo sunt omnes thesauri sapientiæ et scientiæ absconditi—unto the knowledge of the mystery of God the Father and of Christ Jesus: In whom are hid all the treasures of wisdom and knowledge"), like in *Meditatio IV*, AT VII, 53.19–21. I have insisted on the decisive importance of this equivalence between waking and sleeping for the *cogitatio* reduced to itself in Descartes (see my "Les trois songes ou l'éveil du philosophe," *La Passion de la raison. Hommage à Ferdinand Alquié* [Paris: PUF, 1983]; republished under the title, "Does Thought Dream? The Three Dreams, or The Awakening of the Philosopher," *Cartesian Questions: Method and Metaphysics* [Chicago: University of Chicago Press, 1991], 1–19).

37. *Discourse on the Method*, AT VI, 32.9–15; CSM I, 127.

38. *Discourse on the Method*, AT VI, 33.20–24; CSM I, 127.

39. *Discourse on the Method*, AT VI, 39.13–29, emphases added; CSM I, 130–31. See also: "Nam sive vigilem, sive dormiam, duo et tria simul juncta sunt quinque—For whether I am awake or asleep, two and three added together make five" (*Meditatio I*, VII, 20.27; CSM II, 14).

40. *Discourse on the Method*, AT VI, 38.21–24; CSM I, 130, emphasis added. Here, God enters in as the guarantor that the evidence (clarity and distinctness), which he made the supreme criterion for our minds (creation of the eternal truths), is equivalent to the truth. In this sense, he simply intensified the reduction of ideas to the evidence with a reduction of the evidence to the truth.

41. *Meditatio V*, AT VII, 70.31–71.2; CSM II, 49, emphases added. See also: "Concludere quidem potuisset [*sc*. Bourdin] ex meis [*sc*. scriptis], *id omne quod ab aliquo clare et distincte percipitur esse verum*, quamvis ille aliquis possit interim dubitare *somnietne an vigilet*, imo etiam, si lubet, *quamvis somniet, quamvis sit delirus*: quia nihil potest clare ac distincte percipi, a quocunque demum percipiatur, quod non sit tale quale percipitur, hoc est, *quod non sit verum*—Admittedly he [Bourdin] might have inferred from what I wrote that *everything that anyone clearly and distinctly perceives is true*, although the person in question may from time to time doubt whether he is *dreaming or awake*, and may even, if you like, *be dreaming or mad*. For no matter who the perceiver is, nothing can be clearly and distinctly perceived without its being just as we perceive it to be, *i.e. without being true*" (*VIIæ Responsiones*, AT VII, 461.21–28; CSM II, 310, emphasis added).

42. *Meditatio III*, AT VII, 35.14–15. See my commentary, "The General Rule of Truth in the Third Meditation," *On the Ego and on God: Further Cartesian Questions*, chap. 3, 42–62.

43. Husserl, *Ideen, I*, Hua. III/I, §24, pp. 43–44; Dahlstrom, 43.

44. Husserl, *Logical Investigations*, vol. II, trans. J. N. Findlay (London and New York: Routledge, 1970, 2001), VI, appendix, §6, p. 346.

45. Husserl, *The Idea of Phenomenology*, Hua. II, p. 14; English translation: *The Idea of Phenomenology*, trans. William P. Alston and George Nakhnikian (Dordrecht: Kluwer Academic Publishers, 1990), 11.

46. Husserl, *Logical Investigations*, vol. II, V, "Appendix to §11 and §20," p. 127.

47. Husserl: "We thus achieve insights in a pure phenomenology which is here oriented to *real (reellen)* constituents, whose descriptions are in every way 'ideal' and free from 'experience', i.e. from presupposition of real *existence*." In a note, Husserl specifies: "*Real* would sound much better alongside 'intentional' but it definitely keeps the notion of thinglike *(dinghaft)* transcendence which the reduction to *real (reell)* immanence in experience is meant to exclude. It is well to maintain a conscious association of the *real* with the thinglike/the world of things" (*Logical Investigations*, vol. II, V, §16, pp. 112–13, and 354 n26).

48. Descartes, *Regula XII*, AT X, 418.1–17; CSM I, 44. On all of this, see my *On Descartes' Grey Ontology: Cartesian Science and Aristotelian Thought in the Regulæ*', chap. 3, §22–24.

49. *Regula XII*, AT X, 420.14–18, emphases added; CSM I, 45. See: "Ubi notandum est, intellectum a nullo unquam experimento decipi posse, si præcise tantum intueatur rem sibi objectam, prout illam habet vel in se ipso vel in phantasmate, neque præterea judicet imaginationem fideliter referre sensuum objecta, nec sensus veras rerum figuras induere, nec denique res externas tales semper esse quales apparent—We should note here that the intellect can never be deceived by any experience, provided that when the object is presented to it, it intuits it in a fashion exactly corresponding to the way in which it possesses the object, either within itself or in the imagination. Furthermore, it must not judge that the imagination faithfully represents the objects of the senses, or that the senses take on the true shapes of things, or in short that external things always are just as they appear to be" (*Regula XII*, 423.1–8; CSM I, 47). The understanding, or intellect, can never let itself be deceived, provided that it stays with the appearing of things, the appearing *reduced* to the simple natures and to their combinations, leaving aside the seeming that is felt or imagined. In this way, under the rule of the reduction to immanence of the clear and distinct *cogitatio*, we find a veritable *impossibility* of error ("in solo intuitu rerum, sive simplicium, sive copulatarum, falsitatem esse non posse—there can be no falsity in the mere intuition of things, be they simple or conjoined," *Regula XIII*, AT X, 432.18–19; CSM I, 53—see also *Regula II*, 365.16–18; *Regula III*, 368.13–24; *Regula VIII*, 399.13–16).

50. *Meditatio III*, AT VII, 37.7–9; CSM II, 26, emphasis added. Inversely: "Præcipuus autem error et frequentissimus qui possit in illis [*sc.* judicia] reperiri, consistit in eo quod ideas, quæ in me sunt, judicem rebus quibusdam extra me positis similes esse sive conformes; nam profecto, *si tantum ideas ipsas ut cogitationis*

meæ quosdam modos considerarem, nec ad quidquam aliud referrem, vix mihi ullam errandi materiam dare possent—Thus the only remaining thoughts where I must be on my guard against making a mistake are judgements. And the chief and most common mistake which is to be found here consists in my judging that the ideas which are in me resemble, or conform to, things located outside me. Of course, *if I considered just the ideas themselves simply as modes of my thought*, without referring them to anything else, they could scarcely give me any material for error" (ibid., 37.22–28; CSM I, 26, emphases added). See: "Nam per solum intellectum percipio tantum ideas de quibus judicium ferre possum, nec ullus error proprie dictus in eo præcise sic spectato reperitur—Now all that the intellect does is to enable me to perceive the ideas which are subjects for possible judgements; and when regarded strictly in this light, it turns out to contain no error in the proper sense of the term" (*Meditatio IV*, 56.15–18; CSM II, 38).

51. *Meditatio III*, AT VII, 40.7–9; CSM II, 27.

52. *Meditatio III*, 41.26–29; CSM II, 29, emphases added. See: "omnis clara et distincta perceptio *proculdubio est aliquid*, ac proinde a nihilo esse non potest, sed necessario Deum authorem habet, Deum inquam, illum summe perfectum, quem fallacem esse repugnat; ideoque *proculdubio est vera*—every clear and distinct perception is *undoubtedly something*, and hence cannot come from nothing, but must necessarily have God for its author. Its author, I say, is God, who is supremely perfect, and who cannot be a deceiver on pain of contradiction; hence the perception is *undoubtedly true*" (ibid., 62.15–20, emphasis added; CSM II, 43). See *Principia philosophiæ I*, §17, and also the discussion with Caterus, where *esse objective in intellectu* henceforth no longer means, for Descartes, the thing itself completing the operation in an object, but that which "in intellectu eo modo [*sc.* est] quo solent ejus objecta, non quidem formaliter [. . .], sed objective, hoc est eo modo quo objecta in intellectu esse solent—the object's being in the intellect in the way in which its objects are normally there [. . .] not of course formally existing [. . .] but objectively existing, i.e. in the way in which objects normally are in the intellect" (*Iæ Responsiones*, 102.25–103.1; CSM II, 75).

53. Husserl, *Cartesian Meditations*, §8, Hua. I, pp. 59 and 60; Cairns, 19 and 21.

54. Contrary to the initial declaration of Husserl: "The meditator executes this regress [the regress of the ego as subject of his pure *cogitationes*] by the famous and very remarkable method of doubt" (*Cartesian Meditations*, §1, Hua. I, p. 45; Cairns, 3). The regress of the *cogitationes* onto the *ego* comes from the act of the reduction, and *allows* doubt only as one of its applications.

55. *Meditatio II*, AT VII, 29.14–15, on which the best commentary is found in *Principia philosophiæ I*, §9: "sed etiam sentire, idem est hic quod cogitare. Nam si dicam, ego video, vel ego ambulo, ergo sum; et hoc intelligam de visione, aut ambulatione, quæ corpore peragitur, conclusio non est absolute certa; quia, ut sæpe sit in somnis, possum putare me videre, vel ambulare, quamvis oculos non aperiam, et

loco non movear, atque etiam forte, quamvis nullum habeam corpus. Sed si intelligam de ipso sensu sive conscientia videndi aut ambulandi, quia tunc refertur ad mentem, quæ sola sentit sive cogitat se videre aut ambulare, est plane certa—Hence, *thinking* is to be identified [...] also with sensory awareness. For if I say 'I am seeing, or I am walking, therefore I exist', and take this as applying to vision or walking as bodily activities, then the conclusion is not absolutely certain. This is because, as often happens during sleep, it is possible for me to think I am seeing or walking, though my eyes are closed and I am not moving about; such thoughts might even be possible if I had no body at all. But if I take 'seeing' or 'walking' to apply to the actual sense or awareness of seeing or walking, then the conclusion is quite certain, since it relates to the mind, which alone has the sensation or thought that it is seeing or walking" (AT VIIIA, 7–8; CSM I, 195).

56. Husserl, *The Idea of Phenomenology*, Hua. II, p. 14; Alston and Nakhnikian, 11, emphasis added. On the "wonder of wonders" of this correlational a priori, see my *Reduction and Givenness*, chap. 1, §6, pp. 31–35.

57. Husserl, *Crisis of European Sciences*, §48, Hua. VI, pp. 168 and 169; Carr, 165 and 166.

58. Descartes, respectively *Discourse on the Method*, AT VI, 38.18–21; CSM I, 130, and To Mersenne, 6 May 1630, AT I, 150.2–4; CSM III, 24.

59. Husserl, *Cartesian Meditations*, §1, Hua. I, p. 44; Cairns, 2.

60. Ibid., §3, Hua. I, p. 48; Cairns, 7.

61. Ibid., §31, Hua. I, p. 101; Cairns, 66–67.

62. Heidegger, *Sein und Zeit*, respectively §62, p. 305, and §60, p. 297; Stambaugh, 282, 273.

63. Like Husserl later, under the pretext of a supposed deduction *more geometrico* on the basis of the "fundamental axiom" of the *cogito*, an error that a serious reading of the appendix to the *IIæ Responsiones* would have avoided, and which was privileged, it is true, by the German critique since at least Hegel.

64. Husserl, *Cartesian Meditation*, §1, Hua. I, p. 44; Cairns, 2.

65. Heidegger, "Brief über den 'Humanismus,'" in *Wegmarken*, GA 9, 313; English translation: "Letter on Humanism," in *Pathmarks*, ed. William McNeill (Cambridge: Cambridge University Press, 1998), 239.

66. "die phänomenologische Methode bewegt sich durchaus in *Akten der Reflexion*" (*Ideen I*, §77, Hua. III, p. 177; Dahlstrom, *Ideas I*, 139; emphasis added). §36 of *Ideen* thus refers back to "acts in the *widest* sense of the *Logical Investigations*" (Hua. III, p. 80; Dahlstrom, 63),

67. Husserl, *Logical Investigations V*, §10, p. 369; Findlay, vol. 2, p. 97. (see "Akterlebnis, act-experience" §12, p. 376, or §20, p. 413; Findlay, vol. 2, pp. 100, 120). See: "The object is an intentional object: this means there is an act having a determinate intention" (*Logical Investigations V*, §20, p. 412; Findlay, vol. 2, p. 120).

68. Husserl, *Logical Investigations V*, respectively §3, Hua. III, p. 352, and §8, Hua. III, p. 362; Findlay, vol. 2, pp. 84–85 and 93.

69. Husserl: "Instead of becoming lost in the *performance* of acts built intricately on one another, and instead of (as it were) naïvely positing the existence of the objects intended in their sense and then going on to characterize them, or of assuming such objects hypothetically, of drawing conclusions from all this etc., we must rather practise 'reflection', i.e. *make these acts themselves*, and their immanent meaning-content, *our objects* ('*reflektieren*', *d. h. diese Akte selbst und ihren immanenten Sinnesgestalt zu Gegenstände machen*). [. . .] These acts [. . .], though hitherto not objective, must now be made objects of apprehension and of theoretical assertion (*sollen uns die Objekte der Erfahrung . . . werden*)" (*Logical Investigations*, vol. II, "Investigations in Phenomenology and Knowledge Part I, Introduction," §3, Hua. III, p. 9; Findlay, vol. I, p. 170, emphasis added). Husserl specifies it in a 1903 letter to Hocking: "The expression that occurs so frequently, that 'objects' 'are constituted' in an act, always refers to the property of the act to make the object representable; it is not about 'constituting' properly so called" (quoted by Walter Biemel, "Les étapes décisives dans le développement de la philosophie de Husserl," *Husserl. Cahiers de Royaumont* [Paris: Minuit, 1959], 68–69; see Claude Romano, *At the Heart of Reason*, 296).

70. Descartes, *Meditatio I*, AT VII, respectively 18.2–3 and 17.13–18.1; CSM II, 12.

71. Ibid., VII, 18.17–18 and 18.6–10.

72. Ibid.: "Age ergo somniemus . . .—Suppose then that I am dreaming. . ." (VII, 19.23; CSM II, 13).

73. Ibid., respectively: "vetus opinio, Deum esse qui potest omnia . . .—the long-standing opinion that there is an omnipotent God. . ." (VII, 21.1 and following, and 22, 23). Let us note that in this last case, the issue is explicitly that of a mere supposition, a decision all the more arbitrary as it depends precisely on the will: "Quapropter, ut opinor, non male agam, si, voluntate plane in contrarium versa, me ipsum fallam—In view of this, I think it will be a good plan to turn my will in completely the opposite direction and deceive myself" (22.13–14; CSM II, 15), continued by "supponam igitur . . .—I will suppose therefore. . ." (22.23; CSM II, 15). Let us note as well that sometimes the decision plays against doubt: the argument of madness finds itself disqualified without any real reason, for a motive of inter-subjective affinity with the reader, who must not be compared to a madman ("nisi me forte comparem nescio quibus insanis [. . .] nec minus ipse demens viderer—Unless perhaps I were to liken myself to madmen [. . .] I would be thought equally mad," 18.26 and 19.6–7; CSM II, 13).

74. Descartes, respectively, "manebo obstinate" (VII, 23.4); "laboriosum est hoc institutum" (23.9–10); and "quia hoc fieri vix potest" (34.15).

75. Descartes, respectively VII, 21.27; CSM II, 14, emphasis added, and "Denique statuendum sit hoc pronuntiatium, *Ego sum, ego existo* [. . .] *necessario* esse verum"

328 *Notes to Chapters Five and Six*

(25.11–13; CSM II, 17, emphasis added). See: "Nihil nunc admitto nisi quod *necessario* sit verum—At present I am not admitting anything except what is *necessarily* true" (27.12; CSM II, 18, emphasis added).

76. Descartes, VII, 45.17–18; CSM II, 31. Let us remark that, for the demonstration of the existence of material bodies, Descartes very wisely abstains from indicating this necessity: "Ac proinde res corporeæ existunt—It follows that corporeal things exist" (80.4; CSM II, 55), an absence that is all the more significant because at first this necessity was hoped for: "argumentum, quod *necessario* concludat aliquod corpus existere—an argument that can provide any basis for a necessary inference that some body exists" (73.27–28; CSM II, 51, and for the reasons for this pulling back, see Marion, *On Descartes' Passive Thought*, §4).

77. Descartes, respectively VII, 35.14–15; CSM II, 24; and VII, 70.12–15; CSM II, 48, and then *Discourse on the Method*, VI, 33.22–24; CSM I, 127.

78. Descartes, *quoties*: VII, 25.12; 26.2; 36.8, and on the contrary 12; 55.29; 62.1; and a key text, 62.12–15 (CSM II, 43), which ties the decision of the will to the phenomenal manifestation of the true: "Nam *quoties voluntatem in judiciis ferendis* ita contineo, ut ad ea tantum se extendat quæ illi clare et distincte ita ab intellectu *exhibentur*, fieri plane non potest ut errem—for if, *whenever I have to make a judgement*, I restrain my will so that it extends to what the intellect clearly and distinctly *reveals*, and no further, then it is quite impossible for me to go wrong"; then 67.21 and 72.16 (the same thesis in reverse). *Quamdiu*: VII, 22.8; 25.9; 27.9; 36.16; 54.8; 65.7–9 (CSM II, 44): "ea certe est natura mentis meæ ut nihilominus *non possem iis non assentiri*, saltem *quamdiu* ea clare percipio—the nature of my mind is such that *I cannot but assent to these things*, at least *so long as* I clearly perceive them" = 68.5–7 (CSM II, 47): "idipsum nequidem fingere possum, *quamdiu* nihil *volo admitterre* nisi quod clare et distincte intelligo—Indeed, I cannot even imagine this, *so long as* I am *willing to admit* only what I clearly and distinctly understand"; 69.16–18 (CSM II, 48): "Etsi enim ejus sim naturæ ut, *quamdiu* aliquid valde clare et distincte percipio, *non possim credere* verum esse—Admittedly my nature is such that *so long as* I perceive something very clearly and distinctly *I cannot but believe* it to be true"; 69.30–70.1 (CSM II, 48): "nec *possum non credere* id verum esse, *quamdiu* ad ejus demonstrationem attendo—*so long as* I attend to the proof, *I cannot but believe* this to be true."

79. Descartes, AT VII, 47.24–26; CSM II, 32.

Chapter Six

1. I will quote, out of convenience, from the edition of the *Essais* by Pierre Villey and Louis Saulnier (Paris: PUF, 1965) (first ed. 1924) (among other reasons because it is referred to by David B. Leake and Alice E. Leake, *Concordance des Essais de Montaigne* [Geneva: Droz, 1981]), parenthetically indicating in the text the book, essay, and page prefaced by the initial "V" (Villey); reference to the English translation will be indicated by the translator's initial "F" (Donald Frame) followed by the page. Here, "To the Reader," V3; F2.

2. Plato, *Phaedrus* 247e and 249c, or *The Republic VI*, 490b.

3. Montaigne rarely uses the word "paradox," and only as an adjective: "a paradoxical reasoning [*un discours paradoxe*]" (III.5, V875; F667); "It was a paradoxical command [*un commandement paradoxe*] that was given us of old by that god at Delphi: 'Look into yourself, know yourself, keep to yourself'" (III.9, V1001; F766). Nevertheless, this second usage (which challenges the possibility of a self-knowledge) is enough to precede Pascal's *hapax*: "Know then, proud man, what a paradox you are to yourself" (*Pensées*, L. 131; trans. Krailsheimer, 35). See the study by Yves Delègue, "Du paradoxe chez Montaigne," in *Cahiers de l'Association internationale des études françaises*, 14 (1962): 241–53.

4. The anecdote concerning Solon and King Croesus comes from Herodotus, *Inquiry* I, §86, from Aristotle, *The Nicomachean Ethics* I.11, 1100a10 (perhaps through the Latin translation by N. Oresme, as suggested by Edilia Traverso, *Montaigne e Aristotele* [Florence: Le Monnier, 1974], 100), and from Cicero: "Nec expectat [*sc.* the wise man] ullum tempus aetatis, ut tum denique judicetur beatusne fuerit cum extremum vitae diem morte confecerit; quod ille unus e septem sapientibus non sapienter Croesum monuit, nam si beatus umquam fuisset, beatam vitam usque ad ilium a Cyro exstructum rogum pertulisset—Nor does he wait for any period of time that the decision whether he has been happy or not may be finally pronounced only when he has rounded off his life's last day in death—the famous warning so unwisely given to Croesus by old Solon, one of the seven Wise Men; for had Croesus ever been happy, he would have carried his happiness uninterrupted to the pyre raised for him by Cyrus" (*De Finibus Bonorum et Malorum*, with an English translation by H. Rackham [London: William Heinemann / New York: The MacMillan Co., 1914], III.22, §76, pp. 296, 297). But the text of reference remains that of Sophocles: "Count no mortal happy till / he has passed the final limit of his life secure from pain" (*Oedipus the King*, v. 1525–30, in *Sophocles I: Oedipus the King, Oedipus at Colonus, Antigone*, second ed., ed. and trans. David Grene and Richmond Lattimore [Chicago: University of Chicago Press, 1991], 76).

5. The characteristics of death according to Montaigne coincide almost exactly with those also recognized by Heidegger: "dem eigensten, unbezüglichen und unüberholbaren Seinkönnen—the ownmost possibility of being, absolute and unsurpassable" (*Sein und Zeit*, §50, p. 251; cf. rev. trans. Stambaugh, 241).

6. Descartes, *Meditatio II*, AT VII, 25.11–13; CSM II, 17.

7. Descartes, *Meditatio V*, AT VII, 70.31, which the French translation [translated into English] glosses like this: "But even though I might be asleep, everything that presents itself to my mind with evidence is absolutely true" (AT IX-1, 56). Contrary to Plato (*Theaetetus* 190b–c), Saint Augustine (*Contra Academicos* III.11, p. 25), and Descartes (*Discourse on the Method*, AT VI, 39.9–17 and 26–31 or *VIIæ Responsiones*, VII, 461.21–27), Montaigne does not overcome the aporia of an indistinction between waking and dreaming ("How easily we pass from waking to sleeping!" II.6,

V372; F268), even in the case of mathematics. Doubtless not out of ignorance or negligence of this very particular type of object, but simply because it is a matter of objects, and neither my thought, nor my "moi" come under objectivity; so that, even if one admitted the exception of mathematics, it would in no way concern *me*. The whole question then remains that of deciding whether, in dreams, I nevertheless do not already think, and fully so (see *supra*, Chapter One, §3–6; Chapter Three, §7; Chapter Five, §6–7). In fact, Montaigne precisely contests that I ever experience a pure thought that absolutely belongs to me and thus that in thought I ever reach a pure experience of the "moi."

8. *Meditatio II*, AT VII, 25.25ff (see *supra*, Chapter Two, §2–3).

9. A precise allusion to Aristotle's definition: "ἡ ψυχή ἐστιν ἐντελέχεια ἡ πρώτη σώματος φυσικοῦ δυνάμει ζωὴν ἔχοντος" (*De Anima* II.1, 412a27–29, trans. R. D. Hicks [Cambridge: Cambridge University Press, 1907], 50, 51).

10. Saint Bernard of Clairvaux, *Meditationes piissimæ de cognitione humanæ conditione*, chap. I (quoted from *Sancti Bernardi [. . .] Opera*, ed. Venise, 1781, vol. 5, p. 288, n. 361). The reference is misidentified by Pierre Villey (p. XLIII and 1289), but corrected by Vincent Carraud, quoting *De anima seu Meditationes devotissimæ*, according to the Dion-Charpentier edition (Paris: Vivès, 1906), vol. 5, p. 509, in his "Imaginer l'inimaginable: le Dieu de Montaigne," in Emmanuel Faye, ed., *Descartes et la Renaissance: Actes du colloque international de Tours des 22–24 mars 1996* (Paris: Honoré Champion, 1999), 144. The theme of the incomprehensibility of man, which reproduces that of God, goes back at least to Gregory of Nyssa (*On the Making of Man*, XI, PG 44, col. 156b) and is prolonged well beyond Descartes. See my sketch "La raison formelle de l'infini," in Cyrille Michon, ed., *Christianisme. Héritages et destins* (Paris: Librairie générale française, 2002), 109–31, and *Negative Certainties*, chap. I, §6–7, 37–50. In this context, André Comte-Sponville's remark that "we must conclude that 'God alone is,' like Montaigne (II.12, V603), but also that we cannot know what he is, *nor if he is*" ("Montaigne cynique?", *Revue internationale de philosophie*, 1992/2: 241) signals a clear fault of interpretation: God alone exists in the strict sense, but his essence remains *for that very reason* inaccessible to man, since man does not *exist* strictly speaking; there is no "atheism," even latent, in this perfectly Christian position. Thus, the final clause ("nor if he is") has no legitimacy and almost amounts to contraband (a less peremptory position is found in his *Dictionnaire amoureux de Montaigne* [Paris: Plon, 2020]). The same goes for Alain when he speaks of "Montaigne [. . .] or man without God" (*Abrégé pour les aveugles*, in *Les passions et la sagesse* [Paris: Gallimard, Bibliothèque de la Pléiade, 1960], 804) and in Marcel Conche ("Montaigne bets on the non-truth of Christianity," *Montaigne et la philosophie* [Paris: Mégare, 1987], 61). A solid ignorance of Christian theology would seem to be the condition here for doubting Montaigne's Christianity.

11. [Translators' note: As will become evident in this section, this translates the French: "*Se Tenir à Soi*."]

12. Without any doubt, the first allusion refers to Cicero: "Tota enim philosophorum vita, ut ait idem [Plato], commentatio mortis est—For the whole life of the philosopher, as the same wise man says, is a preparation for death" (Cicero, *Tusculan Disputations* I, §30, 74, trans. J. E. King, Loeb Classical Library [Cambridge and London: Harvard University Press / William Heinemann Ltd., 1927], 86, 87), and thus to Plato (*Phaedo*, 67d). The second allusion is less clear; perhaps it refers to Ecclesiastes 3:12: "I know that there is nothing better for man than pleasure and well-being as long as he lives"; or Ecclesiastes 5:17: "Here is what I see as good: It is appropriate to eat and drink and prosper from all the toil a man toils at under the sun during the limited days of life God gives him; for this is his lot" (see 9:5–10 or Sirach 14:14). Other comments on the status of philosophy by Montaigne: I.26, "it is philosophy that teaches us to live" (V163; F120), more appropriate to banquets and worldly life than "ergotisms"; III.8: the uselessness of philosophical technique makes it so that "For being more learned they are none the less inept" (V927; F707); or III.8: "the weak ones, says Socrates, corrupt the dignity of philosophy in handling it" (V932; F711).

13. Whence follows Pascal: "To have no time for philosophy is to be a true philosopher" (*Pensées*, L. 513; trans. Krailsheimer, 184). The interpretation, by Erasmus, of the same Pauline texts (*In Praise of Folly*, 65 and 66) ends up in the same reversal of the relation between philosophy and wisdom. Vincent Carraud has shown definitively (see "Imaginer l'inimaginable: le Dieu de Montaigne," 126) that this passage from the *Apology* (II.12, 449) consists simply of four quotations of Saint Paul (Colossians 2:8; 1 Corinthians 3:19; 1 Corinthians 8:2; and Galatians 6:3). To which one could add, among other passages, "Because the foolishness of God is wiser than men" (1 Corinthians 1:25).

14. Confirmed by the previous analyses, *supra*, Chapters One, §5; Three, §2–3; and Five, §8–9.

15. A transparent allusion to the definition of *epechō* by Sextus Empiricus: "We use 'I withhold assent' as short for 'I do not have the means (*echō*) to say which of the alternatives proposed I ought to believe and which I ought not believe,' indicating that the matters appear equal to us as regards conviction and the absence of conviction. As to whether they are equal, we maintain no firm opinion, but we do state what appears to us to be the case about them when that appearance affects us. And withholding assent is so called from the intellect's being held back in such a way as neither to assert nor deny, because of the equipollence of the matters in question" (*The Skeptic Way. Sextus Empiricus's Outlines of Pyrrhonism*, trans. Mates, I.22, p. 115). And, more generally, Montaigne alludes to all the modes of doubt (ibid., I.14, pp. 94–110). Here I also follow the astute indications of Marcel Conche, *Montaigne et la philosophie* (32 and following). See other references *supra*, Chapter One, §3–4.

16. See the texts examined earlier, Chapter Six, §3.

17. On this reserve, which he indeed characterizes as a "judgment that does not judge," see Marcel Conche, *Montaigne et la philosophie*, chap. II, in particular p. 32, and the excellent study by Emmanuelle Baillon, "Une critique du jugement," *Revue internationale de philosophie*, 1992/2, 138–56.

18. The opening note "To the Reader," even and above all if it overtly counsels him or her not to read the *Essays* ("I have had no thought of serving [...] you would be unreasonable to spend your leisure on so frivolous and vain a subject," V3; F2), nevertheless marks the contrary quite clearly: the entire enterprise takes place inside of a dialogical space, where what is said of "me" pertains in fact and even in principle for everyone. At issue is not the apparatus of the book in general (for most of the time a book does not deal either with its author or with its reader), nor even confessions (which can be addressed to God or, first of all, to the author him or herself), but the "moi" universalized in me, and thus the reader him or herself.

19. Husserl: "It is certainly part of the distinctiveness of the intuition of an essence that a chief element of individual intuition, namely, the appearance or visibility of something individual, underlies the intuition of the essence, although it does so, to be sure, neither as an apprehension of what is individual nor, by any means, as a positing of [the individual] as an actuality. What is certain is that, as a consequence of this, one cannot have an intuition of an essence without being able to shift one's gaze freely toward a 'corresponding' individual and form a consciousness of an example—just as, conversely, one cannot have an intuition of something individual without freely being able to form an idea of it and to focus within the idea on the corresponding essence that is exemplified in what is individually visible. But that changes nothing in the following regard, namely, that *both kinds of intuition are intrinsically different*" (*Ideas I*, §3; trans. Dahlstrom, 13–14, Hua. III, p. 15).

20. Pierre-Maxime Schuhl and Georges Gougenheim (who moreover quite visibly think more of Aristotle than of Plato): "*Forma* here has a philosophical, technical meaning: each man is the subject who supports the essence of man in general; what varies are the accidents; but the form, that is to say the essence, is the same for all. It is through matter that one is individualized. On the contrary, the form of man is common to all men, just as the form of oak is common to all oak trees. Montaigne qualifies this form as 'entire' because it has all the traits that constitute it present in everyone" (*Trois essais de Montaigne* [Paris: Vrin, 1965], 67).

21. M. A. Screech: "[I]t is arguably the most important sentence Montaigne ever wrote. Not that there is anything unusual in the assertion as such; that the whole form of the human race is to be found in every single man and woman is the teaching of Thomist theology and so, in a special sense, the teaching of Montaigne's Church. We may note the categorical nature of Montaigne's assertion. There is no tentative sceptical hesitation here. This is an issue on which he did not need to keep an open mind" (*Montaigne and Melancholy. The Wisdom of the "Essays"* [Lanham, MD: Rowman & Littlefield, 2000], 106).

22. André Tournon, "Le grammarian, le jurisconsulte et l'"humaine condition'," *Bulletin de la société des amis de Montaigne*, July 1990, and "L'*humaine condition*: Que sais-je? Qui suis-je?", in Marie-Luce Demonet, ed., *Montaigne et la condition de l'homme* (Paris: PUF, 1999), in particular p. 29 and following. Let us note that Gougenheim and Schuhl already admitted without any difficulty this juridical meaning: "By *condition* one can understand either the human condition, or the social condition that specifies it" (*Trois essais de Montaigne*, 115). Making recourse to a legal interpretation does not, moreover, offer only advantages: not only does Montaigne hold the "jurisconsultes" in low esteem (III.13, V1066; F816), but *here* he claims precisely to go beyond the status ("not as a grammarian, or a poet, *or a jurist* [*jurisconsulte*]") in view of manifesting "the human condition" in itself.

23. A similar use of "subject" in the precise sense of substrate or *synolon* is verified elsewhere: "I presented myself to myself for argument and *subject*" (II.8, V385; F278); "this plan of using oneself as a *subject* to write about" (II.18, V663; F503); "As much as I can, I employ myself entirely upon myself; and even in that *subject* [. . .], since this is a *subject* that I possess at the mercy of others, and over which fortune has more right than I have" (III.10, V1003; F766–67); "I study myself more than any other *subject*. That is my metaphysics, that is my physics" (III.13, V1072; F821)—where we must take seriously the *hapax* "metaphysics": I have access to only a single essence, and to an essence that is always taken in its matter ("moi"), in short, an essence of the sub-lunar world; thus, my "metaphysics" is limited to this "physical" essence, which is to say endowed with matter, and thus changeable and imprecise. This is why, unable to define it with concepts, I must describe it through narration.

24. Aristotle, *Metaphysics* Z.10, 1035a27–30.

25. Ibid., Z.8, 1034a5–8, in *The Basic Works of Aristotle*, ed. Richard McKeon, 795.

26. It is not enough to say that Montaigne understands "my universal being" as my individual being in its totality (as André Tournon often suggests). First because it would be necessary to prove that "universal" can have this meaning in Montaigne; and then because it would be necessary to understand how "universal" says the individual. Both are perhaps not impossible (as we shall see), but they must be proven.

27. Aristotle, *Posterior Analytics* I.4, 73b25ff; *The Basic Works of Aristotle*, 117.

28. Doubtless the search for explicit thematic comparisons, attempted by Traverso, *Montaigne e Aristotele*, 313 n1, does not open the only possible way; for that matter the description of the image that the *Essais* provide of Aristotle, as man and scholastic idol (the path privileged by Philippe Desan, *Montaigne dans tous ses états* [Fasano: Schena, 2002], chap. XII, "'Ce tintamarre de tant de cervelles philosophiques!': Montaigne et Aristote"), does not exhaust the question.

29. Pierre Villey saw this point: "This Moi is unique; there are not two identical personalities in the universe. The lessons that we draw from our experience thus are, speaking rigorously, only of value for ourselves. But if every Moi is different, they all resemble one another by some aspect, for *every man bears [in himself] the entire form*

of the human condition. In painting himself, Montaigne thus paints in several ways all men, and each of his readers can find himself in him and take profit for himself from the painting of Michel de Montaigne" (*Les* Essais *de Michel de Montaigne* [Paris: Nizet, 1932], 98). Still to ask is how this paradox of a universal ipseity must be able to be understood (for example, through reference to Aristotle's universal by itself, or through a repetition of Saint Augustine), or if it can happen through the sole force of literary labor, without a concept (as for instance in Rousseau, Chateaubriand, and Proust; see Marion, *In the Self's Place*, chapter 1, §8).

30. Aristotle: "Nature participates not only in being, but in being-well" (*The Parts of Animals* II.10, 656a6, trans. A.L. Peck [Cambridge, MA, and London: Harvard University Press / William Heinemann Ltd., 1968], 172, 173). See also *On Generation and Corruption* II.10, 336b28.

31. Quotation from Cicero, *Tusculan Disputations*, I, §30, p. 74, trans. J. E. King, 86 (see above, p. 331 n12).

32. These two verses were, moreover, painted in Montaigne's library; see Pierre Villey, ed., *Les* Essais *de Michel de Montaigne*, LXX.

33. The final quotation—"Frui paratis et valido mihi / Latoe, dones et, precor, integra / Cum mente" (Horace, *Odes I*, 31, v. 17–18)—fits exactly with this request, provided that one translates it correctly: "Grant me, Latona's son [namely, Apollo] to enjoy available goods and also [to enjoy] myself, without waning and with my mind entire." The line clearly does not bear on "the goods I have acquired" (VIII16), nor on "enjoying what I have, and keeping it" (Barral's edition [Paris, 1967], 449), and not on possession, but rather on the request of a gift: *dones*. Horace, like Montaigne, respects grace, more sometimes than their modern commentators do.

Chapter Seven

1. Descartes, AT VII, 196.9; CSM II, 137. On this "underwhelming" debate, see most recently Edwin Curley, "Hobbes contre Descartes," in Jean-Marie Beyssade and Jean-Luc Marion, eds., *Descartes: Objecter et répondre*, 149; as "disappointing," see "Hobbes versus Descartes," in Roger Ariew and Marjorie Glicksman Grene, eds., *Descartes and His Contemporaries: Méditations, Objections and Replies* (Chicago: University of Chicago Press, 1995), 97.

2. A helpful development by Luc Borot, "Du premier état de la philosophie première de Hobbes," *Philosophie* 23 (1989)—in the introduction to his translation of *De Principiis*—and of Yves-Charles Zarka and Jean Bernhardt, eds., *Thomas Hobbes. Philosophie première, théorie de la science et politique* (Paris: PUF, 1990), 16.

3. See also Descartes, AT VII, 183.22–25 and 185.19–21; CSM II, 129 and 130.

4. Thomas Hobbes, *Opera Philosophica Latina* = OPL, ed. Gulielmi Molesworth, vol. 1, p. 54; or ed. K. Schumann (Paris: Vrin, 1999), 53–54; from now on I will cite the pagination from the OPL, as K. Schumann reproduces it in the margin of his reference edition. [Translators' note: for the English, we will follow *The Collected*

English Works of Thomas Hobbes = CEW, vol. I, ed. Sir William Molesworth (London: John Bohn, 1839; reprinted by Routledge/Thoemmes Press, 1992), updated to reflect Marion's translations of Hobbes' original Latin text.]

5. Descartes, AT VII, 37.3–6; CSM II, 25, emphasis added, quoted with cruel precision in the opening of Objection V (179.12–15; CSM II, 126). But Hobbes does not see (or does not want to see) that this first definition of the idea is quickly supplemented by that of the "forms" that refer to the sole *"subjectum meæ cogitationis—* the object of my thought" (37.9; CSM II, 26), such as volitions, fears, affirmations, etc. Above all, he does not suspect that this double determination of the idea as a form will fail to demonstrate the existence of any being other than the *res cogitans*, and thus that Descartes here makes his reader renounce it by indicating another way (*"quædam adhuc via mihi occurrit"* 40.5; CSM II, 27), where all ideas, taken exclusively as *modi cogitandi*, will be distinguished not by their *realitas objectiva* (my thought alone), but by their *realitas formalis*. The confusion between the common and the properly Cartesian definition of the idea, made here by Hobbes, will find a wide and lasting posterity, especially in the English commentaries, where today it still often retains the weight of dogma.

6. Descartes, AT VII, 180.7; CSM II, 127. See 142.2; CSM II, 101 (is this a suggestion of Mersenne or someone close to him, under the influence of Hobbes?) and 189.17; CSM II, 133 (Hobbes against the idea of God again).

7. Hobbes, *Leviathan*, I.12, Latin and English from the Clarendon Edition of the Works of Thomas Hobbes, vol. IV, ed. Noel Malcom, p. 167; see also "donec ad cogitationem hanc veniatur, causam aliquam esse aeternam—until [. . .] he comes to this thought at last, that there is some eternal cause" (I.11, 161).

8. Aristotle, *De anima* III.7, 431a16ff, trans. R. D. Hicks (Cambridge: Cambridge University Press, 1907), 141. See also I.1, 403a3ff. and III.8, 432a9–14.

9. Thomas Aquinas, in *De Anima* I.2.19; trans. Kenelm Foster, O.P., and Silvester Humphries, O.P. (Yale University Press, 1951); rev. ed. Notre Dame, IN: Dumb Ox Books, 1994), 9. See *Contra Gentes*, II, c. 80–81, and Suarez, *De Anima* I, s. 11, n. 6, in *Opera omnia*, ed. C. Berton, vol. 3 (Paris: Vivès, 1857), p. 546.

10. Pietro Pomponazzi, *De immortalitate Animi*, respectively c. 9 and 4; in ed. B. Mojsisch (Hamburg, 1990), 91 and 36; English in *The Renaissance Philosophy of Man*, ed. Ernst Cassirer, Paul Oskar Kristeller, John Herman Randall, Jr. (Chicago: University of Chicago Press, 1948), 319, and 296. On this debate, one will always benefit from reading Étienne Gilson, "Autour de Pomponazzi. Problématique de l'immortalité de l'âme en Italie au début du XVIe siècle," *Archives d'histoire littéraire et doctrinale du Moyen Âge*, vol. 28, 1961.

11. *Regula XIV*, AT X, 440.28–441.8; CSM I, 58.

12. *De Corpore*, IV.26.1, OPL I, 335; CEW, 411–12.

13. Descartes, respectively, to Mersenne, December 24, 1639, AT II, 628.8 (not included in CSMK); and VII, 57.13–14 and 14–15; CSM II, 40; see Chapter Four, §5–7.

14. Descartes, respectively *Meditatio III*, AT VII, 46.17–23; CSM II, 32; then *Væ Responsiones*, 368.1–4; CSM II, 253. An Augustinian origin of the theme seems probable: "Si enim quod vis dicere, si cepisti, non est Deus; si comprehendere potuisti [...] cogitatione tua te decepisti; si autem hoc est, non comprehendisti—For if you have grasped what you want to say, it is not God. If you have been able to comprehend it, [...] you have deceived yourself through your thoughts; so he is not this, if you have comprehended it" (Sermo 52.6.16, PL 38, 360); English translation in *The Cambridge Edition of Early Christian Writings*, vol. 1, ed. Andrew Radde-Gallwitz (Cambridge: Cambridge University Press, 2017), p. 321.

15. Descartes, AT VII, 183.21; CSM II, 129. Spinoza will remember the formulation: "Idea vera (habemus enim ideam veram)—a true idea (for we have a true idea)," *De Intellectus Emendatione*, §33, in Curley I, 17.

16. Hobbes, *Leviathan* I.3, 47, emphasis added.

17. Hobbes, *De Corpore* I.1.8, OPL I, 9; CEW, 10.

18. Hobbes, Objection II in AT VII, 172.15–20; CSM II, 122, citing VII, 27.14; CSM II, 18. Against Curley ("Hobbes versus Descartes," 98ff.), who suggests that Hobbes refuses to pass from thinking to existence, I hold along with Yves-Charles Zarka (*La Décision métaphysique de Hobbes* [Paris, Vrin, 1987], 139ff) that, to be more exact, Hobbes contests the passage of *sum cogitans* to *sum res cogitans*, and therefore *cogitatio*, which will be precisely the objection of Nietzsche.

19. Hobbes, respectively *IIIæ Objectiones*, AT VII, 175.10–11; CSM II, 124; 173.14–15; CSM II, 122; and 185.6–7; CSM II, 130.

20. "A thing, for Hobbes, can only be a body, a matter occupying an extension," as Pierre Guenancia summarizes it in "Hobbes et Descartes—le nom et la chose," in Yves-Charles Zarka and Jean Bernhardt (dir.), *Thomas Hobbes: Philosophie première, théorie de la science et politique*, 68.

21. Hobbes, *IIIæ Objectiones*, AT VII, 173.24; CSM II, 122–23. On Descartes' rejection of this interpretation, see *Seventh Objections*, AT VII, 559.3–560.1; CSM II, 382, and my commentaries in *Cartesian Questions: Method and Metaphysics*, chap. 5, §1–2; *On the Ego and God: Further Cartesian Questions*, chap. 1, §3 and chap. 2, §5–6.

22. Aristotle, *Metaphysics* Z.4, 1029a23; trans. Hugh Tredennick in *Metaphysics, Books I–IX* (Cambridge MA: Harvard University Press, 1989), 318.

23. On these aporias, refer to my analysis in *On the Ego and God: Further Cartesian Questions*, chap. 1, §3, "Substance and subsistence: Suarez and the Treatise on Substantia," p. 80ff.

24. Descartes, AT VII, 176.15, 18, 24, 25; CSM II, 124, confirmed by *Principia philosophiæ I*, §53; CSM I, 210.

25. Descartes: "ipsam substantiam non immediate per ipsam cognoscamus—we do not come to know a substance immediately, through the substance itself" (VII, 176.1–2; CSM II, 124), confirmed by: "non potest substantia primum animadverti

ex hoc solo, quod sit res existens, quia hoc solum nos non afficit—we cannot initially become aware of substance merely through its being an existing thing, since this alone does not of itself have any effect on us (*Principia philosophiæ I*, §52, AT VIII, 25.5; CSM I, 210).

26. A good outline of the relation between Berkeley and Hobbes is found in Yves-Charles Zarka, *La Décision métaphysique de Hobbes*, 55–58.

27. Descartes will again confront the position of Hobbes with Regius' thesis II, which makes the *mens* a simple mode of the body. On this occasion, to refute what in fact turns out to be one of the potentialities of his own—insufficient—doctrine of substance, he will try to link the attribute as strictly as possible to a substance, unlike in the *IIIae Responsiones*, VII, 174.4–176.29, where the *ratio communis* and its *affinitas* (176.23) leave the gap between attribute and substance wide open. This is perhaps why, in order to distinguish the mode and the attribute, he will go as far as suggesting that the attribute too, like the substance, subsists by itself (*Notae in programma quoddam*, AT VIII-1, 348.25ff. and 350.27ff.). Historians of philosophy have yet to carry out a precise study of this text, as well as a comparison between Hobbes and Regius.

28. Hobbes, respectively *De Corpore* I.1.8, OPL I, 9; CEW I, 10; and [*Logica*] (Chatsworth), respectively chap. 1 and 6, following *La Critique du De Mundo de Thomas White*, ed. J. Jacquot and H. W. Jones, 463 and 473.

29. [*De Principiis*], cited after *La Critique du De Mundo de Thomas White*, 457. A parallel text (*De Corpore* II.8.24, OPL I, 105; CEW I, 18) makes the argument even stranger: as Aristotle's *materia prima* is neither a separate body, nor any of the bodies, it should be reduced to a "merum nomen—a mere name"; yet, its usage will be maintained, because it designates the body without considering any form or accident, "*excepta solummodo* magnitudine, sive extensione et aptitudine ad formam et accidentia recipienda—*except only* magnitude or extension, and aptness to receive form and other accidents" (emphasis added). But why make such an exception, by what right can we maintain a characteristic of extension, instead of admitting the indetermination of *materia prima* without remainder? In other words, doesn't the *corpus generaliter sumptum* still have too much determination to be equivalent to *materia prima*, let alone *substantia*? Descartes, let us note, had felt the weakness of such an interpretation of every substance as material by returning to the strict interpretation of matter as prime matter, absolutely undetermined, a matter that is "nempe Metaphysic[a]—namely, metaphysical" (AT VII, 175.13; CSM II, 124); but this appeal to the authority of Aristotle is clearly not sufficient to hold back the assault of Hobbes, who only understands matter as determined (*materia signata*), and, dare we say, always as already material (extended). Spinoza, who will not fall into the incoherence of qualifying the one *substantia* as material or corporal, appears to be the best refutation of Hobbes' choice.

338 Notes to Chapter Seven

30. Descartes, *IIIæ Responsiones*, respectively, AT VII, 176.9–11, and 176.15–19, both in CSM II, 124.

31. Descartes, *Regula XII*, respectively AT X, 419.18–20 and 419.9–15; CSM I, 44–45.

32. On this essential point, see *Descartes's Grey Ontology*, §23, and, for the finally metaphysical extension of these simple natures, *Cartesian Questions: Method and Metaphysics*, chap. 3.

33. Hobbes, *De Corpore*, respectively, I.6.13 and II.8.3, OPL I, 71 and 93; CEW I, 81 and 104. See also [*De Principiis*] in *Critique du* De Mundo, 452–53.

34. Hobbes, *De Corpore*, respectively I.6.14, I.6.2, emphasis added, and I.5.4, "*spiritus*, id est *corpus tenue—spirit*, that is a *thin body*"; in OPL I, 73, 60, and 52; and CEW I, 83, 67 and 59.

35. *Regula* III, AT X, 368.21–22; CSM I, 14. This is extended by evoking Socrates' doubt, which necessarily refers to another simple intellectual nature, intellection (AT X, 421.17ff; 432.26ff; CSM I, 46 and 53) and which anticipates the *dubito, ergo sum*. On the importance of the role of simple intellectual natures in the *Regulæ*, I thus differ from the analyses of Michel Fichant, *Science et métaphysique dans Descartes et Leibniz* (Paris: PUF, 1998), chap. 1. On the return of simple natures in the *Meditationes*, see *Cartesian Questions: Method and Metaphysics*, chap. 3.

36. Descartes, to Mersenne, 21 January 1641, AT III, 283.19–25; CSMK III, 169.

37. According to Descartes' explanation of Hobbes' thesis in *IIIæ Objectiones*, AT VII, 173, 15ff; CSM II, 124 (and 185.6ff; CSM II, 130); then *De Corpore*, I.1.8, OPL I, 9; CEW I, 10.

38. Hobbes, *De Corpore*, I.5.2, and I.6.8, OPL I, 51 and 66; CEW I, 56–78 and 75.

39. Hobbes, *Critique du* De Mundo, XXVII, §1, pp. 312 and 313. In the same way: "Rursus nominibus positivis duo rerum genera denotantur, nimirum *ens* et *esse*: sub *ente* continentur ea quae existunt, vel exiterunt, vel exitura sunt. Sub *esse* continentur modi quibus entia concipiuntur, quae vocari solent accidentia. Sub ente itaque numerantur corpora [. . .]. Sub *esse* vero ordinantur naturae entium sive entitates, sive essentiae, sive ea quae entibus accidere, vel inesse dicimus, qualia sunt *esse corpus*, sive *corporeitas*, essentia corporis.—Again, two kinds of things are denoted by positive names, namely *being* (*ens*) and *being* (*esse*): under beings (*ens*) are contained those things which exist, or have existed, or will exist. Under being (*esse*) are contained the ways in which beings are conceived, which are usually called accidents. Therefore, bodies are numbered under beings [. . .]. But under being (*esse*) are ordered the natures of beings, whether entities, essences, or those things which are accidents of beings, or what we say exist in them, such as being a body (*esse corpus*), or *corporeality*, the essence of a body" (ibid., XXXIV, §2, p. 381).

40. Hobbes, *De Corpore* II.8.1, OPL I, 90 and 91; CEW I, 102. Or: "Corpus is whatsoever not depending upon our cogitation" [*De Principiis*], 452. And: "Corpus est quicquid non dependens a cogitatione nostra cum spatii parte aliqua coincidit

vel coextenditur—the body is whatever coincides or is coextended with some part of space, and is not dependent on our thought" ([*Logica*] (Chatsworth), in *Critique du* De Mundo, 476).

41. Aristotle, *Categories* VII, 8b21, trans. H. P. Cooke and Hugh Tredennick, Loeb Classical Library 325 (Cambridge, MA: Harvard University Press, 1938), 63. On the Cartesian refusal of the absoluteness of substance, see *Descartes' Grey Ontology*, §13–14.

42. Descartes, *Regula VI*, AT X, respectively 381.18 and 13; CSM I, 21.

43. Hobbes, *De Corpore*, respectively I.2.14 and I.3.3, OPL I, 21 and 29, CEW I, 24 and 32 (emphasis added).

44. Hobbes, *Critique du* De Mundo, XXVII, §4, p. 317; et XXVIII, §5, p. 334, emphasis added.

45. Hobbes, *De Corpore* II.7.2, OPL I, 92, CEW I, 104, emphasis added.

46. According to the apt formulation of Martine Pécharman, who adds: "The *esse cogitabile* or *imaginabile* understood purely as *corpus*, is what gives the least hold to an idea; being as it is possible to conceive it is only an object of a residual idea, the *ens corpus* is a minimum conceivable," in "Le vocabulaire de l'être dans la philosophie première," *Hobbes et son vocabulaire*, ed. Yves-Charles Zarka (Paris, Vrin, 1992), 39. Yet one comment: why speak with such insistence and without textual support, of a *minimum*, or a conceivable residue? Without understanding it in the sense of Descartes where simple natures offer atoms of evidence (Hamelin), it seems that we must rather recognize the body (defined as imaginable being) as the first object for a non-illusory idea. Thus, it would be a question rather of the *maximum* conceivable in relation to the least directly representable terms, of the first eidetic and epistemological sufficiency. Of course, admitting this weakens the phantasm sometimes attributed to Hobbes of an *ideatum* without *idea*, even an idea without the power of ideas. But Hobbes has perhaps at times taken (and against his most zealous commentators) the risk of weakening his dogmatic theses to respect the very rigor of reason.

47. Hobbes, *De Corpore* II.7.1, OPL I, 81–82, CEW I, 92, emphasis added. On the numerous parallels of this text, see the analyses of Yves-Charles Zarka, *La Décision métaphysique de Hobbes*, 36ff, which precisely emphasizes that this thesis goes back to the very first moments of Hobbesian philosophy.

48. Hobbes, *De Corpore* IV.25.1, OPL I, 316, CEW I, 389 (emphasis added).

49. Hobbes, *Critique du* De Mundo, IX, §16, p. 170.

50. Hobbes, *De Corpore* I.1.8, OPL I, 9; CEW I, 10, emphasis added.

51. See the recent contributions of Marco Lamanna, "La naissance de l'ontologie à Saint-Gall: *Jacob Lorhard et la métaphysique monastique*. Un état de la question"; Domenico Collacciani, "Devenir cartésien? La méthode de l'ontologie. De Gerhard de Neufville à Johann Clauberg"; and Alice Ragni, "L'ontologie à Genève: de David Derodon à Jean-Robert Chouet"; in Vincent Carraud and Alice Ragni, eds., "Les deux siècles de l'ontologie," *Les Études philosophiques* 3, 2020.

Chapter Eight

1. [Translators' note: We have opted to follow the abbreviations of Edwin Curley: Book numbers are given as Roman numerals or omitted where the context is clear. P = proposition, D (alone or following a book) = definition, D (following a proposition) = demonstration, C = corollary, and S = scholium.]

2. G. W. F. Hegel, *The Science of Logic*, trans. George Di Giovanni (Cambridge: Cambridge University Press, 2010), vol. I, p. 55.

3. Ferdinand Alquié identifies this difficulty: "Among these definitions, one would expect to encounter first that of God, since, as we know, using the method 'in due order' consists in starting from God, from whom the rest can be deduced. However, the definition of God only occupies the sixth place and contains terms (those of substance and attribute) which have already been defined [...]. We must then recognize that the definition of God in the *Ethics* results from a construction undertaken from the elements known before it" (*Le Rationalisme de Spinoza* [Paris: PUF, 1981], 107), citing Martial Gueroult: "The idea of God [...] is a complex notion, although its genetic definition supposes simpler elements whose nature must be defined and properties determined in advance"; but isn't it [the idea of God] there to state the difficulty, rather than to resolve it? The same holds when we see it, *at the same time*, "a culmination and starting point" (*Spinoza*, vol. 1, *Dieu* [Paris, Aubier, 1968], 37 and 177).

4. Like so many others, Harold H. Joachim thought he could unify these four demonstrations (*A Study of the Ethics of Spinoza* [Oxford, 1901], 45), and Martial Gueroult extracted *five* other proofs of the existence of God in *Ethics I* (*Spinoza*, vol. 1, p. 177). Far from seeing this as a success, Ferdinand Alquié discerned in this proliferation the same difficulty that I see: "One might be astonished on the other hand to see Spinoza proposing different definitions [...] to characterize one and the same reality. Do not the laws of logic, as well as the laws of mathematics, require a definition to fit the defined, to the whole of the defined, and nothing but the defined? In my opinion, all of this comes from the fact that Spinoza wanted to unify, by his own system, the notions arising from diverse requirements" (*Le Rationalism de Spinoza*, 132). It remains to identify the origin of these diverse requirements.

5. According to the remarkable concordance of Michel Guéret, André Robinet, and Paul Tombeur, *Spinoza: Ethica* (Louvain-la-Neuve: CETEDOC, 1977), which Spinozist research does not use often enough, I only note two demonstrations for *Ethics IV*, P38, P51, and P59. *Ethics I*, P11, with its four demonstrations, is thus a remarkable exception; it is hard to imagine that this has no theoretical significance.

6. Spinoza, *Principia philosophiæ cartesianæ*, I, P5S, in *Opera omnia*, ed. Carl Gebhardt (Heidelberg: Heidelberger Akademie der Wissenschaften, 1925), vol. 1, p. 158; English trans. Curley I, 246.

7. Descartes, *IIæ Responsiones*, AT VII, 167.3 and 166.25; CMS II, 117; and *Meditatio V*, 65.2–26; CMS II, 45, respectively. See also: "manifestum, non magis posse existentiam ab essentia Dei separari, quam ab essentia trianguli magnitudinem trium ejus angulorum æqualium duobus rectis—it is quite evident that existence can no more be separated from the essence of God than the fact that its three angles equal two right angles can be separated from the essence of a triangle" (66.7–11; CSM II, 46).

8. See again Spinoza, *Principia philosophiæ cartesianæ* I, P5S; and *Prolegomenon* (Gebhardt I, 147ff; Curley I, 236ff). *Ens perfectissimum* (in the same context, Gebhardt I, 145; Curley, 235ff) takes up the Cartesian *ens summe perfectum* (AT VII, 65.21; 66.12ff; 67.9ff.; 166.18; etc.). Harry Austryn Wolfson also relates the first demonstration of PII to the a priori argument of *Meditatio V*. See *The Philosophy of Spinoza* (Cambridge, MA: Harvard University Press, 1934), vol. 1, pp. 179–84 and 212. It is hard to understand why Martial Gueroult relates it instead to the *causa sui*, without textual support.

9. Descartes, AT VII, 164.27–165.3; CSM II, 116 (Spinoza's probable source). Spinoza's recovery of Descartes does not imply his agreement with the principle of causality, or the principle of reason, but it allows us to mark his differences, as Vincent Carraud established in *Causa sive ratio: La raison de la cause de Suarez à Leibniz*, chap. 3.

10. Descartes, *Iæ* and *IVæ Responsiones*, respectively VII, 108.18–22; CMS II, 78; and 238.11–18; CMS II, 166.

11. Descartes, respectively VII, 109.15ff.; CSM II, 79; and 242.10; CSM II, 169. Martial Gueroult makes a number of comparisons between this second demonstration and *IIæ Responsiones* (VII, 152.1–4; CMS II, 108) and especially with the *causa sui* (*Spinoza*, vol. I, pp. 187 and 191); I will follow instead Harry Austryn Wolfson, who sees only a relation to "the second proof of Meditation III" (*Philosophy of Spinoza*, 212).

12. Descartes, *Meditatio III*, AT VII, respectively 40.16ff.; 45.11; and 45.28ff; CSM II, 28, and 31. See as well *substantia infinita*, AT VII, 45.21; 45.27; 166.1; 185.26, etc.

13. Martial Gueroult righty insists on Spinoza's incapacity to conceive it a posteriori (*Spinoza*, 193, 197, 198, and 493).

14. Descartes, *Meditatio III*, AT VII, 47.19ff; CSM II, 32.

15. On these critical points, allow me to refer to my own studies: *On the Metaphysical Prism of Descartes*, chap. 4, §16–20, and *Cartesian Questions II*, chap. 9, "Outline of a History of Definitions of God in the Cartesian Epoch," especially §5–8.

16. The hypothesis of Martial Gueroult, *Spinoza* (184, 204 and 499, etc.). See the concordance of Michel Guéret, Andre Robinet, and Paul Tombeur, *Spinoza: Ethica*, for the *Ethics*, and Emilia Giancotti-Boscherini, *Lexicon spinozianum* (The

Hague: M. Nijhoff, 1970, vol. 1, p. 373, and vol. 2, p. 914) for the rest of his work. The same imprecision is found in Gilles Deleuze: "it is not enough to say that Spinoza privileges *Ens necessarium* over *Ens perfectissimum*. What is actually [?] most important is *Ens absolutum*" (*Expressionism in Philosophy: Spinoza*, trans. Martin Joughin [New York: Zone Books, 1992], 81). It is surprising that prominent interpretations rely on concepts that the text is ignorant of.

17. *Ethics I*, Appendix, Gebhart, p. 80; Curley, p. 446. See also: "quo enim res aliqua plus perfectionis habet, eo etiam magis de Deitate participat, Deique perfectionem exprimit magis—for the more perfection a thing has, the more it has of godliness, and the more it expresses God's perfection" (*Epistula* XIX, Gebhardt IV, 94; Curley I, 360).

18. See among others: "Per realitatem et perfectionem idem intelligo—By reality and perfection I understand the same thing" (*Ethics II*, D6); "nam quo plura ens cogitans potest cogitare, eo plus realitatis sive perfectionis idem continere concipimus—for the more things a thinking being can think, the more reality, *or* perfection, we can see it to contain" (P1S); "nihil ergo realitatis aut perfectionis idea vera habet præ falsa—then a true idea has no more reality or perfection than a false one" (P43S); "unam ideam plus realitatis, sive perfectionis, quam aliam habere—we perceive that one idea has more reality, or perfection, than another" (P49S).

19. See my analysis "L'analogie d'un fondement: causa sui," in *Sur la théologie blanche de Descartes. Analogie, création des vérités éternelles et fondement* (Paris: PUF, 1981), §18.

20. Spinoza, *De Intellectus Emendatione*, §92, in Curley I, 38.

21. As is sometimes said, by forgetting creation of the eternal truths; for the phrase, "Deus, non tantum est causa efficiens rerum existentiæ, sed etiam essentiæ—God is the efficient cause, not only of the existence of things, but also of their essence" (I, P25), is limited to literally citing Descartes (especially in reversing the meaning: "it is certain that he [God] is the author of the essence of created things no less than of their existence" (To Mersenne, 27 May 1630; CSM III, 152.2–4).

22. DVI; see also P10S (which clarifies that each attribute expresses *certam essentiam*, a certain essence, not the whole essence of the substance); and P11, etc.

23. Descartes, *Meditatio III*, AT VII, 45.28–29; CSM II, 31. See Chapter Four, §5–7.

24. Spinoza, *Cogitata metaphysica* I, §3, ed. Gebhardt, vol. 1, pp. 238, 240, and 243, respectively; ed. Curley I, 306, 307, 309.

25. Ibid., respectively, I, §6; II, §2; and II, §7; ed. Gebhardt, 249, 253, and 261, ed. Curley, 314, 319, 327.

26. Ibid., II, §3, ed. Gebhard, 253ff; ed. Curley, 319.

27. Spinoza, Letter 60 to Tschirnhaus, n.d., Gebhardt, vol. 4, p. 270ff.; Curley II, 433.

28. Spinoza, *Cogitata metaphysica*, II, §3, Gebhardt, 253ff; Curley, 319.

29. Spinoza, *Cogitata metaphysica*, respectively *Prolegomena* (and *Ens perfectissimum*); *Axioma VI ex Cartesio depromptum*, §6; Corollary of Lemma I; P10D and P10 (Gebhardt, vol. 1, pp. 145, 155, 165, 168, 169, respectively; Curley, 235, 243, 252, and 254).

30. Spinoza, respectively, Letter 2 to Oldenburg, n.d., Gebhardt II, 7; Curley I, 165; and *Koorte Verhandeling*, I.2, ed. Filippo Mignini, in *Spinoza: Œuvres I. Premiers écrits* (Paris: PUF, 2009), 196, see also 202 (= Gebhardt I, 19 and 22); translation in Curley I, 65; see also 68.

Chapter Nine

1. The opposite principle, that God "simul cum mente humana alterius rei etiam ideam habet—in so far as he also has the idea of another thing together with the human mind" (P11C), confirms quite well the thesis that every affection depends at once on the one affecting and especially on the one affected: "Omnes modi, quibus corpus aliquod ab alio afficitur corpore, ex natura corpori affecti *et simul* ex natura corporis afficientis sequuntur—all modes which by a body are affected by another body follow both from the nature of the body affected and *at the same time* from the nature of the affecting body" (A1, after lem. 3, emphasis added). If, as knowledge of every effect, that of the mind includes that of its cause(s), this inclusion remains essentially confused, so that it refers what is affected especially back to itself. For Spinoza (against Descartes), most of the time, perception is equivalent to passion: hence its inadequacy, where the same representation holds for *plura* (P13S) *simul* (DV7; P16 and P16D; P18D; P29S).

2. Respectively, Aristotle *De Anima* III.4. 429b30, trans. R. D. Hicks. (see also III.8, 431b21: "ἡ ψυχὴ τὰ ὄντα πώς ἐστι πάντα—the soul is in a manner all beings") and Descartes, *Regulæ ad directionem ingenii*, I, AT X, 360.7–10; CMS I, 9. Likewise, see Thomas Aquinas: "anima hominis sit omnia quodammodo secundum sensum et intellectum—the soul of man is, in a way, all things by sense and intellect" (*Summa theologiæ* Ia, q. 80, a. 1, c.), which specifies: "quod Aristoteles non posuit animam esse actu compositam ex omnibus, sicut antiqui naturales; sed dixit quodammodo animam esse omnia, in quantum est in potentia ad omnia—Aristotle did not hold that the soul is actually composed of all things, as did the earlier philosophers; he said that the soul is all things, 'after a fashion,' forasmuch as it is in potentiality to all" (q. 84, a. 2, ad 2m). Edwin Curley rightly insists on this restriction of the mind by exclusive focus on its own body: "it is hard to see how any philosopher could give a greater priority to knowledge of the body than Spinoza has" (*Behind the Geometrical Method: A Reading of Spinoza's Ethics* (Princeton: Princeton University Press, 1988), 72. On the relation between theory and knowledge in Spinoza and Aristotle, see Frédéric Manzini, *Spinoza: une lecture d'Aristote* (Paris: PUF, 2009), Section II: "Les trois genres de connaissance," especially 135ff and 171ff.

3. The problem comes from a sequence of *Meditatio II*: "Manet positio: nihilominus tamen ego aliquid sum. Fortassis vero contingit, ut hæc ipsa, quæ suppono nihil esse, quia mihi sunt ignota, tamen in rei veritate non differant ab eo me quem novi? Nescio, de hac re non disputo: de iis tantum quæ mihi nota sunt, judicium ferre possum. Novi me existere; quæro quis sim ego ille quem novi. Certissimum est hujus sic præcise sumpti notitiam non pendere ab iis quæ existere nondum novi; non igitur ab iis ullis, quæ imaginatione fingo.—Let this supposition stand; for all that I am still something. And yet may it not perhaps be the case that these very things which I am supposing to be nothing, because they are unknown to me, are in reality identical with the 'I' of which I am aware? I do not know, and for the moment I shall not argue the point, since I can make judgments only about things which are known to me. I know that I exist; the question is what is this 'I' that I know? If the 'I' is understood strictly as we have been taking it, then it is quite certain that knowledge of it does not depend on things of whose existence I am as yet unaware; so it cannot depend on any of the things which I invent in my imagination" (AT VII, 27.23–28; CSM II, 18–19, quoted by Arnauld in VII, 192.22ff). *Discourse on the Method* lends itself to the same objection: "de cela même que je pensais à douter de la vérité des autres choses, il suivait très évidemment et très certainement que j'étais; au lieu que si j'eusse seulement cessé de penser, encore que tout le reste de ce que j'eusse jamais imaginé eût été vrai, je n'aurais aucune raison de croire que j'eusse été: je connus de là que j'étais une substance dont toute l'essence ou la nature n'est que de penser et qui, pour être, n'a besoin d'aucun lien ni ne dépend d'aucune chose matérielle—from the mere fact that I thought of doubting the truth of other things, it followed quite evidently and certainly that I existed; whereas if I had merely ceased thinking, even if everything else I had ever imagined had been true, I should have had no reason to believe that I existed. From this I knew I was a substance whose whole essence or nature is simply to think, and which does not require any place, or depend on any material thing, in order to exist" (AT VI, 32.28–33.7; CSM I, 127). Arnauld refuses, and rightly so it seems, the too-easy distinction between what holds "in ordine ad ipsam rei veritatem—in an order corresponding to the actual truth of the matter" and what holds "in ordine ad meam perceptionem—in an order corresponding to my own perception" (VII, 8.6–8; CSM II, 7), since the question is of *knowing* if the distinction by knowledge is equivalent to the distinction in truth; hence Descartes does not invoke it.

4. The general principle of this equivalence (VII, 71.13–20; CSM II) extends the *regula generalis* established by *Meditatio III*—"illud omne esse verum quod valde clare et distincte percipio—whatever I perceive very clearly and distinctly is true" (VII, 35.14–15; CSM II, 24; see also VII, 15.3–4; CSM II, 11, and 65.6–7; CSM II, 45; and *Discourse on the Method*, AT VI, 33.20–22; CSM I, 127; To Morus, 5 February 1649, AT V, 272.21–25; CSMK III, 363)—and prepares its special application to the real distinction of soul and body (AT VII, 88.2–20; CSM II, 60–61).

5. See the Letter to the Abbé de Launay (?), July 1641: "When things are separated only by a mental abstraction, you cannot help noticing their conjunction and union when you consider them together" (AT III, 421.4–7; CSMK, 188); or To Gibieuf, 19 January 1642, III, 474.9–478.12; CSMK, 201–203; and To *X, 1645 or 1646, which, to explain the modal distinction, opposes the distinction "nempe rationis ratiocinatæ" to the distinction "rationis ratiocinantis, hoc est, quæ non habeat fundamentum in rebus—reason ratiocinantis, that is, one which has no foundation in reality" (IV, 349.26–28; CSMK, 280).

6. When Arnauld reads in Descartes's text, *res/mens completa* (as in VII, 121.10, quoted in 200.16; CSM II, 140), he understands *adæquata* and indeed comments on *adæquata rei cognitio* (200.6; CSM II, 140), by "notitiam [. . .] completam et adæquatam*—this knowledge is complete and *adequate*" (201.20ff; CSM II, 141), or by *"ens complete et adæquate conceptum—*a being of which I have complete and adequate conception"(203.24; CSM II, 143). He also blends together completeness and adequacy, while Descartes distinguishes them. The confusion is heightened by the fact that Clerselier translated *adæquata (idea)* by *idée entière et parfaite* [whole and perfect idea], where any trace of intrinsic equality between idea and its ideate has vanished.

7. Arguments drawn from the analogy between the mind/body relation, on the one hand, and on the other, the relation of the triangle/properties of a triangle (AT VII, 201.24–203.26; CSM II, 141–42).

8. Arnauld thus returns Descartes to the program that he himself fixed, perhaps without seeing it so clearly: "In sequentibus autem ostendam quo pacto, ex eo quod nihil aliud ad essentiam meam pertinere cognoscam, sequatur nihil etiam revera ad illam pertinere—I shall, however, show below how it follows from the fact that I am aware of nothing else belonging to my essence, that nothing else does in fact belong to it" (*Præfatio*, VII, 8.12–13, quoted by Arnauld in 199.10–12; CSM II, 7 and 140).

9. *Sufficit*, AT VII, 219.21; CSM II, 155. In the *Regulæ*, sometimes a non-exhaustive enumeration suffices (*sufficit*), in contrast to an *enumeratio completa* (AT X, 390.6–24; CSM I, 26–27). As in this case (in contrast to the *Responsiones*), *completa* is equivalent to *adæquata*, and as one of the examples used is precisely that "animam rationalem non esse corpoream—that the rational soul is not corporeal" (390.14–15), we could find an outline of the situation of 1641 as early as 1627 (against Jean-Paul Weber's estimation that *"sufficient* means *complete*," *La Constitution du texte des Regulæ* [Paris: Société d'Édition d'Enseignement Supérieur, 1964], 55). See my development in *Règles utiles et claires pour la direction de l'esprit*, 187.

10. "substantiæ, hoc est, res per se subsistentes—substances, that is, things which subsist on their own" (AT VII, 222.18; CSM II, 157). See also "vera substantia, sive res per se subsistens—a true substance, or self-subsistent thing" (To Regius, January 1642, AT III, 502.11; CSMK, 206).

11. This is not a verbal quibble, improvised by the *IV_æ Responsiones* to escape Arnauld's objection; in fact, from the *I_æ Responsiones*, the *entia incompleta* (AT VII, 121.18), derived from the formal distinction, are opposed to a *res completa*, the *res cogitans* (121.10), and to *complete* understanding (120.28; 121.6). Arnauld, who cites these texts (200.12–201.18), does not notice that they escape his objection in advance, and thus he comments on them in the wrong way.

12. AT VII, 220.6–7; CSM II, 155, and also, "non requiritur ut nostra de iis cognitio sit adæquata—it is not necessary for our knowledge to be adequate" (220.22–23; CSM II, 155). See the excellent commentary by Johannes Clauberg, *Metaphysica de ente* [...] *Ontosophia*, §189, *Opera omnia philosophica* (Amsterdam, 1691; Hildesheim: Georg Olms, 1968), vol. 1, p. 314ff.

13. However, inadequacy does not only affect human knowledge of God (AT VII, 113.9–17; 140.2–5; 189.17–21; CSM II, 81, 100, 133, respectively), but, as is clarified in a commentary later than this text (200.20; CSM II, 140), knowledge of any object at all, however small: "E.g. sumamus triangulum, rem, ut videtur simplicissimam, et quam facillime adæquare posse videremur, sed nihilominus illum adæquare non possumus. [...] ipse enim auctor [sc. Descartes] nullius rei adæquatam cognitionem sibi tribuit, sed nihilominus certus est se in multis, si non in omnibus, rebus eam habere cognitionem, et ea fundamina, ex quibus adæquata cognitio deduci posset, et forsan deducta est—For example, let us take a triangle. This appears to be something extremely simple, which it seems we should very easily be able to achieve adequate knowledge of. [...] As for the author [Descartes], he has never attributed to himself adequate knowledge of anything whatsoever; but nonetheless he is certain that in many, if not all, cases, he has the sort of knowledge and the sort of foundations from which adequate knowledge could be—and perhaps already has been—deduced" (*Entretien de Burman avec Descartes*, AT V.151–52 = ed. J.-M. Beyssade, §8, pp. 34–37; *Descartes' Conversation with Burman*, trans. John Cottingham [Oxford: Clarendon Press, 1976], 10–11). Yet this surprising reservation simply confirms other statements in canonical works: "conceptu rem adæquato, qualem nemo habet, non modo de infinito, sed nec forte etiam de ulla alia re quantumvis parua—a fully adequate conception of things (and no one has this sort of conception either of the infinite or of anything else, however small it may be)" (AT VII, 365.3–5; CSM II, 252); even knowledge of a triangle, in its exhaustive sense, remains impossible (*Regula XII*, AT X, 422.18–23; CSM I, 46; *V_æ Responsiones*, AT VII, 368.11–20; CSM II, 254); and thus, all the more, "I do not on that account deny that there can be in the soul or the body many properties of which I have no ideas" (To Gibieuf, 19 January 1642, AT III, 478.6–8; CSMK III, 201).

14. In fact, not only is divine power infinite as a determination of God (*immensa potentia*, VII, 111.4; 119.13; 188.23; 237.8–9, etc.; CSM II, 80, 132, 165), but it must be said that it exhibits its ultimate incomprehensibility; for the "puissance incompréhensible—power beyond our grasp" (AT I, 146.4 and 150.22; CSMK, 23 and

25), which appeared *ad extra* in 1630 to create eternal truths, reappeared *ad intra* in 1641 to ensure the *causa sui*, as *immensa et incomprehensibiles potentia* (AT VII, 110.26–27; CSM II, 79).

15. AT VII, 220.12–14; CSM II, 155. Hyperbolic doubt forbids the certitude that "res juxta veritatem sint tales quales ipsas percipimus, [...] quandiu authorem meæ originis ignorare me supponebam—whether things do in reality correspond to our perception of them [...] so long as I was supposing myself to be ignorant of the author of my being" (AT VII, 226.15–18; CSM II, 159); lifting this doubt thus allows the equivalence between the truth of things and my perception; but this equivalence does not, however, imply the adequacy between my perception, on the one hand, and the totality of properties of things, thus the creative power of God, on the other.

16. AT III, 474.20—475.5; CSMK, 201–202.

17. To Gibieuf, 19 January 1642, AT III, 475.19–22, then 23–24 (both CSMK, 202). See the Letter to de Launay, 22 July 1641, in III, 420.25–421.15 (CSMK, 188). It is on this basis that Descartes refutes the arguments where Arnauld conflates the body/mind relation with the relation of triangle/properties (VII, 223.25—225.25; CSM II, 157–58).

18. *Ethica II*, P32, does use *Ethica I*, A6 ("Idea vera debet cum suo ideato convenire—a true idea must agree with its object," the medieval definition often criticized by Spinoza) in its demonstration, and not *Ethica* II, D6: "Per ideam adæquatam intelligo ideam, quæ quatenus in se sine relatione ad objectum consideratur, omnes ideæ proprietates sive denominationes intrinsecas habet—by adequate idea I understand an idea which, insofar as it is considered in itself, without relation to an object, has all the properties, *or* intrinsic denominations of a true idea," which will be defended at length in II, P43 and schol.

19. The expression "*in Deo*" of P32 helpfully refers to "Quicquid est, in Deo est, et nihil sine Deo esse neque concipi potest—whatever is, is in God, and nothing can be or be conceived without God" of *Ethica I*, P15, also mobilized to found the "in Deo adæquata" (II, P38D). The expression "in nobis" refers to God, but only "quatenus nostræ mentis essentiam constituit—insofar as he constitutes the essence of our Mind" (II, P34D). How can we establish their equivalence? Spinoza defines it in this way: "Idea vera in nobis est illa, quæ in Deo, quatenus per naturam mentis humanæ explicatur, est adæquata—an idea true in us is that which is adequate in God insofar as he is explained through the nature of the human Mind" (II, P43), but it remains still to be shown that such an idea—adequate in us, that is, in God explained by our soul alone—is indeed given; Spinoza responds by affirming it without any further explication: "*Ponamus* itaque *dari* in Deo quatenus per naturam mentis humanæ explicatur, ideam adæquatam A—*Let us posit*, therefore, that there is in God, in so far as he has explained through the nature of the human Mind, an adequate idea, A." But positing it is not enough to prove it: we must not only ask if such an adequate idea in God can remain in us, but above all, if God can

348 *Notes to Chapter Nine*

have an adequate idea of anything by remaining confined to the limits "quatenus *nostræ mentis* essentiam constituit—in so far as he constitutes the essence of *our human Mind*" (P34).

20. Commenting on *Ethica II*, P34, Martial Gueroult thought it possible to understand it in this way: "The demonstration consists in identifying [. . .] the *adequate* idea *given in us* to the adequate idea given in God. As the two ideas are only one and every idea in God is true (§32), the *adequate* idea *in us* is factually true" (*Spinoza*, vol. 2, *L'Âme* [Paris: Aubier, 1974], p. 307). This elegant gloss strikes me as fragile because (a) there are not two adequate ideas here, but only one, that which, referred to God, is in God and not in us; (b) it is not then a question of identifying two already adequate ideas, but of identifying the inadequate idea of ours with the adequate and divine idea. In short, the sequence "Cum dicimus dari in nobis ideam adæquatam—when we say that there is in us an adequate idea" in no way can mean "Datur in nobis idea adæquata—an adequate idea is given in us," except by begging the question.

21. There is no doubt that *Ethica II* affirms elsewhere on many occasions the adequacy of the idea that God has, as simply constituting my mind (as in the demonstrations of P34, P38, P40, and P43). But it remains to be seen how to conceive the passage to adequacy of an idea limited to a mode or a finite group of modes. For (a) if "nullæ <ideæ> inadæquatæ nec confusæ sunt, nisi quatenus ad singularem alicujus Mentem referuntur—there are no inadequate confused ideas except in so far as they are related to the singular Mind of someone else" (P36D), then all the ideas related to a single finite mind or (which comes down to the same thing) to God, as constituting this particular mind, are inadequate; (b) this all the more so since my mind cannot be conceived except *simul* with other ideas, and therefore God, as constituting my mind, must also conceive *simul* with other ideas starting from my mind alone, and which are thus inadequate (see §11, corollary). Gueroult himself wanted to distinguish in this last text "God [. . .] in so far as he is infinite and insofar as he is only finite"; but then how can one still admit that this God ("held to be non-infinite, that is, as finite" (*Spinoza*, vol. I, pp. 122 and 125) could have or produce an adequate idea—if not, like the *mens*, which constitutes and explicates it, that is, by reference to infinite God? But once the mask of metonymies is lifted, Spinoza is confronting the Cartesian difficulty of the infinite incommensurable to the finite. Does he really resolve it?

22. Ferdinand Alquié thought that *Ethica II*, P47, has in particular something that should surprise us and concluded that the knowledge of God (even of the third kind!) remains "an agenda and a wish" and that "this agenda was not carried out, this wish was not satisfied" (*Le Rationalisme de Spinoza*, 252ff and 236). From his side, Martial Gueroult recognized in P46 a "bold affirmation" (430); nevertheless, he preferred to resolve a difficulty marginal to the text (how to justify the transition between *being* an idea that includes the adequate knowledge of God and *having* the

adequate knowledge of God, p. 427), rather than face the real aporia: how does the fact that knowledge of any thing whatsoever implies, as a known object, adequate knowledge of God (II, P46), allow an idea (that of the *mens humana*) to have by right, as a knowing subject, adequate knowledge of the divine essence (II, P47)? On the other hand, Jonathan Bennett points out the difficulty clearly: "He [Spinoza] says that all men *can* have knowledge of God, because all men *do*, this being based on 2p47 [...] This is on a par with arguing that because all men eat, it is possible for them all to eat well" (*A Study of Spinoza's Ethics* [Cambridge: Cambridge University Press, 1984], 306; see also 368).

23. Only *arguably* since it would be necessary to reflect on the theoretical support that the doctrine of common notions (sketched in II, P40S1 and P40S2) could bring to the demonstration of the two univocities (as kindly suggested by Alexandre Matheron, with whom I discussed the difficulty). Two facts nevertheless limit the scope of an investigation before it begins. (a) P32 precedes the appearance of common notions and therefore cannot, in good logic, authorize them; (b) P47 does not mention them.

24. See *Ethica II*, P43S: "Sane sicut lux seipsam et tenebras manifestat, sic veritas norma sui et falsi est—as the light makes both itself and the darkness plain, so truth is the standard both of itself and the false"; and already *Cogitata metaphysica*, I, §6: "Si porro quæras quid sit veritas præter veram ideam, quære etiam quid sit albedo præter corpus album—if you should ask what truth is beyond a true idea, ask also what whiteness is beyond a white body" (Gebhart I, 247; Curley I, 313). The starting point could well have been Descartes critiquing *De Veritate* by Herbert of Cherbury (To Mersenne, 16 October 1639, AT II, 596.25–597.9; CSMK, 138).

25. §72, p. 32. Other examples in *De Intellectus emendation* include §74, p. 33 (subtle body, intrinsically false idea), §104–105, pp. 42–43, and Letter LV (deducing the properties of the circle from its idea). The *idea vera* is verified by a "nulla interrupta concatenationem rerum—with no interruption in the connection of things" (§80, p. 35), according to a theme taken up from the *Regulæ III* (AT X, 369.22–26), *VII* (387.11–12), *XI* (407.4), and *XVII* (460); CSM I, 15, 25, 37, 70, respectively. See my notes in *Règles utiles et claires*, 221–23.

26. *Regulæ XII*, AT X, 420.14–15; CSM I, 45; explained in 420.16–421.2; 423.1–30 and 432.27 (CSM I, 45, 47, 53, respectively). Harry Austryn Wolfson (*The Philosophy of Spinoza*, vol. 2, p. 112), Martial Gueroult (*Spinoza*, 602 and 605) and Juan Domingo Sánchez ("Spinoza lecteur des Regulæ: Note sur le cartésianisme du jeune Spinoza," *Revue des sciences théologiques et philosophiques* 71, 1987) make this rapprochement. We must recall that J. H. Glazemaker, Spinoza's Dutch translator (see J. Kingma and A. K. Offenberg, *Bibliography of Spinoza's Works up to 1800* [Amsterdam: Amsterdam University Library, 1977]), was also the translator of the *Regulæ*, which appeared in Amsterdam as *Regulen uan de bestieringe des uerstants* in 1684, in vol. III of *Alle de Werken van de Heer Renatus Des Cartes* and whose publication

had begun as early as 1656 (see C. Louise Thijssen-Schoute, "Le cartésianisme aux Pays-Bas," in *Descartes et le cartésianisme hollandais* [Paris/Amsterdam: PUF, 1950], 191ff., and Giovanni Crapulli, *René Descartes, Regulæ ad Directionem Ingenii*, critical text with the 17th c. Dutch version [La Haye, 1966], pp. XIV–XVI); some of these volumes were in Spinoza's library (see Jacob Freudenthal, *Die Lebensgeschichte Spinoza's* [Leipzig: Verlag von Viet & Comp., 1899], 160–64; and K. O. Meinsma, *Spinoza en zijn kring* [The Hague: Martinus Nijhoff, 1896], *Spinoza et son cercle*, translation by S. Roosenburg and annotation by H. Méchoulan, J.-P. Osier et al. [Paris: Vrin, 1983]).

27. *Regula III*, AT X, 368.2–24; CSM I, 14. By comparison with Descartes' example, Spinoza's example does not seem entirely sound: does the idea of a semi-circle not imply greater complexity than that of a circle of which it is a division? Descartes clearly explained that every limitation of extension produced an idea more complex than that of the extension (*Regula XII*, 418.19—419.5; CSM I, 44).

28. Descartes, To Gibieuf, 19 January 1642, AT III, 474.20ff. See above, p. 318ff.

29. See my hypothesis in Jean-Luc Marion, "Le fondement de la *cogitatio* selon le *De Intellectus Emendatione*. Essai d'une lecture des §104–105," *Les Études philosophiques* 3, 1972: 357–68.

30. *IVæ Responsiones*, respectively, AT VII, 220.13 and 221.8; CSM II, 155 and 156; then *Discourse on the Method*, AT VI, 8.16ff; CSM I, 144.

31. Suarez, *Disputationes Metaphysicæ* XXXV.2.2, in *Opera omnia*, vol. 26, p. 436; then I.5.41, vol. 25, p. 49.

32. Suarez, *De Deo trino et uno* II.VII.2, vol. 1, p. 64. It must be clearly stressed that here, in contrast to Thomas Aquinas, it is no longer the natural desire to see God that supports this thesis, but the achievement of the objective concept of *ens* (see II.VII.10, I, p. 66, and II.VIII.4, p. 70). In this sense, Spinoza is on the side of Suarez (the *substantia* replacing the *conceptus univocus entis*, both sharing the possibility of adequate knowledge).

33. Suarez, *De Deo trino et uno* II.VII.60, p. 69. The preeminence of the concept of *ens* allows us to go to the point of thinking the (foolish) possibility of a quidditative knowledge of the divine essence even without the illumination of grace: "mihi probabilius est, lumen gloriæ non esse necessarium de potentia absoluta ad videndum Deum—it is more probable to me, that the light of glory is not necessary for the absolute possibility of seeing God" (II.XVII.5, p. 111).

34. Suarez, *De Deo trino et uno* II.XVIII.4, p. 114.

35. Ibid. II. XIX.8, then II. XIX.13–14, pp. 176 and 177.

36. Ibid. V.XIX.8, p. 61. See also: "Licet videns essentiam Dei, videat ipsam esse infinite cognoscibilem, tamen simul videt a se non infinite videri, et ita suam visionem non habere modum adæquatum objecto et ideo non comprehendere illud— Even if seeing the essence of God, he sees that it is infinitely knowable, however at

the same time he sees that it is not seen infinitely by himself, and thus his vision does not have a mode adequate to the object and therefore does not comprehend it" (V.XXXIX.14, p. 178). On the fact that Suarez nevertheless comprehends God in the concept of being and on the impossibility of *comprehendere* God in Descartes, see among other recent analyses, my study *Sur la théologie blanche de Descartes*, respectively §7 and §17, p. 135ff and p. 398ff.

37. Spinoza: "Intellectus, actu *finitus* aut actu infinitus, Dei attributa Deique affectiones, *comprehenderi* debet, et nihil aliud—An actual intellect, whether *finite* or infinite, must *comprehend* God's attributes and God's affections, and nothing else" (I, P30, cited in II, P4D, emphasis mine). It is remarkable that Spinoza, who employs *comprehensio* only rarely, uses it this time for the account of *finitude* as well as that of the infinite. But why specify that there is nothing else to understand: what remains other than the attributes of God?

38. Thomas Aquinas, *Summa theologiæ* Ia, q. 12, a. 1, c.

39. Thomas Aquinas, *Contra Gentes* III, c. 51 and c. 52.

40. Ibid., c. 52.

41. Ibid., c. 53 and c. 58. See "lumen divinæ gloriæ," in *Summa Theologiæ* Ia, q. 12, a. 1 and *Compendium theologiæ*, c. 105; "fulgor diuinæ essentiæ" in *De Veritate*, q. 8, a. 1; "ipsa essentia non videbitur, sed quidam, fulgor, quasi radius ipsius—the essence itself will not be seen, but a certain brightness, as it were a radiance thereof" (*Summa Theologiæ, Supplementum*, q. 92, a. 1).

42. Ibid., c. 55. See *De Veritate* q. 8, a. 2; and *Summa Theologiæ* Ia, q. 12, a. 8. Article 7 of this same question gives as an example of comprehension that the sum of the angles of a triangle equals two right angles: this will be taken up often by Descartes and Spinoza, but strangely in order to demonstrate the existence of God from his essence.

43. Ibid., c. 59. See *Summa Theologiæ* Ia, q. 12, a. 8 (non-comprehensive knowledge of the consequences of a principle and cause); and a. 9: "cognoscere eas, prout earum similitudines præexistunt in Deo, est videre eas in Deo—to know them by their similitudes pre-existing in God, is to see them in God." *De Veritate* q. 8, a. 4: "Possibile tamen est ut aliquis intellectus creatus essentiam Dei videns, omnia cognoscat quæ Deus scit scientia visionis, ut de anima Christi ab omnibus tenetur.—However, it is possible for a created intellect which sees God to know all that God knows with his knowledge of vision" (here, Christ ensures the salvation not only of the ignorant, but also of the learned); *Summa Theologiæ, Supplementum*, q. 92, a. 1, ad. 2m: "visio autem illa, qua Deum per essentiam videbimus, est eadem cum visione, qua Deus se videt—Again, the vision whereby we shall see God in his essence is the same whereby God sees himself," and so we see his effects as he sees them. On this doctrine in general, see William J. Hoye, *Actualitas Omnium Actuum, Man's Beatific Vision of God as apprehended by Thomas Aquinas* (Meisenhein a/G: Hain, 1975), and especially the monumental work of Christian Trottman, *La Vision*

béatifique des disputes scolastiques à sa définition par Benoît XII (Paris: Bibliothèque de l'École française de Rome, 1995).

44. Suarez, *De Deo trino et uno* II.XXV.20, p. 151. See also: "Asserimus enim posse creaturas videri in Verbo, visa essentia Dei, propter connexionem quamdam, quæ est inter creaturas ut possibiles et Deum ut omnipotentem, quæ, licet non consistat in relatione, consistit in continentia eminentiali unius in alio, et naturali dependentia creaturæ, a Deo— For we assert that, the essence of God being seen, creatures can be seen in the Word, according to a certain connection between creatures as possible and God as omnipotent, a connection which, although it does not consist in a relation, consists in eminently containing one in the other, and in the natural dependence of the creature on God"; and "probabile esse, visa divina essentia, necessarium esse uidere quidquid est possibile, vel credibile saltem sub hoc communissimo conceptu creabilis seu possibilis—it is a probable opinion that, when the divine essence is seen, it is necessary to see all that is possible, or at least believable, under the most common concept of the creatable and the possible" (II.XXVI.10 and II.XXVI.14, op. cit., pp. 161 and 163).

45. Spinoza, respectively *Cogitata metaphysica* I, §1: "Incipiamus igitur ab Ente, per quod intelligo id omne, quod, cum clare et distincte percipitur, necessario existere, vel ad minimum posse existere, reperimus—Let us begin, therefore, with Being, by which I understand whatever, when it is clearly distinctly perceived, we find to exist necessarily, or at least to be able to exist" (Gebhart I, 233; Curley, 299); then Epistula LXIV (The Hague, 29 July 1675): "Denique exempla quæ petis, primi generis, sunt in cogitatione intellectus absolute infinirus, in extensione autem motus et quies; secundi autem, facies totius Universi, quæ quamvis infinitis modis variet, manet tamen semper eadem—Finally, the examples which you ask for: examples of the first kind are, in Thought, absolutely infinite intellect, and in Extension, motion and rest; an example of the second kind is the face of the whole Universe, which, however much it may vary in infinite ways, nevertheless always remains the same" (Gebhart IV, 278; Curley II, 439); and finally Suarez, *De Deo uno et trino* II.XXVIII.8, t. 1, p. 471. Note that here Suarez cites and comments on Thomas Aquinas: "species et genera rerum et rationes eorum—the species and the genera of things and their types" (*Summa Theologiæ* Ia, q. 12, a. 8, ad 4m).

46. We might nevertheless think of *Korte Verhandling I*, 1, and the commentaries of Fiorenzo Mignini (in his remarkable edition and translation, *Breve Trattato*); *Ethica I*, P29S, citing the *Commentary on Divine Names* by Thomas Aquinas, and the admittedly riskier comments of Wolfson, *The Philosophy of Spinoza*, vol. 1, pp. 16 and 368.

47. "Cum Notis Iacobi Reuii ss. theolog. D." My attention was drawn to this rare work (BNR 2703) by my friend and colleague Theo Verbeek, in his annotated translation of *La Querelle d'Utrecht* by René Descartes and Martin Schoock (Paris: Les Impressions nouvelles, 1988), 471.

48. Both published in Leiden, respectively in 1650 (?) and 1654. On Heereboord, see Herman de Dijn, "Adrian Heereboord en hat Nederlands Cartesianisme," *Algemen Tijdschrift voor Wisjbegeerde* 75, 1989.

49. Suarez, *Disputationes metaphysicæ* XXV.1.43, op. cit., t. 25, p. 910. Cited by Revius, *Suarez repurgatus*, 480.

50. Revius: "anthropolatreia qua beati Deo *adæquantur*" (*Suarez repurgatus*, 480). To avoid it, Revius maintains, by an opposite excess, that the *beati* do not have the *species* of the divine essence. The common presupposition is metaphysical: every vision aims at a representation by concept (of an object).

51. *Cogitata metaphysica* I, §2; Gebhart I, 239; Curley I, 305.

52. Respectively, *Cogitata metaphysica* I, §2; Gebhart I, 239; Curley I, 305; *Korte Verhandeling*, in *Premiers écrits*, ed. Moreau, 190; Curley I, 62; *De Intellectus emendatione*, §49, §92, note, and §99, etc.

Conclusion

1. Edmund Husserl, *Crisis of European Sciences*, §9, p. 1, Hua. VI, p. 59; trans. Carr, 58. The same "zigzag" is found regarding logic in the *Logische Untersuchugen*, II/1, "Introduction," §6, p. 17. See as well: "Phenomenological archeology is the fact of bringing to light the constitutive hidden layers of the constructions [. . .] realized in the world of experience [. . .]. As in regular archeology: reconstruction, understanding by zigzag" (*Phänomenologische Archeologie*, Ms C VI, p. 1, quoted by Francesco Valerio Tommasi, "Quelle antériorité pour la philosophie première? L'histoire husserlienne des idées et la fondation cartésienne de la phénoménologie," in Dominique Pradelle and Camille Riquier, eds., *Descartes et la phénoménologie* [Paris: Hermann, 2018], 139).

2. Edmund Husserl, *First Philosophy*, II, §28, Hua. VIII, pp. 6–7; trans. Sebastian Luft and Thane M. Naberhaus, 210–11.

3. *Ibid.*, I, §9, pp. 62–63; Luft and Naberhaus, 65.

Appendix

1. Andrée Comparot, *Augustinisme et aristotélisme de Sebon à Montaigne* (Paris: Cerf, Thèses, n.d.), 216.

2. Pierre Villey, *Les Sources et l'Évolution des Essais de Montaigne* (Paris: Hachette, 1908; New York: Burt Franklin, 1968), vol. 1, p. 72.

3. Saint Augustine, *La Cité de Dieu* [. . .] *illustrée des commentaires de Jean Louis Vivès, de Valence* (Paris, 1570, second edition 1578). Pierre Villey concludes that "Montaigne retains from St. Augustine only the *City of God*, which makes much room for moral ideas. This was, after all, a classic work: Montaigne had much to draw from it on most of the subjects that interested him" (*Les Sources et l'Évolution des Essais de Montaigne*, 520). There are at least two exceptions, as we shall see.

4. R. E. Leake, D. B. Leake, A. E. Leake, *Concordance des* Essais *de Montaigne* (Geneva: Droz, 1981), 99. See Montaigne, *Les Essais*, ed. Pierre Villey, p. XLIII (speaking of 19 quotations).

5. M. Dreano, "L'augustinisme dans l'apologie de Raymond Sebond," *Bibliothèque d'Humanisme et Renaissance* (Geneva: Droz, 1962), vol. 24:3, p. 574.

6. BA follows another lesson: inserver*a*nt (imperfect), not inserver*u*nt (perfect). [English translations of *De Civitate Dei* are taken from Augustine, *The City of God Against the Pagans*, trans. R. W. Dyson (Cambridge: Cambridge University Press, 1998), and identified in-text by the translator's name, followed by the page number.]

7. See *Essais* II.12, p. 527 and following (F392–93), and my connecting this to Descartes in *On Descartes' Metaphysical Prism*, 303–304.

8. Elisabeth Caron, "Saint Augustin dans les *Essais*," *Montaigne Studies. An Interdisciplinary Forum*, II/2, December 1990: 17–33, in a study that is often too polemical to be useful, nevertheless remarks correctly that "If Montaigne does not quote the *Confessions* of Saint Augustine by name in the *Essais*, while he quotes certain other texts that are well-known (for example *L'Institution [de la religion] chrétienne* by Calvin), there is no reason to think that he had not heard it discussed" (33). And she references Adeodatus (IV.vi.14), regarding whom Augustine "*nearly* thanks God for having taken" his terrifying genius "from him."

9. As Vincent Carraud has established, in particular in "L'imaginer inimaginable: le Dieu de Montaigne," in Vincent Carraud and Jean-Luc Marion, eds., *Montaigne: scepticisme, métaphysique, théologie*, 148ff. See Chapter Six, §8.

10. According to V1283.

11. English translation: Saint Augustine, *The Trinity*, trans. Edmund Hill, O.P. (Brooklyn, NY: New City Press, 1991), 243.

12. Villey here gives an incorrect reference: IV.31, *ad loc.*

13. Blaise Pascal, *Pensées*, trans. Krailsheimer, 17.

14. This point has been established by Vincent Carraud, *Pascal. Des connaissances naturelles à l'étude de l'homme* (Paris: PUF, 2007), Part II, chap. 1, "Le *De Civitate Dei* de... Montaigne," 70–72. Another quotation ("There is no combat so violent among the philosophers, and so bitter, as that which arises over the question of the sovereign good of man, out of which, by Varro's reckoning, two hundred and eight-eight sects were born," *Essais* II.12, V577; F435), attests to a reading of the single indirect source of Varro, Saint Augustine, *The City of God*, XIX.2 (BA 37: 52). Pascal here relies directly on Montaigne, not Saint Augustine (see the demonstration by Vincent Carraud, *Pascal et la philosophie* [Paris: PUF, 1992], 103 and following, and *Pascal: Des connaissances naturelles*, 69).

15. See the French translation, *De la création de l'homme*, by Jean Laplace (Paris: Cerf, 2002), "Sources chrétiennes," no. 6, 122. Complete this with, among others, Basil of Caesarea, *Against Eunomius*, III.6, PG 29, col. 668b (and see the edition by Bernard Sesboüé, *Contre Eunome* (Paris: Cerf 1983), "Sources chrétiennes," no. 305,

166), as well as John Chrysostom, *On the Incomprehensibility of God* V, 259ff (see the edition of Jean Daniélou, A.-M. Malingrey and R. Flacelière, *Sur l'incompréhensibilité de Dieu* (Paris: Cerf, 1951, 1970), "Sources chrétiennes," no. 28 bis, 294 and following). On this incomprehensibility according to Saint Augustine, see the texts analyzed in my study *In the Self's Place. The Approach of Saint Augustine*, §40, pp. 252–60.

16. Richard H. Popkin, *The History of Scepticism from Erasmus to Spinoza* (Berkeley: University of California Press, 1979), 43 (this is the augmented edition of *The History of Scepticism from Erasmus to Descartes*, 1960, 3rd ed. 1968). See: "The marriage of the Cross of Christ and the doubts of Pyrrho was the perfect combination to provide the ideology of the French Counter-Reformation"; and: "He offers total scepticism as a 'defense' of the Catholic rule of faith" ("Theological and Religious Scepticism," *The Christian Scholar* 39 [1956]: 53 and 47). Is it a matter, however, of an ideology or, by contrast, that of employing skepticism in order to preserve Christian faith from every ideology, including nascent scientism or unquestioned "humanism"? The same is found in Elaine Limbrick: "We believe we have found the key to the religious thought of Montaigne by considering him from the point of view of Augustinianism. Having given up on finding the Truth and God through the approaches of human reason, Montaigne will be led to conclude, like Saint Augustine, that it is faith alone that allows one to reach the highest mysteries." Or: "Montaigne goes further than Saint Augustine: he makes use of Saint Paul, his preferred apostle, to turn back the pretensions of the human spirit [quoting 1 Corinthians 8:12]." And finally: "Once again, Montaigne makes use of the texts of the great doctor in order to guarantee his own orthodoxy and avoid any reproach of atheism" (and see an equivalent passage: "[he] sought and found in Saint Augustine the elements of thought that seemed to favor his own opinions, and which guaranteed his orthodoxy"; Elaine Limbrick, "Montaigne et saint Augustin," *Bibliothèque d'Humanisme et Renaissance*, 34, 1972, respectively pp. 56, 53, and 64). But, may one ask, did Montaigne have the need (and even the least awareness of the need) to *guarantee* his own orthodoxy, which he seems never to have doubted?

Index of Names

Adam, Charles, 275n1, 282n37
Agostini, Igor, 313n18
Alain, 330n10
Alquié, Ferdinand, 276n5, 282n32, 289n3, 291n17, 300n68, 302n2, 317n46, 321n21, 323n36, 340n3, 340n4, 348n22
Antisthenes, 176
Arbib, Dan, 99, 276n2, 277n11, 282n38, 291n15, 291n18, 294n35, 298n54, 308n60, 312n15, 312n16, 313n19, 314n22, 314n26, 315n34, 316n38, 318n51
Ariew, Roger, 288n69, 298n54, 319n9, 334n1
Aristotle, 2, 6, 20, 83, 88, 89, 126, 151, 158, 159, 169, 170, 173, 174, 184, 185, 190, 197, 200, 201, 228, 276n5, 329n4, 330n9, 332n20, 333n24, 333n25, 333n27, 333n28, 334n29, 334n30, 335n8, 336n22, 337n29, 339n41, 343n2
Armogathe, Jean-Robert, xiv, 282n38, 291n15, 311n10, 311n11, 314n26, 320n16

Arnauld, Antoine, 25, 112, 229–30, 286n63, 309n74, 344n3, 345n6, 345n8, 346n11, 347n17
Augustine (Saint), 3, 69, 109, 150, 259–73, 276n3, 281n28, 282n34, 292n20, 307n47, 307n51, 307n56, 315n33, 329n7, 334n29, 353n3, 354n6, 354n8, 354n11, 354n14, 355n15, 355n16
Averroes, 185
Azouvi, François, 275n3, 318n1

Bacon, Francis, 1
Baillet, Adrien, 11, 82, 132
Baillon, Emmanuelle, 332n17
Balzac, Jean-Louis Guez de, 282n32, 282n37
Barbaras, Renaud, 292n23
Beaufret, Jean, 253, 303n2, 323n23
Becker, Oskar, 319n5
Belgioioso, Giulia, 320n16, 311n10, 311n11
Bennett, Jonathan, 349n22
Benoist, Jocelyn, 288n67
Bergson, Henri, 142, 150

357

Index of Names

Bernard of Clairvaux (Saint), 159, 276n5, 330n10
Bernhardt, Jean, 334n2, 336n20
Beyssade, Jean-Marie, 280n27, 287n63, 289n3, 291n17, 294n35, 299n62, 300n65, 334n1, 346n13
Biard, Joël, 319n9
Borot, Luc, 334n2
Boulnois, Olivier, 314n22, 314n23
Bourdin, Pierre, 45, 125, 298n54, 299n62, 309n74, 320n15, 323n41
Brunschvicg, Léon, 127, 320n12
Burman, Frans, 25, 47–48, 103, 277n7, 284n44, 288n66, 299n60, 309n72, 314n27, 317n45, 346n13
Buzon, Frédéric de, 277n7

Calderón de la Barca, Pedro, 10, 79, 281n31
Calov, Abraham, 201
Carraud, Vincent, xiv, 26, 275n1, 276n2, 277n8, 277n11, 281n31, 286n62, 288n67, 288n68, 291n18, 292n18, 293n27, 299n58, 306n33, 318n2, 323n36, 330n10, 331n13, 339n51, 341n9, 354n9, 354n14
Caterus, Johannes, 110, 111, 230, 325n52
Cervantes, Miguel de, 9, 79, 280n26
Chanut, Pierre, xii, 64, 303n7, 304n12, 304n17, 305n24, 307n51, 307n53, 307n55, 308n58, 308n64
Charron, Pierre, 1, 2, 5, 6, 21, 277n7, 278n14, 278n16, 283n42, 284n43, 285n54, 316n38
Chassignet, Jean-Baptiste, 10, 177, 281n30
Chateaubriand, François-René de, 334n29

Cicero, 3, 20, 161, 176, 277n12, 278n18, 280–81n27, 281n28, 282n34, 329n4, 331n12, 334n31
Clauberg, Johannes, 47, 100, 201, 257, 321n19, 339n51, 346n12
Clerselier, Claude, 25, 114, 298n54, 311n10, 312n13, 316n43, 345n6
Cohen, Hermann, 124
Collacciani, Domenico, 339n51
Comte-Sponville, André, 330n10
Conche, Marcel, 330n10, 331n15, 332n17
Corneille, Pierre, 79
Costabel, Pierre, 275n1, 294n29, 311n7
Courtine, Jean-François, 314n48
Crapulli, Giovanni, 350n26

D'Auriole, Pierre, 284n43
Deleuze, Gilles, 342n16
Demonet, Marie-Luce, 333n22
Denzinger, Heinrich, 283n41
Derrida, Jacques, 280n27
Desan, Philippe, 333n28
Diogenes Laertius, 20, 277n12, 285n52, 285n53
Doney, Willis, 284n46, 321n21
Duns Scotus, John, 35, 99, 100, 101, 201, 313n21, 313n22

Elizabeth, Princess of Bohemia, xii, 114, 301n72, 303n5, 303n7, 304n15 & 16, 305n21, 305n23, 306n25, 306n29, 307n54, 308n58, 308n62, 310n78, 317n44
Emge, Carl August, 319n5
Erasmus, 161, 265, 331n13, 355n16
Erdmann, Johan Eduard, 124

Faye, Emmanuel, 277n7, 294n33, 319n9, 330n10
Fénelon, François de Salignac de La Mothe, 82, 257, 276n5, 287n63, 310n75 & 76
Ferrari, Massimo, 319n12
Fichant, Michel, 338n35
Fischer, Kuno, 124
Fontialis, Jacobus, 321n19
Foucault, Michel, 53, 280n27, 295n39
Francis de Sales (Saint), 307n51
Freudenthal, Jacob, 350n26

Galilei, Galileo, 92, 322n36
Garnier, Robert, 10, 281n31
Gassendi, Pierre, 1, 27, 31, 104, 106, 108, 112, 113, 114, 115, 116, 190, 251, 285n50, 290–91n14, 304n13, 309n70, 309n74, 312n13, 312n17, 316n39, 40 & 41
Gebhardt, Carl, 340n6, 341n8, 342n17, 342n24 & 25, 342n27 & 28, 343n29 & 30
Giancotti-Boscherini, Emilia, 341n16
Gibieuf, Guillaume, 233, 299n58, 345n5, 346n13, 347n17, 350n28
Gilson, Étienne, 292n21, 319n9, 320n12, 335n10
Glazemaker, Jan Hendriksz, 349n26
Goclenius, Rudolph, 321n19
Gougenheim, Georges, 332n20, 333n22
Gouhier, Henri, 18, 253, 284n45, 289n1
Gregory of Nyssa (Saint), 269, 330n10
Gregory the Great (Saint), 316n38
Gregory of Rimini, 284n43
Gregory, Tullio, xiv, 1, 283n43
Greisch, Jean, 321n26
Grene, Marjorie, 298n54, 334n1

Grimaldi, Nicolas, 288n69, 310n3, 317n47, 321n26
Guéret, Michel, 340n5, 341n16
Gueroult, Martial, 127, 128, 282n35, 284n46 & 47, 291n17, 300–301n68, 302n79, 317n46, 340n3 & 4, 341n8, 341n11, 341n13, 341n16, 348n20, 348n21, 348n22, 349n26

Heereboord, Adriaan, 250, 353n48
Hegel, Georg Wilhelm Friedrich, 8, 55, 121, 142, 203, 204, 257, 279n22, 318n1, 326n63, 340n2
Heidegger, Martin, xiv, 32, 37, 40, 42, 43, 44, 45, 49, 50, 55, 124–28, 141, 144, 155, 156, 257, 276n3, 289n75, 290n6, 292n21, 292n23, 293n26, 296n39, 296n43, 296n45 & 46 & 47, 297n50, 299n63, 300n67, 306n24, 320n15, 320n17, 321n20, 322n26 & 27, 326n62, 326n65, 329n5
Henry, Michel, 128, 138, 287n64, 300n65, 322n27
Herbert of Cherbury, Edward, 349n24
Hermann, Friedrich-Wilhelm von, 319n5, 322n27
Herodotus, 329n4
Hintikka, Jaako, 31
Hobbes, Thomas, xiv, xv, 1, 32, 35, 39, 108, 111, 116, 181–95, 197–98, 200–201, 279n23, 294n35, 309n74, 317n45, 334n1–35n7, 336n16–21, 337n26–29, 338n33 & 34, 338n37–40, 339n43–50
Hooker, Michael K., 321n22
Horace, 334n33
Hume, David, 1

360 Index of Names

Husserl, Edmund, xiv, 33, 49, 121, 122–31, 134–35, 137–42, 144, 147, 167, 254, 257, 276n7, 290n12, 292–93n23, 318–19n3–6, 320n16, 321n20, 322n27, 322n29, 322n31, 323n43–24n47, 325n53 & 54, 326n56–59, 326n63 & 64, 326n 67–27n69, 332n19, 353n1–3
Huygens, Christiaan, xii

Joachim, Harold H., 340n4

Kambouchner, Denis, 275n4, 284n47, 318n47
Kant, Immanuel, 1, 13, 17, 27, 32–33, 37, 39, 40, 42–43, 44–45, 49, 51, 53, 55, 86, 89, 91, 105, 106, 123, 124, 125, 126, 127, 142, 167, 189, 205, 212, 253, 257, 286n62, 287n63, 290n7, 293n26, 297n48, 301n70 & 71, 311n4, 311n6, 311n9, 316n35, 318n2, 319n12, 320n15, 321n20
Kennington, Richard, 284n46
Kepler, Johannes, 92
Kierkegaard, Søren, 142
Koyré, Alexandre, 319n9

La Mothe Le Vayer, François de, 2, 9, 20, 284–85n50, 285n53
Lactantius, 159
Lamanna, Marco, 321n19, 339n51
Laporte, Jean, 282n35, 309n73, 317n46
Launay, Jean de, 345n5, 347n17
Lavigne, Jean-François, 321n26
Leibniz, Gottfried Wilhelm, 53, 76, 124, 257, 293n26, 302n75, 318n2, 320n12
Lentulus, Cyriacus, 288n69
Levinas, Emmanuel, 86, 128, 257, 310n3, 319n5, 321n26
Liard, Louis, 320n12
Locke, John, 1, 76, 142
Lojacono, Ettore, 280n26
Lorhardus, Jacobus, 321n19
Luynes, Louis Charles d'Albert, Duke of, 22, 104, 284n46, 314n29, 315n30, 322n28

Malebranche, Nicolas, 1, 21, 52, 76, 142, 172, 201, 254, 255, 257, 276n5, 276n1, 285n55, 301n75, 302n2, 318n2
Manzini, Frédéric, 343n2
Maritain, Jacques, 320n12
Matheron, Alexandre, 349n23
Méchoulan, Henry, 350n26
Mehl, Édouard, 288n69, 288n71, 289n74, 298n54
Meinsma, Koenraad Oege, 350n26
Merleau-Ponty, Maurice, xiv, 276n6
Mersenne, Marin, 1, 2, 18, 31, 82, 86, 92, 94, 103, 117, 123, 193, 283n40, 284n47, 284n49, 288n74, 290n10, 303n7, 308n57, 308n60, 309n74, 311n10, 312n13, 316n36, 318n48, 318n52, 322n29, 326n58, 335n6, 335n13, 338n36, 342n21, 349n24
Mesland, Denis, 301n72
Michon, Cyrille, 330n10
Mignini, Filippo, 343n30, 352n46
Molière, 282n37
Montaigne, Michel Eyquem de, xiv, xv, 1, 2, 9, 10, 15, 21–26, 62, 64–69, 79, 139, 149–53, 155–59, 161, 163–74, 177–80, 257, 259–73, 276n1, 277n7, 281n29, 283n42, 286n56 & 57, 286n59, 286n62, 288n67, 295n38, 304n9, 304n11–14, 305n22, 305n24, 306–7n31–46,

316n38, 328n1, 329n3–5, 329–30n7, 330n10, 331n12 & 13, 331n15, 332n17 & 18, 332n20 & 21, 333n22, 333n26, 333n28, 334n29, 334n32 & 33, 353n1–3, 354n4, 354n8 & 9, 354n14, 355n16
Moreau, Pierre-François, 353n52
Morin, Jean-Baptiste, 86, 91, 102, 289n3, 302n78, 311n5, 314n26
Morus (or More), Henry, 314n24, 320n13, 344n4

Nancy, Jean-Luc, 289n3, 290n5, 291n17, 295n39, 300n68
Nassau, Maurice of, 14
Natorp, Paul, 124
Nietzsche, Friedrich, xiv, 27, 37, 42, 49, 50, 51, 53, 55, 73, 74, 126, 142, 189, 257, 270, 285n50, 290n6, 293n26, 296n40, 297n48 & 49, 299n63, 301n69, 301n73, 302n76 & 77, 305–6n24, 336n18
Noack, Hermann, 319n5

Ockham, William of, 8, 283n43
Oldenburg, Henry, 222, 343n30
Olivo, Gilles, 26, 275n1, 277n8, 281n31, 299n58, 323n36
Osier, Jean-Pierre, 350n26

Pariente, Jean-Claude, 288n69
Pascal, Blaise, 2, 21, 40, 73–76, 162, 172, 257, 268, 286n58, 286n62, 292n18, 293n27, 295n38, 306n38, 308n63, 329n3, 331n13, 354n13 & 14
Paul, (Saint), 161, 179, 265, 307n45, 323n36, 331n13, 355n16
Pécharman, Martine, 294n35, 339n46
Pellegrin, Pierre, 276n5, 283n39
Perrin, Christophe, 320n17

Plato, 20, 57, 64, 125, 126, 151, 160, 168, 266, 282n34, 329n2, 329n7, 331n12, 332n20
Pollot, Alphonse de, 286n63, 299n59, 303n5
Pomponazzi, Pietro, 185, 335n10
Popkin, Richard H., 1, 273, 355n16
Pradelle, Dominique, 292n23, 353n1
Proust, Marcel, 334n29
Pyrrho, 5, 20, 355n16

Ragni, Alice, 339n51
Raiola, Marilène, 283n43
Rashed, Roshdi, 319n9
Regius (Roy), Henricus, xii, 190, 309n72, 309n74, 337n27, 345n10
Reneri, Henricus, 286n63, 299n59, 303n5
Revius, Jacobus, 250, 251, 353n49 & 50
Ricœur, Paul, 128, 322n26
Robinet, André, 340n5, 341n16
Rochot, Bernard, 275n1, 285n50
Rodis-Lewis, Geneviève, 276n1, 277n7, 281n31, 282n37, 284n47, 289n3, 302n1, 317n46
Romano, Claude, 293n23, 327n69
Roosenburg, Selinde, 350n26
Rotrou, Jean, 281n31
Rousseau, Jean-Jacques, 142, 257, 276n5, 334n29

Saint-Thierry, William of, 111, 316n38
Sánchez Estop, J. D., 349n26
Sartre, Jean-Paul, 127, 128, 321n26
Schelling, Friedrich Wilhelm Joseph, 25–26, 27, 33, 142, 257, 290n11, 301n73
Schmitt, Charles B., 1
Schuhl, Pierre-Maxime, 168, 332n20, 333n22

Index of Names

Screech, M. A., 168, 332n21
Seneca, 159
Sextus Empiricus, 1, 2, 4, 5, 9, 20, 79, 139, 276n5, 277n6, 277n9, 278n13, 278n15, 278n19, 279n24, 282n39, 284n50, 285n51, 286n56, 331n15
Shakespeare, William, 79
Socrates, 3, 20, 69, 168, 170, 172, 286n58, 306n41, 331n12, 338n35
Sophocles, 329n4
Spallanzani, Mariafranca, 282n37
Spinoza, Baruch, xiv, xv, 35, 52, 53, 76, 102, 123, 124, 126, 142, 147, 192, 201, 202–9, 211–19, 221, 223–26, 228–30, 232–40, 242–46, 248–52, 254–55, 257, 301n74, 309n74, 317n44, 318n2, 336n15, 337n29, 340n3–6, 341n8 & 9, 341n11, 341n13, 341n16, 342n20, 342n24, 342n27–43n30, 343n1 & 2, 347n18–49n22, 349n26–50n27, 350n32, 351n37, 351n42, 352n45 & 46
Sponde, Jean de, 177
Suarez, Francisco, 35, 92, 100, 101–2, 201, 244–46, 248, 249–52, 257, 314n23, 320n13, 335n9, 336n23, 350n31–36, 352n44 & 45, 353n49 & 50

Thijssen-Schoute, Louise, 350n26
Thomas Aquinas, (Saint), 35, 83, 99, 184, 246–49, 250, 298n57, 310n79–81, 313n20, 335n9, 343n2, 350n32, 351n38–43, 352n45 & 46
Timpler, Clemens, 201
Tombeur, Paul, 340n5, 341n16
Tommasi, Francesco Valerio, 353n1
Tournon, André, 168, 333n22, 333n26
Traverso, Edilia, 329n4, 333n28

Verbeek, Theo, 352n47
Villey, Pierre, 259, 281n29, 286n57, 328n1, 330n10, 333n29, 334n32, 353n2 & 3, 354n4, 354n12
Vinti, Carlo, 311n11
Voetius (or Voet), Gisbertus, xii, 2, 104, 288n69, 308n60, 309n74

Waelhens, Alphonse de, 319n5
Weber, Dominique, 295n35
Weber, Jean-Paul, 345n9
Wittgenstein, Ludwig, 86, 285, 311n4
Wolff, Christian, 201
Wolfson, Harry Austryn, 341n8, 341n11, 349n26, 352n46

Zarka, Yves-Charles, 334n2, 336n18, 336n20, 337n26, 339n46 & 47

Cultural Memory in the Present

Walter Benjamin, *On Goethe*
Elliot R. Wolfson, *Nocturnal Seeing: Hopelessness of Hope and Philosophical
    Gnosis in Susan Taubes, Gillian Rose, and Edith Wyschogrod*
Severo Sarduy, *Barroco and Other Writings*
David D. Kim, *Arendt's Solidarity: Anti-Semitism and Racism in the Atlantic World*
Hans Joas, *Why the Church?: Self-Optimization or Community of Faith*
Jean-Luc Marion, *Revelation Comes from Elsewhere*
Peter Sloterdijk, *Out of the World*
Christopher J. Wild, *Descartes' Meditative Turn: Cartesian Thought as Spiritual Practice*
Eli Friedlander, *Walter Benjamin and the Idea of Natural History*
Helmut Puff, *The Antechamber: Toward a History of Waiting*
Raúl E. Zegarra, *A Revolutionary Faith: Liberation Theology
    Between Public Religion and Public Reason*
David Simpson, *Engaging Violence: Civility and the Reach of Literature*
Michael Steinberg, *The Afterlife of Moses: Exile, Democracy, Renewal*
Alain Badiou, *Badiou by Badiou*, translated by Bruno Bosteels
Eric Song, *Love against Substitution: Seventeenth-Century
    English Literature and the Meaning of Marriage*
Niklaus Largier, *Figures of Possibility: Aesthetic Experience,
    Mysticism, and the Play of the Senses*
Mihaela Mihai, *Political Memory and the Aesthetics of Care:
    The Art of Complicity and Resistance*
Ethan Kleinberg, *Emmanuel Levinas's Talmudic Turn: Philosophy and Jewish Thought*
Willemien Otten, *Thinking Nature and the Nature of Thinking: From Eriugena to Emerson*
Michael Rothberg, *The Implicated Subject: Beyond Victims and Perpetrators*
Hans Ruin, *Being with the Dead: Burial, Ancestral Politics,
    and the Roots of Historical Consciousness*
Eric Oberle, *Theodor Adorno and the Century of Negative Identity*
David Marriott, *Whither Fanon? Studies in the Blackness of Being*
Reinhart Koselleck, *Sediments of Time: On Possible Histories*, translated
    and edited by Sean Franzel and Stefan-Ludwig Hoffmann
Devin Singh, *Divine Currency: The Theological Power of Money in the West*
Stefanos Geroulanos, *Transparency in Postwar France: A Critical History of the Present*
Sari Nusseibeh, *The Story of Reason in Islam*
Olivia C. Harrison, *Transcolonial Maghreb: Imagining
    Palestine in the Era of Decolonialization*

Barbara Vinken, *Flaubert Postsecular: Modernity Crossed Out*
Aishwary Kumar, *Radical Equality: Ambedkar, Gandhi, and the Problem of Democracy*
Simona Forti, *New Demons: Rethinking Power and Evil Today*
Joseph Vogl, *The Specter of Capital*
Hans Joas, *Faith as an Option*
Michael Gubser, *The Far Reaches: Ethics, Phenomenology, and the Call
    for Social Renewal in Twentieth-Century Central Europe*
Françoise Davoine, *Mother Folly: A Tale*
Knox Peden, *Spinoza Contra Phenomenology: French Rationalism from Cavaillès to Deleuze*
Elizabeth A. Pritchard, *Locke's Political Theology: Public Religion and Sacred Rights*
Ankhi Mukherjee, *What Is a Classic? Postcolonial Rewriting and Invention of the Canon*
Jean-Pierre Dupuy, *The Mark of the Sacred*
Henri Atlan, *Fraud: The World of Ona'ah*
Niklas Luhmann, *Theory of Society, Volume 2*
Ilit Ferber, *Philosophy and Melancholy: Benjamin's Early
    Reflections on Theater and Language*
Alexandre Lefebvre, *Human Rights as a Way of Life: On Bergson's Political Philosophy*
Theodore W. Jennings, Jr., *Outlaw Justice: The Messianic Politics of Paul*
Alexander Etkind, *Warped Mourning: Stories of the Undead in the Land of the Unburied*
Denis Guénoun, *About Europe: Philosophical Hypotheses*
Maria Boletsi, *Barbarism and Its Discontents*
Sigrid Weigel, *Walter Benjamin: Images, the Creaturely, and the Holy*
Roberto Esposito, *Living Thought: The Origins and Actuality of Italian Philosophy*
Henri Atlan, *The Sparks of Randomness, Volume 2: The Atheism of Scripture*
Rüdiger Campe, *The Game of Probability: Literature and Calculation from Pascal to Kleist*
Niklas Luhmann, *A Systems Theory of Religion*
Jean-Luc Marion, *In the Self's Place: The Approach of Saint Augustine*
Rodolphe Gasché, *Georges Bataille: Phenomenology and Phantasmatology*
Niklas Luhmann, *Theory of Society, Volume 1*
Alessia Ricciardi, *After La Dolce Vita: A Cultural Prehistory of Berlusconi's Italy*
Daniel Innerarity, *The Future and Its Enemies: In Defense of Political Hope*
Patricia Pisters, *The Neuro-Image: A Deleuzian Film-Philosophy of Digital Screen Culture*
François-David Sebbah, *Testing the Limit: Derrida, Henry,
    Levinas, and the Phenomenological Tradition*
Erik Peterson, *Theological Tractates*, edited by Michael J. Hollerich
Feisal G. Mohamed, *Milton and the Post-Secular Present: Ethics, Politics, Terrorism*
Pierre Hadot, *The Present Alone Is Our Happiness, Second Edition:
    Conversations with Jeannie Carlier and Arnold I. Davidson*

*For a complete listing of titles in this series, visit the
Stanford University Press website, www.sup.org.*

The authorized representative in the EU for product safety and compliance is:
Mare Nostrum Group
B.V Doelen 72
4831 GR Breda
The Netherlands

www.ingramcontent.com/pod-product-compliance
Lightning Source LLC
Chambersburg PA
CBHW031751220426
43662CB00007B/363